YOUR EYES WILL BE OPENED

SOCIETY
OF BIBLICAL
LITERATURE

DISSERTATION SERIES

J. J. M. Roberts, Old Testament Editor
Charles Talbert, New Testament Editor

Number 97

YOUR EYES WILL BE OPENED
A Study of the Greek (Ethiopic)
Apocalypse of Peter

by
Dennis D. Buchholz

Dennis D. Buchholz

YOUR EYES WILL BE OPENED
A Study of the Greek (Ethiopic)
Apocalypse of Peter

Scholars Press
Atlanta, Georgia

YOUR EYES WILL BE OPENED

Dennis D. Buchholz

Ph.D., 1984
Claremont Graduate School

Advisor
James M. Robinson

Library of Congress Cataloging-in-Publication Data

Buchholz, Dennis D., 1947 –
  Your eyes will be opened.

  (Dissertation series / Society of Biblical
Literature ; no. 97
    Bibliography: p.
    1. Apocalypse of Peter (Greek-Ethiopic version) —
Criticism, interpretation, etc. I. Title
II. Series: Dissertation series (Society of Biblical
Literature) ; no. 97.
BS2920.P6B83   1987   229'.94   86-27900
ISBN 1-55540-024-8
ISBN 1-55540-025-6 (pbk.)

Printed in the United States of America
on acid-free paper

TO MY PARENTS

ACKNOWLEDGEMENTS

Many people have given me help with this dissertation. I cannot name them all here, but I thank them very much.

A few people must be mentioned. I owe a great deal to the late William H. Brownlee who supervised the dissertation until his untimely death in July, 1983. The Ancient Biblical Manuscript Center in Claremont obtained for me the necessary microfilms and photographs, supplied by the Bodleian Library of Oxford, the Bibliothèque Nationale of Paris, and Ernst Hammerschmidt of Hamburg. The members of Lemmon Rural Lutheran Parish granted me a leave of absence in 1981-2, and the members of First Lutheran Church, Pomona, CA showed me many kindnesses during my stay there at that time. Twice the abbot and monks of Assumption Abbey in Richardton, ND supplied me with a place to work. Fr. Terrence Kardong, OSB prepared some translations from Latin for me. Luther-Northwestern Seminary in St. Paul, MN also provided a place to study and use of the library. The South Dakota State Library and its outlet in Lemmon, SD obtained for me material difficult to find. And finally, Wolf Leslau has kindly evaluated the Ethiopic work I have done. Thank you all.

Dennis D. Buchholz
Lemmon, SD

TABLE OF CONTENTS

CHAPTER ONE

INTRODUCTION

I. Which Apocalypse of Peter?

The writing which we call the Apocalypse of Peter was
given that title in ancient times. About 200 CE Clement of
Alexandria quotes from it using the words "Peter says in the
Apocalypse."[1] We first find the exact words 'Apocalypse of
Peter' about 400 CE in a writing of Macarius of Magnesia.[2]
Macarius quotes a pagan writer whom he is refuting. This pagan writer, who is unnamed but who is perhaps Porphyry and in
any case probably wrote during the third century,[3] uses the
words το λελεγμενον εν τη αποκαλυψει του πετρου 'the saying in
the Apocalypse of Peter.' Our Apocalypse of Peter, as we shall
see below, was well known and used throughout the ancient
Roman world. We are certain that whenever we have found a
reference to an Apocalypse of Peter up through the Middle
Ages, it is this document that is meant.

However, in modern scholarly discussions the name

---

[1]Once in Ecl. Proph. 41; twice in Ecl. proph. 48-49.

[2]Apocritica 4.6.

[3]For a discussion of this see the conclusions drawn by
Adolf von Harnack in Kritik des Neuen testaments von einem
griechischen Philosophen des 3. Jahrhunderts (Leipzig: J.
C. Hinrichs, 1911), 107-110,137-144.

1

Apocalypse of Peter without further qualification could also refer to either of two other writings which have become known by that name. In order to avoid confusion, we will first briefly discuss these two other documents and follow that with a similar brief overview of our Apocalypse of Peter before we proceed further.

A. The Gnostic Apocalypse of Peter from Nag Hammadi

Among the documents discovered in 1945 in Egypt near the town of Nag Hammadi is one from codex VII written in Coptic but labelled in Greek αποκαλυψις πετρου 'Apocalypse of Peter.' The Coptic text is available in a facsimile edition.[1] It was edited by Frederik Wisse and translated into English by Roger A. Bullard for The Nag Hammadi Library in English.[2] A new edition and translation of the text have been done by James Brashler.[3] We could distinguish this writing from that which is the subject matter of our dissertation by calling it the Coptic Apocalypse of Peter as is frequently done. However, as Brashler indicates,[4] this work was written originally in Greek and can only be fully

---

[1]The Facsimile Edition of the Nag Hammadi Codices: Codex VII. (Leiden: E. J. Brill, 1972).

[2]James M. Robinson, General Ed., The Nag Hammadi Library in English (San Francisco: Harper and Row, 1977), pp. 339-345.

[3]James A. Brashler, "The Coptic Apocalypse of Peter: A Genre Analysis and Interpretation" (Ph.D. dissertation, Claremont Graduate School, 1977).

[4]Ibid., pp. 8-13.

understood when translation errors are taken into account.
It would be misleading, therefore, to use the designation
Coptic Apocalypse of Peter for one and Greek Apocalypse of
Peter for the other, for both were written in Greek.
Neither would it be appropriate to call one the Coptic
Apocalypse of Peter and the other the Ethiopic Apocalypse of
Peter since portions of the latter are actually preserved in
Greek.

This problem of terminology is no small problem since
much confusion has arisen from lack of standard terminology.
For example, Klaus Berger[1] refers to verse one of the Greek
fragment from Akhmim (which does not appear in the Ethiopic
text) and calls it the Coptic Apocalypse of Peter. Perhaps
because of this, his index lists under Coptic Apocalypse of
Peter all the references to the document which this dissertation studies. In addition, he mentions the "Arabic-
Ethiopic" Apocalypse of Peter which is unrelated to either
of these documents[2] and apparently also unrelated to the

---

[1]Die Gesetzesauslegung Jesu. Ihr historischer Hintergrund im Judentum und im Alten Testament. Teil I: Markus
und Parallelen (Neukirchener Verlag, 1971), p. 23.

[2]This "Arabic-Ethiopic" Apocalypse of Peter is not one
work at all. Rather, Eduard Bratke investigated 20 Arabic,
Syriac, Carshuni, and Ethiopic manuscripts of pseudo-
clementine and petrine character. Many of these are virtually unrelated to each other. A description of his investigation together with translations of extracts from some
of these manuscripts is given in "Handschriftliche Uberlieferung und Bruchstücke der arabisch-aethiopischen Petrus-
Apokalypse," Zeitschrift für wissenschaftliche theologie 36
(1893), 454-493. Bratke was seeking the ancient Apocalypse
of Peter but found no trace of it.

Arabic <u>Apocalypse of Peter</u> discussed below. The confusion
stems from a multitude of various kinds of documents which
claim to be a revelation of Peter. Inconsistent use of
terminology has resulted in the sort of confusion displayed
by Berger.

Since it has become confusing to distinguish these two
documents by their languages, I have chosen to distinguish
one of them by the nature of its contents. Thus I call the
<u>Apocalypse of Peter</u> from Nag Hammadi the Gnostic <u>Apocalypse
of Peter</u>. I could correspondingly call the subject of this
dissertation the Apocalyptic <u>Apocalypse of Peter</u>. This also
seems awkward. Why should we use the adjective apocalyptic
to modify the noun apocalypse? Yet this could be made
acceptable because of the rift in meaning which current
scholarship has drawn between apocalyptic and apocalypse.
Apocalyptic is the adjective applied to a certain historical
movement or to literary works which are defined by characteristics of content, such as imminent eschatology, cosmic
dualism, graphic symbolism, angelology, etc.[1] The historical movement and corresponding worldview are increasingly
known as apocalypticism.[2] Nevertheless, the adjective

---

[1]Cf. D. S. Russell, <u>The Method and Message of Jewish
Apocalyptic</u> (Philadelphia: Westminster, 1964); H. H. Rowley,
<u>The Relevance of Apocalyptic</u> (New York: Association Press,
1964); Walter Schmithals, <u>The Apocalyptic Movement</u> (Nashville: Abingdon, 1975).

[2]Paul D. Hanson, "Apocalypticism," <u>The Interpreters
Dictionary of the Bible</u>, Supplementary Volume (Nashville:
Abingdon, 1976), 28-34.

apocalyptic remains useful in labelling those things which
are related to the movement by having those characteristics.

On the other hand, scholars have become increasingly
dissatisfied with the debate about which documents are apocalyptic and which are not.[1] The end result is that now the
noun apocalypse is being reserved for those works which fit
a form developed from genre analysis.[2] This includes works
such as gnostic apocalypses and Greek and Latin apocalypses
which are not necessarily "apocalyptic" by nature (as "apocalyptic" is understood above). Therefore the use of the
adjective gnostic for one and apocalyptic for the other
would relate the titles to the contents of the documents.
Moreover, in this particular case it would serve to high-
light the contrast between the apocalyptic and gnostic
worldviews evident in these apocalypses.[3] Yet after all
this, the phrase "apocalyptic apocalypse" remains too awkward to use. The Apocalypse Group of the Society of Biblical Literature Genres Project has placed our "apocalyptic"

---

[1]Cf. Klaus Koch, The Rediscovery of Apocalyptic
(Naperville, Illinois: Allenson, 1972).

[2]Philipp Vielhauer, "Introduction" pp. 581-607 and
"Apocalyptic in Early Christianity 1. Introduction" pp. 608-
642 in volume 2, Edgar Hennecke, New Testament Apocrypha,
ed. by W. Schneemelcher, English trans. ed. by R. McL.
Wilson (Philadelphia: Westminster, 1965); Paul D. Hanson,
"Apocalypse, Genre," The Interpreter's Dictionary of the
Bible, Supplementary Volume (Nashville: Abingdon, 1976), 27-
28; James Brashler, "The Literary Character of the Genre
Apocalypse," ibid., 70-120; John J. Collins, ed., Apocalypse:
The Morphology of a Genre, Semeia 14 (1979).

[3]For this contrast see esp. Schmithals, ibid.

Apocalypse of Peter in a group of apocalypses called Early
Christian Apocalypses.[1] I will follow this terminology and
call that document which is the subject of this dissertation
the Early Christian Apocalypse of Peter. I do so with some
regret, for some of the apocalypses from Nag Hammadi are
also rather early in date and are also Christian, though not
orthodox.

This is certainly true of this Gnostic Apocalypse of
Peter. It is a third century CE writing.[2] And it claims to
be from the true Christian community.[3] It is to be classified as an apocalypse.[4] In content, the author shows that
certain problems of persecution suffered by the gnostic community are to be solved by a proper understanding of Jesus'
crucifixion. Here is the well-known picture of the Jesus
whose body is crucified and suffers while the real Jesus,
the heavenly revealer, laughs at his enemies from above the
cross (NH VII, 81:1-82:3). Jesus is the heavenly revealer
who saves those who have a heavenly essence by illuminating
their origin and destiny. The true interpretation of Jesus
is revealed to Peter in three visions with interpretations
of the visions and also three sayings of Jesus with inter-

---

[1]Adela Yarbro Collins, "The Early Christian Apocalypse," John Collins, ed., ibid., 61-121.

[2]Brashler, ibid., 245.

[3]Brashler, ibid., 197-238.

[4]Francis T. Fallon, "The Gnostic Apocalypses," John
Collins, ed., ibid., 123-158; Brashler, ibid., 144-157.

pretation. These are revealed to Peter who is to be the founder of the gnostic community. Brashler concludes that "With these visions and their interpretation as the principle components of this document, the structure of _Apoc. Pet._ could be seen as a carefully constructed juxtaposition of traditional Christian views and Gnostic interpretations.[1]

How does this Gnostic _Apocalypse of Peter_ relate to our Early Christian _Apocalypse of Peter_? The matter will certainly not be settled here and requires a full and detailed investigation. The possibility remains open at present that the careful juxtaposition of views of which Brashler speaks is present precisely because the gnostic author was writing a gnostic substitute for the earlier orthodox apocalypse which he had before him. The following comparisons should be kept in mind. First of all, both documents lay claim to Peter as the transmitter of their teaching and the founder of their respective groups.[2] The theological contrast is stark, therefore, in such things as martyrdom which is seen positively by the orthodox Christians and more negatively by the gnostics. For example, in

---

[1]Brashler, ibid., pp. 241-242.

[2]Pheme Perkins, "Peter in Gnostic Revelation," _Society of Biblical Literature 1974 Seminar Papers_, ed. George MacRae (Cambridge, Massachusetts: Society of Biblical Literature, 1974), v. 2, 1-13; Brashler, "Peter as the Founder of the Gnostic Community," ibid., 206-216; Erik Peterson, "Das Martyrium des hl. Petrus nach der Petrus-Apocalypse," _Frühkirche, Judentum und Gnosis_ (Freiburg: Herder, 1959), 88-91 [originally published in _Miscellanea G. Belvederi_ (Rome: 1953), 181ff.]

EC [Early Christian] <u>Apocalypse of Peter</u> 14:4-5[1] Jesus sends
Peter to his martyrdom at Rome; in NH VII, 82:18-20, 84:6-11
Jesus tells Peter to be strong, for Jesus will be with Peter
so that none of his enemies will prevail against him. Corresponding to this, the orthodox see Jesus as a martyr whose
example they do well to follow (EC <u>Apocalypse of Peter</u> 2:9-
10) while the gnostics see the orthodox as clinging to the
name of a dead man (NH VII 74:13-14) and describe themselves
as "those who are from the life" (NH VII 70:24). Other
theological themes these two documents have in common are
the parousia, the dissolution of the universe, the immortality of souls, life from above, ability to distinguish right
from wrong, apostasy, spiritual blindness, heavenly light,
good fruit (the fig tree). There is also a certain similarity in the form of these two documents. In both Jesus
gives visions to Peter. In the EC <u>Apocalypse of Peter</u> the
resurrected Jesus is sitting on the Mount of Olives at the
opening of the document and the story reaches its high point
in the vision of the heavenly temple (16:8-9) after which
Jesus ascends into the second heaven (17:2-3). In the Gnostic <u>Apocalypse of Peter</u> the Savior before the crucifixion is
sitting in the heavenly temple which is apparently above the
heavens (NH VII, 71:9-14). Even certain words, phrases and
images are alike in these two works. For example, the word
pledge is used for immortal soul in NH VII, 77:3 and for

---

[1]My own verse numbers. See below in this edition of
the text.

the buried bodies of the dead who await resurrection in EC
Apocalypse of Peter 4:11; in the early Christian apocalypse
Peter is chosen by Jesus to be a martyr so that Jesus might
begin his work of destruction,[1] while in NH VII, 71:15-21
Jesus chooses Peter for the beginning[2] of the remnant (=the
gnostics); "eternal destruction" in NH VII, 75:15-23 and
"rooting out" in NH VII, 80:18-21 should be compared with
the rooting out of sinners in EC Apocalypse of Peter 3:2;
and in EC Apoc. Pt. 5:7-8 all people run in vain from the
fire at the parousia while in NH VII, 78:3-6 the gnostics
run in vain until the parousia when they are vindicated. If
this gnostic apocalypse is dependent in this way on the
early Christian one, however, the gnostic writer has taken
orthodox post-resurrection material and treated the same
themes in a pre-crucifixion setting. This is the opposite
of the normal trend in which sayings of Jesus are explained
in gnosticism by the resurrected Jesus, in orthodox material
by the pre-crucified Jesus.[3] But whether the author of the
Gnostic Apocalypse of Peter has actually used the EC Apocalypse of Peter or not remains open to further investigation.
Certainly the relationship is not such that we can gain any
knowledge of the latter by scrutinizing the former.

---

[1]The meaning is not clear.

[2] αρχη

[3]James M. Robinson, "Jesus: From Easter to Valentinus
(or to the Apostles' Creed)," Journal of Biblical Literature
101 (1982), 5-37, esp. pp. 31-32.

B. The Arabic Book of the Rolls

In 1931 A. Mingana published an edition and translation of a work called The Apocalypse of Peter.[1] It is contained in manuscript Mingana Syr. 70 from his personal
collection. The text is in Garshuni (Arabic written with
Syriac characters), and is rather long, 194 leaves. The
work is related by borrowing to several others of different
names, but especially to another group of five much smaller
manuscripts in Mingana's collection which are entitled Apocalypse of Peter. The manuscript which Mingana edits, how-
ver, is called The Book of the Rolls.[2] I will use that name
to distinguish it clearly from our Early Christian Apocalypse
of Peter.

This Garshuni manuscript opens with a history of the
Jewish people down to the birth of the Virgin Mary. Mingana
did not publish this portion of his text because an older
redaction and translation had already been published.[3] Then
follows a more apocalyptic and dogmatic pseudo-clementine
section which contains large portions of a pseudo-clementine
work known in Ethiopic and translated into French in part by

---

[1]A. Mingana, "The Apocalypse of Peter," Woodbrooke
Studies, Bulletin of the John Rylands Library 14-15 (1931-
32); 182-297, 423-562, 179-279. This was reprinted in Woodbrooke Studies, vol. 3 (Cambridge: Heffer and Sons, 1931).
M. R. James reviewed this in Journal of Theological Studies
33 (1932), 76-77; cf. also Journal of Theological Studies 33
(1932), 311-315.

[2]Mingana, ibid., 14, 192.

[3]Margaret Dunlop Gibson, Apocrypha Arabica, Studia
Sinaitica No. VIII (London: C. J. Clay, 1901).

Grébaut.[1] This section also contains an Arabic rescension of the Testament of Adam.[2] Next, after a description of the torment of hell, there is a long obscure section on the kingdoms which will rule this world up to the coming of Antichrist. Then, after a description of Antichrist, comes a history of the apostles and their travels which appears for the most part towards the end of the Gadla Hawāriyāt, an Ethiopic text edited and translated by Budge.[3] Unfortunately, Mingana does not translate all of the manuscript. Particularly folios 124b-145b are omitted by him. He says these contain a vision of Peter, a description of torments inflicted on different types of sinners, and prophetical announcements by Jesus to Peter on the end of the world and on the punishments of sinners.[4] Similarly, he omits 151b-154b which contain "a vision of heaven and of the Ascension of our Lord into it, witnessed by all the Apostles and the

[1]Sylvain Grébaut, "Literature Ethiopienne pseudo-clémentine: III traduction du Qalêmentos," Revue de l'Orient chrétien 16 (1911), 72-84, 167-175, 225-233; 17 (1912), 16-31, 133-144, 244-252, 337-346; 18 (1913), 69-78; 19 (1914), 324-330; 20 (1915-1917), 33-37, 424-430; 22 (1920-1921), 22-28, 113-117, 395-400; 26(1927-1928), 22-31 (with Alcide Roman). Grébaut translates ms. 78 d'Abbadie.

[2]Mingana, ibid., 14, 185. See, besides the bibliography there, A. -M. Denis ed., Introduction aux pseudepigraphorum quae supersunt graece, Pseudepigrapha Veteris testamenti Graece No. 3 (Leiden: Brill, 1970); and James H. Charlesworth, The Pseudepigrapha and Modern Research, Septuagint and Cognate Studies No. 7 (Missoula, Montana: Scholars Press, 1976), 91-92.

[3]E. A. Wallis Budge, The Contendings of the Apostles (London: n.p., v. I, 1898, v. II, 1901).

[4]Mingana, ibid., 15, 190.

Disciples. . . ."[1] These are precisely the sections we
would be most interested in, for they treat the same subject
matter as our EC Apocalypse of Peter. Finally, this Arabic
text closes with a section of early Church discipline and
practices which Mingana omits from his edition because he
wishes to treat it in more detail at another time.

What is the relationship of this Arabic Book of the
Rolls to our EC Apocalypse of Peter? Maurer states categor-
ically ". . . there is no point of contact with the so-called
Apocalypse of Peter translated from the Arabic. . . ."[2] He
is following James, who in his review of Mingana's book says
"The Apocalypse of Peter [Arabic] has no vestige in it of
the old Apocalypse."[3] But this is to put the case too
strongly for several reasons.

First, as I have already pointed out, we do not have
available to us the complete translation of the Arabic text and
are in fact missing two sections which are most important to us.
Secondly, there might perhaps be very distant traces of our
EC Apocalypse of Peter in the material which we do have. I
list the following parallels with chapter and verse numbers
from the latter text and with volume and page numbers from
Mingana's translation: the question about the events at the

---

[1]Mingana, ibid., 15, 191.

[2]Ch. Maurer, "Apocalypse of Peter," Edgar Hennecke, ed.,
New Testament Apocrypha, ibid., vol. II, 664.

[3]In his review of Mingana, ibid., 76.

end of the world (1:2; 14, 189-190); the setting on the Mt.
of Olives with the disciples at the time of Christ's ascension (1:1 and 17:2-6; 14, 191); the vision in Jesus' right
hand (3:1-3; 14, 213-214); God's mercy is a mystery (prologue; 14, 214); the indescribable light, and fruit trees,
and perfume of paradise (15:2 and 16:2-3; 14, 224-226 and
229); the heavenly tabernacle (16:8-9; 14, 226-227); those
who are saved look at the condemned (13:1; 14, 230); everyone is requited according to his deeds (13:6; 14, 234); the
fire which never is extinguished (5:4, 8, cf. 6:5; 14, 238
and 492); the coming of the Son will be like lightning from
east to west (1:6; 14, 429); the punishing worms who eat
sinners and multiply (7:10; 14, 431); torment of continued
biting of the tongue (9:3 and 11:8; 14, 432); worms which
are poisonous (7:9; 14, 432); angels in charge of the fire
(7:4; 14, 433); the punishments do not destroy the sinners,
only torment them (7:2; 14, 433); possible end to eternal
torment (14:1; 14, 433-434); better not to have been born
(3:4-7; 14, 480); the coming of Enoch and Elijah (2:12; 15,
189); the cloud of brightness which overshadows at the ascension (17:2; 15, 193). Many of these parallels, however, are
of a general nature and do not indicate dependence.

Thirdly, at least some of the material in this Arabic
text must be quite old. This includes passages which have
a christology which must precede Nicea,[1] some which have a

---

[1]Mingana, ibid., 14, 185-186, 426-427, and 15, 183.

marked prejudice against the Apostle Paul,[1] one passage
which Mingana says is "certainly the most striking testimony
that I have found in any eastern book in favor of the Church
of Rome,"[2] and one passage where the terminology "The Deceiver and the Error" is such that it must be traced back to
Odes of Solomon 38:10.[3] Using this latter point, J. Rendel
Harris has claimed not only that this must be from the original EC Apocalypse of Peter, but also that the Odes of
Solomon must have borrowed the uncommon phrase from there.[4]
He goes on to observe that the key to understanding Ode 38
is to realize that it is an apocalypse. Finally he asserts
that the Odes of Solomon and the canonical Apocalypse of
John are dependent on EC Apocalypse of Peter and that the
first two letters of John are in turn dependent upon the
Odes of Solomon. This would make the EC Apocalypse of Peter
important indeed. But while it is more than likely that the
unusual phrase "The Deceiver and the Error" must ultimately

---

[1]Mingana, ibid., 15, 179-184.

[2]Mingana, ibid., 15. 184.

[3]Mingana, ibid., 14, 426.

[4]J. Rendel Harris, "The Odes of Solomon and the Apoca-
lypse of Peter," The Expository Times 42 (1930-31), 21-23.
For the text of the Odes of Solomon see J. R. Harris and A.
Mingana, The Odes and Psalms of Solomon (New York: Longmans,
Green & Co.; vol. 1, 1916; vol. 2, 1920); and James H.
Charlesworth, The Odes of Solomon (Missoula, Montana: Schol-
ars Press, 1977). A discussion of date of composition,
original language, and a bibliography is available in Walter
Bauer, "The Odes of Solomon," Edgar Hennecke, ed., New Tes-
tament Apocrypha, ibid., v. 2; pp. 808-810; and in James H.
Charlesworth, The Pseudepigrapha and Modern Research, ibid.,
189-194.

connect in some way the Arabic <u>Book of the Rolls</u> with the
<u>Odes of Solomon</u> and we may also grant that perhaps Harris's
insight that Ode 38 is an apocalypse has much value and
should be pursued, there is no connection visible between
that phrase and the EC <u>Apocalypse of Peter</u>,[1] nor can we call
Harris's theory concerning the relationship of <u>Revelation</u>,
EC <u>Apocalypse of Peter</u>, <u>Odes of Solomon</u>, and the letter of
John anything more than unwarranted speculation based on his
theory of an abrupt end to the apocalyptic period in the
early church.[2] We cannot assign with confidence any specific material from this composite document to a particular
source unless we actually find it in that source.

Yet while we are justified to retain the possibility
that this Arabic <u>Book of the Rolls</u> could be our EC <u>Apoca-
lypse of Peter</u> in a greatly expanded and altered form, it
certainly does not contain the better text of the ancient
apocalypse for which some scholars had been searching.[3]
This altered form and vast expansion have virtually eliminated it from consideration when researching the original
apocalypse. The time span between the two is significant.
Mingana believes the <u>Book of the Rolls</u> to be a <u>mixtum</u>

---

[1]The apocalypse mentions the Deceiver (2:12; cf. also
2:7 and 2:10) but the term is by this time traditional for
Antichrist.

[2]Harris, ibid., 21.

[3]See the lament and yet the statement of hope that
such a text will yet be found in the review of James, ibid.,
p. 77.

compositum whose first layer is from about 800 CE.[1] This first layer was written in Arabic in Egypt by Syrian scribes who used older traditional material.[2] The process of adding layers and subtracting material continued, he believes, until the fourteenth century. It may have been one of these layers or a similar document which James de Vitry saw in Syria and of which he wrote to Pope Honorius III in 1219: "In the present year the Syrians who were with us in the army showed us a very ancient book from their library - chest written in the Saracen language. Its inscription (title) reads: The Revelations of the Blessed Apostle Peter, published in one volume by his disciple Clement. Whoever was the author of this book, he prophesied (praenuntiavit) openly and plainly on the condition of the church of God from the beginning up to the time of the Anti-christ and the end of the world."[3]

C. The Early Christian Apocalypse of Peter

This is the original Apocalypse of Peter and the one treated in this dissertation. Since it will of course be discussed below in great detail, only a short summary for

---

[1]Mingana, ibid., 14, 187.

[2]Mingana, ibid., 14, 187; 14, 428.

[3]Latin text in Johann Ernst Grabe, _Spicilegium ss. patrum ut et haereticum_ (Oxoniae: theatro Shedoniano, 1689-90), vol. 1, 76-77. The translation quoted here is taken from a private translation of the de Vitry text prepared for me by Fr. Terrence Kardong, OSB and appended to this dissertation.

purposes of comparison will be given here.[1]

This apocalypse was well known in the early church of the third and fourth centuries. It was written sometime before 150 CE. Some church fathers refer to it, and it is even quoted as scripture. The oldest list of the Canon of the New Testament, the Muratorian Canon, includes it. With the passing of time, however, it fell into disfavor and the text was lost.

We have recovered two important rescensions of the text. The first is a large fragment in Greek which was discovered near Akhmim in Egypt in 1886. This is the text referred to as the Akhmim Apocalypse of Peter. It is fragmentary and incomplete and has a corrupted form of text. The second text is an Ethiopic translation first brought to light in 1910. It has the advantage of being complete, as far as we know, but may contain additions or alterations. There are two other small fragments in Greek. These texts will be thoroughly discussed below. When I refer to the Apocalypse of Peter hereafter without any qualifications, I am referring to this Ethiopic text.

This document is thoroughly apocalyptic in content. Seated on the Mt. of Olives, Jesus is approached by his

---

[1]Compare the summaries with bibliography in Berthold Altaner, Patrology (New York: Herder and Herder, 1960), 83-84; Johannes Quasten, Patrology (Westminster, Maryland: The Newman Press, 1950), vol, I, 144-146; Ch. Maurer, ibid., 663-668; Morton S. Enslin, "Peter, Apocalypse of," George A. Buttrick, ed., The Interpreter's Dictionary of the Bible (Nashville: Abingdon, 1962), vol. 3, 758.

disciples and questioned by them about the signs of the parousia and the end of the world. He replies with a warning
about false christs and about the swiftness of his coming
and also with the parable of the fig tree, which he explains
to them is about martyrs. Jesus then shows to Peter the
final outcome of souls, the good and the bad. This causes
all of them to weep at the fate of the condemned. When
Peter quotes a saying of Jesus to the effect that it would
have been better if they had not been created, Jesus defends
the mercy of God by saying that Peter does not understand
because he has not seen their works. He describes the judgment day. First, there is the physical resurrection of the
bodies from the dead. Then the universe is dissolved with
fire which brings all the risen dead to the place of judgment. Finally, Christ comes to take his throne for judgment.
He orders the wicked to go through the River of Fire. The
evil spirits who are false gods are sentenced. Then people
are brought to the place of punishment each deserves for his
or her specific crime. There are six chapters devoted to
describing various punishments. The righteous are given
eternal life. The condemned, seeing this, plead for mercy,
but their plea is rejected and they admit that their sentence is just. Apparently the righteous are able to request
salvation for at least some of the condemned, who are then
baptized in the Acherusian Lake and placed in the Elesian
Fields. Jesus announces that he is about to go into his
eternal kingdom. He commands Peter to go to martyrdom in

Rome and gives him assurance. Jesus takes his disciples to
the holy mountain where Moses and Elijah appear to them in
heavenly form with radiant bodies. Peter asks after the
patriarchs and he is shown a garden with beautiful, sweet-
smelling fruit trees. When Peter wishes to make three
temples for Jesus and Moses and Elijah, he is rebuked. Then
Jesus shows them the heavenly temple, which is not described.
A voice comes from heaven announcing that Jesus is God's son.
A shining cloud descends, picks up Moses and Elijah and
Jesus, and carries them into the second heaven. This ful-
fills some scripture prophecies. The disciples descend from
the mountain rejoicing because God writes the names of the
righteous in the heavenly book of life.

II. The EC Apocalypse of Peter
in the Early Church

There are many witnesses to our apocalypse in the
early church. We will divide them between direct and indirect witnesses. Direct witnesses are references in which
the document is mentioned by name or quoted directly.
Actual texts of the apocalypse are also included here. Indirect witnesses are those which use, refer to, or allude to
the apocalypse without revealing that this is their source.
It should be understood that the witnesses in this latter
category can be as certain and as important as those in the
first, though many of them are not. We will take each category in chronological order.

A. The Direct Witnesses for EC
Apocalypse of Peter

There are twelve direct witnesses. For convenience we
list them here with their dates (all CE).

1.	The Muratorian Canon	170-200
2.	Clement of Alexandria	c. 200
3.	a. The pagan writer quoted in Macarius Magnes	270?
	b. Macarius Magnes	c. 400
4.	The Rainer and Bodleian fragments of the Greek text	3rd or 4th century
5.	Methodius of Olympus (or Philippi)	c. 300
6.	Eusebius of Caesarea	before 303
7.	Homily on the Parable of the Ten Virgins	4th century
8.	Sozomen	439-450

9.	Catalogue in Codex Claromon-tanus	4th-6th centuries
10.	The List of the Sixty Books	c. 600?
11.	The Akhmim fragment of the Greek text	6th-9th centuries
12.	The Stichometry of Nicephorus	850?

1. The Muratorian Canon

The Muratorian Canon was apparently written shortly after the Shepherd of Hermas in Rome. It was originally composed in Greek and translated into Latin. It is the earliest of all existing catalogues of the New Testament.

Lines 68-80 read:

cruit epistola sane iude et superscrictio
iohannis duas in catholica habentur et sapi
entia ab amicis salomonis in honore ipsius
scripta apocalapse etiam iohanis et pe
tri tantum recipimus quam quidam ex nos
tris legi in eclesia nolunt pastorem uero
nuperrime temporibus nostris in urbe
roma herma conscripsit sedente cathe
tra urbis romae aeclesiae pio ēps fratre
eius et ideo legi eum quide oportet se pu
plicare uero in eclesia populo neque inter
profetas completum numero nequ inter
apostolos in finē temporam potest

Further an epistle of Jude and two with the title (or:
    two of the above mentioned)
John are accepted in the catholic Church, and the Wisdom
written by friends of Solomon in his honour.
Also of the revelations we accept only those of John and
Peter, which (latter) some of our
people do not want to have read in the Church. But Hermas
wrote the Shepherd quite lately in our time in the city
of Rome, when on the throne of the
church of the city of Rome the bishop Pius, his brother,
was seated. And therefore it ought indeed to be read, but
it cannot be read publicly in the Church to the people
    either among

the prophets, whose number is settled, or among the apostles to the end of time.[1]

From this catalogue we learn that the EC Apocalypse of Peter was known before 200 CE in Rome where it was being read as scripture in the churches there. But some people objected to its liturgical use. Whether they objected to its content or disputed its authenticity we do not know. Neither do we have any idea when it ceased to be so read or why. It must have been considered authentically petrine by some.

2. Clement of Alexandria

Twice Clement quotes from the Apocalypse of Peter. Both quotes are found in the Eclogae Propheticae. This latter work has passed down to us appended to the Stromateis of Clement. It is generally agreed that the work is Clement's, but there is some disagreement concerning its nature. Clement wrote a commentary on the writings of the Old and New Testaments (including the Apocalypse of Peter) which is called Hypotyposeis and which was known to Eusebius.[2] M. R. James was among those who believed the Eclogae Propheticae

---

[1]Latin text in G. Bardy, "Muratori (Canon de)," Pirot, L., Robert, A., and Cazelles, H., eds., Dictionnaire de la Bible. Supplement. (Paris: Librairie Letouzey et Ane, 1957), vol. 5, cols. 1399-1408. English translation from Wilhelm Schneemelcher, "The Muratori Canon," Edgar Hennecke, ed., New Testament Apocrypha, ibid., vol. 1, 42-45.

[2]Eusebius, Historia Ecclesiastica 6, 14, 1.

to be excerpts from the Hypotyposeis.[1] Zahn thought they
were taken from lost parts of Clement's Stromateis, while
Quasten assumes they are a collection of excerpts from gnostic writings with short studies by Clement for use in preparing further books of the Stromateis which were never
written.[2] In any case, the Eclogae Propheticae consists of
quotes from other, mostly gnostic writings with comments by
Clement. Of these it is said ". . . their highly compressed
form makes it very difficult to identify which words are
Clement's own."[3] Clement died in 215 CE. If the Stromateis
remained unfinished because of his death, then the Eclogae
Propheticae would probably originate shortly before. But
perhaps they stem from before Clement's flight from Alexandria in 202 CE.

The first quote comes from section 41:

η γραφη φησι τα βρεφη τα εκτεθεντα τημελουχω παραδιδοσθαι
αγγελω υφ ου παιδευεσθαι τε και αυξειν και εσονται φησιν
ως οι εκατον ετων ενταυθα πιστοι διο και πετρος εν τη
αποκαλυψει φησι και αστραπη πυρος πηδωσα απο των βρεφων
εκεινων και πλησσουσα τους οφθαλμους των γυναικων

The Scripture says that the children exposed by parents
are delivered to a protecting (= temelouchos) angel, by
whom they are brought up and nourished. And they shall
be, it says, as the faithful of a hundred years old here.
Wherefore Peter also says in his Apocalypse, "and a flash
of fire, coming from their children and smiting the eyes
of the women."

---

[1]M. R. James, The Apocryphal New Testament (Oxford:
Oxford University Press, 1975 (1924)), 506.

[2]Johannes Quasten, ibid., vol. 2, 14-15.

[3]F. L. Cross, The Early Christian Fathers (London:
Duckworth, 1960), 120.

The second quote is from sections 48-49:

αυτικα ο πετρος εν τη αποκαλυψει φησιν τα βρεφη <τα>
εξαμβλωθεντα της αμεινονος εσομενα μοιρας ταυτα αγγελω
τημελουχω παραδιδοσθαι ινα γνωσεως μεταλαβοντα της
αμεινονος τυχη μονης παθοντα α αν επαθεν και εν σωματι
γενομενα τα δ ετερα μονης της σωτηριας τευξεται ως
ηδικημενα ελεηθεντα και μενει ανευ κολασεως τουτο γερας
λαβοντα το δε γαλα των γυναικων ρεον απο των μαστων και
πηγνυμενον φησιν ο πετρος εν τη αποκαλυψει γεννησει θηρια
λεπτα σαρκοφαγα και ανατρεχοντα εις αυτας κατεσθιει δια
τας αμαρτιας γινεσθαι τας κολασεις διδασκων

For example Peter in the Apocalypse says <u>that the
children born abortively</u> receive the better part. These
<u>are delivered to a care-taking (temelouchos) angel</u>, so
that after they have reached knowledge they may obtain
the better abode, as if they had suffered what they would
have suffered, had they attained to bodily life. But the
others shall obtain salvation only as people who have
suffered wrong and experienced mercy, and shall exist
without torment, having received this as their reward.
<u>But the milk of the mothers which flows from their
breasts and congeals</u>, says Peter in the Apocalypse, <u>shall
beget tiny flesh-eating</u> beasts and they shall run over
them and devour them--which teaches that the punishments
will come to pass by reason of the sins.[1]

These passages must be compared to the relevant section of the Akhmim Greek fragment (section 26):

πλησιον δε του τοπου εκεινου ειδον ετερον τοπον
τεθλιμμ[εν]ον εν <ω> ο ιχωρ και η δυσωδια των κολαζομενων
κατερρεε και ωσπερ λιμνη εγινετο εκει κακει εκαθηντο
γυναικες εξουσαι τον ιχωρα μεχρι τ[ω]ν τραχηλ[ων] και
αντικρυς αυτων πολλοι παιδες ο[ιτινε]ς αωροι ετ[ι]κτοντο
καθημενοι εκλαιον και προηρχοντο εξ αυ[των φλογ]ες πυρος
και τας γυναικας επλησσον κατα τω[ν] οφθαλμων αυται δε
ησαν αι α[γαμως τα βρεφη τεκο]υσαι και εκτρωσασαι

[1]Greek text of Stählin in Erich Klostermann, <u>Apocrypha
I. Reste des Petrus-evangeliums, der Petrus-Apokalypse und
des Kerygma Petri</u>, Kleine texte für Vorlesungen und Ubungen
3 (Berlin: Walter de Gruyter, 3rd ed., 1933), 12-13; English
trans. from Maurer, ibid., 674-675.

And near that place I saw another place jammed full in
which the matter and filth of the tortured flowed down
and became like a lake there. And women were sitting
there who had the matter up to their throats. And opposite them were many children who were born before their
time. While they sat they wept. And flames of fire came
out from them and struck the women in the eyes. These
were those who [unmarried had born infants] and caused
abortions.[1]

This should also be compared with the quotation below

from Methodius and, of course, to the Ethiopic text.

In the extant writings of Clement of Alexandria, the

Apocalypse of Peter is not cited often. Nevertheless, ac-

cording to Eusebius he did include it in the books of the

Bible upon which he commented.[2] He also cites it in the

same manner in which he cites Scripture.[3] But when in our

first fragment he says "the Scripture says," does he mean

our apocalypse? In this same fragment he does specifically

quote it by name. This might lead us to suspect that it is

another work he is quoting at the beginning of the fragment.

But then in the second fragment he again brings up the care-

taking angel and says it is found in the Apocalypse of Peter.

In the first fragment, however, Clement was speaking of ex-

posure of infants by their parents. In the second he is re-

ferring to abortion. Yet again on the other hand, these

passages are connected by their common use of the word

---

[1]Greek text of Klostermann, ibid., 10-11; English
translation my own.

[2]Eusebius, Historia Ecclesiastica 6, 14, 1.

[3]John M. Norris, "The Functional New Testament of
Clement of Alexandria" (Ph.D. dissertation, University of
Chicago, 1942).

τημελουχος 'caretaking' to an uncommon degree because that adjective is to be found only in these two passages and in the related one from Methodius (see below) in all of Greek literature. It is not found in the Akhmim text. But the translator of the Ethiopic apparently thought it was a name and transliterated it as Temlakos. The Greek Apocalypses of Paul and John also both understood it as a proper name.[1] This is a good example of how difficult it is to distinguish which words in these <u>Eclogae Propheticae</u> are excerpts from the <u>Apocalypse of Peter</u>, which are excerpts from some other writings, and which are Clement's own words.

This is not the place for a detailed comparison of all the relevant passages from Clement, Methodius, later apocalypses, the Akhmim fragment, and the Ethiopic translation. But a careful comparison yields the following results: (1) The original Greek text must have used the word τημελουχος. The confusion in Clement about whether this use was in connection with abortion or exposure of infants is to be explained by looking at the Ethiopic. There in Chapter 8 the aborted children receive justice first and then the exposed children. At the end of the chapter appears the sentence "But their children will be given to the angel Temlakos, but those who killed them will be punished forever, for (it is) God who has required it." Clement may have interpreted that

---

[1]See the discussion in M. R. James, "A New Text of the Apocalypse of Peter," <u>The Journal of Theological Studies</u> 12 (1911): 36-55, 157, 352-383, 573-583.

sentence to include both groups of children. That may also have been the intention of the original author. The Akhmim text omits any mention of the exposed infants. It does not use the word τημελουχος because the word was in the section omitted. This is a powerful witness that Clement had in this part of his Apocalypse of Peter a text closer to the Ethiopic than to the Akhmim fragment.

(2) In fragment one, the flash of fire (or lightning) which punishes the women was in the original apocalypse. The Ethiopic and the Akhmim fragment agree against Clement that this involved the aborted and not the exposed children. Clement apparently was refusing to distinguish them clearly. So too it is virtually certain that the punishment of the congealing milk from which beasts came and bit the women was also in the original. It appears in the Ethiopic in the same form (in the section omitted in the Akhmim text). Here again Clement has changed the group to which it referred, since the punishment itself is much more appropriate for the mothers of children already born than it is for women who have had abortions.

(3) The lesson which the apocalypse teaches is said by Clement at the end of the second fragment to be "the punishments will come to pass by reason of the sins (δια τας αμαρτιας). Corresponding to this in the Ethiopic text are those places where it is explicitly said "Punishment is according to the deed"(1:8, 6:3, 6:6, 13:3, 13:6). In light of this, it is likely that Clement read this sentence in his

text of the apocalypse and that it should be translated "The punishments will take place by means of the sins."

(4) In fragment one Clement says that the exposed children will be brought up and nourished by the angel. In the second fragment we apparently have an expansion of this. It seems to say that they are allowed to mature, giving them a chance to obtain the "better abode." If they do not reach that better abode, however, they remain unpunished out of mercy because they have been wronged. This may be Clement's own elaboration and probably reflects his own theology, carried out logically from that of the apocalypse; that is, these children too must be tested by life for their own reward or punishment.

(5) The most puzzling item is in fragment one of Clement--"And they shall be, it says, as the faithful of a hundred years old here." James thinks this to have originated from a combination of Isaiah 65:20 and Wisdom 4:6-9.[1] But regardless of its origin, was it in the Apocalypse of Peter? Clement appears to say that it was, but we do not find it in any of our texts or references. The matter must remain unresolved. A speculative suggestion would be that Clement is actually commenting on another unknown text to which he relates quotations from the Apocalypse of Peter. The "it says" would then refer to this unknown text. This would also help to explain the use here of δıο 'wherefore' which does not

---

[1]M. R. James, "A New Text of the Apocalypse of Peter," ibid., 371, 376.

fit well here as a particle used to indicate conclusions
drawn.[1] διο would then mark the return to quotations from
the apocalypse.

From these fragments in Clement we learn that the EC
Apocalypse of Peter was known, read, quoted, and commented
upon by a scholar in Egypt c. 200 CE. Clement used it as
scripture and drew theological conclusions from it. His
quotes reflect the form of the text we have in the Ethiopic
translation.

3. The Pagan Writer Quoted in Macarius Magnes

We do not have a great deal of information about Macarius Magnes. He probably was bishop of Magnesia around
400 CE and wrote the Apocritica about that time.[2] This work
is written in dialogue form. A pagan philosopher has his
objections refuted by Macarius. But the words of the pagan
philosopher are all taken verbatim from a widely-read attack
on Christianity. Von Harnack has shown that this attack was
a shortened revision of the fifteen books of Porphyry called
Against the Christians.[3] Porphyry was a Neo-Platonist, a

---

[1]James was particularly troubled by this διο and insisted that it indicated a whole new section in the Eclogae
Propheticae. He apparently won his way with Stählin when
that text was reedited. See J. Montague Robinson and M. R.
James, The Gospel According to Peter, and The Revelation of
Peter (London: C. J. Clay, 1892), 72; and James, "A New Text
of the Apocalypse of Peter," ibid., 369-370.

[2]Quasten, ibid., vol. 3, 486-488.

[3]Adolf von Harnack, Kritik des Neuen Testaments von
einem griechischen Philosophen des 3. Jahrhunderts, ibid.,
137-144.

student of Plotinus from 262/3 onwards. Plotinus had sent
him to Sicily where he wrote his attack on Christianity apparently sometime before 270 CE.[1] We assign the references
in Macarius, then, to two different sections, depending upon
whether they are from Porphyry or from Macarius himself.

a. From Porphyry c. 270 CE

While quoting passages from the New Testament, after
he has repudiated the saying from the synoptics "Many will
come in my name saying I am the Christ" and before he at-
tacks some of Jesus' parables, Porphyry digresses to treat
the topic of the destruction of heaven and earth. He quotes
twice from the Apocalypse of Peter in order to refute two of
its teachings.

The first of these is in Apocritica 4, 6:

περιουσιας δ ενεκεν λελεχθω κακεινο το λελεγμενον εν
τη αποκαλυψει του πετρου εισαγει τον ουρανον αμα τη γη
κριθησεσθαι ουτως η γη (φησι) παραστησει παντας τω θεω
κρινουμενους εν ημερα κρισεως και αυτη μελλουσα κρινεσθαι
συν και τω περιεχοντι ουρανω

By way of superfluity let this word also be quoted
from the Apocalypse of Peter. He introduces the view
that the heaven will be judged along with the earth in
the following words, "The earth will present before God
on the day of judgment all men who are to be judged and
itself also will be judged with the heaven that encom-
passes it."

The second quote is in Apocritica 4, 7:

και εκεινο δ αυθις λεγει ο και ασεβειας μεστον υπαρχει το

---

[1]Frederick Copleston, A History of Philosophy (Westminster, Maryland: Newman Press, 1950), 463-464 and 473-475.

ρημα φασκον και τακησεται πασα δυναμις ουρανου και ελιχ-
θησεται ο ουρανος ως βιβλιον και παντα τα αστρα πεσειται
ως φυλλα εξ αμπελου και ως πιπτει φυλλα απο συκης

And again he says this statement which is full of impiety, saying "And every power of heaven shall burn, and
the heaven shall be rolled up like a book and all the
stars shall fall like leaves from a vine and like leaves
from a fig-tree."[1]

The first of these quotations is found in the Ethiopic

text, 4:13 "And the earth will give back all on the day of

judgment, for in it (the day) it (the earth) must be judged

at the same time, and heaven with it." The second has in

the Ethiopic an imperfect parallel at best and then only to

the first part "Even the stars will melt in a flame of fire

like they had not been created. And the firmaments of heaven

(will be) in a lack of water and go and become like what were

not created" (5:4-5). There are significant problems with

the state of the Ethiopic text here. But the real problem

is that this quote is not actually found in any of our texts

of the Apocalypse of Peter. It is an almost exact quote

from the LXX of Isaiah 34:4 as it is found in Vaticanus.

Maurer, assuming that the melting of the stars corresponds

to "Every power of heaven will burn" in that passage from

Isaiah, suggests that the pagan writer had the complete

quote of Is 34:4 in the manuscript he was using.[2] We have

no way of determining if it was part of the original Greek

---

[1]Greek text in Klostermann, ibid., 13; English trans.
Maurer, ibid., 671.

[2]Maurer, ibid., 671.

text, but its omission in the Ethiopic suggests that perhaps some scribe added it as a proof text in one of the Greek manuscripts.

But we are not yet finished with Porphyry as a witness. The remainder is less direct because the apocalypse is not mentioned by name as the source. Nevertheless, there can be little doubt that when Porphyry turns to the subject of resurrection in Apocritica 5, 24 he is criticizing that doctrine as it is presented in the Apocalypse of Peter.[1] He begins by saying that the creation must be eternal since it has derived from an immortal being. Then he criticizes the idea that the body can be returned after being eaten by birds or fish or beasts or after being burned. Anticipating that the Christians will reply with "It is possible for God" (τουτο τω θεω δυνατον), he denies that God can do all things and gives several examples of things God cannot do. Then he asserts as absurd the very idea that God would destroy the beautiful heaven and the earth while at the same time he is raising up old dead bodies, some of which were gruesome even before they died. Besides the earth would have no room for all those who had died since its creation.[2] Porphyry was basing his criticism on the destruction of heaven and earth and the description of a very physical resurrection in chapters 4 and 5 of the Ethiopic text. There it is said that

---

[1]M. R. James, "The Recovery of the Apocalypse of Peter," The Church Quarterly Review 80 (1915), 29-31.

[2]Greek text and German translation in von Harnack, Kritik des Neuen Testaments, ibid., 92-95.

the beasts and birds will give back at the resurrection the flesh they have eaten when God commands it, for nothing is impossible for God.

From these fragments of Porphyry we learn that c. 270 CE the Apocalypse of Peter was targeted for criticism by an opponent of the Christians who probably saw it as easy prey. He quotes from the apocalypse in about the same way he quotes from other scriptures. He may have found it among the other Christian scriptures in Rome where his teacher Plotinus had his school. He was acquainted with chapters 4 and 5 which are missing from every Greek text we possess.

b. From Macarius Magnes

How did Macarius respond to these criticisms of Porphyry? We will quote the translations of James[1]:

> Let us examine this "trumped-up" (κεκομψευμενην) statement in the Apocalypse of Peter (which he repeats). Of course it is obvious that heaven and earth are not to be judged because of any sin they have committed; but it is equally plain that the divine word contains no lie. For even if we rule out the Apocalypse of Peter, the words both of the prophet and of the gospel combine to drive us into agreement with the Apocalypse whether we will or no, since the prophet says "The heaven shall be rolled up," etc. and the gospel, "Heaven and earth shall pass away" etc.

James goes on to say that Macarius nowhere shows any signs of having read the Apocalypse of Peter.[2] From the reply of Macarius and from the study made by James, we learn

---

[1]M. R. James, "The Recovery of the Apocalypse of Peter," ibid., 31; from Apocritica 4, 16.

[2]Ibid.

that c. 400 CE in Magnesia (Asia Minor) Macarius was not
well acquainted with the Apocalypse of Peter. He seems to
agree with it rather reluctantly and probably did not treat
it as Scripture.

4. The Rainer and Bodleian Fragments of the Greek Text

A discussion of the Rainer fragment and its importance
for editing the Ethiopic, as well as the text itself, is
given in Chapter 4 in the comments on Apocalypse of Peter
14. The text of the Bodleian fragment is presented and discussed in Chapter 2 in the description of the manuscripts.
In this latter chapter I also discuss the reasons for assuming that these fragments both come from the same manuscript.

Since both these fragments are from Egypt, we learn
from them that a Greek text of the Apocalypse of Peter was
current there in the 3rd or 4th century. The manuscript is
in the same tradition as our Ethiopic text, but the Greek by
this time already shows signs of being corrupt. Perhaps the
original parent manuscript was already poorly written.

5. Methodius of Olympus (or Philippi)

According to Quasten[1] Methodius was thought in ancient
times to have been bishop of Olympus in Lycia and to have
died a martyr in Chalcia in 311 CE. More recently it has
been held that he was bishop of Philippi in Macedonia. Altaner questions that he was a bishop at all and the fact and

---

[1]Johannes Quasten, ibid., vol. 2, 129-137.

place of his martyrdom, believing that he was an itinerant teacher.[1] The date of his death must be generally correct, however. He was an opponent of Origen.

He wrote a Symposium modelled on Plato's work. It deals for the most part with the topic of virginity. The Apocalypse of Peter is quoted (but not by name) to defend the proposition that all human generation is the work of God, even the births which result from adultery.

This is from Symposium 2, 6:

οθεν δη και τημελουχοις αγγελοις καν εκ μοιχειας ωσιν τα αποτικτομενα παραδιδοσθαι παρειληφαμεν εν θεοπνευστοις γραμμασιν ει γαρ την γνωμην εγινοντο και τον θεσμον της μακαριας εκεινης φυσεως του θεου πως αγγελοις ταυτα παρεδιδοτο τραφησομενα μετα πολλης αναπαυσεως και ραστωνης πως δε και κατηγορησοντα σφων αυτων τους γονεις ευπαρρησιαστως εις το δικαστηριον εκικλησκον του χριστου συ ουκ εφθονησας ημιν ω κυριε το κοινον λεγοντα τουτο φως ουτοι δε ημας εις θανατον εξεθεντο καταφρονησαντες της σης εντολης

Whence, also, we have received from the inspired writings, that those who are begotten, even though it be in adultery, are committed to guardian angels. But if they came into being in opposition to the will and the decree of the blessed nature of God, how should they be delivered over to angels, to be nourished with much gentleness and indulgence? and how, if they had to accuse their own parents, could they confidently, before the judgment seat of Christ, invoke Him and say, "Thou didst not, O Lord, grudge us this common life; but these appointed us to death, despising thy command?"[2]

---

[1]Berthold Altaner, ibid., 242-244.

[2]Greek text from Klostermann, ibid., 23; English trans. by William R. Clark in Alexander Roberts and James Donaldson, eds., The Ante-Nicene Fathers (New York: Charles Scribners Sons, 1925), vol. 6, p. 316.

This fragment is related to the two in Clement (see above). They all have the same form: (1) mention of the caretaking angel (or angels); (2) other material probably relating to the more general context; and, (3) a quote from the Apocalypse of Peter itself. But in each of them the quotation is different. All three quotations are found in the Ethiopic text. The quotation in Methodius, missing in the Akhmim fragment, is found in 8:5-7.

From this fragment we learn that c. 300 CE probably in Macedonia or Asia Minor the Apocalypse of Peter was highly regarded, even considered inspired Scripture by a competent theologian. Methodius felt free to use it in a philosophical treatise written in defense of the faith. He does not quote it by name. Perhaps this reveals a reluctance to use this apocalypse openly, but equally it could be said that perhaps the Apocalypse of Peter was so well known that it was unnecessary to name it, as is also often true of the other Scriptures.

6. Eusebius of Caesarea

The famous church historian Eusebius needs little introduction. He apparently was born and educated in Caesarea in Palestine at the school which Origen founded there. He seems to have written the earlier section of his Ecclesiastical History before 303 CE. Twice in book three he gives his opinion of our apocalypse. We quote these only in translation.

The first is found in Historia Ecclesiastica 3, 3, 2.

Eusebius discusses the writings of Peter. He accepts the

first epistle, rejects the second but notes that many have

found it useful and then continues:

> On the other hand, of the Acts bearing his name, and
> the Gospel named according to him and Preaching called
> his and the so-called Revelation [Apocalypse], we have
> no knowledge at all in the Catholic tradition, for no
> orthodox writer of the ancient time or of our own has
> used their testimonies. [1]

Later in the same book at 3, 25, 4-6 he summarizes the

writings of the New Testament as he uses them. He lists the

four Gospels, Acts, the Epistles of Paul, I John, and I

Peter. Following that (after saying that possibly the Rev-

elation of John belongs with these recognized books), he

lists the disputed books which are the Epistles of James,

Jude, II Peter, and II and III John. He continues:

> Among the books which are not genuine must be reckoned
> the Acts of Paul, the work entitled the Shepherd, the
> Apocalypse of Peter, and in addition to them the letter
> called of Barnabas and the so-called teaching of the
> Apostles. And in addition, as I said, the Revelation of
> John, if this view prevail. For as I said, some reject
> it, but others count it among the Recognized Books. Some
> have also counted the Gospel according to the Hebrews in
> which those of the Hebrews who have accepted Christ take
> a special pleasure. These would all belong to the dis-
> puted books, but we have nevertheless been obliged to
> make a list of them, distinguishing between those writ-
> ings which, according to the traditions of the Church,
> are true, genuine, and recognized, and those which differ
> from them in that they are not canonical but disputed,
> yet nevertheless are known to most of the writers of the
> Church, in order that we might know them and the writings
> which are put forward by heretics under the name of the

---

[1] Kirsopp Lake, trans., Eusebius. The Ecclesiastical
History, Loeb Classical Library No. 153 (Cambridge: Harvard
University Press, 1926), Vol. 1, 193.

apostles containing gospels such as those of Peter, and Thomas, and Matthias, and some others besides, or Acts such as those of Andrew and John and the other apostles.[1]

From these reports of Eusebius we learn that Eusebius did not hold a favorable view of the Apocalypse of Peter. His own view is probably that of the first report, though he overstates the case when he claims that no orthodox writer had used it. In the second passage, he has, if I read him right, four categories: (1) the recognized books; (2) the books whose authorship was disputed; (3) those which are spurious but yet of orthodox teaching; and finally, (4) those books which are heretical. From the tone which he uses, those books in the third category which includes the Apocalypse of Peter are despised by Eusebius. He probably gives them a separate place because of public opinion. This may be a clue, though it is indefinite, that our apocalypse about 300 CE in Palestine had fallen out of favor with church leaders (but note Methodius' quotation given above) while it retained a more popular appeal.

7. Homily on the Parable of the Ten Virgins

This writing is a Latin sermon, probably from North Africa. Its discoverer Wilmart places it in the 4th century. It is an allegorical explanation of the parable of the Ten Virgins from Matt. 25:1-13.

Lines 58-60 read:

Ostium clausum flumen igneum est quo impii regno Dei

---

[1]Ibid., pp. 257-259.

arcebuntur, et apud Danielum et apud Petrum--in Apocalypsi
cius--scriptum est.

The closed door is the river of fire by which the ungodly
will be kept out of the kingdom of God, as it is written
in Daniel and by Peter in his Apocalypse.

Lines 77-78:

Resurget et illa stultorum pars, et inveniet ostium
iam clausum, opposito scilicet flumine igneo.

That party of the foolish shall also arise and find
the door shut, that is, the river of fire lying before
them.[1]

In this case the parallels to a river of fire are

clearly from our apocalypse because it is mentioned by name.

The river of fire is found in 5:8-6:5 and 12:4-7. The Ten

Virgins are found in the Ethiopic manuscripts at 11:6 in a

context in which they do not seem to belong.

This is an important witness for the use of our apocalypse

as scripture in the churches of North Africa in the 4th cen-

tury CE.

8. Sozomen

The lawyer Sozomen was born in Palestine, travelled in

Italy, and settled in Constantinople. In this city he wrote

between 439 and 450 CE his Historia Ecclesiastica. In book

6, chapter 19 while reviewing various regional customs of

churches, he has the following:

---

[1]Latin text from André Wilmart, "Un anonyme ancien De
X Virginibus," Bulletin d'ancienne littérature et archéologie
chrétiennes 1 (1910), 35-49 and 88-102; English trans. from
Maurer, ibid., 678; see also M. R. James, "A New Text of the
Apocalypse of Peter," ibid., 383

ουτω γουν την καλουμενην αποκαλυψιν πετρου ως νοθεν
παντελως προς των αρχαιων δοκιμασθεισαν εν τισιν
εκκλησιαις της παλαιστινης εισετι νυν απαξ εκαστου ετους
αναγινωσκομενην εγνωμεν εν τη ημερα παρασκευης ην ευλαβως
αγαν ο λαος νηστευει επι αναμνησει του σωτηριου παθους

So, at any rate, we have discovered the so-called
Apocalypse of Peter, proved entirely spurious by the
ancients, being read in some churches of Palestine even
now once each year during the day of preparation on which
the people most reverently fast in commemoration of the
saving passion [i.e., on Good Friday].[1]

We learn from Sozomen that the Apocalypse of Peter was
read as Scripture, i.e., was part of the lectionary, at some
churches of Palestine slightly before the middle of the 5th
century CE. This was for Sozomen an abberation, so we can
assume it was quite uncommon elsewhere. Even "the ancients"
knew it was spurious. Did he get this last information from
Eusebius, whose writings he knew? The tradition that this
apocalypse was scripture took a long time to die out. Why
was this apocalypse thought to be appropriate for Good Fri-
day? Perhaps to make the deliverance won by Christ on the
cross seem more vivid; and perhaps also to drive people more
deeply into repentance on the day when they "most reverently
fast."

9. The Catalogue in Codex Claromontanus

In Codex Claromontanus there is a stichometry of the
biblical writings in which the name Apocalypse of Peter

---

[1]Greek text in J. P. Migne, Patrologia Graeca (Paris:
Bibliothecae Cleri universae, 1864), Vol. 67, col. 1477;
English trans. my own.

appears in last place. It may be as early as the fourth
century CE, but is sixth century at latest because the manuscript is that old. Since it is difficult to date and since
we cannot determine with certainty the place of origin, we
learn only that the Apocalypse of Peter was being copied and
that it was about 270 lines long. That is roughly the size
of II Timothy, listed at 288 lines. The exact length of
these lines is not known. For purposes of making copy,
probably the average length of a line of Homer (36-38 letters) was standard.[1]

10. The List of the Sixty Books

This list is found in several manuscripts and may be
from c. 600 CE. It names 60 canonical books, then a few
writings outside the sixty, and finally 25 apocryphal books.
The Apocalypse of Peter is the sixteenth on the list of
apocrypha. The list probably reflects the attitude among
church leaders of its time. It also shows us a trend--this
apocalypse had lost its battle for recognition.[2]

11. The Akhmim Fragment of the Greek Text

This was discovered in Egypt in 1886/7. It has been
variously dated from the sixth to the twelfth centuries,
with current opinion preferring the earlier dating. See the

---

[1]Wilhelm Schneemelcher, Edgar Hennecke, ed., New Testament Apocrypha, ibid., vol. 1, 45-46.

[2]Ibid., 51-52.

discussion of it in chapter two. It is certainly a different rescension of the text than we have in the Ethiopic or the earlier church fathers. How valuable it is for restoring the original Greek of our apocalypse is open to question. It demonstrates the popularity of the Apocalypse of Peter in Egypt at this late date. The fact that this fragment was found buried with a monk may indicate an association of our apocalypse with funeral practices, perhaps almost of a magical sort.

12. The Stichometry of Nicephorus

The origin of this list of canonical books is not certain. It is probably from Jerusalem c. 850 CE. The list divides the writings in three groups--recognized, disputed, and apocryphal. Four New Testament writings are said to be disputed. They are the Apocalypse of John, the Apocalypse of Peter, the Epistle of Barnabas, and the Gospel of the Hebrews. The length of each work is given, and the Apocalypse of Peter is said to have 300 lines. Apparently even in the middle of the 9th century CE our apocalypse continued to be copied in Palestine and was treated with more esteem than the apocryphal books. The difference between the 270 lines mentioned in the Codex Claromontarus and the 300 lines given here should not be taken to have any significance.[1]

---

[1]Ibid., 49-51.

B. Indirect Witnesses for the EC
Apocalypse of Peter

There are many writings in the early church which have some parallels to the Apocalypse of Peter. Some of these, such as those in the Pistis Sophia, the Testament of Our Lord, the Apocalypse of Zosimus, and in Commodian are matters of form or general subject matter only and do not witness direct knowledge of our apocalypse. Others are no real parallels at all. These include those found by James in II Clement and the Shepherd of Hermas.[1] There are yet others which are so late in date that similarity of content with our apocalypse is most likely due to general public views or to borrowing from the Apocalypse of Paul. This latter apocalypse became very popular in the Middle Ages and made many of the earlier traits in the Apocalypse of Peter well known. Such late writings as the Greek Apocalypse of the Virgin, the Apocalypse of Esdras, the Ethiopic Conflict of Matthew, the Apocalypse of John, the Ethiopic Apocalypse of the Virgin, and the story of Barlaam and Joasaph need not concern us here. There remain 18 witnesses or supposed witnesses of various sorts that need to be discussed.

1. The Sibylline Oracles, Book 2   c. 150

2. The Epistula Apostolorum   2nd century (160-170?)

3. Theophilus of Antioch   shortly after 180

4. Celsus   c. 180

---

[1]M. R. James, "A New Text of the Apocalypse of Peter," ibid., 380-383.

5.	The Acts of Paul	c. 190
6.	The Acts of Thomas	c. 200
7.	The Passion of Perpetua and Felicitas	202
8.	Hippolytus of Rome	220-235
9.	Pseudo-Cyprian, De laudi martyrii	3rd century
10.	The Coptic Apocalypse of Elijah	3rd century
11.	Pseudo-Cyprian, Adversus aleatores	c. 300?
12.	Ephraem Syrus	4th century
13.	Cyril of Jerusalem	c. 350
14.	The Apocalypse of Paul	late 4th century
15.	The Apocalypse of Thomas	c. 400
16.	The Pseudo-Titus Epistle	5th century
17.	Carmen de Iudicio Domini	c. 500?
18.	The Ethiopic Apocalypse on the Tübingen Manuscript	date unknown

1. The Sibylline Oracles, Book 2

The earliest and the most valuable of all these witnesses to the Apocalypse of Peter is the second book of the
Sibylline Oracles. The parallels are given by James who
places the Greek lines from the oracles beside the corresponding lines of the apocalypse (translated from the Ethiopic).[1] The nature of the parallels is such that there can
be no doubt whatsoever that the author of the oracles used
the apocalypse. The generally accepted date for book 2 is

---

[1]M. R. James, "A New Text of the Apocalypse of Peter,"
ibid., 39-52.

c. 150 CE.[1] We will list the parallels in a general way,

not pointing out the borrowing of details, and then discuss

them briefly.

	Ap. Pt.	Sib. Or. 2
coming of deceivers	2:7-8	165-166
miracles done by a deceiver (or Belier) (not given by James)	2:8, 13	167-168(176)
confusion among early Christians and Jews (not given by James)	2:9-12	168-170
raising of dead bodies	4:2-9	221-237
river of fire burns all heaven and earth	5:2-9	194-220
Christ comes to hold judgment	6:1-6	238-254
torments of sinners in hell	7:1-12:7	255-308
righteous are given their reward by angels	13:1-2	313-329
appeal by the punished for mercy is rejected	13:4-6	309-312
sinners are saved from torment by the prayers of the righteous and placed in Elysium	14:1-3	330-338

The first three parallels went unnoticed by James.

The first two are certain but could possibly be attributed

to common tradition rather than to dependence. The third is

indefinite, but both writings may be alluding to a recent

[1]Alfons Kurfess, "Christian Sibyllines," Edgar Hennecke, New Testament Apocrypha, ibid., vol. 2, 703-745; Alfons Kurfess, "Oracula Sibyllina I/II," Zeitschrift für die neutestamentliche Wissenschaft 40 (1941), 151-168; Adella Yarbro Collins, "Early Christian Apocalypses," John Collins, ed., Apocalypse: The Morphology of a Genre, Semeia 14 (1979), 97-98.

political event, the Bar Kochba rebellion (see the discussion below on the date of the Apocalypse of Peter).

Of the remaining parallels, the major differences are one of order of events. In the Apocalypse of Peter the dead are raised before the conflagration and then all are driven by the fire to the place of judgment. In the Sibylline Oracles 2 the conflagration occurs first, the angels bring the souls of living people to the judgment seat, and then the dead are raised and brought to join the living for the judgment. Again, in the Apocalypse of Peter the tormented sinners plead for mercy and are denied it while the righteous watch, having received their heavenly life. But in the oracles, the plea for mercy precedes the description of the rewards. As a result the prayer of the righteous in the oracles is made from their heavenly paradise which is wonderfully described. But in the apocalypse the prayer is made before the righteous enter into their kingdom, which is never described.

By c. 150 CE our apocalypse was used as a major source for Book 2 of the Sibylline Oracles, which follows it closely for about 150 lines. Thus we have conclusive evidence that Apocalypse of Peter 4:2-14:3 was known at that time in a form similar to that which is found in the Ethiopic text. Perhaps also 2:7-12 was used but this is less certain.

2. The Epistula Apostolorum

This Epistle of the Apostles is preserved for us in
Coptic and in Ethiopian. No early Christian writers mention
it. Carl Schmidt dates it 160-170 CE, but others have
thought it even earlier.[1] In form it is parallel to our
apocalypse, i.e., it is a conversation which Jesus carried
on with his disciples after the resurrection. Besides this
the following should be noted:

1) In chapter 16 we read: And we said to him, "O Lord,
great is this that you say and reveal to us. In what kind
of power and form are you about to come?" And he said to
us, "Truly I say to you, I will come as the sun which bursts
forth; thus will I, shining seven times brighter than it in
glory, while I am carried on the wings of the clouds in
splendour with my cross going on before me, come to the
earth to judge the living and the dead." See Apocalypse of
Peter 1:6-7.

2) In chapter 26 the flesh rises with the spirit at
the final resurrection, judgment takes place according to
deeds and is eternal, and the reward of the righteous is
rest in the kingdom of the Father. This appears to be a
summary of Apocalypse of Peter and is the final answer to the
question asked as early as chapter 19, "In what form [will
we belong to the Father's incorruptibility]? Of an angel or

---

[1]Carl Schmidt, Gespräche Jesu mit seinen Jüngern nach
der Auferstehung, (Leipzig: J. C. Hinrichs, 1919); J. Quasten, ibid., vol. 1, 150-153.

that of flesh?" There is considerable stress on the resurrection of the flesh in both documents. Cf. Apocalypse of Peter 4-6.

3) When Jesus says at the end of chapter 39 "I, the word became flesh and died, teaching and guiding, that some shall be saved, but the others eternally ruined, being punished by fire in flesh and spirit," his disciples (ch. 40) express concern for the punished. To this Jesus says:

> "You do well, for so are the righteous anxious about sinners, and they pray and implore God and ask him." And we said to him, "O Lord, does no one entreat you?" And he said to us, "Yes, I will hear the requests of the righteous concerning them."[1]

See Apocalypse of Peter 14:1-3.

4) In chapter 51 the heavens divide, and a bright cloud comes and carries Jesus away while the angels rejoice. This is similar to Apocalypse of Peter 17.

In the Epistula Apostolorum we have a document from c. 160-170 CE which uses the EC Apocalypse of Peter chapters 1, 14, and 17 and also indicates acquaintance with chapters 4-6. We might ask further if chapter 26 does not show acquaintance with chapter 16 of the apocalypse. Thus the author of the later document probably knew well the whole apocalypse.

3. Theophilus of Antioch

Theophilus was bishop of Antioch in Syria. He wrote a defense of Christianity shortly after 180 CE. It is known

---

[1] English trans. from Hugo Duensing, "Epistula Aposto-

as Ad Autolycum. Quispel and Grant[1] noticed there an

allusion to the Apocalypse of Peter in 2,19:

μετα δε το πλασαι τον ανθρωπον ο θεος εξελεξατο

αυτω χωριον εν τοις τοποις τοις ανατολικοις διαφορον

φωτι διαυγες αερι λαμπροτερω φυτοις παγκαλοις εν ω

εθετο τον ανθρωπον

> After man's formation, God selected for him an area
> in the eastern regions, distinguished with light,
> radiant with shining air, with exquisite plants, and
> he placed man in it.[2]

The alleged parallel would exist with the Akhmim

fragment 15:

> And the Lord showed me a widely extensive place
> outside this world, all gleaming with light, and the
> air there flooded by the rays of the sun, and the
> earth itself budding with flowers which fade not, and
> full of spices and plants which blossom gloriously
> and fade not and bear blessed fruit.[3]

The evidence is not convincing because it was normal

at that time to describe paradise with much light and beau-

tiful plants. Compare, for example, Enoch 28-33, 108:11-15.

However, most of chapter 14 of book one of Ad Autolycum is

concerned with warning Autolycus to believe in order to

escape the eternal punishments. If Autolycus does not

believe now, he will come to believe when he is in eternal

lorum," Edgar Hennecke, ed., New Testament Apocrypha, ibid.,
vol. 1, 189-227.

[1]G. Quispel and R. M. Grant, "Note on the Petrine
Apocrypha," Vigiliae Christianae 6 (1952), 31-32.

[2]Greek text in J. P. Migne, Patrologia Graece (Paris:
Bibliotheca Cleri Universae, 1857), vol. 6, col. 1084; Eng.
trans. my own.

[3]Translation in Maurer, ibid., 681-682.

torment. But the prophets and other ancients who stole from them have told about such punishments so that no one will be able to say, "We have not heard, and we did not know." With this should be compared Apocalypse of Peter 7:8 where adulterers say, "We did not know that we had to come into eternal punishment;" 7:11 where the murderers say, "For we heard and did not believe that we would come into this eternal place of punishment;" and 13:4 where all the tormented say together, "Have mercy on us, for now we have learned the judgment of God which he told us beforehand and we did not believe."

While this evidence is still not conclusive, it is likely that Theophilus was acquainted with the Apocalypse of Peter and even, if I gather the full sense of Ad Autolycum 1,14, that it may have played a role in his conversion to Christianity. When Theophilus appeals in that chapter to prophets who preceded the Greek poets and philosophers, he may have in mind the Sibylline Oracles, particularly Book 2. Yet we do not find there the theme of forced belief for those in torment. If we accept this as evidence, then Theophilus knew of the torments in hell, at least in chapter 7 and/or the appeal for mercy in chapter 13.

4. Celsus

Celsus wrote an attack on Christianity called True Discourse about 178 CE. We have large portions of it preserved because Origen quotes it at length in his apology

Contra Celsum. M. R. James[1] believes that Celsus had in
mind the Apocalypse of Peter when he said (Contra Celsum
5,14):

> Another piece of silliness is their notion that
> when God lights up, like a cook, the rest of the race
> will be roasted and they only will escape--not only
> those that are alive, but those too who have died
> long since, popping out of the ground in their orig-
> inal bodies. It is a worm's hope, absolutely. What
> human soul could ever want its rotten body back? and
> you do not even all agree in the belief.

Immediately following this, Celsus says that the
Christians have no answer but need to resort to the absurd
notion that all things are possible with God. Origen's
reply to Celsus (6,15) involves the condescension that this
is a doctrine for the simple people to drive them away from
vice.[2] It is the combination of the fire, the resurrection,
and the appeal to God's omnipotence in raising dead bodies
which convinces James that Celsus wrote with a view to our
apocalypse. And he could very well be right, since we find
this combination seldom at this early time. Later these
ideas would be more widespread, as indeed they probably were
by Origen's time. But the evidence is far from conclusive.

5. The Acts of Paul

Tertullian relates a story in which the author of the

---

[1]M. R. James, "The Recovery of the Apocalypse of
Peter," ibid., 28-29.

[2]We have no evidence that Origen himself knew the
Apocalypse of Peter. Yet this has been conjectured. See
the brief discussion by Hugo Duensing, "Apocalypse of Paul,"
in New Testament Apocrypha, ed. Edgar Hennecke, rev. ed. by
Wilhelm Schneemelcher, ibid., vol. 2, 755.

Acts of Paul was discovered and because of his forgery was removed from his office as a presbyter. From the story we learn that these acts were composed before 190 CE in Asia Minor.[1] The Acts of Paul was a large collection of traditions about Paul which was early divided and has come down to us in three independent pieces--The Acts of Paul and Thecla, The Correspondence of St. Paul with the Corinthians, and the Martyrium Pauli. None of the supposed parallels are convincing and we cannot claim the Acts of Paul as a witness. They do not show that the author used our apocalypse, only that he was acquainted with some similar popular material.

The supposed allusions are these: a) In The Acts of Paul and Thecla 3,28-29 the virgin Thecla prays for the dead girl Falconilla, that the latter may be transferred to the place of the just. This is similar to Apocalypse of Peter 14:1-3 where the righteous are given leave to spring the sinners from torment by prayer. b) Thecla is thrown to the beasts and survives. As she is released the governor gives her clothing, to which she responds "he who clothed me when I was naked among the beasts shall clothe me with salvation in the day of judgment" (Acts of Paul and Thecla 3,37-38). In Apocalypse of Peter 13:1 the righteous and elect receive the clothing of celestial life. c) In the correspondence,

---

[1]Wilhelm Schneemelcher, "Acts of Paul," Edgar Hennecke, ed., New Testament Apocrypha, ibid., vol. 2, 322-390; Quasten, ibid., vol. I, 130-133. The quotations which follow are from this edition.

in the letter known as III Corinthians, the resurrection of
the body is defended with the analogy of the seed sown into
the ground and rising with life. This is followed with the
question "How much more. . .will he raise up you who have
believed in Jesus Christ, as he himself rose up?" (24-31).
Compare the same image and question in Apocalypse of Peter
4:10-12. d) The final judgment is more often mentioned in
the Martyrium Pauli than elsewhere, particularly in chapter
4. There we find mention of the living God who comes from
heaven as judge because of the lawless deeds that are done
in the world. "He comes to burn the world until it is
pure." Compare this with Apocalypse of Peter 5-6. e) In
the Coptic fragments edited by R. Kasser,[1] Paul is destroying the gods of Ephesus. The popular report of his activ-
ities is "This man destroys the gods, saying: Ye shall see
them all burned with fire." In the Apocalypse of Peter 6:7-
9, 10:5-7 the idols and the demons that inhabited them are
burned.

6. The Acts of Thomas

The Acts of Thomas comes from Edessa in Syria towards
the beginning of the 3rd century CE. It represents a gnostic Christianity centered in Mesopotamia.[2]

The relevant section is the Sixth Act. A young

---

[1]Ibid., 387-390.

[2]Günther Bornkamm, "The Acts of Thomas," Edgar Hennecke, ed., New Testament Apocrypha, ibid., vol. 2, 425-531;
Quasten, ibid., vol. 1, 139-140.

Christian man has killed his girlfriend because she has refused to live celibate with him and he cannot bear to see her defiled by sexual intercourse. She is raised from the dead and reports on her trip around hell. There are wheels of fire with souls hung on them (see Apocalypse of Peter 12:5-7), sexual perverts (see 10:2-4), babies testifying (see chapter 8), adulterers (see 7:5-8), mire and worms (see 8:1 and 9:2), people hung by the tongue and by the hair (see 7:2 and 7:5), and a hateful black man with dirty clothes (see Akhmim Fragment 21).

It is clear that the author of the Acts of Thomas was acquainted at least with Apocalypse of Peter 7-12 (the visions of hell). This is an important witness because it comes from the east and from among a less than orthodox group. These Acts became widespread and were used in the much later Barlaam and Joasaph legends.

7. The Passion of Perpetua and Felicitas

Saturus, Saturninus, Revocatus, Perpetua, and Felicitas all suffered martyrdom in Carthage c. 202 CE. Very shortly after this someone collected the personal accounts of prison life and visions from God which Perpetua and Saturus themselves had written while imprisoned and added to these accounts the story of their deaths in the arena. This author may have been Tertullian.[1]

---

[1]R. E. Wallis, trans., "The Martyrdom of Perpetua and Felicitas," A. Roberts and J. Donaldson, eds., The Ante-Nicene Fathers, ibid., vol. 3, 691-706; Quasten, ibid., vol. 1, 181-183.

In the second of her visions Perpetua sees her dead
brother Dinocrates "going out from a gloomy place . . .
parched and very thirsty, with a filthy countenance and
pallid colour." This may be compared with the gloomy place
where were the angels who wore dark clothing in Akhmim
Fragment 21. The vision of Saturus has some parallels to
the description of paradise in Akhmim Fragment 15-20. This
garden was an extensive space outside the world, brightly
illuminated, with flowers and trees and angels and an in-
credibly sweet odor.[1]

It is difficult to say if these parallels indicate a
dependence on the Apocalypse of Peter. The description is
closer to the Greek than to the Ethiopic, which seems corrupt and abridged at this point. In particular the bright
light and the angels are missing from the Ethiopic (16:2-5).
However, the Ethiopic perhaps indicates the presence of
martyrs (16:5) which are also present in Saturus's vision
but not in the Greek. I am inclined to attribute the parallels to the standard paraphernalia of paradise rather than
to dependence of the vision on our apocalypse.

8. Hippolytus of Rome

Hippolytus was a presbyter in Rome who opposed Pope
Callistus (217-222) and led a schismatic movement in that

---

[1]M. R. James and J. A. Robinson, The Gospel According
to Peter, and the Revelation of Peter, ibid., 60-61; J. A.
MacCulloch, Early Christian Visions of the Other-World
(Edinburgh: St. Giles, 1912), 17-23, esp. 21.

city that apparently continued until shortly before his
death in 235 CE. It is likely that while he spent most of
his life in Rome, he was not a native but came there from
somewhere in the east.[1] In any case he writes in Greek.
There are two relevant passages in the surviving works.

a) The first is the remains of a work mostly lost
called On the Universe (περι του παντος) written before 225
CE. The extant fragment concerns Hades. Hades is an
underground world with no light. It is a prison for souls
who are kept there until the final judgemnt. Angels lead
the sinners to the left and down to temporary places of torment based on the deeds of each soul. There is a lake of
unquenchable fire (Gehenna) with hot terrible smoke. The
wicked see it and know that it is for them on judgment day.
They also see paradise, a place of shining light and complete joy where the righteous wait for judgment day. On
that judgment day everyone, righteous and unrighteous will
be brought before Christ when he comes as judge. He assigns
to each what is righteous according to his works. "And
being present at His judicial decision, all, both men and
angels and demons, shall utter one voice, saying, "Righteous
is thy judgment."[2] The punishing angels (7:4), the picture
of the judgment day (chapter 6), the proximity of the pun-

---

[1]Quasten, ibid., vol. 2, 163-207.

[2]English trans. from S. D. F. Salmond, "Against Plato,
On the Cause of the Universe," A. Roberts and J. Donaldson,
eds., The Ante-Nicene Fathers, ibid., vol. 5, 221-223; see
also M. R. James and J. A. Robinson, ibid., 67-69.

ishments to the righteous (13:1-4), and the praise of God's righteous judgment by all (13:6) are found in the Apocalypse of Peter. This last detail in particular makes it likely that Hippolytus was using his knowledge of the Apocalypse of Peter in this treatise.

b) In Hippolytus' work The Refutation of All Heresies 10,30 (or 34), written after 222 CE, we find εκφευζεσθε

. . . ταρταρουχων αγγελων κολαστων ομμα αει μενον εν απειλη "You will escape the ever-continual menacing eye of the angels of torment who are in charge of hell (Tartaros)."[1] James points out that the adjective ταρταρουχος "in charge of Tartaros" is very rare and that Hippolytus probably got it from the Apocalypse of Peter. The Ethiopic translator treats it as a proper name (13:5).

These two passages taken together make it likely that Hippolytus knew our apocalypse. We should consider him a witness to the currency of the Apocalypse of Peter (particularly chapters 7-13) in Rome c. 225 CE.

9. Pseudo-Cyprian, De laudi martyrii

Among the writings attributed to Cyprian is a sermon On the Glory of Martyrdom. It is from the 3rd century CE.[2]

---

[1]Greek text from M. R. James, "A New Text of the Apocalypse of Peter," ibid., 370; English trans. my own; Cf. J. H. MacMahon, trans., Roberts and Donaldson, eds., The Ante-Nicene Fathers, ibid., vol. 5, 9-153, esp. 153.

[2]Quasten, ibid., vol. 2, 370-371; E. Wallis, trans., "On the Glory of Martyrdom," A. Roberts and J. Donaldson, eds., The Ante-Nicene Fathers, ibid., vol. 5, 579-587; Adolf von Harnack, "Die Petrusapokalypse in der alten abendländ-

Here we will only summarize the possible points of contact
with our apocalypse. They are found in chapters 19-21:
What is bad points out what is good. That is why one of
the rewards of the saints is to know that the sinners are
punished for their evil deeds. Gehenna is a place of wail-
ing, fire, and darkness. Each separate offence receives a
different appropriate punishment. Some of these are being
hurtled over a precipice (see Apocalypse of Peter 10:2-4),
heavy chains (see 10:6), a whirling wheel (12:4-6), and
severe crowding (12:1). On the other hand, the verdant
fields of the righteous have fragrant flowers, trees with
continual fruit (15:2-3), mild climate, joy, and the martyrs (15:5). This is not absolute proof, but it seems more
likely than not that the author knew the Apocalypse of
Peter, because the punishments are so much alike in details
that are not common to other descriptions.

10. The Coptic Apocalypse of Elijah

a. There are extant an Apocalypse of Elijah in Hebrew
and one in Coptic. Both of these appear to be extensive
developments of Jewish work by that name from the first
century BCE.[1] The Coptic text in transliteration with an

---

ischen Kirche," Texte und Untersuchungen zur Geschichte der
altchristlichen Literatur 13 (Berlin: Berlin Academy, 1895),
71-73.

[1]James H. Charlesworth, The Pseudepigrapha and Modern
Research, ibid., 95-98; Wilhelm Schneemelcher, "Later Apocalypses," Edgar Hennecke, ed., New Testament Apocrypha,
ibid., vol. 2, 752; E. Yarbro Collins, ibid., 99-100; Heinrich Weinel, "Die später christliche Apokalyptik," Hans

English translation has been published by Houghton.[1] It is probably from the third century AD.

In 13:10-14:9 the coming of the Messiah is described very much like the coming of the Son of God in Apocalypse of Peter 1:5-7. It is significant that in this parallel each such description follows a claim "I am the Christ" made falsely and that in each is the warning "Do not believe!" A second section of the Apocalypse of Elijah, 18:1-20:15, has several more distant parallels in the Apocalypse of Peter. This section deals with the persecution of the righteous by the false messiah/antichrist and so finds parallels with Apocalypse of Peter 2:7-13. In both texts the false messiah deceives people through miracles, but eventually the people recognize that he is not the expected Messiah and reject him. In the Apocalypse of Peter those who have been deceived by him yet later reject him and then are martyred by him are still reckoned among the faithful. The author of the Apocalypse of Elijah has a somewhat similar problem with those who have fled the persecution in order to save themselves. Those who fled will fall asleep. Their souls and spirits will go to the Lord while their bodies turn into stone to preserve them from being eaten by wild

Schmidt, ed., Ευχαριστηριον. Festschrift für Herman Gunkel (Göttingen: Vandenhoek und Ruprecht, 1923), 162-167; Wolfgang Schrage, Die Elia-Apokalypse (Gütersloh: Gerd Mohn, 1980).

[1]Herbert Pierrepont Houghton, "The Coptic Apocalypse, Part III, Akhmimite: 'The Apocalypse of Elias,'" Aegyptus revista italiana di Egittologia e di papirologia 39 (1959), 179-210. I use Houghton's page and line numbering.

beasts until the Judgment (see Apocalypse of Peter 4:4). At the Judgment they will have a place of rest but will not inherit the kingdom itself. The kingdom is reserved for those who endured to the end. This distinction between the place of rest and the kingdom is possibly the same as that intended by the author of the Apocalypse of Peter 14:1-3 when the sinners who have been punished are given salvation in the Elysian Fields and the righteous enter the kingdom. Finally, "The Lord will take their spirit and their souls to himself," Apocalypse of Elijah 18:17-18, should be compared to Apocalypse of Peter 6:4, "But each of the elect, those who have done good, will come to me when they have died."

In addition, there are two more important parallels. The first of these is found in 23:1-10. A person who has escaped coming to the judgment finds his sins "will range themselves against him at that place where they had been committed." In Apocalypse of Peter 6:3, where the judgment cannot be escaped, the sinners find "the works of each one of them will stand before them."

Secondly, immediately following, in Apocalypse of Elijah 23:11-24:2, we read:

> The righteous will behold the sinners in their punishment, with those who have persecuted them and delivered them up. Then will the sinners on their part behold the place of the righteous and will be partakers of grace. In that day will that for which the (righteous) shall often pray, be granted to them.[1]

---

[1]English translation and discussion by M. R. James, "The Recovery of the Apocalypse of Peter," ibid., 32.

James is almost certainly right when he interprets this to
mean that the salvation of sinners will be granted at the
request of the righteous. This doctrine is not found widely
distributed. It was taught in Apocalypse of Peter 14:1-3
(the Rainer fragment) and in Sibylline Oracles book 2, 330-
338, which apparently took it from the Apocalypse of Peter.
The other parallels with the Apocalypse of Peter, and the
fact that the righteous behold the sinners in torment just
preceding the plea for mercy (Apocalypse of Peter 13:1-2)
here but not in the Sibylline Oracles, make it likely that
in the Apocalypse of Elijah we have the influence of the
Apocalypse of Peter. Some confirmation of this view comes
with the words "those who have persecuted and delivered them
up" (Apocalypse of Elijah 23:13-14). The persecutors and
betrayers of the righteous are distinguished from other sinners. The same phrase is used in Apocalypse of Peter 9:1-2
where these offenders are said to be in Gehenna, apparently
a more severe punishment than other sinners receive, and
probably understood to be a separate geographical location
from the other punishments.

Thus it is likely that the author of the Apocalypse of
Elijah was acquainted with the Apocalypse of Peter itself or
steeped in a tradition which made use of it.

b. Very briefly should be mentioned here the Apocalypse of Zephaniah. The manuscript evidence is confusing
and there is little agreement on its date or even on which

material belongs to it.[1] The Coptic text in transliteration
with English translation has been published by Houghton.[2]
This document is closely related to the Apocalypse of Elijah
and, given the corruption of the manuscripts, may actually
be only a later revision of it. It bears also an uncertain
relationship to the Apocalypse of Paul, and the distant parallels to the Apocalypse of Peter may come through acquaintance with that document. No parallel of the Apocalypse of
Zephaniah with the Apocalypse of Peter is close enough to
warrant pursuing here.

11. Pseudo-Cyprian, Adversus Aleatores

This sermon Against Dice-Throwers has come down to us
among the works of Cyprian. Harnack assigns it to Pope
Victor (189-199 CE) but it is more likely from North Africa
c. 300 CE.[3]

The Latin text of Adversus Aleatores 8 reads:

> Aleae tabula qui ludit et maleficia nosse debet, quod
> a dei servos longe sit scientes quoniam foris est male-
> ficus et uenenarius et iteram in iudicii dei igne rotante
> torquebitur.

> He who plays dice has to know evil things which are
> not fitting (far from) the servants of God; he should
> know that an evildoer and poisoner (will remain) outside
> (the kingdom) [Rev. 22:15] and again: "on the day of

---

[1]James H. Charlesworth, The Pseudepigrapha and Modern
Research, ibid., 220-223; Wilhelm Schneemelcher, "Later
Apocalypses," ibid., 751-52.

[2]Herbert Pierrepont Houghton, ibid., 40-67 and 68-91.

[3]Quasten, ibid., vol. 2, 368-369.

judgment, he will be tortured on a fiery wheel." [Apoca-lypse of Peter 12:5-6][1]

It is possible that the sermonizer is here quoting from the two apocalypses which had authority for him and his congregation. But the same connection of sorcery with fiery wheels on the judgment day is also found in Sibylline Oracles 2, 283-286. Dependence on the Apocalypse of Peter is likely but not proven.

12. Ephraem Syrus

Ephraem the Syrian was born in 306 CE at Nisibis. He lived there until 363 when he moved to Edessa. He died in 373. There are many writings which bear his name, often in metrical form. Unfortunately there exist no critical editions of the texts nor any standard translations. "Much material bearing his name is spurious, dubious, or has been altered."[2]

In this situation it is not possible to evaluate the information with which M. R. James supplies us about parallels in his works with the Apocalypse of Peter. We will just note them.

One work seems to contain the sections on the command to Hades, the beasts and birds, etc., to give up their dead (4:2-5), the rejoining of the bones (4:7-9), the river of

---

[1]Latin text from M. R. James, "A New Text of the Apocalypse of Peter," ibid., 50 and 383; English trans. by Terrence Kardong, OSB.

[2]Berhold Altaner, ibid., 401-405; see also Otto Bardenhewer, Patrology (St. Louis: B. Herder, 1908), 387-393.

fire (5:8-6:5), and the admission by sinners of the justice
of God (13:6).[1] Judgment Day is described in one of
Ephraem's sermons in much the same way as in our apocalypse
--a conflagration, return of Christ, restoration of bodies
eaten by animals, and a description of hell.[2]

James thinks the dependence is clear and he may be
right. If these writings do come from Ephraem Syrus we have
here a witness to the use of much of our apocalypse in Syria
during the 4th century CE.

13. Cyril of Jerusalem

This bishop of Jerusalem wrote some Catechetical Lectures c. 350 CE which were delivered to those seeking baptism.[3]

There are two places in lecture 15 where Cyril departs
from the canonical passages he is quoting to agree with the
Apocalypse of Peter. a) In 15,20 we find "Then shall they
see the Son of Man coming on the clouds of heaven; and they
shall mourn tribe by tribe." Compare this to Apocalypse of
Peter 6:1-2 where Jesus comes on the clouds and then each
nation weeps when they see him crowned. Probably the Ethiopic ያንኅይ : ስስ : ሐHስ.Uσ- translates an original κοψονται
φυλαι κατα φυλας. b) In 15, 21 we have "The Son of Man

---

[1]M. R. James, "A New Text of the Apocalypse of Peter,"
ibid., 40 and 51.

[2]M. R. James, "The Recovery of the Apocalypse of
Peter," ibid., 19.

[3]Quasten, ibid., vol. 3, 362-377.

shall come to the Father, according to the Scripture which
was just now read, on the clouds of heaven, drawn by a
stream of fire, which is to make trial of men."[1] The Scripture mentioned is Dan. 7:9-14 which Cyril had read at the
beginning of his lecture. He was using it to expound that
portion of the Nicene Creed which reads "He shall come in
glory to judge the quick and the dead; of whose kingdom
there will be no end." James notes that the stream of fire
which in Dn 7:10 was part of the paraphernalia of the divine
throne has become an instrument of punishment and a means of
separating the righteous from the wicked as in Apocalypse of
Peter.[2] It is highly likely that these are traces of the
Apocalypse of Peter on the thought of Cyril. He is a witness to the use of our apocalypse in Jerusalem the middle of
the 4th century CE.

14. The Apocalypse of Paul (non-gnostic, apocalyptic)

According to Barhebraeus (13th century CE) Origen mentions c. 250 CE an Apocalypse of Paul which was accepted by
the Church. However, if this is true, it is not that apocalypse as we know it. The present form of this work clearly
comes from the late 4th century CE. Unfortunately, of the

---

[1]English trans. from E. H. Gifford, "The Catechetical
Lectures of S. Cyril Archbishop of Jerusalem," Philip Schaff
and Henry Wace, eds., A Select Library of Nicene and Post-
Nicene Fathers of the Christian Church (Grand Rapids: Eerdmans, 1952; reprint of edition of 1893), vol. 7, 110.

[2]M. R. James, "A New Text of the Apocalypse of Peter,"
ibid., 383.

original Greek only a summary survives in that language.
The best text is in Latin followed by the Coptic and then
the Syriac. It may have originated in Egypt. This Apocalypse of Paul became very popular and widespread. It is
heavily dependent on our Apocalypse of Peter and is largely
responsible for making well known material from the latter.
It is usually held that Dante knew and used the Apocalypse
of Paul.[1]

When comparing the Apocalypse of Paul with that of
Peter we should keep in mind an approach to this material by
the former which is given in the document itself. In chapter 15 an ungodly man dies and his soul is brought up for
immediate judgment. When he is forced to face his evil
deeds which stand before him he is described thus: "I saw
that that hour was more bitter to him than the future judgment." The author of the Apocalypse of Peter had been oriented completely toward the future judgment at the end of
the world. The author of the Apocalypse of Paul is oriented
to a personal judgment immediately following death. What
material he has taken from Peter has been moved in time from
future to present and may have been altered to fit the new
point of view. The fact of a future resurrection when the
soul must return to its body is maintained, however (chapters 14 and 15).

---

[1]Hugo Duensing, "Apocalypse of Paul," Edgar Hennecke,
ed., New Testament Apocrypha, ibid., 755-798; Quasten, ibid.,
146-149; Altaner, ibid., 88-89; Heinrich Weinel, ibid., 146-
149; Yarbro Collins, ibid., 85-86.

The following parallels should be noted:

a) The evil deeds of sinners stand before them at the judgment; Paul 15, Peter 6:3.

b) The soul of an ungodly man says at his judgment "O that I had not been born nor been in the world" (Paul 15). Peter is rebuked by Jesus for saying "It were better for them [the sinners] not to have been created" (Peter 3:4-6). At the end of Paul 40 we have an exact parallel with Peter 3:4-6. There is weeping for sinners. The question is asked why they were ever born (created). The answer is that God has more mercy than Paul (Peter). Visions of punishments follow. See also Paul 33. In Paul this comes to a head in chapters 43-44. At the end of chapter 42 Paul says, "It would be better for us if we who are all sinners had not been born." Paul and the angels and Michael join the sinners in pleading for mercy, and God grants them every Sunday off from their punishments. This seems to be the author's answer to why the sinners were ever born, i.e., they had been given a chance to do good even if they had done only evil and so by their deeds made it true that they should never have been born. At the same time relief from punishment for one day a week appears to be a replacement for the permanent release implied in Apocalypse of Peter 14:1-3. See also i) below.

c) The time for repentance is past and it has been wasted (Paul 16, Peter 13:5). In each case it is an angel who informs the sinner(s). Cf. Paul 40, 44.

d) The angels Tartaruchus and Temeluchos are set over the punishments (Paul 16, 18, 40; Peter 8:10, 13:5). See Paul 34.[1]

e) God's judgment is pronounced just by the angels in Paul, by the sinners in Peter (Paul 16, 18; Peter 7:11, 13:6).

f) In Paul 19 the names of the righteous are written on golden tablets which are above the pillars of the gate of Paradise. In Peter 17:7 the names of the righteous are known to be written in the book of life in heaven.

g) Paradise has incredible fruit (Paul 22; Peter 16: 2-3).

h) Baptism for sinners in Lake Acherusia (Paul 22; Peter 14:1).

i) In Paul 24 those who have renounced the world but yet have pride are not allowed to enter the city. But when Christ comes the righteous will pray for them and then they will enter the city. This should be compared to Peter 14: 1-3 where the righteous ask for sinners out of torment.

j) There is a punishing river of fire (Paul 31-40; Peter 5:8, 6:2-5, 12:4-7).

k) Many punishments are the same or similar. For the punishment in Paul 34 of the fiery prongs piercing the intestines, cf. Peter 9:4. For the worms in Paul 36-37, 39, 42, cf. Peter 7:10. For cutting the lips in Paul 36, cf.

---

[1]M. R. James, "A New Text of the Apocalypse of Peter," ibid., 370-371.

Peter 9:4. Compare the usurers in Paul 37 and Peter 10:1;
the tongue-chewers in Paul 37 and Peter 7:2, 9:3, 11:8; the
magicians in the pit where all punishments flow together in
Paul 38 and Peter 12:4-7; adulterers in Paul 38-39 and Peter
7:5-8; the very deep pit in Paul 32 with that in Peter 7:
3-4; those dressed in black who did not keep their virginity
in Paul 39 and Peter 11:6-7; those who harmed or neglected
widows and orphans in Paul 39, 40 and Peter 9:5-7; hanging
by the hair in Paul 39 and Peter 7:5-8 (both in connection
with adultery and possibly cosmetics); homosexuality in Paul
39 and Peter 10:2-4; those who are blind and dressed in
bright clothing, who give alms and yet are not right with
God in Paul 40 and Peter 12:1-3; the fiery pyramid or pillar
of Paul 40 and Peter 9:5; wild animals tearing people to
pieces in Paul 40 and Peter 11:6; the very close agreement
between the abortionists and/or those who expose children in
Paul 40 and Peter 8; the angels who make their rounds in the
pits, Paul 40 and Peter 7:4; the hypocrites in Paul 40 with
those in Peter 12:1-3.

1) Abraham and Isaac and Jacob, the patriarchs, etc.,
are shown to Paul in paradise, Paul 47-51. To this compare
Peter 15:2-16:6.

m) If the ending in the Coptic is from the original
Apocalypse of Paul, then there is a parallel to Apocalypse
of Peter 1:1, for the setting of the revelation was then a
meeting of the apostles on the Mount of Olives.

For our purposes, it is especially important that

there are so many parallels to Apocalypse of Peter 3. This
chapter has so far remained unattested in the literature we
have examined. But there can be little doubt that the
author of the Apocalypse of Paul knew this chapter in a form
such as we have it in the Apocalypse of Peter and probably
got it from there, since he shows so many signs that he was
well acquainted with that work. Indeed it should be said
that the Apocalypse of Paul is organized as we have it in
order to give an answer to the question why God would create
people whose only future was to be punished eternally after
a life of wicked deeds. His answer is that God out of mercy
gives them a life during which they can choose good or evil
(cf. Paul 33). Thus the Apocalypse of Paul is a commentary
on Apocalypse of Peter chapter 3 and the solution (in chapter 14) to the problem expressed there.[1]

15. The Apocalypse of Thomas

    This apocalypse has two sections. The first describes
history up to the final days (e.g., "a king shall arise,"
etc.). This section is probably from c. 450 CE.[2] Section
two describes the events of the last seven days which take

---

[1]If indeed the "better to have never been born" theme
is the raison d'être of the Apocalypse of Paul, then James's
theory that Paul may have really ended with chapter 44 is
given more support. See M. R. James, The Apocryphal New
Testament (Oxford: Clarendon Press, 1924), 555. For a more
detailed comparison of the Apocalypse of Paul to the Akhmim
Fragment see Robinson and James, ibid., 65-67.

[2]M. R. James, The Apocryphal New Testament, ibid., 557
where Arcadius and Honorius (d. 423) are mentioned.

place following a voice from heaven each day (cf. Apocalypse

of Peter 4:5-6). This second section is probably the

earlier Apocalypse of Thomas which may have originated c.

400 CE. It was written either in Latin or Greek.[1] It may

have some connections with Manichean or Priscillian circles.[2]

It is the events of the sixth day (from section two)

which draw our interest. Christ descends from heaven in (a

cloud of) light with the power and honor of the holy angels.

The eternal fire which surrounds paradise is let loose and

devours all the elements of the world. The souls of the

saints are released. They return to their bodies. "Then

their bodies will be changed into the image and likeness and

honour of the holy angels and into the power of the image of

my holy Father. Then they will put on the garment of eter-

nal life: the garment from the cloud of light which has

never been seen in this world; for this cloud comes down

---

[1]A. de Santos Otero, "Apocalypse of Thomas," Edgar
Hennecke, ed., New Testament Apocrypha, ibid., vol. 2, 798-
803; Quasten, ibid., vol. 1, 149-150; Altaner, ibid., 89;
Weinel, ibid., 154-155; Yarbro Collins, ibid., 100.

[2]D. de Bruyne published the Latin text of a homily he
associated with Priscillianism ("Apocryphes Priscillianistes," Revue Bénédictine 24 (1907), 318-335). In it are
quotations from the first section of the Apocalypse of
Thomas. It also utilizes (twice) the very rare adjective
"tartarucho" which according to James indicates that the
Apocalypse of Peter was at least ultimately the source. See
M. R. James, "A New Text of the Apocalypse of Peter," ibid.,
370-371. But this homily does not seem to be related to the
second section of the Apocalypse of Thomas. Exactly how the
homily is related to the Apocalypse of Peter, if at all, is
uncertain. I have not discussed it as a witness because of
its uncertain date and origin. By 1923 James thought it was
Irish (The Apocryphal New Testament, ibid., 556 and 558).

from the upper kingdom of the heavens by the power of my
Father, and will invest with its glory every spirit that has
believed in me. Then they will be clothed and, as I said to
you before, borne by the hands of the holy angels. Then
they will be carried off in a cloud of light into the air,
and rejoicing go with me into the heavens and remain in the
light and honour of my Father. Then there will be great joy
for them in the presence of my Father and in the presence of
the holy angels."

We see here some similarities in language: the image
of my holy Father (cf. Apocalypse of Peter 3:6), the cloud
of light which has never been seen in this world (cf. 15:3),
the upper kingdom (cf. the second heaven in 17:3, 6). But
what is impressive is the same correspondence in language
when it is coupled with the almost identical order of events
from the Apocalypse of Peter: 1) Jesus descends in light
with the angels (chapter 1, also chapter 6), the fire from
heaven dissolves the elements (chapter 5), the dead are
raised in their bodies (chapter 4), their bodies are transformed (chapter 5), the righteous are given the garments of
eternal life as they are carried by the angels (chapter 13),
the cloud of light carries them off into the air (cf. chapter 17), they go rejoicing with Jesus into the heavens
(chapter 14). It also seems as if the light cloud which in-
vests each spirit with its glory (an interpretation of the
garment of life) should be seen in relation to the shining
bodies and clothes of Moses and Elijah (chapter 15).

Apparently the torments of hell are not present because the wicked will simply be destroyed (Apocalypse of Thomas, the eighth day; cf. the seventh day).

This combination of similarity in form and in details of expression makes it virtually certain that the author of the Apocalypse of Thomas knew and used the Apocalypse of Peter, at least all those sections which describe salvific rather than condemnatory events. The Apocalypse of Thomas is a witness that heretical, probably Manichean-related groups were interested in the Apocalypse of Peter c. 400 CE.

16. The Pseudo-Titus Epistle

The title of this work makes the claim that this is a letter written by Titus the disciple of Paul. This Latin writing is actually an exhortation to virginity. It probably originated in the Priscillianist controversies of 5th and 6th centuries Spain.[1] It is interesting in that it quotes many sayings from unknown apocrypha.

On pp. 157-158 we find:

Thou knowest that different judgments must be passed on sinners. In the member with which each man has sinned, in the same also shall he be tormented. The prophet Elias bears witness to a vision: The angel of the Lord, he says, showed me a deep valley, which is called Gehenna, burning with brimstone and pitch. In this place the souls of many sinners dwell and are tormented in different ways. Some suffer hanging from the genitals, others by the tongue, some by the eyes, others head downwards. The women are tormented in their breasts, and the young hang

---

A. de Santos Otero, "The Pseudo-Titus Epistle," Edgar Hennecke, ed., New Testament Apocrypha, ibid., vol. 2, 141-166; Quasten, ibid., vol. 1, 156-157; Altaner, ibid., 83. All references are to page numbers in Santos Otero.

from their hands. Some virgins are roasted on a
gridiron, and other souls undergo an unceasing torment. The multiplicity of the torments answers to the
diversity of the sins of each. The adulterers and the
corrupters of such as are under age are tormented in
their genitals. Those who hang from their tongues are
the blasphemers and false witnesses. They have their
eyes burned who have stumbled through their glances
and who have looked at foul things with craving for them.
Head downwards there hang those who have detested the
righteousness of God, who have been evil-minded, quarrel-
some towards their fellows. Rightly then are they burned
according to the punishment imposed upon them. If some
women are punished with torment in their breasts, then
these are women who for sport have surrendered their own
bodies to men, and for this reason these also hang from
their hands.[1]

The author states a general principle: "In the member
with which each man has sinned, in the same also shall he be
tormented." Then he illustrates the truth of this by quoting a report of a vision which Elijah had. This vision of
Gehenna has a number of parallels with the inferno in Apocalypse of Peter 7-12. They are the burning deep valley (cf.
7:3-4), adulterers hanging by the genitals (cf. 7:7), blasphemers and false witnesses hanging by the tongue (cf. 7:2,
9:3, 11:8, 9:4), burning of the eyes (cf. 9:3, 8:4), those
who detest God's righteousness (cf. 12:1-3), punishments involving breasts (cf. 8:8-9).

The parallels are not exact, nor do certain punishments always apply to the same crime. Nevertheless, the
resemblances are striking and imply some connection between
these two infernos. What is it? Unfortunately we are

---

[1]A. de Santos Otero, trans., ibid.

unable to say. The passage has every indication that it has
been taken from an Elijah apocryphon, probably verbatim.

D. de Bruyne, who first published this section,
asserted that it was from a Jewish Apocalypse of Elijah from
which stem both the Coptic Apocalypse of Elijah (see no. 10
above) and the extant but much later Hebrew Apocalypse of
Elijah.[1] But this section does not appear in either of
them. Therefore we cannot say with any assurance that this
is from an Apocalypse of Elijah at all.[2] There is nothing
particularly Christian about this quotation. We must leave
undecided for the time being whether it is earlier or later
than our Apocalypse of Peter. It is at least as old as the
5th century CE composition in which it is found, and it may
be much earlier.

17. Carmen de Iudicio Domini

This Latin rhyme of over 400 lines is found among the
works of Tertullian and Cyprian. It was written by neither.
Some anonymous author is responsible for this less than mas-
terful poem on the Judgment Day. The full name is Carmen ad
Flavium Felicem de resurrectione mortuorum et de iudicio
Domini. It was probably written c. 500 CE.[3]

---

[1]D. de Bruyne, "Nouveaux fragments des Actes de
Pierre, de Paul, de Jean, d'André, et de l'Apocalypse d'Elie,"
Revue Bénédictine 25 (1908), 149-160.

[2]James H. Charlesworth, "Apocalypse of Elijah [and
Elijah Cycle]," ibid., 95-98.

[3]Quasten, ibid., vol. 2, 319; Altaner, ibid., 600; S.
Thelwall, trans., "A Strain of the Judgment of the Lord,"

Lines 1-48 are an appeal for inspiration. There follows in lines 48-133 a recounting of God's act of creation, the fall of mankind, and the misery of human beings who are subject to death. The parallels to the Apocalypse of Peter follow. Lines 133-165, the God who can do all things can raise the dead at his word, for the earth will give everyone back. And the beasts and birds, etc., will give back what they have eaten, for all must appear at the judgment seat. It is like the seed put in the ground arid but yet it lives. To this section compare Apocalypse of Peter 4.

After a discussion of the rising and setting of the heavenly bodies and of the phoenix, and the tree which shoots forth its leaves (lines 165-178), the judge arrives with his angels and again the bodily resurrection is described and judgment is given (lines 178-242). The members of the body come together and the soul is restored to them (lines 200-209), much as in Apocalypse of Peter 4:7-9.

Martyrs and Seers in bright clothes are mentioned (133-135). Then the righteous are taken to paradise in the east, which is vaguely described at length (lines 135-339). Included in paradise are much sunlight, flowers, fragrance,

A. Roberts and J. Donaldson, eds., The Ante-Nicene Fathers (New York: Charles Scribner's Sons, 1925), vol. 4, 135-141. I use the numbering and translation of Thelwall. He believes the poem may have been written by Verecundus (d. 552 CE). See his notes, p. 166 of that work. Latin text in Migne, Patrologia Latina, ibid., vol. 2, col. 1089-1098.

gems, trees, roses, etc. In lines 340-473 the sinners are thrown into tartarus. Their plight is described only in a general way--darkness, fire, pain, grief, etc. A list of evildoers in 430-450 is also nonspecific and has no corresponding punishments. Included are idolaters, adulterers, robbers, murderers, thieves, etc. It is emphasized how God through his law and prophets had warned these sinners (lines 451-473), and finally there is an exhortation to prepare oneself for death by pious deeds (lines 473-512).

The parallels with the Apocalypse of Peter are real, but they are not convincing. Perhaps the author has destroyed many of the telltale words and phrases by putting the story into restrictive verse. In any case, we lack evidence to claim that the author of this work was personally acquainted with the Apocalypse of Peter, though he may have had much knowledge of it second-hand.

18. The Ethiopic Apocalypse on the Tübingen Manuscript

In 1893 Eduard Bratke reported on a search he had made among Arabic, Syriac, Carshuni and Ethiopic manuscripts for the Apocalypse of Peter.[1] He had only attained negative results. During the course of his investigation, Bratke asked A. Dillmann to translate certain sections of an (apparently now lost) manuscript in Tübingen of which

[1] Eduard Bratke, ibid. See especially pp. 477-486 for our discussion.

Dillmann had given a précis in 1858.[1] Fortunately, Bratke
includes in his report a few pages of Dillmann's translation. He judges these pages closest to the original Greek
Apocalypse of Peter, but yet distant from it. Yet there are
parallels with our Ethiopic text, chapters 2 and 3 of which
Bratke could not be aware of since he did not have it
available to him. I have appended my English translation
of Dillmann's German to this dissertation and numbered
sections of it for easy reference.

The parallels lie not in matters of detail which have
apparently been altered to fit a new historical situation,
but in the general outline of the course of events:

Tübingen Ms.	Event	Apocalypse of Peter
1, 3	false messiahs corrupt people through their wicked deeds	2:7-8
5	a certain one of these (in Tüb. Ms. a king) will arise and they will hold him to be Christ	2:8-9
6-12	the followers of the false messiah reject him	2:10
12-13	the false messiah makes martyrs of those who reject him; these martyrs fulfill the prophecy about the sprouting of the fig tree	2:10-11

---

[1]August Dillmann, "Bericht über das äthiopische Buch
Clementinischer Schriften," Nachrichten der Akademie der
Wissenschaften zu Gottingen (1858), 185-199, 201-215, 217-
226.

Tübingen Ms.	Event	Apocalypse of Peter
14	Enoch and Elijah come	2:12
- - - - - - - - - - - - - -		
15-18	Christ comes in judgment	missing here, but implied in context of 3:1 (the last day)
- - - - - - - - - - - - -		
19	the righteous, the sinners, and the angels all weep at the fate of the sinners	3:3
- - - - - - - - - - - - -		

This parallelism in the course of events coupled with a claim by each document to the tradition of Peter makes it likely that this section of the Tübingen Ms. is a later expansion of the Apocalypse of Peter 2-3. Unfortunately we are unable to date the writing which appears on the Tübingen Manuscript. We can only say that it is probably several centuries later than the composition of the Apocalypse of Peter and then infer that the latter continued to exert an influence in Ethiopia, either directly or through the traditions which later came to Ethiopia. Perhaps it could be a late indication of the independent existence of chapters 2-3. The relationship of the Tübingen Manuscript to the Arabic Book of the Rolls discussed above is not clear.

C. A Summary of the Evidence for the Apocalypse
of Peter in the Early Church

The Apocalypse of Peter was widely used among
Christians from the second to the sixth centuries of our
era. There are witnesses to its use in Egypt, North Africa,
Rome, Asia Minor, Syria, and Palestine. From the middle of
the second century we find it used and quoted frequently,
and apparently it continued to be copied at least until the
sixth century in Egypt (the Akhmim fragment) and until the
ninth century in Jerusalem (the Stichometry of Nicephorus).

But speaking more exactly, what in our present
Ethiopic text is attested? The question involves the trustworthiness of the Ethiopic as against the Akhmim text. The
thesis of this dissertation is that the Ethiopic text in
spite of some corruption is the more faithful of these two
texts and can be relied upon (with due caution at particular
points in the text) for purposes of New Testament and Early
Church History investigations.

Recently scholars have been quite hesitant to use
material from the Ethiopic text because it was under suspicion of being later material. We therefore continue this
chapter with a history of the research done on the Apocalypse of Peter. Then in chapter two we describe the various
Greek and Ethiopic manuscripts involved. Chapter three
presents a new edition of the Ethiopic text with two translations, one rather woodenly reflecting the Ethiopic style,
the other designed to read more easily. We include here an

index of Ethiopic words. Following this, chapter four is a short commentary dealing with various problems, mostly those of vocabulary and grammar and those arising from textual variants. Finally, other significant problems concerning the faithfulness of the Ethiopic text are taken up and a case is made for its usefulness.

III. The History of Research

All copies of the Apocalypse of Peter had long since
disappeared before the rise of modern scholarship. Little
was done before the Akhmim text was found in 1886. The
various small fragments found among the Church Fathers were
collected.[1] Some Ethiopic manuscripts had been examined for
traces of it.[2] Theodor Zahn attempted to show that the
Apocalypse of Peter was not mentioned in the Muratorian
Canon, but his theories and emendations were not later
accepted.[3] The most detailed study of which we are aware
was done by M. R. James,[4] but only a brief summary of the results has ever been published. James recognized from the
fragments that the Apocalypse of Peter contained an inferno
but he also suggested incorrectly that it contained a scene
of judgment for individual souls such as we find in Origen

---

[1]First by Johann Ernst Grabe, Spicilegium ss. patrum
ut et haereticum (Oxoniae: theatro Shedoniano, 1689-90),
vol. 1, 74-77. See Adolphus Hilgenfeld, Novum Testamentum
extra canonem receptem, fasc: cle 4 (Lipsiae: T. O. Weigel,
1884), 71-74.

[2]August Dillmann, "Berichte über das äthiopische Buch
clementinischer Schriften," Nachrichten von der königlichen
Gesellschaft der Wissenschaften zu Göttingen (1858) pp. 185-
200, 201-215, 217-226. See also H. Ewald, "Ueber die
Aethiopischen Handschriften zu Tubingen," Zeitschrift für
die Kunde des Morgenlandes 5 (n.d.), 165-201.

[3]Theodor Zahn, Geschichte des neutestamentlichen
Kanons, Vol. 1 (Erlangen: Deichert, 1888), 307-310.

[4]M. R. James, The Testament of Abraham. Texts and
Studies, vol. 2, no. 3 (Cambridge: Cambridge University
Press, 1892), 21-26.

and Macarius. James was to play a large role in <u>Apocalypse</u>

<u>of Peter</u> studies for the next forty years.

    A. Research on the Akhmim Fragment to 1910:
        A Time of Enthusiasm

In the winter of 1886/7 a French archaeological team

opened a grave near Akhmim in Upper Egypt. The manuscripts

which contain our most important Greek texts of the <u>Book of</u>

<u>Enoch</u>, the <u>Gospel of Peter</u>, and the <u>Apocalypse of Peter</u> were

found in this grave. Both the manuscripts and the grave

were dated anywhere from the sixth to the twelfth centuries

CE. The manuscripts were not prepared for publication until

1892. When the find was made public it caused a great deal

of excitement among scholars.[1] The <u>Gospel of Peter</u> drew

---

[1]Of the many journal notices and preliminary reports,
the following should be consulted: H. Lüdemann, <u>Theo-
logischer Jahresbericht</u> (Braunschweig: C. A. Schwetschke)
vol. 13 (1893), 171-183 and vol. 14 (1894), 184-187; Hans
von Schubert, "Neue Funde auf dem Gebiete der urchristlichen
Litteratur," <u>Die christliche Welt</u>, No. 1 (29 Dec., 1892),
col. 7-12 and No. 3 (12 Jan., 1893), col. 50-55; D. Nösgen,
"Der Fund von Akhmim," <u>Evangelische Kirchenzeitung</u>, 1893,
No. 8 (Feb. 19), col. 125-128, No. 9 (Feb. 26), col. 141-
144, No. 10 (Mar. 8), col. 149-156; F. P. Badham, "The New
Apocryphal Literature," <u>The Athenaeum</u> No. 3399 (Dec. 17,
1892), 854-855; Edward B. Nicholson, "The Revelation of
Peter," <u>The Academy</u> No. 1079 (Jan. 7, 1893), p. 14; F. P.
Badham, "The Origin of the Peter Gospel," <u>The Academy</u> No.
1108 (July 29, 1893), pp. 91-93 and No. 1109 (Aug. 5, 1893),
p. 111-112; Eduard Bratke, "Studien über die neu entdeckten
Stücke der jüdischen und altchristlichen Literatur," <u>Theo-
logisches Literaturblatt</u> 14, No. 7 (Feb. 17, 1893), col. 73-
79 and No. 9 (Mar. 3, 1893), col. 97-102; Arthur C. Headlam,
"The Akhmîm Fragments," <u>The Classical Review</u> 7 (1893), 458-
463; P. Chapuis, "L'Evangile et l'Apocalypse de Pierre,"
<u>Revue de théologie et de philosophie</u> (1893), 338-355. See
also the reviews by Emil Schürer on the various important
studies which were beginning to appear: <u>Theologische Liter-
aturzeitung</u>, vol. 17, No. 25 (Dec. 10, 1892), 609-612 and
612-614; vol. 18, No. 2 (Jan. 21, 1893), 33-37; vol. 18,

much of the attention at that time and is even now considered by some to be much more important for New Testament research than the Apocalypse.[1] But the latter was certainly not ignored, and the excitement over its discovery sparked investigations of several kinds including the above-mentioned search conducted by Bratke for an Arabic, Syriac, or Ethiopic text.[2]

The pages of parchment containing the apocalypse were considerably more damaged than those of the gospel. Therefore the first important task was to establish the Greek text and translate it for general distribution. The earliest edition, appearing even before the official transcriptions of the archaeological team but based upon an early unpublished version of them, was published by M. R. James.[3] James divided the material into twenty sections for easy reference. Shortly thereafter followed the official transcriptions of Bouriant who had been in charge of the team

No. 7 (April 1, 1893), 187-188; and Vol. 18, No. 19 (Sept. 16, 1893), 477-478.

[1]Helmut Koester, Introduction to the New Testament (Philadelphia: Fortress, 1982), vol. 2, 49, 68, 160-164; idem., "Apocryphal and Canonical Gospels," Harvard Theological Review 73 (1980), 105-130.

[2]Eduard Bratke, "Handschriftliche Uberlieferung und Bruchstucke der arabisch-Ethiopischen Petrus-Apokalypse," Zeitschrift für wissenschaftliche Theologie 36 (1893), 454-493.

[3]J. Armitage Robinson and Montagne Rhodes James, The Gospel According to Peter, and the Revelation of Peter (London: C. J. Clay and Sons, 1892).

which had made the discovery.[1] Adolf von Harnack followed

with his edition and comments.[2] Harnack divided the text

into thirty-four sections. In later editions these

numbering systems of James and Harnack were sometimes

combined into a hybrid system as if James' numeration were

"chapter" and Harnack's "verse."[3]

In France Adolphe Lods published the text with com-

ments and a Latin translation.[4] The Apocalypse of Peter was

translated into Italian along with comments by Chiapelli.[5]

Suggestions for textual emendations also came from

Wilamowitz-Möllendorff.[6] Harnack revised and expanded his

---

[1]U. Bouriant, Fragments grecs du livre d'Enoch,
Memoires publiées par les membres de la mission archéo-
logique française au Caire sous la direction de M. U.
Bouriant 9, fascicle 1 (Paris: Ernst Leroux, 1892).

[2]Adolf von Harnack, "Bruchstücke des Evangeliums und
der Apokalypse des Petrus," Sitzungsberichte der Königlich
Preussischen Akademie der Wissenschaften zu Berlin 44 (1892),
895-903 and 949-965. This has been reprinted in Kleine
Schriften zur alten Kirche: Berliner Akademieschriften 1890-
1907 (Leipzig: Zentralantiquariat der DDR, 1980), 83-108.

[3]As in the edition of Klostermann cited below. Unfortunately this practice can result in confusion. For example,
Apocalypse of Peter 20:34 gives the false impression that
"chapter" 20 has at least 34 "verses" when in fact both numbers together or separately refer to a single short section.

[4]Adolphe Lods, Evangelii secundum Petrum et Petri
Apocalypseos quae supersunt ad fidem codicis in Aegypto
nuper inventi (Paris: Leroux, 1892).

[5]Alessandro Chiapelli, Il nuova frammento dell'
Apocalisse di Pietro, Nuova antologia di scienze, lettere,
ed arti, series 3, volume 47 (1893), 112-122.

[6]U. von Wilamowitz-Möllendorff in Index scholarum in
Academie Georgus Augustus per Semester aestos anni 1893
habendarum, pp. 31-33. I was unable to obtain this article
or even to ascertain its correct title. Fortunately, Oscar

work on the text to form a short commentary[1] and Lods followed suit shortly thereafter, this time in French and
including a French translation. [2] Lods had the advantage in
that he had access to the as yet unpublished photographs of
the manuscript. Funk issued an edition with Latin translation also at about this time. [3]

It was Lods who helped to publish the official photographs of Bouriant and who wrote an introduction to accompany them. [4] These photographs had been retouched by the
publisher to make them easier to read. However, the re-
touching brought into question the reliability of these
photographs and raised a great deal of controversy about
Bouriant's handling of the whole project. Oscar von Gebhardt sped off to Egypt and returned with new photographs
which he published along with transcriptions and a short
commentary on the condition of the manuscript and paleo-

von Gebhardt lists Wilamowitz-Möllendorff's suggestion on
page 41 of the work cited below.

[1]Adolf von Harnack, Bruchstücke des Evangeliums der
Apokalypse des Petrus, Texte und Untersuchungen zur Ges-
chichte der altchristlichen Literatur 9, 2 (Leipzig: J. C.
Hinrichs, 1893).

[2]Adolphe Lods, L'évangile et l'apocalypse de Pierre
publiés pour la 1re fois d'après le photographies du manuscrit de Gizéh (Paris: Leroux, 1893).

[3]Funk, "Fragmente des Evangeliums und der Apokalypse
de Petrus," Theologische Quartalschrift 75 (1893), 255-288.

[4]Adolphe Lods, L'Evangile et l'Apocalypse de Pierre.
Le Texte grec du livre d'Enoch, U. Bouriant, ed., Mémoires
publiés par les membres de la mission archéologique fran-
caise au Caire 9, fascicle 3 (Paris: Ernst Leroux, 1893).

graphic matters.[1] Von Gebhardt's photographs are the basis of the best edition even today.

The initial frantic activity of 1892/3 culminated in the edition which Albrecht Dieterich included in his magnificent study of pagan Hellenic afterlife,[2] and then began to subside. In 1897 Andrew Rutherford published an English translation for The Ante-Nicene Fathers.[3] Piccolomini made some useful suggestions concerning the Greek text in 1899.[4] The German translation of H. Weinel became the most accessible of the translations.[5] Preuschen issued a new edition with a German translation in 1905.[6] The string of editions

---

[1]Oscar von Gebhardt, Das Evangelium und die Apokalypse des Petrus (Leipzig: J. C. Hinrichs, 1893).

[2]Albrecht Dieterich, Nekyia: Beitrage zur Erklärung der neuentdeckten Petrusapokalypse (Leipzig: B. G. Tuebner, 1893; second edition unchanged but with an added section of notes by Richard Wünsch, 1913).

[3]Andrew Rutherford, trans., "The Revelation of Peter," Allan Menzies, ed., The Ante-Nicene Fathers (reprint Grand Rapids: Wm. B. Eerdmans, 1951), v. 10, 141-147.

[4]E. Piccolomini, "Sul testo dei frammenti dall' evangelio e dell' apocalissi del pseudo-pietro," Rendicoti della reale academie dei Lencei 8 (1899), fascicles 7-8, pp. 389-404.

[5]Heinrich Weinel, "Offenbarung des Petrus," Edgar Hennecke, ed., Neutestamentliche Apokryphen (Tubingen: J. C. B. Mohr, 1904), 211-217. See also Weinel's notes and remarks in the companion volume, Edgar Hennecke, ed., Handbuch zu den neutestamentliche Apokryphen (Tubingen: J. C. B. Mohr, 1904), 285-290.

[6]Erwin Preuschen, Antilegomena: Die Reste der ausserkanonischen Evangelien und urchristlichen Überlieferungen (Gieszen: Alfred Töpelmann, second edition, 1905), Greek text pp. 84-88, German translation, pp. 188-192.

finally came to an end with that of Erich Klostermann.[1] The
latter's edition, which includes an apparatus with all the
notable suggestions which preceded its appearance, now serves
as the standard text of the Akhmim Fragment.[2]

The issues which the Akhmim Fragment raised were es-
sentially four: 1) What is the relationship of the Apocalypse
of Peter to the Gospel of Peter also found at Akhmim, and
indeed, bound together with it in the same volume and written by the same scribe?; 2) What is the relationship of the
Apocalypse of Peter to the Second Letter of Peter found in
the canon?; 3) Were the sources used in the Apocalypse of
Peter Jewish or Greek?; and, 4) How widely known and used
was the Apocalypse of Peter in the early church?

The first of these issues was raised by Bormann[3] who
suggested that the second fragment from Akhmim was from the

---

[1]Erich Klostermann, Apocrypha I. Reste des Petrus-
evangeliums, der Petrusapokalypse und des Kerygma Petri,
Kleine texte für Vorlesungen und Übungen 3, 3rd edition
(Berlin: Walter de Gruyter, 1933). The third edition is an
unaltered reprint of the second edition of 1908, except for
the surprising unfulfilled notice that the Ethiopic and
Arabic texts will be included in a forthcoming edition. The
first edition appeared in 1903.

[2]Used, for example, by Walter Bauer, A Greek-English
Lexicon of the New Testament and Other Early Christian Lit-
erature, trans. William F. Arndt and F. Wilbur Gingrich
(Chicago: U. of Chicago Press, 1957).

[3]E. Bormann, Deutsche Zeitung, Vienna, No. 7516 (No-
vember 30, 1892). This is cited by von Harnack, Bruchstücke,
2nd ed., ibid., p. IV and elsewhere in the above-mentioned
literature of the time. I was unable to obtain a copy of
this article, which apparently appeared in something on the
order of an evening newspaper. Bormann apparently included
a German translation his article.

Apocalypse of Peter while the latter formed a part of the
Gospel of Peter. Dieterich[1] presented sophisticated arguments which indicate that the Akhmim fragments were parts of
the Gospel of Peter. The later Apocalypse of Peter developed
out of the Gospel at the point where the latter contained an
apocalyptic speech of Jesus, he said. Most scholars continued to treat these two fragments as portions of separate,
independent writings, however. Carl Schmidt, in a review of
Dieterich's book,[2] attempts to refute Dieterich's arguments
on this score one by one and in doing so states well the
case for the independence of the two documents. In spite of
this, the evidence is still in favor of the view that these
two fragments may be from a single writing. This is so for
two reasons: 1) the external evidence that they are found
bound together and written by the same scribe; and, 2) the
internal evidence of similarity in style and vocabulary,
particularly the use of "Lord" whenever one might expect
"Jesus" and the appearance of the phrase "we the twelve disciples" in both fragments though each claims to tell the
story from the vantage point of the apostle Peter rather
than from that of the twelve. Thus Theodor Zahn[3] was to

---

[1]Albrecht Dieterich, Nekyia, ibid., 10-18.

[2]Carl Schmidt, review of Nekyia by Albrecht Dieterich,
in Theologische Literaturzeitung 19 (1894), col. 560-565.

[3]Theodor Zahn, "Kanon des Neuen Testament," Herzog-
Hauck, Realencyclopädie für protestantische theologie und
Kirche, 3rd edition (Leipzig: J. C. Hinrichs, 1901), v. 9,
p. 779; Grundriss der Geschichte des neutestamenitichen
Kanons, 2nd edition (Leipzig: A. Deichert, 1904), p. 25,

suggest that the two fragments were both from the <u>Gospel of Peter</u> but that it was the <u>Gospel</u> which had used the older <u>Apocalypse</u> as a source.

It is important to note that these basic discussions occurred prior to the discovery of the Ethiopic text. They did not arise from an attempt to legitimate the Ethiopic as over against the Akhmim text. But of course the Ethiopic provided a new opportunity to evaluate the reliability of the Akhmim fragment and in that context to reassess the relationship of the Akhmim <u>Apocalypse</u> to the <u>Gospel of Peter</u>. N. Bonwetsch drew the conclusion that the new discovery excluded from consideration the possibility that the Akhmim text might be part of the <u>Gospel of Peter</u>.[1] But James, who had earlier supported the independence of the two fragments, changed his mind. In a thorough study James concluded in agreement with Zahn that the Akhmim text was part of the <u>Gospel of Peter</u> and that its source was the <u>Apocalypse of Peter</u>.[2] Without prejudice to which arose earlier, the <u>Gospel</u> or the <u>Apocalypse</u>, H. Stocks also concluded from an otherwise

---

note 17. See also F. Crawford Burkitt, <u>The Gospel History and Its Transmission</u> (Edinburgh: T. & T. Clark, 1906), 332-337, esp. p. 336, note 2.

[1]N. Bonwetsch, "Zur Apokalypse des Petrus," <u>Theologisches Literaturblatt</u> 33 (1912), col. 121-123.

[2]M. R. James, "A New Text of the Apocalypse of Peter," ibid., 577-582. He reiterates this view in "The Recovery of the Apocalypse of Peter," ibid., 20-23.

rather speculative study that both Akhmim fragments were
parts of the Gospel of Peter.[1]

That somehow these two, the Akhmim Apocalypse of Peter
and the Akhmim Gospel of Peter (our only extant source for
this apocryphal gospel) are closely connected became generally accepted. L. Vaganay in a lengthy commentary on the
Gospel of Peter denied that they had any connection with
each other.[2] But his views are refuted in a reply by James.[3]
Today the issue is not yet thoroughly resolved, particularly
with regard to which document might be dependent upon the
other. But no one recently has taken a stand against any
connection between the Akhmim fragments, and their possible
close connection has seriously weakened the position of anyone who would favor the Akhmim text as a reliable witness to
the text of the Apocalypse of Peter. Ch. Maurer proposes
that it was only a later editor, possibly even the copyist
of the Greek Akhmim fragments, who brought together the
Gospel of Peter and the Apocalypse of Peter, adapting the

---

[1]H. Stocks, "Quellen zur Rekonstruktion des Petrus-
evangeliums," Zeitschrift für Kirchengeschichte 34 (1913),
38-41 and 47-50.

[2]Léon Vaganay, L'Evangile de Pierre, second edition,
(Paris: Librairie Lecoffre (J. Gabalda et Fils), 1930), 187-
192. Also in agreement is A. F. Findlay, Byways in Early
Christian Literature: Studies in the Uncanonical Gospels and
Acts (Edinburgh: T. & T. Clark, 1923), pp. 114-115 and notes
98-99, pp. 317-318.

[3]M. R. James, "The Rainer Fragment of the Apocalypse
of Peter," Journal of Theological Studies 32 (1931), 275-
278.

latter to the former. [1] We can only agree at present with P.
Vielhauer that the evidence is too scanty for certainty on
this question and it will only be resolved by new dis-
coveries rather than further studies. [2]

A second issue during this early period of research
was the relationship of the Apocalypse of Peter to the canonical 2 Peter. Already James in his earliest publication on
this writing lists 15 resemblances between 2 Peter and the
Apocalypse of Peter Akhmim Fragment. [3] He extends three possible explanations for this. Either the author of the Apocalypse copied 2 Peter by design, or the two are products of
the same school, or the resemblances do not exist. James
was cautious on this score, and only twenty years later in
his commentary on 2 Peter do we find him finally opting for
the second explanation. [4] Adolf von Harnack presents a
similar list of the resemblances without comment. [5] Others
were not so cautious.

---

[1]Ch. Maurer, ibid., 666-667.

[2]Phillipp Vielhauer, Geschichte der urchristlichen
Literatur (Berlin: Walter de Gruyter, 1975), 507-513. It
still remains to be investigated in what ways the Ethiopic
version might be related to the Gospel of Peter. Surely,
for example, the shining cross which precedes Christ at his
return in Apocalypse of Peter 1:6 must be the same as that
which follows him out of the tomb in Gospel of Peter 10:39
and which actually speaks in 10:42.

[3]M. R. James and J. A. Robinson, The Gospel according
to Peter, and the Revelation of Peter, ibid., 52-53.

[4]M. R. James, The Second Epistle General of Peter and
the General Epistle of Jude (Cambridge: Cambridge U. Pr.,
1912), pp. xxvi-xxviii.

[5]A. von Harnack, Bruchstücke des Evangeliums und der
Apokalypse des Petrus, 2nd ed., ibid., 87-88.

W. Sanday proposed that the Apocalypse of Peter and 2 Peter were written by the same author.[1] E. Kühl found too little evidence for a final decision, but agreed that nothing stood in the way of identity of authorship.[2] The suggestion made later by von Harnack, that the only late attested Second Letter of Peter had used the more widely and earlier attested Apocalypse as one of his sources when he wrote, was seriously entertained.[3] This position was vehemently disputed by A. Simms in his attempt to defend the authenticity of 2 Peter,[4] and Simms insists that no resemblances exist which cannot be explained by a common religious milieu, attempting to refute in detail the list which James had composed. But F. H. Chase left open the position of Harnack even as he himself leaned to the position that the two documents were the work of two writers who belonged to the same

---

[1]W. Sanday, Inspiration. Eight Lectures on the Early History and Origin of the Doctrine of Biblical Inspiration; being the Bampton Lectures for 1893 (London: Longmans, Green & Co., 1894), 346-348 and 384. H. von Schubert agreed with him; see reference in Spitta (below).

[2]Ernst Kühl, Die Briefe Petri und Judae. Kritisch-exegetischer Kommentar über das Neue testament begründet von. H. A. W. Meyer, sixth ed. (Göttingen: Vandenhoeck und Ruprecht, 1897), 375-376.

[3]Adolf von Harnack, Geschichte der altchristlichen Literatur bis Eusebius, Part 2: Die Chronologie (Leipzig: J. C. Hinrichs, 1958; reprint of edition of 1897), v. 1, pp. 470-472. Jülicher agreed with Harnack (reference in Spitta, below).

[4]A. Ernest Simms, "Second Peter and the Apocalypse of Peter," The Expositor (London), Fifth Series 8 (1898), 460-471.

school.[1] And Heinrich Weinel inclined to the view that the
author of the letter used the Apocalypse of Peter as a
source,[2] as did R. Knopf.[3]

The tide began to turn with the commentaries of Bigg
and Mayor,[4] both of whom point to the vast differences between the two writings. Bigg suggests, and Zahn later
agrees,[5] that it was certain remarks in 2 Peter which led to
the creation of the Apocalypse of Peter and possibly also
other Petrine pseudepigrapha. The whole discussion ground

---

[1]F. H. Chase, "Peter, Second Epistle," James Hastings,
ed., A Dictionary of the Bible (New York: Charles Scribner's
Sons, 1900), v. 3, 814-816. Chase thinks it impossible that
the author of the Apocalypse borrowed from the letter.

[2]Heinrich Weinel, "Offenbarung des Petrus," ibid., 212.
Weinel also expressed the possibilities that either a commor
Petrine stream of tradition or a common dependence of both
documents on the same non-Christian sources could also account for the resemblances.

[3]Rudolf Knopf, Die Briefe Petri und Judä. Kritisch-
exegetischer Kommentar über das Neue testament begründet von.
H. A. W. Meyer, seventh edition (Göttingen: Vandenhoeck und
Ruprecht, 1912), 255.

[4]Charles Bigg, A Critical and Exegetical Commentary on
the Epistles of St. Peter and St. Jude. International Critical Commentary, 2nd ed. (Edinburgh: T. & T. Clark, 1902),
pp. 207-209, 242-244, and 265; Joseph B. Mayor, The Epistle
of St. Jude and the Second Epistle of St. Peter (New York:
Macmillan and Co.: 1907; reprint ed., Grand Rapids: Baker
Book House, 1979), CXXX-CXXXIV.

[5]". . . the emphasis upon the parousia as an integral
element of the Petrine preaching (2 Pet. i.16), and the prophetic character of 2 Pet. ii.-iii. probably supplied the
impulse for the fabrication of the ἀποκάλυψις πέτρου."
Theodor Zahn, Introduction to the New Testament, trans.
Melanchton W. Jocobus, et. al. (Edinburgh: T. & T. Clark,
1909), v. 2, 273.

virtually to a halt with an essay by F. Spitta[1] which is
generally accepted as proving the priority of 2 Peter.[2]
According to Spitta the Apocalypse of Peter 1-7 (Akhmim) is
closely related to 2 Peter 1:16-2:3. The source of the saying about false prophets is the synoptic tradition where it
is connected to the parousia of Christ. This connection is
found in 2 Peter but not in the Apocalypse where it is God
himself who comes in judgment. Then too, the author of the
Apocalypse is only interested in using the transfiguration
to show the glory of the departed saints while the author of
2 Peter finds importance in the glory of Jesus himself (who
is not transfigured in the Apocalypse) to make his point
concerning the certainty of the parousia. This, according
to Spitta, demonstrates that 2 Peter has not been influenced
by the Apocalypse of Peter. Either the influence is the
other way around or the (still demonstrable) relationship
must be due to a use of other literature or ways of religious
expression which the two have in common.

Since the appearance of Spitta's essay commentators on
2 Peter have often ignored the existence of the Apocalypse
of Peter altogether. Others have gone beyond this to claim

---

[1]F. Spitta, Die Petrusapokalypse und der zweite
Petrusbrief," Zeitschrift fur die neutestamentliche
Wissenschaft 12 (1911), 237-242.

[2]See, for example, Ch. Maurer, "Apocalypse of Peter,"
ibid., 664.

with no further proof that the author of the Apocalypse knew and used 2 Peter.[1] This would make the apocalypse the earliest witness to the letter. The date of 135 CE (derived from the Ethiopic text and bearing no relationship to the Akhmim Fragment here in question!) is being used as a terminus ante quem for 2 Peter because dependence of the Apocalypse on the letter is assumed.[2]

The following comments about Spitta's essay should be kept in mind: 1) Spitta does not prove nor does he claim to prove the dependence of the Apocalypse of Peter on 2 Peter. His methodology is to show that from the context of 2 Peter 1:16-2:3 it is unlikely that its author would have developed the scheme of his argument out of Apocalypse of Peter 1-7 (Akhmim). It would more likely be the other way around. It is not completely clear that he has established his case. 2) Spitta leaves untreated the verbal resemblances shown by James and Harnack. If he were to complete his topic he would need to deal with them one by one to show how they fit his proposal. 3) It is clear that virtually none of Spitta's reasoning applies to the Ethiopic text which was available at the time his essay was published but which remains unmentioned. A thorough investigation of the relationship of the Ethiopic text to 2 Peter is much to be desired. A few brief

---

[1]J. N. D. Kelly, A Commentary on the Epistles of Peter and of Jude (New York: Harper and Row, 1969), 236.

[2]John H. Elliott in R. A. Martin, James and John H. Elliott, I-II Peter/Jude, Augsburg Commentary on the New Testament (Minneapolis: Augsburg, 1982), 130.

remarks on this subject are made by M. R. James,[1] but these
are rather offhandedly dismissed by D. H. Schmidt in his
study on the Peter Writings.[2] The desired investigation is
still awaited.[3]

---

[1]M. R. James, The Second Epistle General of Peter,
ibid., LVII-LVIII.

[2]David Henry Schmidt, "The Peter Writings: Their Redactors and Their Relationships" (Ph.D. dissertation, Northwestern University (Evanston, Illinois), 1972), 112-116.

[3]There are more connections between the Apocalypse of
Peter (Ethiopic text) and 2 Peter than have been noticed.
Besides the use of the phrase "way of righteousness" (2 Pt.
2:21, cf. 2:2; Apoc. Pt. 7:2), the heavy reliance on the
transfiguration account (2 Pt. 1:16-21; Apoc. Pt. 15-17),
and the destruction of the earth and the heavens by fire
(all of which are closer ties than Schmidt indicates), there
are: 1) the prediction of Peter's death (2 Pt. 1:12-15;
Apoc. Pt. 14:4); 2) the "better than" saying (better never
to have known the way of righteousness 2 Pt. 2:21; better
never to have been created Apoc. Pt. 3:4-5); 3) the false
prophets/christs who will entice people into denial of their
Master/Christ (2 Pt. 2:1-2; Apoc. Pt. 2:7-9); 4) the emphasis upon the promises of Christ especially regarding future
glory (2 Pt. 1:2-4, cf. 3:13; Apoc. Pt. 14:2-6); 5) an emphasis upon Christ's parousia (2 Pt. 1:16 and 3:4; Apoc. Pt.
1:6-8, 6:1); 6) an association of the water flood with the
coming destruction by fire (2 Pt. 3:5-7; the destruction is
consistently pictured as if the fire were flowing water in
Apoc. Pt. 5-6); 7) an emphasis upon the creative power of
God's word (2 Pt. 3:5-7; Apoc. Pt. 4:5-6, cf. 4:3); and 8)
the mention of the gloom of darkness in the nether world
(2 Pt. 2:17; Apoc. Pt. 5:2, 6:5, 9:1). The harangue against
the loose morals of the false teachers (2 Pt. 2:1-22) serves
somewhat the same function as the inferno (Apoc. Pt. 7-12).
There is even the possibility that the judgment of the earth
(Apoc. Pt. 4:13) is reflected in the difficult textual tra-
dition of 2 Pt. 3:10. (See the views of F. W. Danker in
Frederick W. Danker, et. al., Hebrews, James, 1 and 2 Peter,
Jude, Revelation, Proclamation Commentaries (Philadelphia:
Fortress, 1977), 90-91; and also in Walter Bauer, A Greek-
English Lexicon of the New Testament and Other Early Chris-
tian Literature, trans. and ed. William F. Arndt and F.
Wilbur Gingrich; 2nd ed., edited by F. Wilbur Gingrich and
Frederich W. Danker (Chicago: U. of Chicago Press, 1979),
s. v. ευρισκω; but see further the discussion in Tord Fern-
berg, An Early Church in a Pluralistic Society: A Study of

Are the notions concerning the afterlife in our
apocalypse of Jewish or Greek background? This third issue
arose when scholars of the classical Greek literature recognized in the Akhmim fragment conceptions and images related
to more ancient Greek religion. In an essay devoted to
sketching this background, E. Norden in 1893 concludes the
Apocalypse of Peter to be the result of a mixture of the
morality oriented Orphich mysteries, with their emphasis on
rewards or punishments in the afterlife, and the glowing,
effusive imagination of the oriental mind.[1] In that same
year, Albrecht Dieterich published Nekyia,[2] the only full-
length study on the Apocalypse of Peter which has ever been
done. There, beginning with Greek folk religion, the doctrines of the blessed and the damned in the underworld are
traced in the Eleusinian Mysteries, through the remnants of
the Orphich-Pythagorean books found in a broad spectrum of
ancient Greek literature, and into Jewish apokalyptik, particularly the Book of Enoch and 4 Esdras. Dieterich demonstrates the development of these doctrines both with regard
to the classes of sinners and the types of punishments. Of

2 Peter [Lund: Gleerup, 1977], 75-77 who finds a juridical
meaning for ευρισκεσθαι questionable.) A closer examination
might explain these resemblances and discover yet still
others.

[1]Eduard Norden, "Die Petrus-Apokalypse und ihre antiken Vorbilder," Allgemeine Zeitung, Beitrage 98 (1893), Nr.
107, pp. 1-6; reprinted in Kleine Schriften zum Klassischen
Altertum (Berlin: Walter de Gruyter, 1966), 218-233.

[2]Albrecht Dieterich, Nekyia. Beitrage zur Erklarung
der neuentdeckten Petrusapokalypse (Leipzig: B. G. Teubner,
1893; reprinted with supplements by Richard Wünsch, 1913).

the fourteen groups of these which are represented in the
Apocalypse, Dieterich distinguishes seven which undoubtedly
go back to Orphic influence, seven which were added by the
Christian author. This influence came about, says Dieterich,
when members of Orphic communities in Egypt converted to
Christianity and brought with them their pagan beliefs on
the afterlife. He also thinks that gnosticism originated
in much the same way.

This study of Dieterich came under fire immediately.
Carl Schmidt suggested it was possible that such ideas may
have arisen independently or even that older Egyptian ideas
of the dead were the source both for the Greek Orphic
material and for that found in Apocalypse of Peter.[1] It
is further intimated that there exist purely Jewish documents such as the Apocalypse of Elijah which more likely
served as forerunners for the apocalypse which goes by the
name of Peter. Though Schmidt does not refer to it, Moses
Gaster had already published an article in which he translates from Hebrew eight Jewish apocalypses that in his
estimation were pre-Christian and served as sources for the
Apocalypse of Peter.[2] But Gaster's apocalypses originated
actually many centuries later than he believes, and, though
the parallels with the Apocalypse of Peter are striking with

---

[1] Carl Schmidt, review of Nekyia, ibid.

[2] Moses Gaster, "Hebrew Visions of Hell and Paradise,"
Journal of the Royal Asiatic Society of Great Britain and
Ireland (1893), 571-611.

regard to form, there are no connections in detail.

A. Marmorstein has demonstrated some quite general agreements between our apocalypse and the descriptions of hell in three Jewish mystical tractates which in his opinion rely upon an old fragment found in the Mishna.[1] Later, S. Liebermann made the best case for the early Jewish inferno.[2] He finds a fragment from such an inferno in the Palestinian Talmud. Then too, he establishes that an undatable midrash of this type and the apocryphal Elijah story found in the Pseudo-Titus Epistle[3] "drew from one Jewish source." Finally, in this vein, K. Berger in a brief comparison of seven Jewish and Christian descriptions of hell, including the Apocalypse of Peter, concludes that here we have a sure example of the connection of post-New Testament Jewish and Christian apocalyptic material.[4] Berger believes the punishments of hanging by a member of the body to be a development of the talio combined with the ten commandments. And he further suggests that the oldest of the texts which he

[1]A. Marmorstein, "Jüdische Parallelen zur Petrusapokalypse," Zeitschrift für die neutestamentliche Wissenschaft 10 (1909), 297-300.

[2]Saul Liebermann, "On Sins and Their Punishments," Texts and Studies (New York: KTAV, 1974), 29-51; originally published in Hebrew in Louis Ginzberg Jubilee Volume (New York, 1945).

[3]Discussed above as no. 16 in "Indirect Witnesses for the E.C. Apocalypse of Peter."

[4]Klaus Berger, Die Gesetzesauslegung Jesu, Teil I, Neukirchener Verlag, 1971), 349-353.

surveyed may be one of the Jewish apocalypses[1] because it offers the punishments without the explanations of each, a form which developed later. With regard to the pursuit of this Jewish background, we can only observe that extreme caution is necessary when this Jewish material is used. None of these Jewish visions of hell can be accurately dated, there is a likelihood that they are some centuries later than the Apocalypse of Peter, and Berger has not given sufficient reason to date any of them so early.[2]

Returning now to Dieterich's work, his conclusions of Greek influence were generally accepted. The appearance of the Acherusian Lake and Elysium in the later discovered Ethiopic text confirmed the Greek influence which "must be direct, not filtered through a Jewish source."[3] But James was willing to accept such influence only for the description of Hell. For Paradise and the Last Judgment, James contends, the influence of Enoch, Wisdom, and Daniel are the

---

[1]Found in August Wünsche, Aus Israels Lehrhallen (Hildesheim: Georg Olms, 1967; reprint of edition of 1907), v. 3, pp. 70-71.

[2]No actual date is indicated by Berger for any one of the apocalypses he surveys, but he does intimate their time period by relating them to the Apocalypse of Peter and to the Acts of Thomas. Berger's survey deals only with punishments by hanging which play only a minor role in Apocalypse of Peter and appears to me to be a special development of the specific punishments by hanging used incidentally in older material.

[3]M. R. James, "The Recovery of the Apocalypse of Peter," ibid., p. 25.

immediate sources.[1] Certainly the greatest challenge to the
thesis of Dieterich came with the growing skepticism concerning Orphism. The very existence of Orphic mysteries
and thus also Orphic doctrine, Orphic books, and Orphic communities came under sharp attack. The scholarly debate has
been very long and involved.[2] Even as the debate continues,
new evidence supporting the existence of Orphic doctrine and
books has appeared in the discovery of the Derveni Papyrus.[3]
The conclusion of Guthrie that it was precisely in eschatological matters that the Orphic books influenced Christianity
is a reasonable evaluation of the available evidence and an
acceptance of the jist of the argument of Dieterich.[4] The
curt treatment of Dieterich's case by Schmidt in his search
for sources of the Apocalypse of Peter is unjustified.[5] For
the sake of completeness it should be added here that a suggestion by Weinel to search for the sources in the oriental,

---

[1]Ibid., 25-28. Cf. also G. H. Macurdy, "Platonic
Orphism in the Testament of Abraham," Journal of Biblical
Literature 61 (1942), 213-226 where the author traces
Orphic and Platonic elements also in the Judgment scene of
the Testament of Abraham and related literature.

[2]See the discussion in W. K. C. Guthrie, The Greeks
and Their Gods (Boston: Beacon Pr., 1950), 307-332; idem.,
Orpheus and Greek Religion (New York: W. W. Norton, 1935;
second revised edition, 1952).

[3]Walter Burkert, Orphism and Bacchic Mysteries: New
Evidence and Old Problems of Interpretation (Berkeley:
Center for Hermeneutical Studies in Hellenistic and Modern
Culture, 1977).

[4]W. K. C. Guthrie, Orpheus and Greek Religion, ibid.,
269.

[5]David H. Schmidt, ibid.

particularly Babylonian, religions played no significant
role in the discussions.[1]

The final issue of this period, the use of the apocalypse in the early church, will be described here only in
the briefest way since the survey in part two of this chapter includes much of the relevant information. The early
articles by James and von Harnack were already quite thorough in their surveys.[2] The information from these was
absorbed by the histories of the literature and the patrolo-
gies.[3] The impact made by the Apocalypse of Peter was also
traced through the extensive medieval literature on heaven
and hell.[4] It was James again who took up the same task

---

[1]Heinrich Weinel, "Offenbarung des Petrus," ibid.,
213-214.

[2]M. R. James and J. Armitage Robinson, The Gospel According to Peter, and the Revelation of Peter, ibid., 39-82;
Adolf von Harnack, Bruchstucke des Evangeliums und der Apokalypse des Petrus, ibid., 80-87; idem., "Die Petrusapokalypse in der alten abendländischen Kirche," Texte und Untersuchungen zur Geschichte der altchristlichen Literatur 13
(1895), 71-73.

[3]E.g., Adolf von Harnack, Geschichte der altchristlichen Literatur, ibid., Part 1, v. 1, pp. 29-33 and Part 2,
v. 1, pp. 470-472; Otto Bardenhewer, Patrology: The Lives
and Works of the Fathers of the Church, trans. Thomas J.
Shahan (St. Louis: B. Herder, 1908), 113-114.

[4]E.g., Ernest J. Becker, A Contribution to the Comparative Study of the Medieval Visions of Heaven and Hell, with
Special Reference to the Middle-English Versions (Baltimore:
John Murphy, 1899); Philippe de Félice, L'autre Monde; mythes
et légendes le purgatoire de Saint Patrice (Paris: Honoré
Champion, 1906), esp. pp. 171-187 which includes a French
translation of the Akhmim Fragment; J. A. Macculloch, Early
Christian Visions of the Other-World (Edinburgh: St. Giles,
1912).

with enthusiasm after the discovery of the Ethiopic text.[1]
From that time to this little progress has been made in this
regard.[2]

B. Research from the Discovery of the Ethiopic Text
    through the Discovery of the Rainer Fragment
    (to 1932): A Time of Cooling Down

The enthusiasm generated by the discovery of the Akhmim Fragment was not duplicated upon the discovery of the
Ethiopic text. This latter text placed in jeopardy the conclusions of the prior research, for it differed considerably
from the Akhmim text and was written in a language open to
fewer scholars. The first notice about it was given by F.
Nau in 1908.[3] Nau knows only by report that a pseudo-
Clementine work "of little importance" is contained in manuscript 51 d'Abbadie in Paris. Shortly thereafter Sylvain
Grébaut published his synopsis of this work and some brief
remarks on grammatical matters.[4] The Ethiopic text itself
with a French translation appeared in 1910.[5] It was a

[1]M. R. James, "A New Text of the Apocalypse of Peter,"
ibid.; idem., "The Recovery of the Apocalypse of Peter,"
ibid., esp. 28-35.

[2]But see G. Quispel and R. M. Grant, "Note on the
Petrine Apocrypha," ibid.

[3]F. Nau, "Clémentine (Apocryphes)," A. Vacant and E.
Mangenot, eds., Dictionnaire de Théologie Catholique (Paris:
Letouzey et Ané, 1908), v. 3, col. 223.

[4]Sylvain Grébaut, "Litterature éthiopienne pseudo-
clementine," Revue de l'Orient chrétien 12 (1907), 139-151,
285-287.

[5]Idem., ibid., v. 15 (1910), 198-214, 307-323, 425-
439.

pseudo-Clementine composition, and the text appeared to be corrupt in a number of places. M. R. James recognized immediately that the text of the Apocalypse of Peter was embedded in this work. In a series of three articles in 1911 James analyzed the text and established beyond doubt that this is a text of our apocalypse.[1] At the same time he announced the discovery of a new small Greek fragment in the Bodleian Library.[2] The lack of excitement can be seen in the notices given of the discovery.[3]

There was yet another small Greek fragment brought to light by Charles Wessely in 1924.[4] It is in the Rainer collection in Vienna and was incorrectly identified by Wessely as a fragment of the Acts of Peter. F. J. Dölger first identified it correctly.[5]

---

[1]M. R. James, "A New Text of the Apocalypse of Peter," Journal of Theological Studies 12 (1911), 36-66 and 157, 362-383, 573-583.

[2]Ibid., pp. 157, 367-369. James edits this text and translates it.

[3]F. Nau, "Note sur <<Un nouveau texte de l'Apocalypse de Saint Pierre>>," Revue de l'Orient chrétien 15 (1910), 441-442; Bartlett, "Survey of Recent Books bearing on Church History," Review of Theology and Philosophy 7 (1911), 334-336; N. Bonwetsch, "Zur Apokalypse des Petrus," Theologische Literaturblatt 23 (1912), 121-123; Otto Bardenhewer, Geschichte der altkirchlichen Literatur (Darmstadt: Wissenschaftliche Buchgesellschaft, 1962; reprint of edition of 1913), v. 1, 614-615. Cf. H. Stocks, ibid., 43-50.

[4]Charles Wessely, "Les plus anciens monuments du Christianisme: Ecrits sur Papyrus II," Patrologia Orientalis 18 (1924), 481-483.

[5]Franz Joseph Dölger, Sol Salutis. Gebet und Gesang im christlichen Altertum (Munster, Aschendorff, 1925), 354. Unfortunately a notice that Fr. Dölger would treat the text

Meanwhile, a German translation with extremely valuable notes concerning the Ethiopic text was made by Hugo
Duensing.[1] Another German translation with chapter numbers
depending on Grébaut's paragraph divisions was published by
Weinel in 1924.[2] Weinel also places a translation of the
Akhmim text adjacent to that of the Ethiopic for easy comparison. In that same year, M. R. James included an English
translation in his collection of New Testament apocrypha.[3]

E. Winstanley used the Apocalypse of Peter as a sort
of outline to present the point of view of many early Christian eschatological works.[4] J. R. Harris sought to relate
the Book of the Rolls (see Part I above) to the EC Apocalypse of Peter.[5] But the real issues of this period were

---

in detail in a forthcoming essay has not to my knowledge
been fulfilled. See Albert Ehrhard, Überlieferung und Bestand der hagiographischen und homiletischen Literatur der
Griechischen Kirche von den Anfangen bis zum Ende des 16.
Jahrhunderts (Leipzig: J. C. Hinrichs, 1937), v. 1, p. 708.

[1]Hugo Duensing, "Ein Stücke der urchristlichen Petrus-
apokalypse enthaltender traktat der äthiopischen Pseudoklementinischen Literatur," Zeitschrift für die neutestamentlichen Wissenschaft und die Kunde der älteren Kirche 14
(1913), 65-78.

[2]Heinrich Weinel, "Offenbarung des Petrus," Edgar
Hennecke, ed., Neutestamentlichen Apokryphen, 2nd ed.
(Tübingen: J. C. B. Mohr, 1924), 314-327.

[3]M. R. James, The Apocryphal New Testament (Oxford:
Clarendon Pr., 1924), 314-327.

[4]Edward William Winstanley, "The Outlook of Early
Christian Apocalypses," The Expositor, series 8, 19 (1920,
I), 161-184.

[5]J. Rendel Harris, "The Odes of Solomon and the Apocalypse of Peter," The Expository Times 42 (1930/1931), 21-
23.

two: 1) How does the Greek Akhmim text relate to the Ethiopic? and 2) How is the transfiguration account in the Apocalypse of Peter 15-17 related to the transfiguration accounts in the synoptic gospels and in 2 Peter 1:16-19?

We owe again to M. R. James the earliest (and probably still today the best) discussions of the first of these two problems.[1] He found the Ethiopic text to be superior to Akhmim in almost every way by attestation from outside sources. Especially important for later studies was his contention that the Akhmim order of events (the description of heaven before that of hell) was secondary to the Ethiopic and that the Ethiopic, a prophetic speech in the mouth of Jesus in form, was to be preferred to the vision form of Akhmim. Bartlet disagreed with both conclusions, but did not give his reasons.[2] Hugo Duensing suspects both that we still do not have the entire Apocalypse of Peter before us in the Ethiopic text and that much material has been added.[3] He wishes to solve the problem of order of events by suggesting that perhaps the descriptions of Paradise were not originally there at all and were both added later but in different places. E. Klostermann in a very short article

---

[1]M. R. James, "A New Text of the Apocalypse of Peter," ibid., pp. 53-54, 366-367, and esp. 573-577; "The Recovery of the Apocalypse of Peter," ibid., 10-20.

[2]Bartlet, ibid., p. 334.

[3]Hugo Duensing, ibid., 76-78.

favors the Ethiopic as the better text.[1] In a (not completely scholarly) M.A. dissertation, G. L. Luecke finds the
Ethiopic text too long and suggests where additions must
have been made.[2] The Akhmim text is incomplete but more
closely reflects the original than does the Ethiopic according to Weinel.[3] He finds in the latter a much reworked
text, and Amann agrees with him.[4] In a closer study of the
two texts, Goguel weighs the evidence, finds it to be nearly
equal in weight on either side, and decides that the two
texts must be independent recensions of the same original.[5]

    After the discovery of the Rainer Fragment, K. Prümm
made a detailed comparison of that brief text with the corresponding Ethiopic.[6] Prümm believes the new fragment to
speak out strongly for the reliability of the Ethiopic text,
and precisely there where it was highly suspect.   James

----

[1]Erich Klostermann, "Zur Petrusapokalypse," Hundert
Jahre A. Marcus und E. Webers Verlag 1818-1918 (Bonn:
Marcus & Weber, 1919), 77-78.

[2]George Lewis Luecke, "A Reconstruction of the Text of
The Apocalypse of Peter," (M.A. dissertation: U. of Chicago,
1921).

[3]Heinrich Weinel, "Offenbarung des Petrus," ibid.,
2nd ed., 316-317.

[4]E. Amann, "Apocryphes du Nouveau Testament," Louis
Pirot, ed., Dictionnaire de la Bible--Supplement (Paris:
Letouzey et Ane, 1928), col. 525-527.

[5]Maurice Goguel, "A propos du texte nouveau de l'Apocalypse de Pierre," Revue de l'histoire des religions 89
(1924), 191-209.

[6]K. Prümm, "De genuino apocalypsis Petri textu examen
testium iam notorum et novi fragmenti Raineriani," Biblica
10 (1929), 62-80.

again takes to pen and carries Prümm's investigation even
further, speaking out strongly for the trustworthiness of
the Ethiopic.[1] The debate continues with Maurer supporting
the reliability of the Ethiopic text in the tradition of
James, and Vielhauer more skeptically following the path of
Weinel and Goguel.[2] We sincerely hope this dissertation
will advance the discussion on this topic.

Meanwhile, the Apocalypse of Peter played a controver-
sial role in research on the Transfiguration. We cannot
here enter into detail on the Transfiguration investigation
as such. The literature there is quite extensive and
scholars have certainly not reached a consensus on either
the history of the tradition or its function in the synoptic
gospels.

Spitta had made a study of the gospel accounts of the
transfiguration in which he compared them with the Akhmim
Fragment. He demonstrated that this latter is a revelation
of the heavenly world and not a glorification of Jesus or a
revelation of him.[3] The first to use the Ethiopic text for
comparison was M. Goguel. Favoring the Akhmim text over
that of the Ethiopic, which appeared to him to harmonize the

---

[1]M. R. James, "The Rainer Fragment of the Apocalypse
of Peter," Journal of Theological Studies 32 (1931), 270-279.

[2]Ch. Maurer, "Apocalypse of Peter," ibid., 664-667;
Philipp Vielhauer, Geschichte der urchristlichen Literatur,
ibid., 508-511.

[3]F. Spitta, "Die evangelische Geschichte von der Verklärung Jesu," Zeitschrift für wissenschaftliche Theologie
(1911), 97-167.

earlier Greek with the gospel accounts, he concluded that in neither the Akhmim Fragment nor in the Ethiopic was Jesus transfigured. Therefore at least this primitive trait must be older than the synoptic accounts.[1] After Dibelius suggested the connection with the Transfiguration in the Ethiopic text was an attempt to identify the heavenly figures unnamed in the Greek text and to connect the story more closely to the story of Jesus,[2] and when Bultmann also had expressed the same opinion,[3] Goguel analyzed the Ethiopic text still more closely from the long-entertained position that the Transfiguration tradition was a misplaced resurrection account.[4] Goguel emphasizes that the saying concerning the one temple (Apoc. Pt. 16:9) comes from the influence of the synoptics. On the other hand, K. Goetz asserted that the original account of the Transfiguration was best preserved in the Ethiopic version.[5] He believes this to be

---

[1]Maurice Goguel, "A propos du texte nouveau de l'Apocalypse de Pierre," ibid., 208-209.

[2]Martin Dibelius, Geschichte der urchristlichen Literatur (Munich: Chr. Kaiser, 1975; reprint of 1926 edition), p. 84 [p. 97 of the original edition].

[3]Rudolf Bultmann, The History of the Synoptic Tradition, trans. John Marsh (New York: Harper and Row, 2nd edition of 1968; trans. from edition of 1931 with supplementary notes from 1962), 258-261 and 432-433.

[4]Maurice Goguel, La Foi la Résurrection de Jésus dans le christianisme primitif (Paris: Ernest Leroux, 1933), 326-330.

[5]Karl Gerold Goetz, Petrus als Gründer und Oberhaupt der Kirche und Schauer von Gesichten nach den altchristlichen Berichten und Legenden, Untersuchungen zum Neuen

true in part because it explains details in the synoptic
story for which otherwise we cannot account and in part
because there are details in the reference of 2 Pt. 1:16-19
which obviously are in harmony with those in Apocalypse of
Peter 15-17 over against the synoptic accounts.

This issue sometimes found mention then, in more
recent studies of the Transfiguration, but was not given
serious consideration. J. Blinzler believes that 2 Peter
cannot be dependent upon the Apocalypse of Peter because
2 Pt. 1:16 obviously refers to a transfigured Jesus and in
the apocalypse he is not transfigured.[1] Boobyer attempts
to answer most of the points that Goetz has made.[2] The
Transfiguration, he says, is an expanded form of the Ascension story intending to emphasize the Ascension as an illustration of the Second Coming. Ramsey agrees with Boobyer
and pushes for the historicity of the Transfiguration,[3]

Testament 13 (Leipzig: J. C. Hinrichs, 1927), 76-92.
Goetz's attempt to explain Peter's vision in Apoc. Pt. 3,
14 as a Call Vision ultimately to be traced back to the
vision mentioned by Paul (1 Cor. 15:5) should also be kept
in mind (pp. 95-98).

[1]Joseph Blinzler, Die neutestamentlichen Berichte über
die Verklärung Jesu (Münster: Aschendorff, 1937), pp. 73-76
and 20-22. See also Heinrich Baltensweiler, Die Verklärung
Jesu: Historisches Ereignis und synoptischer Bericht (Zürich:
Zwingli, 1959), 24-25.

[2]G. H. Boobyer, St. Mark and the Transfiguration Story
(Edinburgh: T. & T. Clark, 1942), 11-16 and 30-40.

[3]Arthur Michael Ramsey, The Glory of God and the
Transfiguration of Christ (New York: Longmans, Green, & Co.,
1949). On the historicity of the Transfiguration account,
though in a very different way than intended by Ramsey, see

while J. G. Davies treats this connection between the Transfiguration, Ascension, and Parousia on the level of Lukan
redaction.[1] Basing his conclusions on Riesenfeld's theory
that the Transfiguration was originally an account of Jesus'
enthronement,[2] H. M. Teeple believes that the original story
was used by 2 Peter and by the Apocalypse of Peter and was
altered by Mark in connection with Exodus 24 and 34 and with
Deuteronomy 18:15.[3] The Apocalypse of Peter is used several
times by C. E. Carlston in his defense of the theory that
the Transfiguration was originally a misplaced Resurrection
account.[4] Challenging Carlston and insisting that in the
pre-Markan tradition the Transfiguration referred to an
event within the lifetime of the historical Jesus was R.
Stein.[5] Recently Neyrey has used the Apocalypse of Peter to
aid him in exegeting the Transfiguration references in 2

---

also now Morton Smith, "The Origin and History of the Transfiguration Story," Union Seminary Quarterly Review 36 (1980),
39-44.

[1]J. G. Davies, "The Prefigurement of the Ascension in
the Third Gospel," Journal of Theological Studies, new
series 6 (1955), 229-233.

[2]Harald Riesenfeld, Jésus Transfiguré: L'Arrière-plan
du récit évangélique de la transfiguration de Notre-Seigneur
(Kobenhavn: Ejnar Munksgaard, 1947).

[3]Howard M. Teeple, The Mosaic Eschatological Prophet
(Philadelphia: Society of Biblical Literature, 1957), 84-86.

[4]Carles Edwin Carlston, "Transfiguration and Resurrection," Journal of Biblical Literature 80 (1961), 233-240.

[5]Robert H. Stein, "Is the Transfiguration (Mark 9:2-8)
a Misplaced Resurrection-Account?," Journal of Biblical
Literature 95 (1976), 79-96.

Peter.[1] Neyrey maintains that in the latter document also
the Transfiguration is a foreshadowing of the Second Coming.
All this shows at the present time is that there has been a
great reluctance since the time of Goetz to rely very
heavily on evidence from the Apocalypse of Peter and yet
when exegeting the difficult account of the Transfiguration
in the synoptics one can hardly avoid it.

C. Research during the Last Fifty Years:
A Time of Great Caution

Little has been happening in the last fifty years in
studies on the Apocalypse of Peter. No new texts have been
discovered and no major investigations have appeared.

Erich Fascher briefly points out the difficulties in
the Ethiopic text but reminds us that apocalypses often are
mixed compositions by their nature.[2] Edsman in a study on
the baptism with fire pointed to the three functions of the
river of fire in the Apocalypse of Peter: it annihilates the
cosmos, it serves as an instrument of ordeal at the final
judgment, and it then becomes an instrument of torture.[3]
He points out that the function is exactly the same in the

---

[1]Jerome H. Neyrey, S. J., "The Apologetic Use of the
Transfiguration in 2 Peter 1:16-21," Catholic Biblical Quarterly 42 (1980), 504-519.

[2]Erich Fascher, "Petrusapokryphen," Wilhelm Kroll,
ed., Paulys Real-Encyclopädie der classischen Altertumswissenschaft (Stuttgart: J. B. Metzler, 1938), v. 19, part
2 (38th halfband), col. 1373-1381, esp. 1375-1377.

[3]Carl-Martin Edsman, Le baptisme de feu (Uppsala:
A-B. Lundequistska, 1940), 57-63.

Sibylline Oracles 2 where the identical order of events
serves as a valuable check on the tendency we might have to
posit reediting of the text where it would seem more reasonable from our standpoint. Edsman also points out the origin
of such a river of fire in Ethiopian Enoch, Daniel 7, and
Greek mythology.

Two valuable articles have been contributed by Erik
Peterson. The first of these points out that Apocalypse of
Peter 14:3b-6 is the oldest text we have which clearly speci-
fies Peter's death in Rome.[1] The discovery of the Rainer
Fragment relieves this section of the Ethiopic text of the
suspicion of being an addition. This confirms the reference
to Peter's death in the Ascension of Isaiah which is also
placed in the eschatological thought-world of the beginning
of the second century. Peterson contends this speaks both
for the age of the Apocalypse of Peter and as a testimony to
Peter's martyrdom in Rome. In a second article Peterson
deals with the special privilege of prayer for the damned,
Apocalypse of Peter 14:1-6a, also from the Rainer Fragment.[2]
Here he seems on less firm ground when he connects this
prayer with "All Israel has a share in the future world" and

---

[1]Erik Peterson, "Das Martyrium des hl. Petrus nach der
Petrus-Apokalypse," Miscellanea G. Belvederi (Rome: 1953),
181ff.; reprint in Frühkirche, Judentum und Gnosis (Freiburg: Herder, 1959), 88-91.

[2]Erik Peterson, "Die "Taufe" im acherusischen See,"
Vigiliae Christianiae 9 (1955), 1-20; revised and expanded
in Frühkirche, Judentum und Gnosis (Freiburg: Herder, 1959),
310-332.

with a passage from the Apocalypse of Moses. He connects
the "good bath of salvation in the Acherusian Sea" with the
Jewish conception of living water, and he believes both the
Apocalypse of Peter and Hermas are an attempt to Christian-
ize a pre-Christian washing in the apocalyptic stream. Even
though some of the terminology used may be Greek, the background and the topography are Jewish.

In a study of the use of Psalm 24 in the early church,
Ernst Kähler includes a section on the use of that psalm in
the Apocalypse of Peter.[1] This psalm is used at the very
end of the apocalypse in the Ascension scene. Kähler demonstrates that the "men in the flesh" (Apoc. Pt. 17:3) must
refer to the righteous (Psalm 24:3-5) who have died and are
now awaiting Jesus in the first heaven. They are led by
Jesus into the second heaven while the angels call for the
doors to be opened (Psalm 24:7) that the king of glory might
enter. The disciples who watch are the generation of those
that seek him (Psalm 24:6). Kähler says that this is the
earliest christological interpretation of Psalm 24. He
believes this to be original to the Apocalypse of Peter
because it must have been used liturgically in the early
churches of Palestine, a use to which Sozomen testifies.

L. Kretzenbacher produced a study on the use of the
stream of fire in Christian art in the eastern Mediterra-

---

[1]Ernst Kähler, Studien zum Te Deum und zur Geschichte
des 24. Psalms in der Alten Kirche (Göttingen: Vandenhoeck
und Ruprecht, 1958), 53-55.

nean.[1] He found some very distant connections there with
the Apocalypse of Peter, mainly connections through other
writings. M. McNamara sought traces of our apocalypse in
the apocrypha of the Irish church but found nothing
definite.[2]

Two editions of the New Testament Apocrypha containing
the Apocalypse of Peter appeared during this time. The
first, by Michaelis, unfortunately translates only the Akhmim text, but it contains a valuable introduction.[3] The
second was the new edition of Hennecke reedited by Schneemelcher. There Ch. Maurer presents a well-organized translation of both texts and all other fragments as well as the
best available short introduction to this apocalypse.[4] One
should mention here also again the short introduction provided by Philipp Vielhauer in his history of early Christian
literature.[5] Also the noteworthy brief introduction by A.

---

[1]Leopold Kretzenbacher, "Richterengel am Feuerstrom,"
Zeitschrift fur Volkskunde 59 (1963), 205-220.

[2]Martin McNamara, The Apocrypha in the Irish Church
(Dublin: Dublin Institute for Advanced Studies, 1975),
pp. 102-103 and 108.

[3]Wilhelm Michaelis, Die apokryphen Schriften zum Neuen
Testament, 2nd ed. (Bremen: Carl Schunermann, 1958), 469-
481.

[4]Ch. Maurer, "Apocalypse of Peter," Edgard Hennecke,
ed., New Testament Apocrypha, 3rd ed. edited by Wilhelm
Schneemelcher, trans. and ed. R. McL. Wilson (Philadelphia:
Westminster, 1965), vol. 2, pp. 663-683.

[5]Phillip Vielhauer, Geschichte der urchristlichen Literature: Einleitung in das Neue Testament, die Apokryphen,
und die apostolischen Väter (Berlin: de Gruyter, 1975), 507-
513.

Yarbro Collins who has analyzed this writing against the background of a certain definition of the genre "apocalypse."[1]

The most extensive work to come out of this period was a dissertation on the Petrine writings by D. H. Schmidt.[2] Schmidt analyzed the relationship between 1 Peter, 2 Peter, the Apocalypse of Peter and the Gospel of Peter and found no important connections between them. I believe he has ignored some basic connections between the Apocalypse of Peter and 2 Peter. But his most important suggestion may be that the Apocalypse of Peter is based on the Gospel of Matthew with other traditions taken from the Enoch literature.[3] A thorough investigation of the relationship of the Apocalypse of Peter to the gospel literature has not yet been done. Schmidt, who has adopted a methodology largely dependent on tracing the sources used by a given author, has not been adequate in isolating the sources utilized by the author of the Apocalypse of Peter.

Inadequate studies of this apocalypse continue to cause much misunderstanding among scholars. Two examples

---

[1] Adela Yarbro Collins, "The Early Christian Apocalypses," John Collins, ed., Apocalypse: The Morphology of a Genre, Semeia 14 (1979), 72-73 and 107-108. See also the tables, pp. 104-105.

[2] David Henry Schmidt, "The Peter Writings: Their Redactors and Their Relationships" (Ph.D. dissertation, Northwestern University (Evanston, Illinois), 1972), esp. pp. 106-135, 173-179, and 185-202.

[3] Ibid., 134-135.

will suffice here. First of all, it is sometimes said that the Apocalypse of Peter is found among those Books of Clement which form a sort of closing section to the Ethiopic New Testament.[1] This is not so. The pseudo-Clementine work containing our apocalypse is very rare and an entirely different writing from the usual Clementine works found in Ethiopic. Secondly, an unfortunate thing occurred when Klaus Berger recently included the Apocalypse of Peter in his study of the Amen-sayings of Jesus.[2] For in fact there is no Amen-saying in that apocalypse, even though such a saying is supposed and is included in the standard translations.[3] The misunderstanding arose when H. Duensing, mistakenly believing the text (Apoc. Pt. 2:7) to be senseless, introduced those words for no apparent reason into his translation.[4] They have remained with us until now.

---

[1] Edgar J. Goodspeed, A History of Early Christian Literature, revised and enlarged by Robert M. Grant (Chicago: U. of Chicago Pr., 1966), 34-37.

[2] Klaus Berger, Die Amen-Worte Jesu: Eine Untersuchung zum Problem der Legitimation in apokalyptischer Rede (Berlin: Walter de Gruyter, 1970), pp. 120-121 and 137-138.

[3] Ch. Mauer, "Apocalypse of Peter," ibid., 669; M. R. James, The Apocryphal New Testament, ibid., 511.

[4] Hugo Duensing, "Ein Stücke der urchristlichen Petrusapokalypse enthaltender Traktat der äthiopischen Pseudoklementinischen Literatur," ibid., p. 67. See also footnote 5 on that page.

CHAPTER TWO

INTRODUCTION TO THE TEXT

The Ethiopic text of this edition is a mixed text;
that is, it is not the text of any one manuscript. It has
been reconstructed from the Ethiopic and Greek manuscripts
described below, where also are discussed related texts
which have not been utilized. The intention of this edition
is to present the earliest Ethiopic text which the material
at our disposal allows, and at the same time to make available, using the critical apparatus, all of the variants of
the manuscripts. This results in a text reflecting no particular stage of the manuscript tradition, but it does
represent the current progress in research. Unfortunately,
while some portions of the text, for example chapter fourteen, have been greatly advanced, other sections obviously
corrupt, like chapter eleven, remain obscure.

I. Manuscript P

The manuscript for which we use the abbreviation P is
housed in Paris at the Bibliothèque Nationale. It is number
51 in the collection of Antoine d'Abbadie. D'Abbadie had
spent many years in Ethiopia and returned to France with a
large collection of manuscripts, two hundred thirty-four in

number.[1] Many of these had been gathered on a twelve-year
campaign (1837-1849) by his brother Arnould. He himself
catalogued these works,[2] and tells us that ms. 51 came into
his hands lacking the usual case for transporting Ethiopic
books. D'Abbadie rebound and recovered the book (or had
this done). The manuscript is incomplete at the end, but
d'Abbadie suspected that no more than one page was missing,
and a comparison with manuscript T (described below) shows
that this is very likely the case. Perhaps more information
on the acquisition of this manuscript is to be found in his
notes and journals which are yet unedited.

The whole collection was recatalogued by Chaîne and
Conti Rossini working independently in 1912-1915.[3] Ms. 51
contains the following writings:

(1) Sargis of Aberga. This is an apology for Christianity in question-and-answer form. A newly converted Jew
asks questions about his new faith in nine meetings. The

---

[1]Described briefly in Edward Ullendorff, The Ethiopians: An Introduction to Country and People (London:
Oxford University Press, 1965), p. 17.

[2]Antoine Thompson d'Abbadie, Catalogue raisonné de
manuscrits éthiopiens appartenant à Antoine d'Abbadie
(Paris: Imprimerie Impériale, 1859). Ms. 51 is described
on pp. 60-63.

[3]Marius Chaîne, Catalogue des manuscrits éthiopiens
de la collection Antoine d'Abbadie (Paris: Bibliothèque
Nationale, 1912), esp. pp. v-x, 34-37; Carlo Conti Rossini,
"Notice sur les manuscrits éthiopiens de la collection d'
Abbadie." Journal asiatique, ser. 10, 19 (1912): 551-578;
20 (1912):5-72; 448-494; ser. 11, 2 (1913):5-64; 6 (1915):
189-238, 445-494; esp. ser. 10, 20:37-38.

first meeting is slightly more than half the text and has
been edited and translated into French by Sylvain Grébaut.[1]
We know of no other manuscript where this work is found.
It purports to be from the time of Harāqāl king of Rome, by
which is apparently meant Heraclius, Byzantine emperor from
610-641. Grébaut believes it to be an original Ethiopic
composition while Conti Rossini thinks it was written in
Greek and translated into Ethiopic from an Arabic version.
There exists no detailed study of this writing.

(2) The Testament of Our Lord. This is a work well
known in Ethiopic manuscripts but also in Arabic and Syriac.
The Syriac text was published by Raḥmani.[2] An English
translation with introduction and extensive notes was published by Cooper and Maclean.[3] This testament purports to
be written down by Clement of Rome, the last words of Jesus
given to his disciples after his resurrection but before
his ascension. It is in form a Church Order consisting
mostly of liturgical directions. It was probably written
in Greek in Asia Minor about 350 A.D. To my knowledge no
thorough study of the Ethiopic version exists; the text in
d'Abbadie 51 has never been published or used in an edition

---

[1]Sylvain Grébaut, "Sargis d'Aberga," Patrologia Orientalis 3, fascicle 4 (1909):551-643.

[2]Ignace Ephrem II Raḥmani, Testamentum Domini nostri
Jesu Christi (Mainz: Kirkheim, 1899).

[3]James Cooper and Arthur John Maclean, The Testament
of Our Lord (Edinburgh: T. & T. Clark, 1902).

of a text.

(3) The Testament in Galilee of Our Lord Jesus Christ.
The text of this work appears in several Ethiopic manuscripts. These manuscripts, including that of d'Abbadie 51,
were edited and translated into French by Guerrier.[1] The
major part of this testament is better known as the Epistula
Apostolorum, a second-century, anti-Gnostic composition.
The Ethiopic text was reedited and compared with the Coptic
text by Isaak Wajnberg.[2] A convenient German translation
has been made by Duensing.[3] The Ethiopic translation may
have been made from Arabic which may in turn have been
translated from the Coptic or the original Greek.

(4) The Second Coming of Christ and the Resurrection
of the Dead. This is a pseudo-Clementine work known only
from this manuscript and manuscript T (see below). It was

---

[1]L. Guerrier, "Le testament en Galilée de Notre-
Seigneur Jésus-Christ," Patrologia Orientalis 9, fascicle 3
(1912):141-236. A useful preliminary report on this work
was published by Guerrier in "Un 'Testament de Notre-
Seigneur et Sauveur Jésus-Christ' en Galilée," Revue de l'
Orient chrétien 12 (1907):1-8.

[2]German translation and notes in Carl Schmidt, Gespräche Jesu mit seinen Jüngern nach der Auferstehung (Leipzig: J. C. Hinrichs, 1919; reprint ed., Hildesheim: Georg
Olms, 1967); pp. 6-20, 26-155, 47*-66*.

[3]Hugo Duensing, Epistula Apostolorum nach dem Athio-
pischen und Koptischen Texte, Kleine Texte für Vorlesungen
und Übungen, no. 152 (Bonn: Marcus and Weber, 1925).

edited and translated into French by Grébaut.[1] It is not clear when it was written. But it contains in its first seven folios the Ethiopic translation of the Apocalypse of Peter of which we give here a new edition. Its main theme is God's mercy to sinners. While there have been some investigations of the Apocalypse of Peter (described in chapter one above), no research has been done on this pseudo-Clementine work which contains it. A short introduction and summary of this and the following composition have been written by Grébaut.[2]

(5) The Mystery of the Judgment of Sinners. Also a pseudo-Clementine composition, this work like the preceding is known to us only in mss. P and T. The text has been edited and translated into French by Grébaut.[3] No research has been done on it. The date is uncertain. The principle theme is God's mercy toward human beings. In this it seems to have some relationship to the preceding pseudo-Clementine writing, though the Second Coming seems to deal particularly with sinners while the Mystery treats human beings in

---

[1]Sylvain Grébaut, "Littérature éthiopiénne pseudo-clémentine," Revue de l'Orient chrétien 15 (1910); 198-214, 307-323, 425-439.

[2]Sylvain Grébaut, "Littérature éthiopiénne pseudo-clémentine," Revue de l'Orient chrétien 12 (1907); 139-151, 285-287.

[3]Sylvain Grébaut, "Littérature éthiopiénne pseudo-clémentine," Revue de l'Orient chrétien 12 (1907), 380-392; 13 (1908) 166-180, 314-320.

general. This work is incomplete in d'Abbadie 51 as we
learn by comparing it with T.

Manuscript P is of parchment measuring 34 x 27 centimeters. It has some holes and repairs, but these were
present before the text was written on the parchment, for
no part of the text is missing because of them. There are
157 folios, two columns per page, 21-27 lines per column,
and 10-12 letters per line. The letters are for the most
part easily distinguished, but I found it hard to tell η
from $\hbar$. D'Abbadie calls it "belle écriture ancienne."[1]

The writings are clearly separated by signs such as
:: ≡ ::. It appears that five different scribes have worked
on this manuscript. The first scribe copied Sargis and
finished with a scribal colophon on folio 77v. A second
scribe copied the two Testaments and left some empty space
at the end of column 130vb where there is now a sketch of
some faces crudely drawn in what we might term an 'Egyptian'
style. A third scribe appears at the beginning of the
Second Coming (131ra), then a fourth at 131vb line 7, but
only for eight lines, whereupon the third scribe has returned. But the fourth scribe comes back and writes all of
column 132ra, after which the third scribe again continues.
I take a note at the bottom of column 132ra to refer to that
fourth scribe who interrupted the work of the third. The

---

[1]Antoine d'Abbadie, ibid., p. 60.

note reads ሐበሮ፡ሐአልበ 'This is the pen of Lasibala'.
The third scribe writes through column 141vb where there is
a gap of seven lines at the end of the column but where no
text seems to be missing. Finally, a new scribe, the fifth,
begins at the top of column 142ra, finishes the Second Coming, and completes the manuscript with the Mystery.

The Apocalypse of Peter, which runs from 131ra to
137rb thus is copied by the third and fourth scribes mentioned above, and mostly by the third, since the fourth has
copied only one and one-third columns altogether. This
third scribe often omits single letters from words. Sometimes these omissions remain, but just as often this scribe
corrected his omissions by writing the omitted letter above
the line of writing (which is marked by tiny dots or pin
pricks in the margins) in the place where it should appear.
It is possible to tell that sometimes (but not very often)
the scribe has erased and written over that erasure. In
folio 136rb (14:1) ፕፍቀተ፡ወሰይኅ ተ has been written
as a correction above line 13. It is very likely that the
scribe omitted a whole line from the manuscript he was copying and then wrote it in. This tells us that the manuscript
from which he was copying had about ten letters per line in
it.

In the text of the Apocalypse no numbers appear in the
columns. The numbers are written in the left margins before
the line in which they belong, and a space is left for them

at the appropriate place in the line of text. An exception
is in column 136va (15:1) where the number ፩ is written in
the margin but the scribe has failed to leave the appropriate space before ስብእ. Why are the numbers in the
margin? Apparently the numbers were to have been rubricated. The space was left for this and the numbers were
written in the margin to indicate what belonged in the
space. But the rubrication was never done in this part of
the text. In fact in all of the Second Coming only the
last section which contains a type of liturgical calendar
has there been any rubrication. The numbers in the margins
have the usual lines above and beneath the numeral itself.
The numeral one, which is written ፩, is to be understood
as 'each one' where it is duplicated ፩፩ in analogy with
ኅኅ and ናሁ.

The punctuation consists of the word divider : and
the mark :: which usually marks the end of a sentence. But
seldom does this latter mark appear at the end of a sentence
in our apocalypse. Most sentence endings go unmarked. On
the other hand, the mark :: sometimes seems to have a different function than to mark the end of a sentence. For example, in ዕደ::ወአንስት 'men and women' (12:1), መንኮራ
ኵሮ::ዘእሳት 'wheel of fire' (12:5) and ከመወርኅ::ከመ:
ውፅዕ:ፍትሑ 'we have learned that his judgment is good'
(13:6), to mention just a few of many instances, the mark ::
appears to connect sentence parts which belong together.

Such a mark would have been the most helpful when the text
was read orally, and we may entertain the thought that this
text may have been read aloud at some stage of its transmission, probably at its earliest period. A full study of
the use of this mark in Ethiopic manuscripts is badly
needed.

The texts of the Second Coming and the Mystery were
originally edited by Grébaut for Patrologia Orientalis. It
says something about the state of these texts that the editor of that series changed his mind about including them
when he learned how corrupt they were. The nature of these
corruptions is described by Grébaut.[1] He cites missing
syllables, faulty and incomplete vocalization, unknown
words, ⍭ for ⍭ on the plural of the imperfect, the misuse
of the conjunctions ሕሶ and እⰊሶ, etc. I believe that
he overstates the case when he says that "the imperfect replaces the perfect and vice versa," that the first person
pronouns are used one for another, and that the text is
often obscure. For while there exist many difficulties in
the text, much of the obscurity is relieved when strict attention is given to the numbers of the pronouns and the
tenses of the verbs and when due consideration is paid to
the fact that this is an apocalyptic text.

A new edition of the text of the Apocalypse of Peter

---

[1]Sylvain Grébaut, "Littérature éthiopiénne pseudo-
clémentine," 12 (1907):151, 285-287.

was needed not only because a new Ethiopic manuscript has
been discovered and because the Greek texts deserve consideration, but also because Grébaut in his edition has not
always adequately reflected the manuscript. For example,
none of the numbers in chapters 1-14 are included in his
edition. The several places where more than one vowel appears on a letter stem are not indicated. Some letters are
simply misread, and punctuation is not correctly indicated.
There is no need to elaborate on this, since all cases where
the edited text of Grébaut differs from manuscript P are
given in my textual apparatus. Yet Grébaut has been very
helpful in restoring missing letters and repairing the forms
of words obviously written incorrectly.

There are a number of places where the margins contain
notes. Few of these have any importance for our <u>Apocalypse</u>.
But in the bottom margin of 144va (which is in the <u>Second
Coming</u> but later than the <u>Apocalypse of Peter</u>), there is an
undecipherable note about the transformation of lightning
which does not seem to be related to anything directly above
it but may somehow be connected with the transformations in
5:5. There is also an important note at the very beginning
of the manuscript. It reads ሐመጽሐፍ፡ ዘጓ ፡ ኅመክኅ ፡ ኅ
ንm ፉ ፆ ∏ 'This book belongs to the sanctuary of Steven
in Dāgā'. Dāgā is an island in Lake Ṭana, and our manuscript P was at one time part of a church library there.
Indeed, it is likely that it was made in this area.

The copyist does not date this manuscript, and it is
not easy to date Ethiopic manuscripts by other means.
Chaine says it is from the sixteenth century.[1] Conti Rossini stipulates the end of the fifteenth or the beginning
of the sixteenth century.[2]

II. Manuscript T

This manuscript is to be found on the island of Kebrān
in Lake Tānā. It was photographed in 1968 along with many
others during an expedition for that purpose to the area,
an expedition led by the well-known Ethiopic scholar Ernst
Hammerschmidt. Hammerschmidt reports on his trip in a
catalogue of the manuscripts which were filmed. The manuscript is apparently in good condition and the letters are
clear.

The following writings are included in Tānāsee 35:

(1) The Testament of Our Lord. This is described
above in the discussion of manuscript P, where it comes
second.

(2) The Testament in Galilee of Our Lord Jesus Christ.
This has also been described above in the discussion of

---

[1]Chaine, ibid., p. 37.

[2]Conti Rossini, ibid., p. 38.

[3]Ernst Hammerschmidt, Athiopische Handschriften vom
Tānāsee 1, Verzeichnis der orientalischen Handschriften in
Deutschland, v. 21, I, (Wiesbaden: Franz Steiner, 1973).
What is here called manuscript T is number 35 in this cata-
logue. The description is found on pp. 163-167

manuscript P, where it is third.

(3) <u>The Second Coming of Christ and the Resurrection of the Dead</u> which contains the Apocalypse of Peter, described above as the fourth document in P.

(4) <u>The Mystery of the Judgment of Sinners</u>, described above as the fifth document of P. Here it is complete, about a full folio longer.

(5) The <u>Hexameron</u>, a pseudo-Epiphanic work. Hammerschmidt believes this to be a ⁻ferent rescension from the one more commonly in use. T⸺ ₋xt is unpublished.

(6) <u>The Story of the Annunciation of the Archangel Gabriel and his Conversation with Mary.</u> The title explains the contents. It is a text corresponding to chapters 10-12 of a work about Mary published in English translation by Budge.[1] The text is unpublished.

(7) <u>The Story of the Conception of the Savior by Mary.</u> Hammerschmidt indicates that this text is paralleled at least in part by another text and translation published by Budge.[2]

---

[1]Ernest Alfred Wallis Budge, <u>Legends of Our Lady Mary The Perpetual Virgin and Her Mother Hannâ</u> (London: printed privately for Lady Meux, 1900; reprint ed., London: The Medici Society, 1922), pp. 117-121.

[2]Ernest Alfred Wallis Budge, <u>The Miracles of the Blessed Virgin Mary and the Life of Hannâ (Saint Anne), and the Magical Prayers of Aheta Mîkâêl</u> (London: published privately for Lady Meux, 1900), p. 95.

(8) A hymn to Christ praising his incarnation. It remains unstudied.

(9) A tractate by Cyril of Jerusalem on the resurrection of the Lord. This is incomplete at the end. It also remains uninvestigated.

An empty column between works (5) and (6) has been filled with a text in Amharic. This text is squeezed into its space by putting 15-16 letters into a line and 54 lines into the column. But the text is blotted and is no longer legible in many places.

The manuscript is parchment, 22 x 23 centimeters with some repairs made before the text was written on it. There are no holes and no places where the text is missing except at the very end, the conclusion of the Cyril tractate. The manuscript has been rubricated, but one is not always able to tell from the microfilms available to me what is in red and what is not. T has 106 folios, three columns per page, 25 lines per column, and 8-10 letters per line. The letters are quite well written, easy to distinguish. It is a carefully written manuscript, in Hammerschmidt's description.[1] The various documents are clearly separated by marks similar to those in P, and usually also with some blank spaces.

Unlike P, T has been written entirely by the same scribe, with the exception of the short Amharic work which

---

[1]Ernst Hammerschmidt, ibid., p. 167.

has been added later. The scribe has erased a few times, but he never corrects himself, as P does, by writing letters above the line or by putting more than one vowel marking on a letter stem. In a few cases letters which are inadvertently omitted remain uncorrected. The margins of the manuscript remain empty. The numbers are written where they belong in the body of the text. In 15:1 the number Ⴆ is written before ኽርፅኽሆ 'his disciples' rather than before ሰነኽ 'men' where it belongs. The result is that in T only two disciples go with Jesus to the Holy Mountain and an indeterminate number of men appear to them. That this is incorrect is clear not only from the fact that the related transfiguration text of the synoptic gospels also has two men and that they are named in both traditions, but also by the fact that the text immediately following it describes first one heavenly figure and then the other. The number clearly belongs with ሰነኽ.

The punctuation of T is more elaborate than that of P. There is the standard word divider : and the mark :: which normally indicates the end of the sentence. The latter is usually found in T with a red cross in it thus :+:, and the few instances where this is not so the cross seems to be omitted inadvertently, as I could find no pattern to these omissions. This mark is also usually found after proper names, a mark of piety. In addition, there are the marks ǀ and ⁝ . The first of these is made by a vertical line

drawn through the word divider : and also marks the end of
a sentence. It appears often where the end of sentence is
unmarked in P. Yet even with this additional mark, many
sentence endings are still left unmarked. The mark ⁝ is
infrequent and serves somewhat like the English semicolon.
I have not made a complete study of these marks, but their
occurrences are noted in the critical apparatus. The pecul-
iar mark ·|· in 4:7 and 4:9 I believe to mark an apocryphal
quotation.

The text follows rather closely that of P, but the
distinction between ዐ and ዑ is carefully maintained. See
the discussion of this below at 1:4 in the "Notes on the
Ethiopic Text." At the bottom (but not in the margin) of
column 70va, which is at the conclusion of the Mystery, is
written the following:

ኦሐተ ፡ መፍሕፍ ፡ ዘኽፍሕፉ ፡ [most of one line left
ወሰዘፍሕፉ ፡ ኽፍመ ፡ ዘየርዘ ኹ ፡ ዓ ፡ በኽኝ ፡ ይመሐይ ወ ፡ blank here]
ኽግዘኽብ ፡ በመኝግ ፡ ሰ ፡ ሰ ᎙ ፡ ኽ ᎙ ፡ ወ ፡
᎙ ᎙ ፡ ※ = ※.

"May God have mercy in the kingdom of heaven on the
person who commissioned this book to be written . . . .
and upon poor Aṣma Georgis who wrote it. Amen and
amen."

Hammerschmidt[1] interprets this to be traces of the owner's
name which cannot be made out, and thinks it is added later.
But it appears to me to be in the same handwriting as the
main body of the manuscript. I think this may rather indi-

---

[1]Ernst Hammerschmidt, ibid., p. 167.

cate that the manuscript was written before it was commissioned, that the name of the buyer was left empty to be
filled in later, and that no name was ever put into the
blank space. This scribal colophon was probably intended to
be at the end of the book, where such colophons are often
found. This is supported by the fact that the remainder of
the folio, columns 70vb and c, is empty, the only place in
the manuscript where such a large gap is found. If that is
true, the name of the owner may never have been inserted
here because the colophon was no longer at the end of the
book after the same scribe added further material to the
book. If this theory is correct, the noun ጦ ኀኊ፣ 'pauper,
poor person' may have been well used by Aṣma Georgis to describe his own condition--a scribe copying works which had
not been commissioned in the hopes of selling them later.

The manuscript is not dated, but its style of letter
formation is quite different from that in P. Hammerschmidt
ventures to guess the eighteenth century but follows this
with a question mark to indicate how uncertain is the date.

III. How P and T Are Related

Clearly P and T are in the same manuscript tradition.
That is evident from the many cases where they agree in
readings which are obviously errors. The following instances of that agreement in the Apocalypse of Peter are
enough to establish the case:

1. The use of ያኅበር for ያኅበር at 1:7 (cf. 6:1)

2. The appearance of ወዘከሞ at the beginning of 3:3

3. The omission of the negative particle ኢ at 3:5

4. The use of ምኅት for ወትኅ at 4:8

5. The corruption ወበርቀጶተሙ ፡ ይደኅጸ ፡ ዓኅም at 5:5

6. The long dittography (in which appears a variant common to both) at 5:8

7. The corruption involving ቀት at 6:4

8. The corruption of ኅቆኅት and of ኅአ፡ከቆኅሀኅ at 7:5 and 8:3 respectively

9. The omission of ህ in ያኅሀኍ at 8:6

10. The omission of ኅ in ኅምት at 8:6

11. The misplacement of the phrase ኅጵ፡ኅሞኅት፡ ሞኅፀቀኅ at 10:2

12. The appearance of the probably corrupt forms ቦቆ and ምሀር at 10:5 and 11:1

13. The corruption of the name ዐዘረኮቆ at 10:5

14. The number ፩ at 11:6

15. The corruption of ያኅበኍ at 13:2

16. The many corruptions in chapter 14 where P and T are in almost complete agreement (See the discussion of these below in "Notes on the Ethiopic Text.")

But these agreements should not be allowed to obscure a few revealing differences. The variant ያኅበሙ/ያኅኍ at 1:3 is a fairly certain indication that behind both manuscripts lies a tradition in which the third person plural imperfect of verbs with ወ as a third radical was written

with **ⲱ** rather than **ⲁ**. See the discussion in "Notes on the
Ethiopic Text" at 1:3. The many variants of the case of
nouns, for example **ጎⵊⳞ** / **ጎⵊⳞ** at 2:5, indicate that
the probably more original tradition of P where many objects are in the nominative case has been corrected in the
tradition of T, though not in all instances. At 2:10 the
suffix **ⵓ** has been added in the tradition of T in an attempt
to add sense to the passage, even though it actually creates
a conflict with what is said in v. 11. The tradition represented in T is thus a corrected edition. Likewise the numbers of chapter six which appear in P are also really superfluous and so are not present in T, even though elsewhere
such numbers appear in both.

   A particularly revealing variant is the position of
the number **ⳅ** '2' in 15:1-2. The correct place is obvious,
as I have already said just above in discussing T. Why was
the mistake made? In P there is no space left in the text
before **ⲛⲛⲏ** for the number in the left margin. Faced with
such a situation, a scribe in the T tradition has placed it
before **ⲕⳞⲏ** rather than where it should be. This
tells us first of all that the practice of writing the numbers in the margin is the older practice. Secondly it tells
us that manuscript P was not used as the immediate ancestor
of manuscript T. For the number in the left margin in P is
on the line before **ⲛⲛⲏ** but two lines below the line containing **ⲕⳞⲏ** and would not have been moved up that far

by accident. The displacement of the number must have taken
place when a copy was made from a manuscript with a long
line, one which would have contained both ꜧ𝐶ꝗꜧ 𝑈 and
ꞁꞁꜧ so that there was some real question about where the
number belonged.

Thus we have shown that while P and T are in the same
manuscript tradition, T is not copied directly from P itself. P may be either a direct ancestor of T or they may
both share another ancestor. The evidence from the Apocalypse of Peter to decide between these two possibilities is
not conclusive. Perhaps a complete investigation of all
variants in all of the documents common to both would help
decide the issue.

The tradition common to P and T includes the four
writings The Testament of Our Lord, The Testament in Galilee
of Our Lord Jesus Christ, The Second Coming of Christ and
the Resurrection of the Dead, and The Mystery of the Judgment of Sinners. This is clear from the fact that these four
documents are found together in the same order in both. And
the colophon at the end of the last of these in T (described
above) is also an indication that these four are separate in
T from those which follow. It should be noticed that chapters 1-14 of the Testament of Our Lord contain an apocalypse
which is not easily dated but is possibly second or third

century.[1] This same apocalypse in another rescension
appears as the first eleven chapters of the Testament in
Galilee and there serves as an introduction to the second
century Epistula Apostolorum. Then in the Second Coming we
find the Apocalypse of Peter of which the original Greek is
early second century. Can it be accidental that we find in
these three writings three early Christian (probably second
century) works, one of them twice? On this basis too it
should be said that a thorough study of the fourth document,
the Mystery of the Judgment of Sinners is urgently needed.
We are unable to say when these four writings became connected in the manuscript tradition.

Since P and T are the only manuscripts known to contain the Second Coming and the Mystery, and since both of
these manuscripts come from the Region of Lake Ṭānā, it
seems likely that these two writings were never widely
spread in Ethiopia. But the turbulent history of that country leaves even that uncertain, for sometimes manuscripts
were systematically destroyed. Then too, the climate there
is not conducive to manuscript preservation. That is why
although the literary activity was great during the Aksumite
Kingdom (first to sixth centuries A.D.) only a limited number of writings from that period survive, and these are on

---

[1]A very short discussion of it is included by Adela
Yarbro Collins, "The Early Christian Apocalypses" in John J.
Collins, ed., Apocalypse: The Morphology of a Genre, Semeia
14 (Missoula: Scholars Press, 1979), pp. 77-78.

much later manuscripts. Only a small number of manuscripts survive from the fourteenth and fifteenth centuries or before. Ethiopic manuscripts are all of recent date compared to those of many other countries.[1] Seen in this light, the date of P, if late fifteenth or early sixteenth century is correct, places it among those Ethiopic manuscripts which have survived the longest.

IV. The Akhmim Fragment

The story of the discovery of this fragment of the Apocalypse of Peter has been told above in the section on the history of research. The manuscript, which may have been unbound when it was found, is incomplete and breaks off in the middle of a sentence, but yet neither the line nor the page is complete and the manuscript is marked as if it were complete. This has often been taken to mean that the scribe was copying from a fragmentary source or that it was copied hurriedly for the grave near Akhmim in which it was found. The manuscript is P. Cair 10759 housed in the Museum of Egyptian Antiquities in Cairo.[2] It has many holes in the section containing our apocalypse.

This manuscript contains:

---

[1]See Edward Ullendorff, The Ethiopians: An Introduction to Country and People (New York: Oxford U. Press, 1965), pp. 136-157.

[2]Described in Joseph van Haelst, Catalogue des papyrus littéraires juifs et chrétiens (Paris: La Sorbonne, 1976), pp. 201-202, 219.

1. The only fragment of the Gospel of Peter, a gospel from the second century. The text has been edited a number of times. The best edition is that of Erich Klostermann.[1] An English translation based on the German by Ch. Maurer is readily available.[2] Many studies have been done on this text. The most detailed and valuable is that of Léon Vaganay.[3]

2. A fragment of the Apocalypse of Peter. This has also been edited a number of times from this manuscript, and Klostermann's edition is best.[4] Here again an English translation based on Maurer's German is available.[5] Most of the studies done on the Apocalypse of Peter have been based on this Greek fragment.

3. Fragments of the Book of Enoch. These are in two parts. The first part is Enoch 19:3; 20:2-21:9; 1:1-16:22. The second, Enoch 16:22-32:6. These fragments are the chief

[1]Erich Klostermann, Apocrypha I. Reste des Petrus-evangeliums, der Petrusapokalypse und des Kerygma Petri, Kleine texte für Vorlesungen und Übungen 3 (Berlin: Walter de Gruyter, 1933), pp. 4-8.

[2]Ch. Maurer, "The Gospel of Peter" in Edgar Hennecke and Wilhelm Schneemelcher, eds., New Testament Apocrypha (Philadelphia: Westminster, 1963), vol. I, pp. 179-187.

[3]Léon Vaganay, L'Évangile de Pierre, 2nd. ed. (Paris: Librairie Lecoffre (J. Gabalda et Fils, 1930).

[4]Erich Klostermann, ibid., pp. 8-13.

[5]Ch. Maurer, "Apocalypse of Peter," ibid., Vol. II, pp. 663-683. This Greek text is translated in parallel columns with the Ethiopic.

witness for the Greek text of Enoch which has been most recently edited by Black.[1] They were used by R. H. Charles in his translation of the Ethiopic text.[2] The text of Enoch has been edited again more recently by Knibb.[3]

The manuscript is parchment and measures 15 x 12 centimeters. There are 33 folios, with the Apocalypse on folios 7-10 bound in upside down from the rest of the manuscript. There is one column of 18 lines per page with 26-35 letters per line. The Gospel and the Apocalyspe are clearly by the same hand, a cursive difficult to read. The two Enoch fragments are each in a different uncial writing. Ch. Maurer says, "The same hand worked on all three texts in the 8th-9th century."[4] But I do not think it possible to say that. Nor can we say if the Enoch fragments were written at the same time as those of the Gospel and Apocalypse. Various dates ranging from the fourth to the eleventh centuries have been offered for the Enoch fragments while the eighth century is usually given for the rest.[5] All we are certain

---

[1]Matthew Black, Apocalypsis Henochi Graece (Leiden: Brill, 1970).

[2]R. H. Charles, ed., The Apocrypha and Pseudepigrapha of the Old Testament in English (Oxford: Clarendon Press, 1913), Vol. 2, pp. 188-281.

[3]Michael A. Knibb, The Ethiopic Book of Enoch, two volumes (Oxford: Clarendon Press, 1978).

[4]Ch. Maurer, "The Apocalypse of Peter," ibid., p. 663.

[5]Joseph van Haelst, ibid., pp. 202, 619.

about is that the date is uncertain, as is the date of the
grave in which the manuscript is found. The debate about
whether these fragments of the Gospel of Peter and of the
Apocalypse of Peter are really here part of the same document has been described above where the history of research
is told.

No complete and thorough detailed comparison of this
Akhmim text and the Ethiopic Apocalypse of Peter has been
made. They are clearly different rescensions of the same
text, as one can easily see from Maurer's translation where
they stand side by side.[1] The following are important differences which should be noted:

1. The Ethiopic is much longer and has a long section
on the Second Coming and the Final Judgment (chapters 1-6)
and a shorter one on Jesus' ascension (chapter 17) which are
not present in the Akhmim text, though the former is hinted
at in Akhmim 1-3. Nor is there anything comparable in the
Greek to chapters 13-14 of the Ethiopic.

2. In the Ethiopic the description of the punishments
in hell (chapters 5-12) precedes that of the blessedness of
the saved (chapters 15-16). In the Akhmim text, on the
other hand, the order is reversed with the punishments appearing in vv. 21-34 and the blessings in vv. 4-20.

3. The description of hell is fuller and longer in

---

[1]Ch. Maurer, ibid., pp. 668-683.

the Ethiopic while the description of the garden of blessing
is fuller and longer in the Greek.

4. In the Akhmim text both descriptions, those of
hell and of blessedness, are in the form of a vision and are
told in the past tense. In the Ethiopic also this is true
of the latter, but the punishments are part of a longer
prophesy of Jesus in the imperfect (future) and appear only
after the description of the Judgment.

In details too, the two texts differ. For example,
the Ethiopic reads in 15:1-2 ወይቤለኒ፡ እንዘኔዖ፡ ኔፆሱጠ፡
ክርስቶስ፡ ንጉሥነ፡ ንሑር፡ ውጠተ፡ ደብC.ቀዳጠ፡ወመፅኩ፡
ኤርዳኩሁ፡ ምስለሁ፡ ኤንዘ፡ ይዴልዖ፡፡ ወናሁ፡ ፪ ሰብኣ፡ ወ
ኔኔነ፡ ሳሕርተ፡ 7ጶ ሙ፡ ፫ ኤምውስተ ተሙ፡ ኔ7ሙ፡ ይመፅኩ፡
ብርሃነ፡፡ ዘይበCሁ፡ ኔም ፀሐይ And my Lord Jesus Christ
our King said to me, "Let us go to the Holy Mountain." And
his disciples came with him praying. And behold, (there
were) two men. And it was not possible to look at their
face. For from one of them comes a light which gives more
light than the sun.

The corresponding Akhmim text reads και προσθεις ο
κυριος εφη αγωμεν εις το ορος ευξωμεθα απερχομενοι δε μετ
αυτου ημεις οι δωδεκα μαθηται εδεηθημεν οπως δειξη ημιν ενα
των αδελφων ημων των δικαιων των εξελθοντων απο του κοσμου
ινα ιδωμεν ποταποι εισι την μορφην και θαρσησαντες παραθαρ-
συνωμεν και τους ακουοντας ημων ανθρωπους και ευχομενων ημων
αφνω φαινονται δυο ανδρες εστωτες εμπροσθε του κυριου προς

ους ουχ εδυνηθημεν αντιβλεψαι εξηρχετο γαρ απο της οψεως
αυτων ακτιν ως ηλιου And continuing, the Lord said "Let us
go to the mountain (and) pray." And we the twelve disciples, going with him, asked that he show us one of our
righteous brothers who had departed from the world in order
that we might see what sort of form they have and, taking
courage (from that), might encourage also those men who
hear us. And while we were praying, suddenly two men appeared, standing before the Lord, at whom we were not able
to look. For there came out from their face a ray like the
sun.

Comparing the Greek and Ethiopic of this passage, we
see that the Greek is longer in large part because it contains a question put by the disciples to Jesus which is
wholly absent in the Ethiopic. In the Greek Jesus 'continues,' something which has no correspondence in the Ethiopic. The Greek has 'the Lord' while the Ethiopic uses
both the first person singular and the first person plural
in its titles 'my Lord Jesus Christ our King'. In the Greek
Jesus and his disciples go to 'the mountain', in Ethiopic to
'the Holy Mountain'. The Ethiopic has 'his disciples', the
Greek has 'we the twelve disciples'. In the Greek the two
men appear standing before Jesus. In the Ethiopic this is
expressed just with 'two men'. The Greek expresses the inability to look at these men in the first person 'we were
not able' compared with the Ethiopic third person indefinite

'it was not possible.' The Ethiopic singles one of the men out in its description while the Greek does not. Finally, the light coming from the men shines 'like the sun' in the Akhmim text but 'brighter than the sun' in the Ethiopic.

As we can see, the differences between these two texts are too great for us to use the Akhmim to edit the Ethiopic. For it is clear that, whatever may be the relationship of these texts to the original second century Greek, it was not a text of the Akhmim tradition which was translated into Ethiopic. The tradition of the Greek which came to be translated into Ethiopic was that of the manuscripts R and B which we will now describe.

V. Manuscripts B and R

A. Manuscript B

The manuscript fragment which we call B is Ms. Gr. theol. f. 4 in the Bodleian Library at Oxford. First notice of it was given by James,[1] who shortly thereafter made a brief study of it.[2] B is one leaf of a codex of indeterminate length. It is vellum, 7.8 x 4.8 centimeters with 13 lines to a page and 8-10 letters to a line. It was acquired in 1894 or 1895 in Egypt. The Greek text is fragmentary, with many missing letters, some doubtful letters, and the

---

[1]M. R. James, "Additional Notes on the Apocalypse of Peter," Journal of Theological Studies 12 (1911):157.

[2]M. R. James, "A New Text of the Apocalypse of Peter," Journal of Theological Studies 12 (1911):367-369.

whole of the verso difficult to read. It contains 10:6-7 of
the Ethiopic.

The text is very uncertain. The recto is reconstructed
by James as follows (with < > enclosing missing letters):

<γυ>ναικες κ<ρατο>υντες αλυ<σ>εις και μα<στ>ιγουυντε<s>
<ε>αυτους ε<μπρ>οσθεν τ<ου τ>ων
ειδω<λων τ>ων πλαν<ων> και αναναπαυστως
<ε>ξουσιν τη<ν> κολασιν και εγγυs

The text of the verso is so tentative that I dispense
with the brackets and give the hesitatingly reconstructed
text of James who was helped in this by J. Vernon Bartlett:

αυτων ετεροι εσονται ανδρες και γυναικες καιομενοι τη
καυσει των ειδωλομανων ουτοι δε εισιν οιτινες κατελιπον
οδον του θεου ολωs(?) και προε...

Putting these together, we may translate as follows:

[men and] women holding chains and beating themselves
before the deceiving images. And they will have torment
ceaselessly. And near them will be other men and women
burning from the heat of the images. And these are those
who have forsaken the way of God wholly (?) and . . .

The corresponding Akhmim text (vv. 33-34) is as follows[1]:

και παρ εκεινοιs ανδρες ετεροι και γυναικεs ραβδουs
πυροs εχοντες και αλληλους τυπτοντες και μηδεποτε παυομενοι

----

[1]Erich Klostermann, ibid., p. 12.

της τοιαυτης κολασεως και ετεροι παλιν εγγυς εκεινων γυναικες
και ανδρες φλεγομενοι και στρεφομενοι και τηγανιζομενοι ουτοι
δε ησαν οι αφεντες την οδον του θεου

And beside them were other men and women who had rods
of fire. And they were beating one another and never resting from such punishment. And others again near those women
and men were burned and turned and fried. And these were
those who have forsaken the way of God.

Finally, the Ethiopic (10:6-7) reads:

ወእለሂ ፡ ገብርዎሙ ፡ ምሳሌሆሙ ፡ ዕደ ፡ ወእንበተ ፡ በ
ሰንበል ፡ እሳት ፡ ዘይት ፡ ቀወፆ ፡ በበሐተቶሙ ፡ በ
ቀደሜሆሙ ፡ ወከመዝ ፡ ዘናቱ ፡ እግአም ፡ ወእቤሆ
ሙ ፡ ካልኣን ፡ ዕደ ፡ ወእንበተ ፡ ወያውዕዩ ፡ በሀሀበ ፡
ዘናቴ ፡ እግአም ፡ ደይኖሙ ፡ እት ፡ እሙንተ ፡ እለ ፡
ያንደጉ ፡ ተእዛዘ ፡ እግዚአብሔር ፡ ወተለዉ ፡ ፉ
ቃተ ፡ እጋንንት

But those men and women who made their images are in
chains of fire with which they beat themselves in their error before them. And thus is his punishment forever. And
near them are other men and women, and they burn up in the
heat of judgment. Their punishment is forever. These are
they who abandon the commandment of God and followed harsh
(?) demons.

This is unfortunately the only opportunity we have to
compare all three texts of the Akhmim, B and R (which belong
together, see below), and the Ethiopic. From such a comparison the following points are worthy of discussion:

TABLE 1

COMPARISON OF THE AKHMIM, B, AND
ETHIOPIC TEXTS AT 10:6-7

B	Ethiopic	Akhmim
men and . . . women	those men and women who made their images	and beside them other men and women
holding chains and beating themselves	(are) in chains of fire with which they beat themselves	having rods of fire and beating one another
before the de- ceiving images	in their error before them	
and they will have torment ceaselessly	and thus is his punishment forever	and never resting from such punishment
and near them will be other men and women	and near them are other men and women	and others again near those women and men
burning (from) the heat of the images	and they burn up in the heat of judgment	being burned and turned and fried
	their punishment is forever	
and these are those who have forsaken the way of God (wholly?) and . . .	these are they who abandon the com- mandment of God and (follow harsh demons?)	and these were those who have forsaken the way of God

1. In the Ethiopic version the description of sinners is cast as a prediction of the future while in Akhmim it is part of a vision described in the past tense. What was the original literary form? The two verbs governing the participles in B (εσονται and εξουσιν) are both future tense, agreeing with the Ethiopic against Akhmim. The one exception is the last verb in this passage. Akhmim uses an imperfect construction, B the aorist, while the Ethiopic indicates present or future. However, since this verb is intended in all three to include all who ever have or ever will abandon God's way, the difference in tense is in this case insignificant for the larger issue of the literary form of the Apocalypse of Peter.

2. The Ethiopic and B agree against the Akhmim in that they have "chains" where Akhmim has "rods." They also agree in that the men and women beat themselves while in the Akhmim they beat each other. However, the Akhmim and the Ethiopic both have "of fire" to describe the chains/rods and this seems to be missing in B. I say "seems to be" because the evidence is not clear. The participle κρατουντες 'holding' is suspicious because so much of it has been restored. The κ is very faint and uncertain; the letters ρατο are missing altogether; the remainder is more definite. κρατουντες is the suggestion of James, but there does not appear to me to be sufficient space for four letters between the κ (if that is what it is) and the υ (which is very clear). In

other places with the same amount of space James restores two letters. I am unable to suggest another reading which fits both this context and this space, but the possibility must remain open that there might be some reference to fire (πυρος ουντες is too many letters) or to burning (καιουντες is not only an incorrect form but syntactically inappropriate).

3. In B and the Ethiopic the men and women have committed some offense regarding idols. In Akhmim neither idol making nor any offense at all is mentioned for either of the two separate groups of people being punished. In connection with this, በበ፩ተ ተሞ 'in their error' in the Ethiopic must be an attempt to translate των πλανων 'deceiving'. The translator understood πλανων to be from πλανη 'error' rather than from πλανος 'deceiving', and he connected it with the men and women rather than with the idols. Akhmim has no reference to an error or deception.

4. The ceaselessness of the torture is similar in B and Akhmim. In its place the Ethiopic has "thus is his punishment forever." Further, in the second group of those being punished, where the Akhmim and B have nothing at all corresponding to this, the Ethiopic adds "Their punishment is forever." In the "Notes on the Ethiopic Text" to chapter 14 of the text (below) I have a short discussion about the likelihood that the form of universal salvation which the Apocalypse of Peter originally taught was erased from the

document. We do not know when this took place, but it is
likely that at the same time the quite numerous references
to the eternity of the punishments were also added. We seem
to have two cases here, one where the eternity of punishment
replaces the ceaselessness of a punishment which could have
been limited in time, and the other where there was nothing
at all in the text to suggest it.

5. The three connected participles "burned and turned
and fried" in the Akhmim could not possibly fit into the
text of B, corrupt as it is, and thus have no place in its
tradition. The Akhmim has τον οδον του θεου 'the way of
God' where the Ethiopic has "the commandment of God." B is
entirely illegible at this point. There does not seem to be
enough space for εντολην. It may be that the translator of
the Ethiopic translated οδος with 𝔗𝔥𝔥𝔥 which seemed to
him a synonym in this context and also a clearer allusion to
the second of the ten commandments. Akhmim ends at this
point while it is clear that both B and the Ethiopic continue, though the latter is especially corrupt for the next
few lines. There is no justification at all for ολως in B.
It just is not there.

6. It is striking that quite frequently when B and
Akhmim agree in meaning they differ in the expressions used.
For 'beating' B uses μαστιγουντες while Akhmim has τυπτοντες;
to describe the ceaseless punishment B uses και αναναπαυστως
εξουσιν την κολασιν where Akhmim has και μηδεποτε παυομενοι

της τοιαυτης κολασεως; those forsaking the way of God are οιτινες κατελιπον οδον του θεου in B, οι αφεντες την οδον του θεου in Akhmim. It seems strange that so many synonyms are used in such a short passage. It is obvious that one or the other text of B or Akhmim reflects considerable change from the original text of the Apocalypse of Peter. Or perhaps both are distant from the original. We might even entertain the possibility that one of these was a retranslation into Greek from another language. Be that as it may, B is four or five centuries older than Akhmim, and the Ethiopic clearly stands closer to B than does Akhmim.

We may conclude again that the Akhmim text is a different rescension of the Apocalypse of Peter than the Ethiopic, and that the Ethiopic is a translation of the same tradition we find in B. Except for the insistence of the Ethiopic upon eternal punishment, the texts of B and the Ethiopic are really very close indeed.

B is dated by James and those working with him to the fifth century.[1]

B. Manuscript R

The fragment of the text which we call R is labelled P. Vindob. G. ? by van Haelst.[2] It is part of the Rainer

---

[1]M. R. James, ibid., p. 367.

[2]Joseph van Haelst, ibid. The question mark seems to reflect some cataloguing difficulties.

collection housed in Vienna. The Greek text with brief remarks and a French translation was first published by Wessely, who thought it was a fragment of the Acts of Peter.[1]
Recognizing that it was from the Apocalypse of Peter, Prümm
gives the text with a Latin translation in his attempt to
bolster the value of the Ethiopic text as a witness to the
original Greek.[2] Finally, James has further edited the text
and translated it into English.[3] James's edition is the
best and he goes some way in discussing the relationship
between this text and the Ethiopic. The text corresponds to
that of chapter 14 of the Ethiopic (a section which is not
present at all in the Akhmim text) and is very useful for
restoring the Ethiopic of that chapter. Therefore I have
presented the Greek and an English translation below where
I discuss chapter 14 in "Notes on the Ethiopic Text." It
need only be said here that the text is of the same tradition as that from which the Ethiopic was translated.

R, like B, is one leaf from a codex. It is of vellum,
7.8 x 5.3 centimeters and has 13 lines to the page with 8-10

---

[1]Charles Wessely, "Les plus anciens monuments du
Christianisme: Ecrits sur papyrus II," Patrologia Orientalis
18 (1924):345-511. Our text is found on pp. 482-483.

[2]K. Prümm, "De genuino apocalypsis Petri textu examen
testium iam notorum et novi fragmenti Raineriani," Biblica
10 (1929):62-80. The Greek text is on p. 78, the Latin
translation on p. 77.

[3]M. R. James, "The Rainer Fragment of the Apocalypse
of Peter," Journal of Theological Studies 32 (1931):270-279.

letters per line. It is better preserved than B with fewer
missing letters and with fewer letters illegible. It is
dated by Wessely to the third or fourth century.[1] Van
Haelst guesses that it might be from Oxyrhynchus.[2] It was
acquired during the 1880s in Egypt.

C. The Relationship of B and R

M. R. James has said, ". . . the Bodleian and Rainer
fragments of the AP. must be parts of one and the same MS."[3]
Surely he must be correct. Certainty on this matter could
only be obtained by a rigorous examination of the manuscripts themselves. But the two texts agree in size, in
number of lines to the page, and in line length. The agreement in size carries weight because the size is so small and
requires such small writing. While other codices the same
size are not unheard of, they are certainly not plentiful.
Would there be two codices of that size containing the Apocalypse of Peter? The difference in dating does not speak
much against the possibility that these leaves are from the
same manuscript, for not only are the assigned dates from
that period yet subject to review, but the poor condition of
the Bodleian fragment makes the assignment of its date even

---

[1] Charles Wessely, ibid., p. 482.

[2] Joseph van Haelst, ibid., p. 220.

[3] M. R. James, ibid., p. 278.

more uncertain.[1] We are led by this to believe that the
earlier date of the third or fourth century assigned by
Wessely is more likely correct, since it is a judgment based
on a more legible text. This is important for the value of
the Ethiopic text, for since it translates the tradition
present in RB, it reflects (certainly not always exactly)
an early Greek text.

VI. The Quotations in the Church Fathers

Five times various Church Fathers quote the Apocalypse
of Peter by name:

1. Clement of Alexandria (late 2nd century) Ecl. Pr.
   41 and Ecl. Pr. 48f

2. Methodius of Olympus (late 3rd century) Symposium
   2.6

3. Macarius of Magnesia (about 400 A.D.) Apocritica
   4.6 and Apocritica 4.7

These quotations can be found in the edition of the Greek
text by Klostermann.[2] I will not give them here, for while
at an earlier stage of research they were helpful to determine the nature of a document the text of which had not yet
been discovered, they are of no importance to establish the
details of the Ethiopic text. The Church Fathers were not
interested in quoting the text exactly. All the difficulties (which are well known) involved in using the quotations

---

[1]As James has observed, ibid., p. 278.

[2]Erich Klostermann, ibid., pp. 12-13.

of Church Fathers to establish the text of the New Testament also apply here. The quotations are helpful in writing the history of the fate of this writing, however. See above in the Introduction.

CHAPTER THREE

THE APOCALYPSE OF PETER:

TEXT AND TRANSLATION

ABBREVIATIONS AND CONVENTIONS

I. The Ethiopic Text

(2) etc.: Large arabic numerals enclosed in parentheses
indicate chapter divisions. These are the
same as those now in common use, first im-
plemented by Weinel. [1]

2. etc.: Large arabic numerals without parentheses but
followed by a period are verse divisions
made by the present editor.

Ṿ[2] etc.: Small raised arabic numerals to the right of
a reading are indications of notes in the
critical apparatus.

[   ]: Square brackets indicate that the enclosed
reading is suspect or misplaced.

As suggested by Lambdin[2] spelling has been normalized

to conform with that of Dillmann's Lexicon Linguae Ethio-

picae for the following variants:

1. the consonants ሐ and ኀ

2. the vowels ä and ā following a gutteral consonant

3. the consonants ሀ, ሐ, and ኀ

4. the consonants ወ and ዐ

5. the consonants ኅ and ዐ

6. ኢየሱስ is always spelled ኢየሱስ in this
text.

---

[1]Heinrich Weinel, "Offenbarung des Petrus" in Neutestamentliche Apokryphen (Tübingen: J. C. B. Mohr, 2nd edition
1924), pp. 314-327. Weinel used, but did not conform exactly to, the paragraph divisions in the edition of Grébaut.

[2]Thomas O. Lambdin, Introduction to Classical Ethiopic (Geʿez) (Missoula: Scholars Press, 1978), pp. 13-14.

All other spelling variations are given in the critical apparatus. Any reading about which there might be the slightest ambiguity due to the above spelling variations is included in the apparatus. Proper names are spelled as in P with all variations in T given in the apparatus. The punctuation :: has been retained in the text whenever either P or T has it. The punctuation marks in T other than : or :: are given in the apparatus.

II. The Critical Apparatus

P: The text of manuscript d'Abbadie 51 in Paris

T: The text of manuscript Kebran 35 from Lake Tānā

G: The text of P as it has been edited by Sylvain
          Grébaut in Revue de l'orient chrétien XV (1910):
          198-214, 307-323, 425-439

Gn: The footnotes in G

R: The unnumbered fragment of the Greek text in the
          Rainer collection in Vienna. This is a witness
          only for 14:1-5. The edition used here is that
          of M. R. James, "The Rainer Fragment of the
          Apocalypse of Peter," Journal of Theological
          Studies 32 (1931): p. 271.

B: The text of the manuscript fragment Gr. th. f. 4
          (P) in the Bodleian at Oxford. This is a wit-
          ness only for 10:6-7. I have not made any
          changes in the Ethiopic text due to the read-
          ings in B, but the Greek words corresponding
          to the Ethiopic are given in this apparatus.

Editor: The editor of the present text

[   ]:   Square brackets are from the text of G and are
          used there to indicate letters which have been
          omitted by the scribe of P. These brackets do
          not indicate lacunae in the manuscript P.

(   ):   Parentheses enclose explanatory comments on the
          variant readings.

The critical apparatus gives first the reading adopted in the text followed by those witnesses which agree with it. Then the variants are given in the following order: P first, because it is the older witness; T next, as the only other Ethiopic manuscript witness; G third, as a modern critical edition of the Ethiopic; Gn fourth, as a reading rejected by Grébaut or a discussion by him of the text; and finally B or R as non-Ethiopic readings pointing to a possible Ethiopic translation.   All variations in punctuation are listed using the apparatus.   Where it is clear that there has been an erasure, this is indicated.   All blank spaces and all markings in the margin except numbers (see the discussion of numbers above in the section describing the manuscripts) have been given.

III.   The English Translations

(Prologue):   Designates the short section of text preceding the chapter and verse numbers

(2) etc.:   Numerals in parentheses indicate chapter divisions

^{2} etc.:   Smaller raised numerals indicate verse divisions

(   ):   Words in parentheses do not appear in Ethiopic but have been added in English to complete the sense which is intended

[   ]:   Words enclosed in square brackets appear in Ethiopic but are superfluous in English and can be safely ignored in establishing the sense of the passage.

< >: Words enclosed in pointed brackets translate the suspect or misplaced readings which are enclosed in the square brackets of the Ethiopic text

. . .: A dotted line indicates an untranslatable word. The words of the literal translation in the parentheses following the dots are explanations.

Two English translations are presented on pages facing the corresponding Ethiopic text. A literal translation is at the top of the page. This translation is rather wooden and attempts to reflect the Ethiopic grammar and word order where this is possible in English. It is meant to facilitate comparison with the Ethiopic. A free translation is provided at the bottom of the page. This latter translation, while remaining faithful to the intention of the Ethiopic text, provides comparatively smooth English reading and expresses more clearly many meanings which are not so easily seen by the more wooden translation.

ናግም፡ምጹኡቸ፡ለክርስቶስ፡ወትን ሣኬ፡
ምወተን፡፡ዘናገር፡ስሌናብ፡ኡለ፡ይመወ
ቸ፡በኡንተ፡ናጢኡቶመ፡ኡክመ፡ኡዐቀቡ፡
ተኡዘዘ፡ለኡንዘኡብሔር፡ረማረሀመ፡[2]
ወዘነተ፡ናአP[3]፡ከመ፡[4]ዶኡግር፡ምሠጡር
መ[5]፡ለወብዶ፡ኡግዘኡብሔር፡መካሬ፡ወ
መፍቀሬ[6]፡ምሐረተ፡፡(I)I. ወኡንዘ፡ይናብር፡
ወከተ፡ዶብሬ፡ዘዶተ፡ቀርቡ፡ናቤሁ፡ኡለኡ
ሁ፡ወሰገዶና፡ንሐና፡[7]ወኡከተብዻዕናሁ[8]፡በበ፡
ገሐተትነ[9]፡[10]2. ወሰኡልናሁ፡ኡንዘ፡ንብ

---

1. ምጹኡቸ T; ምጹኡቸ (with vowels both ĕ and ū) P; ምጹኡቸ G.
2. : PG; ′ T.
3. ናአP editor. ሐአP PG; ሁአP T.
4. : TG; P omits.
5. ምሠጡርመ PG; ምሠጡር (with a blank space after C where a still legible መ has been erased) T.
6. ወመፍቀሬ T; ወመፍቀሬ PG.
7. : PG; ′ T.
8. ወኡከተብዻዕናሁ PG; ወኡከተብዻዕናሁ T.
9. ገሐተትነ T; ገሐቴተነ P; ገሐተትነ G.
10. : PG; ′ T.
11. ወሰኡልናሁ PG; ወሰኡና:ሁ T.

Prologue-1:2

Literal Translation

(Prologue) The Second Coming of Christ and the Resurrection of the Dead which he told to Peter, those who die on
account of their sin for they did not keep the commandment of
God their creator. And this he pondered that he might know
their mystery.

To the Son of God, the merciful and the lover of mercy.*

(1) [1]And while he was sitting on the Mount of Olives,
his own came up to him. And we bowed down and besought him
each alone. [2]And we asked him, saying to him,

*or: and this he pondered that he might know the mys-
tery of the Son of God, the merciful and the lover of mercy.

Free Translation

(Prologue) The Return of Christ and the Resurrection
of the Dead.

Christ told this to Peter. It is about those dead who
die from their sins because they did not observe the laws of
God who made them. Peter reflected on this in order to
learn their hidden fate.

This is dedicated to the Son of God who is merciful
and compassionate.

(1) [1]Jesus was sitting on the Mount of Olives when his
followers approached him. We knelt down and made a request
of him individually. [2]We asked him,

ሎ፡ ነገር[1]፡ ምንተ፡ ተኣምሪሁ፡ ለምጽኣቲከ፡
ወለኅልቀተ[2]፡ ዓለም፡፡[3] ከመ፡ ናእምር፡ ወንለቡ፡
ጊዜ፡ ምጽኣቲከ[4]፡[5] ወናለብዎሙ፡ ለእለ፡ ይመ
ጽኡ፡ እምድኅሬነ፡ 3. እለ፡ ንሰብክ፡ ሎሙ፡ ቃ
ለ፡ ወንጌልከ፡ ወንሠይሞሙ፡ ውስተ፡ ቤተ፡ ክር
ስቲያንከ፡፡ ከመ፡[6] እሙንቱኒ፡ ሰሚዖሙ፡
ይትዐቀቡ[7]፡ ከመ፡ ያለብዉ[8]፡ ጊዜ፡ ምጽኣቲከ፡፡
4. ወአውሥአነ፡ እግዚእነ፡ እንዘ፡ ይብለነ፡ ዑ
ቁ፡ ኢያስሕትክሙ፡ ወኢትኩኑ፡ ኑፋቃነ፡
ወኢታምልኩ፡ ገዕደ፡ አማልክተ፡፡ 5. ብዙኃን[9]፡

---

1. ነገር editor. ነገበር PTG.
2. ወለኅልቀተ T; ወለ፡ ሕልቀተ PG.
3. ፡፡ PG; ፡ T.
4. ምጽኣቲከ T; ምጽኣተከ PG.
5. ፡ PG; ፧ T.
6. ፡ PG; T omits.
7. ይትዐቀቡ PG; P has had an erasure at ዐ; ይት ዓቀቡ T.
8. ያለብዉ editor. ያለብው PG; ያለቡ T.
9. ብዙኃን TG; ብዙኃነ P.

1:2-1:5

Literal Translation

"Tell (us), what (will be) the signs of your coming and of the end of the world, that we might know and understand the time of your coming and might cause to understand those who will come after us, [3]whom we will preach to them the word of your gospel and will place them in your church, that they also having heard (it), might guard themselves that they will understand the time of your coming?"

[4]And our Lord answered us, saying to us, "Take heed that they do not lead you astray and that you do not become doubters, and that you do not worship other gods. [5]Many

---

Free Translation

"Tell us the signs of your return at the end of the world. Then we will know and be aware of that time and may inform our successors, [3]those to whom we will preach your good news and install in your church. After they have heard it, they too will be able to keep watch and will be alert to the time of your return."

[4]Our Lord answered, "Watch out! Do not let them mislead you. Do not let yourselves doubt. And do not worship other gods. [5]Many men

ዳመጽኡ ፡ በእምየ' ፡ እንዘ ፡ ይብሉ ፡ እና ፡ ወእ
ተ ፡ ካርስቶስ ፡ ኪተተእመንዎመ ፡ ወኪተቀረብ
ዎመ ፡፡ 6. እክመ ፡ ምጽእተስ ፡ ለወልደ ፡ እገዚ
ኡብሔር ፡ ኪዶተዐወቅ² ፡ እግ ፡ ከመ ፡ መብረቆ ፡
ዘዶስተርኪ ፡ እምጽገሕ ፡ እስክ ፡ ምዕራብ³ ፡ ከ
ማሁ ፡ መጽእ ፡ በዶመና ፡ ሰማይ ፡ ምስለ ፡ ኅ
ዶል ፡ ብዙኅ ፡ በከብሐተዮ ፡ እንዘ ፡ መስቀልዮ ፡ የ
ሐወር ፡ ቀደመ ፡ ገጽዮ ⁴ 7. እመጽኡ ፡ በከብሐተ
ዮ ፡ እንዘ ፡ ምክብገተ ፡ ካበርሁ ፡ እምፀሐይ ፡ እ
መጽእ ፡ በከብሐተዮ ፡ ምስለ ፡ ኩሉመ ፡ ቀዱስ
ንዮ ፡ መላእክተዮ ⁵ እመ ፡ ዶናብር⁶ ፡ እቡዮ ፡

---

1. በከምየ TG ; በስምየ (with ሰ or ስ and with
   both vowels ā and ĕ on መ) P.
2. ኪዶተዐወቅ T; ኪዶተግቅ P; ኪዶተጓ[ወ]ቅ G.
3. ። PG ; ፣ T.
4. ። PG ; ፣ T.
5. ። PG ; ፣ T.
6. ዶናብC G ; ዶናብር PT.

1:5-1:7

Literal Translation

will come in my name saying 'I am the Christ.' Do not believe them and do not go near them. [6]For the coming of the
Son of God will not be revealed but like lightning which
appears from the east to the west. Thus I will come in a
cloud of heaven with great power in my glory while my cross
goes before my face. [7]I will come in my glory while giving
out light seven times brighter than the sun. I will come in
my glory with all my holy angels when my Father will set

Free Translation

will come forward using my name, claiming 'I am Christ.' Do
not trust them. Do not even get close to them. [6]For when
the Son of God returns notice will not be given. Instead,
he will appear like a bolt of lightning flashes from east to
west. Just like that I will return in my glory riding the
clouds of heaven accompanied by my vast heavenly army. My
cross will go in front of me. [7]I will be shining seven
times brighter than the sun. And at my return in glory all
my holy angels will be with me. Then my Father will

ኡክሲስ፡ፈበ፡ርኡስP፡ከመ፡ኡኬንን፡ሐረ
ዋነ፡ወምወተነ፡8.ወኡረደP[1]፡ስዞኡ፡በከመ፡
ምጉገሩ፨(2)1.ወኡንተመስ፡ኡኡምሩ፡ኡምበ
ስከ፡ኡPሳኤሁ፡ኡምከመ፡ወፀኡ፡ሠርፁ፡ወ
ስምስመ፡ኡዕፁቂሁ[2]ኡኘሃ፡ይከወን፡ሃልቀተ
ዓስም፨[3]2.ወኡወሣኡከዋ[4]፡ኡነ፡ቤፕርከ፨[5]
ኡቤሑ፡ረክር፡ሊተ፡በኡንተ፡በስከ፡ወበኡይቴ፡
ነኡምር፡3.ኡከመ፡ስስ፡መዋዕሊ ሁ[6]፡ይሠርፁ፡
በስከ[7]ወስስ፡ዓመቻ፡ደገብኡ፡ፍሬሁ፡ወስኡ
ጋኡዘተ ሁ፡ምንተ፡ወኡቻ፡ኡምሳኤሁ[8]፡ስበ
ስስ፡ኬይኡኡመርነ፨[9]4.ወኡወሣኡሌ[10]፡ሊቀ፨[11]

---

1. ወኡረደP T ; ወኡረፁP PG.
2. : PG ; ፤ T.
3. :: PG ; ፤ T.
4. ወኡወሣኡክፀ TG ; ወኡወሠኡክፀ P.
5. :: T ; : PG.
6. መዋዕሊሁ TG ; መዋዕኤሁ P.
7. : PG ; ፤ T.
8. ኡምሳኤ ሁ TG ; ኡምሳኤሁ P.
9. :: PT ; : G.
10. ወኡወሠኡኬ PG ; ወኡወሠኡነ T.
11. :: T ; : PG.

1:7-2:4

Literal Translation

a crown upon my head that I might judge the living and the
dead. [8]And I will pay back everyone according to his deed.

(2) [1]"But you (pl.) learn from the fig tree its
parable: as soon as its shoot has gone out and its branches
have sprouted, then will be the end of the world."

[2]And I, Peter, answered him and said to him, "Explain
to me about the fig tree. And how will we recognize (it)?
[3]For each of its days the fig tree sprouts and each of its
years it gives forth its fruit [and] for its masters. What
is the parable of the fig tree? We have not known it."

[4]The teacher answered me

Free Translation

crown me to judge the living and the dead. [8]I will
reward everyone in a manner appropriate to his actions.

(2) [1]"But you are to learn the parable of the fig
tree: as soon as it buds and its branches leaf, then the
world will end."

[2]I, Peter, addressed him. "Interpret the fig tree
for me, or how else will we learn it? [3]The fig tree has
buds on it every day of its life and it bears fruit for its
owner every year. What is the parable of the fig tree? We
are not acquainted with it."

[4]The teacher answered me,

ወይቤለኒ[1]፡ኢያኩመርክኑ፡[2]ከመ፡[3]ዐፀ፡በለክ፡
ቤት፡ኢስራኬል[4]፡ወኑቸ፡። 5.በከመ፡ተከለ፡ብ
ኡሴ፡ወበተ፡ጋሩቸ፡[5]በለሶ[6]፡ወኢፈረይቶ[7]፡ወኑ
ሠሠ፡ፉረሃ፡ኍንዱየ፡ዓመተ፡ወኢፈኪሮ፡ዶቤ
ኍ፡ለዐቃቤ፡ጋሶቸ፡ሠርቀ፡እዘተ፡በለክ፡ከመ፡
ኢተዐርዐ[8]፡እሳ፡ምድረሳ[9]፡። 6.ወይቤኍ፡ዐቃ
ቤ፡ጋሶቸ፡እኑጋዚኢብጤር፡እኪኪ[10]ንዓሐዶያ[11]፡
ወንከረ፡ሐመደ፡በታሐቱሃ፡ወንሰቀያ[12]፡ማየ።ወ
እኪመ፡ኪፈረይቶ[13]፡በእዘተ፡ሰዓቸ፡ናቤከጠ፡ሠ
ረዋሃ፡እምውበተ፡ጋሶተ፡ወንተክጠ፡ካልኢ፡

---

1. ወይቤለኒ PG; ወይቤለሳ T.
2. ፡ PG; ፤ T.
3. ፡ PG; T omits.
4. ኢስራኬል T; ኢሳራኬል P ; ኢ[ስ]ራኬል G.
5. ፡ PG; ፤ T.
6. በለሶ editor; በለክ PTG.
7. ወኢፈረይቶ PG; ወኢፈርይቶ T.
8. ኢተዐርዐ editor; ኢተሽ[ር]ዐ G; ኢተሽዐ P; ኢተሽንዐ T.
9. ምድረሳ T; ምድርሳ PG.
10. እኪኪ editor; እኪኪ PG; እዐኪ T.
11. ንዓሐዶያ P; ንዳሐየያ T; ንዓሐዶያ G.
12. ወንሰቀያ T; ወንሰዐያ PG.
13. ኪፈረይቶ PG; ኪፈርይቶ T.

2:4-2:6

Literal Translation

and said to me, "Did you (s.) not know that the fig tree is
the house of Israel? [5]Accordingly, a man planted in his
garden a fig tree, and it did not bear fruit. And he sought
its fruit many a year. And not having found it, he said to
the keeper of the garden, 'Uproot this fig tree that it
should not make our land worthless.' [6]And the keeper of the
garden said to God, 'Send (us). We will weed it and dig the
earth under it and water it (with) water. And if it does
not bear fruit at that time we will remove its roots from in
the garden and we will plant another

Free Translation

"Were you unaware that Israel is the fig tree? [5]It is like
this: A man planted a fig tree in his garden but it did not
produce fruit. For many years he looked for fruit on it and
never found any. Finally he said to his gardener, 'Pull
this fig tree out so our soil is not depleted for us.' [6]The
gardener said to the landlord, 'Have us weed it and dig the
earth around it and water it. Then if it fails to produce
we will take it out of the garden and plant

ሀየንቴሁ፡ 7. ኢለበዉ ክኑ፡ ከሞ፡ ዐፀ፡ በለክ፡
ቤተ፡ኢክሬኤል፡ ወኧቸ፡፡ ወሮ፡ኧቤለክ፡ሶበ፡ለ
ምለሙ፡ኅዕሩ ቂሁ፡በደነረ፡ይመጽኡ፡ሐገወያሳ፡
መሊ ሐ፡ 8. ወይቤ ፈሙ፡ ከሙ፡ ኧነ፡ ወኧቸ፡ክር
ከቶክ፡ዘመባኧኩ፡ ወጠተ፡ ዓለም፡፡ ወሶበ፡ርኧዩ፡
ኧከየ፡ምግገፉ፡ይገብኩ፡ ድሳፈ ሆሙ፡ 9. ወይ ከ
ሐድ ዩ፡ዘይብኁ፡ከበሐተ፡ኧበዊ ነ፡፡ ዘለ ቀልዩ፡
ለ ቀ ዳ ማዊ፡ክርከቶክ፡፡ ወ ፀገ ዖ፡፡ ፈ ድ ፈ ይ ፡ 10. ወ
ዘንተለ፡ሐገዊ፡ኢ ኩ ነ፡ክርከቶክ፡፡ ወሶበ፡ክ በ
ዩ ዖ፡ይ ቀ ተ ል ፡በመናገ ሐተ ፡ ወይ ከ ወ ኑ ፡ብዘ ነ ን ፡

---

1. ሀየንቴ ሁ   TG; ሀየ፡ንቴ ሁ   P.
2. ከ ሙ has been written over an erasure in P.
3. :: T ; : PG.
4. ሐገው ያ ሳ   T ; ሐለ ዊ ያ ሳ   P ; ሐገዊ ያ ሳ   G.
5. ወይ ቤ ፈ ወ   PG; ወይ ቤ ፈ ወ   T.
6. :: T ; : PG.
7. ክርከቶ ክ TG; ክርከቶ ክ P.
8. :: T ; : PG.
9. :: PG ; : T.
10. ይ ቀ ተ ል G ; ይ ቀ ተ ፡ ል   P ; ይ ቀ ተ ል ዖ T.

2:6-2:10

Literal Translation

in its place.'

[7]"Did you not understand that the fig tree is the
House of Israel? And by its means I have told you (s.):
when its branches have sprouted at the last (time) falsi-
fiers of the messiah (= false christs) will come. [8]They
will promise that 'I am the Christ who has come into the
world.' And when they have seen the wickedness of his deed
they will turn away after them. [9]And they will deny him to
whom our fathers gave praise whom they crucified (or: who
was crucified), the first Christ, and sinned exceedingly.
[10]But this liar was not Christ. And when they have rejected
him he will kill with the sword and many will become

Free Translation

another tree there.'

[7]"Were you unaware that Israel is the fig tree? I
have used it to tell you that when its leaves shoot out for
the last time men will come impersonating the messiah.
[8]They will give assurances by claiming, 'I am the Christ
who came into the world.' When the people see what evil he
has done they will leave to follow them. [9]They will deny
the one that our fathers worshipped, the first Christ who
they sinned against monstrously when they crucified him.
[10]But that imposter was not the Christ. When they reject
him he will turn violent, killing, and making many

ለማዕት ፦¹ ፲፩. አ ሜ ሃ ኬ² ፦ ለምለሙ ፦ አዕሉ ቂሁ ፦
እበለከ ፦ ዘ ወ ኅቸ ፦ ቤተ ፦ ኢስራኬል ፦ ገሐቱቸ ፦
ይከ ወ ሩ ፦ ለማዕት ፦ በአይ ፦ ዚ አሁ ፦ በ ዘ ጎን ፦ ይ
መ ወ ቸ ፦ ወይ ከ ወ ሩ ፦ ለማዕት ፦፦ ፲፪. ኧ ክ ሙ ፦ ይ
ተ ረ ሳ ወ³ ፦ ሃ ና ክ ፦ ወ ኤ ል ያ ክ ፦ ክ ሙ ፦⁴ ያ ለ በ ወ
ቀ ሙ⁵ ፦ ክ ሙ ፦ ው ኅ ቸ ፦⁶ መ ከ ሐ ተ ፦ ዘ ሀ ለ ወ⁷ ፦ ይ መ
ሰ ኧ ፦ ው ከ ተ ፦ ዓ ለ ም⁸ ፦ ወ ይ ገ በ ር ፦ ተ ኽ ም ረ⁹ ፦ ወ መ
ን ከ ረ¹⁰ ፦ ለ አ ክ ሐ ቸ ፦¹¹ ፲፫. ወ በ ኧ ን ተ ዘ ፦ ኧ ለ ፦ ሞ ቸ ፦
በ አ ይ ፦ ዘ ኢ ሁ ፦ ይ ከ ወ ሩ ፦ ለ ማ ዕ ት ፦ ወ ይ ተ ኧ ለ ቀ¹²

---

1. ፦፦ PT ; ፦ G.
2. ኧ ሜ ሃ ኬ TG; ኧ ሚ ሃ ኬ P.
3. ይ ተ ረ ሳ ወ T; ይ ተ ረ ሳ ወ PG.
4. ክ ሙ፦ G ; ክ ሙ ፦ ክ ሙ P ; ክ ሙ ፦ ክ ሙ ፦ T.
5. ያ ለ በ ወ ቀ ሙ PG; ያ ለ ወ ቀ ሙ T.
6. ፦ TG ; P has a mark like ዘ. Note : at this point there is a change of handwriting in P.
7. ዘ ሀ ለ ወ . In P three shadowy letters are written above ሀ ለ ወ, one above each letter. A ሀ can be made out above ለ . The others are illegible.
8. ፦ PG ; ፣ T.
9. ተ ኽ ም ረ TG; ተ ኽ ም ረ P.
10. ወ መ ን ከ ረ TG; ወ መ ን ከ ር P.
11. ፦ PG ; ፣ T.
12. ወ ይ ተ ኧ ለ ቀ G ; ወ ይ ተ ኧ ለ ቀ P ; ወ ይ ተ ኽ ለ ቀ T.

2:10-2:13

Literal Translation

martyrs. [11]So then the branches of the fig tree will
sprout. This is the house of Israel only. There will be
martyrs by his hand. Many will die and become martyrs.
[12]For Enoch and Elijah will be sent that they might teach
them that this (is) the Deceiver who must come into the
world and do signs and wonders to deceive. [13]And on
account of this those who die by his hands will be martyrs
and will be reckoned

Free Translation

martyrs. [11]So then the fig tree's branches will have shot
out. This is only Israel. There will be martyrs at his
instigation. Many people will die and become martyrs.
[12]Enoch and Elijah will be sent to inform people that he is
the seducer decreed to enter the world in order to lure
people away by performing miracles. [13]This is why those
that he is responsible for killing will be martyrs and will
be classified

ምክስለ፡ሰማዕት፡ቄረኅ፡ወዓድቃን፡[1]ኤል፡ኤሡ
መርዖ፡እኽንግዚ፡አብሔር፡በሕይወቶሙ፡[2](3)1.ወ
ኡርኣይሬ[3]፡ውስተ፡የማኑ፡ነፍሶ፡ዞሉ፡ወውስተ፡
የማኑ[4]፡እሪሑ፡ኤንተ፡ተተገመር፡እምሳልጸ፡በይ
ነረ፡ዕለት፡2.ወዘክሙ፡ይተሌስይ፡ዓድቃን፡ወ
ነኝኣን፡ወዘክሙ፡ይገብሩ፡ርቸ9ኝ[5]፡ልብ፡ወዘክ
ሙ፡ይሠረወ[6]፡0ማዕያን፡እዓለሙ፡ዓእም፡፡[7]3.[8]ር
ኬኅ፡ዘክሙ፡ይበክዮ፡ነኝኣን፡በዐቢያ፡ምንዳቤ፡
ወሐዘን፡ኤስክ፡ዞሉ፡ዘርኬዮ፡በኣዕይንቲሆሙ፡
ይበክዮ፡፡[9]ኤመሬ[10]፡ዓድቃን፡ወኤመሬ፡መኣኤክት፡

---

1. : PG ; ፤ T,
2. : PG ; ፤ T,
3. ወኡርኣይሬ PT; ወኡርኣ የሬ G.
4. የማኅ P TGn;ዐጋመ G.
5. ርቸ9ኝ TG; ርቸ9ኝ P.
6. ይሰረወ T; ይሰረ ወ PG.
7. After ዓእም:: T leaves blank most of one line.
   The next word begins a new line.
8. Both P and T have ወዘክሙ: before Cኬኅ ; G omits
   as here.
9. :: T ; : PG.
10. ኤመሬ PG; ኤመ ሬ (with a space of one letter
    between መ and ሬ) T.

2:13-3:3

Literal Translation

with the good and righteous martyrs who have pleased God in their life."

(3) [1]And he showed me in his right hand the soul of all and in his right-hand palm the image which will be fulfilled in the last day; [2]and how the righteous and the sinners will be separated and how the upright of heart will do and how the evildoers will be rooted out forever and ever. [3]We saw how the sinners will weep in great affliction and sorrow until all who saw (it) with their eyes weep whether the righteous or the angels

---

Free Translation

with those martyrs who have pleased God their whole life."

(3) [1]He showed me in his right hand all souls and a picture of what will happen on the final day. [2]I saw how those who were good will be separated from those who are evil. I saw what will happen to the pure in heart and that the criminals will be permanently annihilated. [3]We saw further how the sinners will grieve in intense torment and anguish so that all of us watching it began to weep, the righteous, the angels,

ወዓዲ፡ለጊሁ፨፬. ወአንሰ፡ተከእልክዮ፡ወአቤ
ሉ፡እግዚኡ፡አብሐኒ፡ከመ፡እንብብ፡ቃልከ፡
በእንተ፡²እጊ፡ኃናኳን³፡እክመ፡ኣየሎመ፡ሶበ፡ኢ
ተፈኗፉ፨⁴5.ወአወሥአኒ⁵፡መደቡን፡ወይቤለ
ኒ⁶፨⁷ኡቤ ኃርክ፡ልምንት፡ከመዝ፡ተብል፡ያሳይሎመ፡
ኢተፈኗር⁸፡⁹አክመ፡አንተ፡ⁱ⁰ዘተቃወሞ፡ለአ
ግዚአብሔር፡6.ወኢኩኑ፡አንተ፡ዘተምሐርሙ፡
አምኔሁ¹¹፡ልሕከተ፡ዘኢሁ፡¹²አክመ፡ወእቻ፡ፈ
ጠርሙ፡ወአምሳኩ ሙ፡ኃበ፡ኢ ሀለዉ¹³፨7.ወሶበ፡

---

1. ቃልከ T; ቃልከ PG.
2. ። TG; P omits.
3. ኃናኳን TG; ኃናኳን (with vowels ā, ă, and ĕ all on ኳ) P.
4. ። T; ። PG.
5. ወአወሥኣኒ T; ወአወሥኒ P; ወአወሥ[ኣ]ኒ G.
6. ወይቤለኒ T; ወቤለኒ P; ወ[ይ]ቤለኒ G.
7. ። T; ። PG.
8. ኢተፈኗር editor. ተፈኗር PT; [ኢ]ተፈኗር G.
9. ። PG; ፣ T.
10. አንተ T; አተ P; አ[ን]ተ G.
11. አምኔሁ T; አኔሁ PG. Cf. Gn.
12. ። PG; ፣ T.
13. ኢ ሀለዉ T; ኢ ሀለዉ PG.

3:3-3:7

Literal Translation

or even himself.

[4]But I asked him and said to him, "O Lord, permit me that I should speak your word concerning these sinners. For, 'It was better for them when they had not been created.'"

[5]And the Savior answered me and said to me, "O Peter, why do you speak thus, 'Non-creation were better for them'? For (it is) you (s.) who are opposing God. [6]And it was not you who have had more mercy on them, his formation, than he. For he created them and brought them forth where they had not been. [7]And when

---

Free Translation

and even Jesus himself.

[4]I asked him, "Lord, let me repeat what you said about these sinners, that it would have been better for them if they had never been created."

[5]The Savior answered, "Peter! Why would you say such a thing, that they should never have been created? You are rebelling against God! [6]You are his own creation. You have not had more mercy on them than he has had. For he created them out of nothing. [7]When

ርኢክ፡ሰቆቃው፡ዘያከውን፡እንገኛኸን፡በደኃ

ሪ፡መዋዕል፡፡²ወበኤንተዝህ³፡ሐዘነ፡ልብከ፡ወዘሰ፡

ከበሱ፡በልዑል፡ኢርኢየከ፡ምግባሮሙ፡(4) ፩.

ወርኢክ፡ያኢዚ፡ዘያረከሶሙ፡በደኃሪ፡መዋዕል፡⁴

ኸሙ፡ያመሱኽ፡ዐለተ፡ኢግዚኢብሔር፡፪. ወዕ

ለት⁵፡ያይን፡ኢንተ፡ኲነኔ፡ኢግዚኢብሔር፡ኢ

ምዳገሐ፡ወሀተ፡ምዕራብ፡⁶ወያተጋብኡ፡ኲሎሙ፡

ኢጓለ፡ኢመሐያው⁷፡ቅድሙ፡ለከቡP፡ዘለዓለም⁸፡

ሐያው፡፡⁹3. ወያኢዘዘ፡ልጉህነያም¹⁰፡ከሙ፡ታርኑ፡

መናሥግተ Y፡ዘኢያማክ፡ወያጋብኡ፡ኲሎ፡ዘሰቻ¹¹፡

---

1. በደኃ T; በደሐሪ PG.
2. :: T; : PG.
3. ወበኤንተH PG; ወበኤንH T.
4. : PG; ፩ T.
5. ወዕለት T; ወዕት P; ወዕ[ለ]ት G.
6. : PG; ፩T.
7. ኸመሐያው TG; ኢምሐያው P.
8. ዘለዓለም T; ዘለዓም P; ዘለዓ[ለ]ም G.
9. :: T; : PG.
10. ልጉህነያም PG; ልጉነያም T.
11. ዘሰቻ TG; ዘበ ቻ (with a space of one letter between በ and ቻ) P.

3:7-4:3

Literal Translation

you (s.) saw the lament which will be for sinners in the
last days [and], on account of this your heart became sad.
But those who have done wrong against the Most High, I will
show you their works.

(4) [1]"And see now what will happen to them in the last
days when the day of God comes:

[2]"And (on) the day of judgment which is the punishment
of God, from the east to the west [and] all the children of
men will be gathered before my Father who lives forever.
[3]And he will command Gehenna that it open its bars of
adamant and give back all which is his

Free Translation

you saw how sinners will lament on the final day it made
you sad. But now I will show you how by their actions they
have transgressed against the Most High.

(4) [1]"Now look at what is in store for them in the
final days when God's day comes:

[2]"On that day when punishment will be given according
to God's decision, all human beings from east to west will
be brought together before my Father who lives forever. [3]He
will order Hades to open its adamantine bars, and he will
take back everyone in it who is his.

ወስቴታ ፡ 4. ወለእኦሪ ዩተኒ ፡ ወለእ ዕፀኑኒ ፡ [1] ወ
ዩኬዘዘሙ ፡ ያገብኡ ፡ ኮ ሎ ፡ ዘበልዑ ፡ ሥጋ ፡ እ
ነዘ ፡ ዩሬ ቀይ ፡ ከሙ ፡ ያስተርኪ ፡ ሰብእ ፡ 5. እከሙ ፡
እልፎ ፡ ዘዩተሀጐል ፡ ስእንጊዜ እብ ሔር ፡ ወ ኦል
ፎ ፡ ዘዩለእኝ ፡ ኮ ሎ ፡ ከሙ ፡ ዘእሁ ። ኮ ሎ ፡ በዕለ
ተ ፡ ይዩነ ፡ በዕለተ ፡ ኮ ነኬ ፡ እከሙ ፡ ምክለ ፡ ብሂ ሎ
ተ ፡ ስእ ን ጊ ዜ እብ ሔር ፡ [2] 6. ወ ኮ ሎ ፡ ይከውን ፡ በ
ከሙ ፡ ዩ ሬ ኝ ር ፡ ? ለ ሙ ፡ [3] ወ ኮ ሎ ፡ ዘ ወ ስቴ ታ ፡ ከ ዘ
ዘ [4] ፡ ወ ኮ ሎ [5] ፡ ኮ ነ ፡ ከ ማ ሁ ኬ ፡ በ ይ ነ ሪ ፡ መ ዋ ዕ ል ፡
7. እከ ሙ ፡ ኮ ሎ ፡ ይ ተ ከ ሁ ሎ ፡ ስ እ ን ጊ ዜ እ ብ ሔ ር ፡ [6] ወ
ከ ማ ሁ ኬ ፡ ይ ብ ል ፡ ወ ስ ተ ፡ መ ጽ ሐ ፍ ፡ ወ ል ይ ፡ እ ኝ

---

1. ፡ PG; [T.
2. ፡ PG; [T.
3. ፡ PG; [T.
4. ኮ HH [PG; ኮ HH T.
5. ወ ኮ ሎ PG; ወ ኮ ሎ (with a space of one letter between ወ and ኮ containing an erasure perhaps
   of ለ or ዩ) T.
6. ፡ PG; [T.

4:3-4:7

Literal Translation

in it. [4]And as for the beasts and the birds, [and] he will command (that) they bring back all the flesh which they have eaten since he wants that men appear. [5]For there is nothing which perishes for God and there is nothing which is impossible for him. All is as his. All (will be) on the day of punishment, on the day judgment for (it is) with the word of God. [6]And all will be in accordance with (how) he creates the world. [and] Everything in it he commanded (to be) and everything was. So likewise it (will be) in the last days. [7]For everything is possible for God and therefore thus it says in scripture: the son

---

Free Translation

[4]Then he will order the animals and birds to return all the human flesh they have eaten because he requires human beings to make their appearance. [5]For nothing is ever destroyed from God's point of view. Nothing is impossible for him. All that is is his. Everyone will be there on judgment day, the day of punishment, because it will happen when God speaks. [6]Everything will occur according to his way of creating: he gave his command, and the world and everything in it came to be. It will be just like that in the final days. [7]Everything is possible for God. As it says in scripture: the son

ለ፡ኣመሐያወ፡ተላበየ[1]፡ጎዐሔሀወ፡ለለ፡ኣዕፀ

ምት፡[2]፰.ወተቤጎ፡ለዐፀም፡ዐፀም፡ኣበ፡ኣዕፀ

ምት፡ወበተ፡መለያልያ፡መተን[3]፡ወሥርወ፡ወሥጋ፡

ወማኣበ፡ወሥዐርተ፡ወበተታ፡[4]፱.ወላፍበ፡ወመ

ንረበ፡ወያሀብ፡ዐበየ፡ኡረኬል፡በተኣዛH[5]፡

ኣጎዚኣብሔር፡[6]ኣበመ፡ኪያሀ፡ሠርዐ፡ኣጎዚኣ

ብሔር፡በተንዛኬሀ[7]፡ምወተን፡ኣመ፡ዐለተ፡ዞለ

ኬ፡[8]፲.ወርኣየ፡ወኣኣምፈ፡ኣHCኣተ[9]፡ዞተዞ

Cኣ፡ወበተ፡ምየር፡ከመ፡ያቡበ፡ዞኣልበ፡ላፍ

በ፡ዮHCኣየ፡፡ወበተ፡ምድር፡ወየሐበ፡ወየፈፈ፡

፲፩.ወየጎብኣ፡ምድር፡በከመ፡ማሐፀንተ፡ዞኣማ

---

1. ተላበየ PTGn ; ተላበይ G.
2. ፡ PG ; + or ·/· T.
3. መተን G ; ምንት PTGn.
4. ፡ PG ; T uncertain.
5. በተኣዛH T ; በተኣዛH PG.
6. ፡ PG ; + or ·/· T.
7. በተንዛኬሀ TG ; በተን፡ዛኬሀ P.
8. ፡ PG ; I T.
9. ኣHCኣተ T ; ኣHCተ P; ኣHC[ኣ]ተ G.

4:7-4:11

Literal Translation

of man prophesied to each of the bones.   8'And you said to
the bone, "Bone (be) to bones in limbs, tendons and nerves,
and flesh and skin and hair on it."   9And soul and spirit
the great Uriel [and] will give at the command of God,' for
him God has appointed over his resurrection of the dead at
the day of judgment.

10"And see (pl.) and understand (pl.) the seeds which
were sown into the ground. Like a dry thing which is without soul it is sown into the ground and it lives and bears
fruit.   11And the earth will give back in accordance with
(its) pledge what

Free Translation

of man prophesied to the various bones 8saying, 'Bones, join
together into limbs and let there be tendons and nerves and
muscles and skin with hair on it.   9And the great Uriel will
distribute soul and spirit when God commands it,' because
God has put him in charge of the resurrection of the dead on
judgment day.

10Look at the seeds which are planted in the ground
and learn from them. A seed is arid and lifeless when it
is put into the ground, but it comes to life and bears fruit.
11So too the earth will return what it has in custody

ሕፀንዮ፡፡ ወዘንቸ፡ ውኁቸ፡ ዘይመውት፡ ዘተዘ
ርኪ፡ ዘርኢ፡ ውስተ፡ ምድር፡ ወዖሰዖ፡ ወዖተወሀ
ብ፡ ለሕዖወት[1]፡ ሰብኢ፡፡ 12. ኤሮ፡ ፈዳፈዳ፡ ለ
ኢለ፡ ዖ፟ኗምኑ፡ ቦቸ፡ ወለሣሩዖኔ ሁ[2]፡ ለኢለ፡ ባኁ
ንተ ኢሀሙ[3]፡ ገብረ፡ ኤግዚ ኢብሔር[4]፡ ዖሳሥኩ ሙ፡
ኩሙ፡ ዐለተ፡ ዖዖን[5] 13. ወዙኡ፡ ተ ገብኢ፡ ምድር፡
ኩሙ፡ ዐለተ፡ ዖዖን፡ ኢክሙ፡ ሀለዋ፡ ባቲ፡ ተተ ኩሳ
ን፡ ሳቡረ፡ ወለማዖ ኔ[6]፡ ምክቤዖ፡[7](5) 1. ወዖ ከሙ
ን፡ ኩሙ፡ ዐለተ፡ ዙነኔ፡ ኢለ፡ ዐለ ወ[8]፡ ሃዖማኗቸ፡ ለ
ኤግዚ ኢብሔር፡፡[9] ወ ለኢለ፡ ገብሩ፡ ሳጢ ኢተ፡

---

1. ለሕዖወት T; ለሕዖወተ PG.
2. ወለሣሩዖኔ ሁ TG; ወለሣሩዖኔ ሁ P.
3. ባኁንተ ኢሀሙ TG; ባኁንተ ኢሁሙ P.
4. ኤግዚ ኢብሔር T; ኤግዚ ብኢብሔር PG.
5. ፡ PG; ዘ T.
6. ወለማዖ ኔ PG; ወለማዖ፡ ኔ T.
7. ፡ PG; ዘ T.
8. ዐለ ወ T; ዐለ ወ PG.
9. ፡፡ T; ፡PG.

4:11-5:1

Literal Translation

has been entrusted to it: and this is what dies. The seed
which has been sown into the ground and revives and is given
life (is) man. [12]How much more (will he not revive) those
who believe in him and his elect ones, for whose sake he
made (the earth)? God will raise them up on the day of
judgment. [13]And all (things or people) the earth will give
back on the day of judgment, for in it (the day) it (the
earth) must be judged at the same time, and heaven with it.

(5) [1]"And (this) will happen on the day of judgment to
those who pervert the faith of God and to those who have
committed sin:

Free Translation

according to its pledge. That which dies, the seed sown in
the ground, and then revives and is given life is the human
race. [12]How much more certain it is that God will resurrect
on judgment day those who believe in him and are chosen by
him, for he made the earth for them. [13]The earth will return everyone on judgment day because then it will have to
be judged at the same time, and heaven too.

(5) [1]"To those who have perverted God's faith and who
have sinned this will happen:

2. ወይተረኘዋ[1]፡መንብሐብጣተ[2]፡ኡሳት፡ወይከ
ወን፡ጣቃ[3]፡ወሾልመተ፡[4]ወያስብከ፡ወይተገስበ
ብ፡ኩሉ፡ዓለመ፡[5]3. ወማያተኒ፡ያተመየጡ፡ወይ
ተወሀብ፡በኡፋሳሐመ፡ኡሳተ፡ወይወ፪፡ኩሉ፡Hወ
ከቴታ፡ወገሐርኒ፡ኡሳተ፡ተከወን፡4. ኡምታሐ
ተ፡ሰማይ፡ኡሳተ፡መሪ፪[6]፡Hኢይጠፍኡ፡ወይወ
ሐH፡ስኩነኔ፡መወተ፡[7]ወከዋኩብተኒ፡ያተመሰ
ወ[8]፡፡በነይ፡ኡሳተ፡ከመ፡ኢተረኛፉ፡5. ወምሾን
ዓተ[9]፡ሰማይ፡በነጢኡ፡ማይ፡[10]ወየሐወሩ፡ወይከመ
ኑ፡ከመ፡Hኢተረኛፉ፡ወኢይዕዕልወ[11]፡መገርቃተ፡

---

1. ወይተረኘዋ G ; ወይተረኘዋ P ; ወይተኘዋ T.
2. መንብሐብጣት editor. መንብሐብነት P ; መንብነብነት
   T ; መንብሐብነት G.
3. ጣቃ TG; ጣቃ P.
4. ፡ PG ; ፲T.
5. ፡ PG ; ፲T.
6. መሪረ T ; መሪC PG.
7. ፡ PG ; ፲T.
8. ያተመሰወ editor. ያተመሰወ PTG.
9. ወምሾንዓት T ; ወምሾነዓት PG.
10. ፡ PG ; ፲T.
11. ወኢይዕዕልወ T ; ወኢይዕስወ PG.

5:2-5:5

Literal Translation

[2]"Cataracts of fire will be opened up and there will
be fog and darkness and the whole world will veil and clothe
itself. [3]And the waters will be turned and will be given
into coals of fire and everything which is in it will burn
up and even the ocean will become fire. [4]From under heaven
(there will be) a bitter fire which does not go out and it
will flow for the judgment of wrath. Even the stars will
melt in a flame of fire like they had not been created.
[5]And the firmaments of heaven in a lack of water will go and
become like what were not created. And there will not be
lightnings

Free Translation

[2]"Waterfalls of fire will be let loose. There will be
gloom and murk overlying and obscuring the whole world.
[3]The fresh water will be transformed into live coals and
everything in it will burn up. Even the ocean will become
fire. [4]Beneath the sky will be a bitter fire which never
goes out, and it will flow out in fury to punish. A flame
will dissolve the stars so it will be as if they had never
been. [5]The supports for the sky will lack water and will
vanish as if they had never been. The lightnings in the sky

ሰማይ፡ ¹ወበዋር ቀያቶሙ፡ ያደሳግዉ፡ ዓስመ፡ 6.ወ
መንረሰ፡ በይን፡ ያተመሰሎሙ፡ ²ወያከውን፡ እሳ
ተ፡ በተእዛዘ፡ እእግዚ እብሔር፡፡ ³ወእምዘ፡ተ
መከወ⁴፡ ዙሉ፡ ፍ ናረተ፡ 7.ያጐይ፡ እንስ፡ እመሕ
ያወ⁵፡ እስ፡ ውበተ፡ መንገስ፡ ሠርቀ፡ ውበተ⁶፡ መንን
ስ፡ ዐረብ፡ ውበተ፡ ሠርቀ፡ያጐይ፡፡ ወእስ፡ውበተ፡
ሰሜን፡ያጐይ፡ ያቡበ፡፡ ⁷ወእስ፡ውበተ⁸፡ ሰሜን፡ 8.
ወበዘለዩ⁹፡ ተረ ክሮሙ፡ መዐተ፡ እሳተ፡ ገሩም፡ ¹⁰ወ
እንዘ፡ያስዮሙ፡ ሳይ¹¹፡ ዘእያመናእኸ፡ ያመጽኡሙ፡
እዘነኀ፡ መዐተ፡ ውበተ፡ ፈስገ፡ እሳተ፡ዘእያመ

---

1. : PG ; ፤ T.
2. : PG ; ፤ T.
3. :: T ; : PG.
4. ተመከወ T ; ተመከወ PG.
5. እመሕያወ TG ; እምሕያወ P.
6. ውበተ TG ; ወበተ P.
7. :: PG ; ፤ T.
8. ውበተ TG ; ውኈበተ P.
9. ወበዘለዩ TG ; ወበዘሉዩ P.
10. : PG ; ፤ T.
11. ሳይ PT ; ሳይ G.

5:5-5:8

Literal Translation

of heaven and through their exorcism they (or: one) will as-
tonish the world. [6]And the spirit of the corpse will be
made like them and will become fire at the command of God.
And then the whole creation has been melted. [7]The children
of men who are in the east will flee to the west; they (in
the west) will flee into the east. And those in the south
will flee north, and those (in the north) to the south.
[8]Everywhere the awesome wrath of fire will find them [and]
while it pursues them, the flame which does not go out will
bring them to the judgment of wrath in the river of fire
which does not

Free Translation

will go out of existence and their exorcism will dumbfound
the world. [6]The spirits of the dead will become like them
and will be changed into fire at God's orders. Then the
whole creation will have been dissolved. [7]The people in
the east will try escaping to the west and vice versa, and
those in the south will try the north and vice versa. [8]But
everywhere the furious fire will find them, driving them
out. The flame which never goes out will bring them to the
judgment of wrath in the river of fire which never

5:8-6:2

ፉኣ፡ ዘያወሕዝ፡ኣ ሳተ፡ኣነዘ፡ይሳድይ፡ ገቲ፡ ዓ
ወክከተፈሊ ሞስ፡ ኣነዘ፡ያሬ ልሑ፡ ምገፉ፡ወይ
ከውን፡ሕፀ፡ከነነ፡፡ ብዘሩ፡ለኣንገለ፡ኣመሕያው፡
(6) I. ወያሬኣዩ፡ ኩ ሎሙ፡ኣነዘ፡ኣመሸኣ፡በያመኅ፡
ብሩህ፡ዘለጓገም፡ ወመጋኣ ከተ፡ ኣግዚኣብሔ
ር፡ዘምስሌይ፡፡ ይሳብሩ፡ መንበሬ፡ከበጠተዩ፡በ
የማሩ፡ኣ ቡዩ፡፡ ሰማያዊ፡2. ወያሳብር ፡ ኣ ከሊ
ል፡ ሬበ፡ር ኣከዩ፡ ኣ ዔ ሃ፡ር ኣዩሙ፡ ኣ ሐሳብ፡ያበ
ከዩ፡ በበ፡ ሕዘበ ሆሙ፡ ወያ ዜ ዘሙ፡ ያ ሳልያ ፡ ኣ

---

1. ፡ PG ; ' T. At this point P T continue with ወዖመ
   ፝፝፝ ቶ ሙ (ወይ መፀ ኩ ሙ T): ለዞንኅ:ወመዓተ:ወከተ:ፈ ገገ:ኣ
   ሳተ: ዘኣይጠፍኣ (ዘኣይጠ ኣ P). The letters with dots
   above them (e.g. ይ) are uncertain in T because of shadows
   in the microfilm image. Cf. Gn.

2. ያሳዩ PG ; ያሳዩ T.

3. ፡ PG ; ' T.

4. ሕፀ PG ; ሕፀ T.

5. ፡፡ PG ; ፡ T.

6. ፡ PG ; ' T.

7. ፡ PG ; ' T.

8. ፡፡ PG ; ፡፡ T.   9. ያሳብፈ P T G ; editor suggests ያሳብፈ.

10. ፡ PG ; ' T.

11. ያበከዩ T G ; ያበኪዩ P.

12. ፡ PG ; ' T.

5:8-6:2

Literal Translation

go out, a fire which flames as it burns. [9]And the waves having separated, while boiling, [and] there will be much gnashing of teeth for the children of men.

(6) [1]"And all of them will see as I come on a shining cloud which is eternal. And the angels of God who are with me will sit on the throne of my glory at the right hand of my heavenly Father. [2]And he will place a crown upon my head. Then, the nations having seen (this), each of their nations will weep, and he will command them (that) they pass

---

Free Translation

goes out. There the fire flows in flames. [9]Its waves separate and then boil up, and for human beings there is much gnashing of teeth.

(6) [1]"They will all see it when I come on shining everlasting clouds, and the angels of God accompanying me will set up my glorious throne on the right hand of my heavenly Father. [2]God will crown me, and when the peoples see that, they will wail, every one of them. Then God will order them to go

ኃተ፡ማእከለ፡ፈለገ፡እሳት፡3.ወምግባራቲሆ
ሙ።[1] ለለ፩ እምኔሆሙ[2]፡ይቀውም፡ቅድሜሆሙ፡ለለ
፩ በከመ[3]፡ምግባሩ፡4.ወለለሣሩያንሰ[4]፡ለእለ፡
ሠናየ፡ገብሩ፡ይመስኡ፡ኀቤየ፡እንዘ፡ሞቱ[5]፡ክል
ቦ፡ዘይሬእዮሙ፡እሳት፡በገዲ፡[6]5.ወዐማፅያንሰ[7]፡
ወኃጥኣንሰ፡ወመደልዋንሰ፡ይቀውሙ፡ማእከለ፡
መዓምቀተ[8]፡ጽልመት፡ዘኢይጠፍእ፡[9]ወደይዎሙ፡
እሳት፡6.ወያመስኡ፡መላእክት፡ኀጢአቶሙ፡ወ
ያከተዓልዉ[10]፡ሎሙ፡መካነ፡ኀበ፡ይደይኑ፡ለዓለ
ም።ለለ፩ በከመ[11]፡አበሳሆሙ፡7.ያመስእ፡መል

---

1. ። T; ፡ PG.
2. ለለ፩ እምኔሆሙ editor. ለለ፩ እምኔሆሙ፡እምኔሆሙ P (Cf. Gn); ለለ፡እምኔሆሙ TG. There is an erasure in P after the first እምኔሆሙ፡.
3. ለለ፩ በከመ P; ለለ፡በከመ TG.
4. ወለለሣሩያንሰ T; ወለሣሩያንሰ PG.
5. ሞቱ editor. ሞቷ PTG.
6. ፡ PG; ' T.
7. ወዐማፅያንሰ T; ወዓማፂያንሰ PG.
8. መዓምቀተ PG; ማእምቀተ T.
9. ፡ PG; ' T.
10. ወያከተዓልዉ editor. ወያከተ፡ዓልው P; ወያከተልዉ T; ወያከተዓልው G.
11. ለለ፩ በከመ P; ለለ፡በከመ TG.

6:2-6:6

Literal Translation

through the river of fire. ³And the works of each one of
them will stand before them, each one according to his deed.
⁴But each of the elect, those who have done good, will come
to me when they have died. The devouring fire will see
nothing of them. ⁵But the evildoers and the sinners and the
hypocrites will stand among the abysses of the darkness
which does not go out and their punishment (is) the fire.
⁶And the angels will bring their sins and prepare for them a
place where they will be punished forever, each one according to his guilt.

Free Translation

through the river of fire. ³The evil deeds of each individual will be there in front of him, each one matching what
he has done. ⁴But each of the chosen, those who have done
good deeds, will come to me at the moment of death. The
destroying fire will see none of them. ⁵But the criminals
and the sinners and the hypocrites will be put among the
deep pits in the pitch darkness which never sees light.
Their punishment is fire. ⁶The angels of God will bring
their sins and prepare for the guilty places of everlasting
punishment, for each individual a place appropriate to his
offense.

ኅክ፡እግዚ ኅብሔር ፡¹ኄሪኤል፡²ናፋሮሙ፡ለኅስ፡
ተሀጉኡ፡ኗ ኛኳን፡በኅይሳ፡ወዠሎሙ፡³ለኅስ፡ሀ
ለዉ⁴፡ሙበተ፡ዠኡ፡ማየተ⁵፡ሙበተ⁶፡ዠኡ፡ከበኩ፡ሙ
በተ፡ዠኡ፡ናቀር፡ወሙበተ፡ሥዕል፡፡⁷8.ወሙበተ⁸፡ዠ
ኡ፡ኅወግር፡ወኅብን፡⁹ወሙበተ፡ናኃተ፡ኅለ፡ይነ
ብሬ፡ሰመያዋሙ፡ኅማልካተ፡9.ያወዪዋሙ፡ምጠ
ሔዋሙ¹⁰፡በኅሳተ፡ዘለዓልም፡፡ወኅምድዛሬ ፡ኃል
ቄ፡ዠሎሙ፡ወመካኗሙ፡ኃበ፡ይነብሩ፡ወዪዪን
ዋሙ፡ለዓልም፡፡(7) 1.ወኅምዘ፡ይመብኵ፡ዕዪ፡ወ
ኅንበተ፡ሙበተ፡መካን፡ዘዪይልዋሙ፡2.በልሰ

---

1. ፡ PG; ፤ T.
2. ፡ PG; ፤ T.
3. ፡ PG; ፤ T.
4. ሀለዉ T; ሀለሙ PG.
5. ማየተ TG; ማየተ P.
6. ሙበተ TG; ወበተ P.
7. ፡፡ PT; ፡G.
8. ወሙበተ TG; ወመበተ P.
9. ፡ PG; ፤ T.
10. ምበሔዋሙ TG; ም፡በሔዋሙ P.

6:7-7:2

Literal Translation

[7]"The angel of God, Uriel, will bring the soul of those sinners who perished in the Flood and of all of them who existed in every idol (and) in every poured metal work, in every love, and in imitation [8]and who lived on all hills and stones and in the road, (who) have been called gods. [9]And they will be burned up with them in eternal fire. And after all of them and the places where they dwell have come to an end, they will punish them forever.

(7) [1]"And then men and women will come to the place proper for them.

"By

Free Translation

[7]"Uriel, God's angel, will bring forward the spirits of all those sinners who died in the Great Flood. And he will bring the spirits who have been in idols, statues and love objects as well as portraits, [8]and those who lived on the hills, in the stones, and along the roads, who were called gods. [9]These spirits will be burned with the idols in everlasting fire. After they have all been exterminated together with their dwellings, they will be punished forever.

(7) [1]"Then men and women will come to their proper places.

ዓሙ ፡¹ ²እንተ ፡ ባቲ ፡ ፀረፉዋ ፡ ለፍናተ ፡ ኳደቅ ፡ ዪ
ሰቆልዎሙ ፡ ያሳዐርዎሙ ፡³ ሎሙ ፡ ዘኪዶጠፍኍ ፡
ክሙ ፡ ያምሥኙዎሙ ፡ ዘልሪ ። 3. ወሳዋ ፡ ካዕበ ፡ መ
ክኇ ፡⁴ ወሆዬ ፡ ግብ ፡ ዐቢዮ ፡ ወምኍኽ ፡ ወክቴተ ፡ ለኽ
ል ፡ ክሐደ ዎ ፡⁵ ለቋደቅ ፡⁶ 4. ወመግእክተ ፡ ይዓን ፡ ዮ
ዋሕዮ ፡ ወሆዬ ፡ ወክቴተ ፡ ወያሳየዱ ፡ ኽሳተ ፡ ደዮፍ
ሙ ። 5. ወ ካዕበ ፡ ካልኽቼ ፡⁷ ኽንክተ ፡ ዮሰቆልዎን ፡
በክሳዶን ፡ ወሥዐርተን ፡ ወክተ ፡ ግብ ፡ ዮወደዮ
ዎን ፡⁸ 6. ወኽሳ ፡ ኽሙንቼ ፡ ኽሳ ፡ ዮፀፍረ ፡ ፀፍር ፡⁹
ወኽኩ ፡ ለፍኛሬተ ፡ ሠናዩ ፡ ኽሳ ፡ የዐወዱ ፡ ለዘሙቼ ፡
ክሙ ፡ ያሥግሬ ፡ ሳፍስ ፡ ሰብኽ ፡ ልሀጒል ፡¹⁰ 7. ወዐዩ

---

1. በልሳናሙ TG; በልሰናሙ P.
2. ፡ PG; ፤ T.
3. ያሳዐርዎሙ editor. ያሳዐርዎሙ PTG.
4. መክሳ PG; መ፡ክሳ T.
5. ካሐደዎ PG; ክሀደዎ T.
6. ፡ PG; ፤ T.
7. ካልኽቼ editor. ካልኬቼ PTG.
8. ፡ PG; ፤ T.
9. ፡ PG; ፤ T.
10. ፡ PG; ፤ T.

7:2-7:7   Literal Translation

their tongue with which they blasphemed the way of righteousness they are hanging them, tearing them to pices for them,
which does not perish that they might snatch them continually.

[3]"And behold, again a place! And there (is) a pit,
large and full. In it (are) those who have denied righteousness.   [4]And angels of punishment go around [and] there
in it and ignite the fire of their punishment.

[5]"And again, other women are hung by their neck and
their hair. Into the pit they are put.   [6]And these are they
who wove braids and not for the creation of good but to go
around for adultery that they might capture the soul of men
for destruction.   [7]And

Free Translation

[2]"They will dangle blasphemers by the tongue with
which they blasphemed the way of God, tearing their tongues
to pieces. The tongues do not perish so they can be grabbed
continually.

[3]"Look! Again there is a place! There is a large
hole filled up. In it are those who have denied the truth.
[4]Torturing angels make rounds there in the pit and light
fires which torment them.

[5]"Look again! Other women! They dangle them by their
neck and hair and put them in the pit.   [6]These women braided
their hair not to make themselves more beautiful but to prom-
enade for adultery, to net men's souls to perdition.   [7]And

ወሬ፡ኢፃ፡ያሰክቡ፡ምበሌሆሙ፡በዘሞት፡ያሰቅ
ልዎሙ፡ውበተ፡መንቃዕተሙ፡ውበተ፡ኢኅተ፡መካ
ን፡ዘያሳደድ፡[1]8.ወያበኡ፡በበያናቲ፡ሆሙ፡ወኊ
ያኊመርኡ፡ከመ፡ንመጹኢ፡ሀለወኡ፡ውበተ፡[2]ያ
ን፡ዘልጎኣጎም፡[3]9.ወልቀተልተ፡ናፍክ፡ወኢልሬ፡
ኃብሩ፡ምበሌሆሙ፡ያወደያዎሙ፡ውበተ፡ኢሳተ፡
ኃበ፡ዘምኡኢ፡ውበቴተ፡ኢሪዊተ፡ሕምዘ[4]ወያያ
የኡ፡ዘኢንበል፡ዐሬናተ፡ኢንዘ፡ያተዐወቀሙ፡
ሕማሞሙ፡10.ወያበዘሩ፡ዐፀሆሙ፡ከመ፡ኢንተ፡
ያመና፡ጾልመተ፡[5]ወያመጹኢ፡መልኢከ[6]ዐዘሪኤል፡
ናፍሶሙ፡ልኢፃ፡ተቀተኡ፡[7]ወርኢያዎሙ፡ያያሬ

1. ፡ PG ; ˈ T.
2. ፡፡ PG ; ፡ T.
3. ፡፡ T ; ፡ PG.
4. ፡ PG ; ˈ T.
5. ፡ PG ; ˈ T.
6. መልአክ TG; መልአከ P.
7. ፡፡ PG ; ⊤ T.

7:7-7:10

Literal Translation

the very men who lay with them in adultery, they hang them by their thighs in that place which burns. [8]And they will say to each other, '[And] we did not know that we had to come into eternal punishment.'

[9]"And the killers of life and those associated with them will be put into a fire which is full inside of poisonous animals. And they are punished without rest while their pain is felt by them. [10]And their worm multiplies like through a cloud of darkness. And the angel Ezrael brings the soul of those whom they killed and they saw them (get) their punishment.

Free Translation

there are the men who committed adultery with them. They dangle them by their thighs in that scorching place. [8]They tell each other, 'We did not realize that we would have to endure eternal punishment.'

[9]"Murderers and their accomplices are put in a fire full of venomous snakes. They are given no rest from their torture, feeling their pain. [10]The worms multiply so it is like going through murky clouds. The angel Ezrael brings the spirits of the murdered victims so they can watch the punishment.

መ : 11. ቀተልዎሙ : ወይብልዎሙ : በበያና ቲ ሆ
መ : ሾደቅ : ወርቶ ፅ : ኍናኄ ሁ : ጔ ኽ ግዚ ኽ ብ ሔ
ር : ኽከመ : ሰማዕ ኒ : ወ ቄ ኽ መ ኒ : ከመ : ን መ ሾ ኽ :
ወ በተ : ዘን ቸ : ም ኇ ና ን : ዘ ጔ ዓ ጔ ም :: (8) 1. ወ ን
በ : ዘን ቸ : ጔ ህ ብ : ግ ብ : ዐ ረ ያ : ወ ዕ መ ቅ : ና ቅ : ወ
ከ ቴ ች : ወ ያ ወ ሕ ዘ : ኇ ሉ : ዘ ኽ ም ኇ ሉ ኋ :: ኍ ና ኄ :
ወ ሰ ቅ ፈ ረ ር [2] : ሾ ብ [3] : 2. ወ ኽ ን ከ ተ ያ ሀ ሙ : ወ ኍ ጣ ቸ :
ኽ ከ ከ : ክ ሳ ወ ፄ ሀ ሙ [4] : ወ ያ ደ ያ ና : በ ሳ ዕ ር : ዐ ረ
ያ ::[5]ኽ ኍ ኄ : ኽ መ ን ቸ : ኽ ጔ : ያ መ ሾ ኇ [6] : ወ ሕ ጐ ን :
ወ ያ ማ ከ ና [7] : ግ ብ ረ : ኽ ግ ዚ ኽ ብ ሔ ር : ዘ ጔ ሐ ኩ :
3. ወ ኽ ን ዳ ረ [8] : ግ ዖ ን : መ ካ ና : ካ ጔ ኽ : ና በ : ያ ና ብ ረ :

1. : PG; ' T.
2. ወሰቅፈረር G; ወሰቅፈረር (with a misshaped ረ) P;
ወሰቅፈረ T.   3. ሾብ PTG; editor suggests ጸ ወብ.
4. ክሳወፄሀሙ P; ክ ፘ ወ ፄ ሀ ሙ T; ክ ሳ ወ ፄ ሀ ሙ G.
5. :: PG; ፲ T.
6. ያመሾኇ G; ያ መ ሾ ኽ PT.
7. ወያማከና TG; ወያከና PGn.
8. ወኽንዳረ PG; ወኽንዳረ T.

7:11-8:3

Literal Translation

[11]They killed them, and they will say to one another, 'Justice and righteousness (are) the judgment of God. For we heard and did not believe that we would come into this eternal place of punishment.'

(8) [1]"And near to this flame (is) a pit, large and very deep. Into it [and] there flows all which is from everywhere, judgment and abomination, discharge. [2]And their women (are) swallowed up to their necks and are being punished with great pain. Therefore these are they who abort their children and wipe out the work of God which he had formed. [3]And opposite them (is) another place where sit

---

Free Translation

[11]The killers will say to them together, 'God's sentence was just and right because we heard that we would come to this place of retribution, but we did not believe it.'

(8) [1]"Near this fire is a huge pit, very deep. All sorts of punishments flow into it from everywhere, loathsome menstruations. [2]The women there are swallowed up to their necks, tortured with intense agony. These women abort their children, wiping out the work which God has molded. Facing them is another place where the children

ውሉዶን፡ እለ፡ ክልኣሆን[1]፡ ሐደው፡[2] 4.ወይገዕ
ሩ፡ ኀበ፡ እግዚአብሔር፡ ወይመጽእ፡ መብረ
ቅ፡ ወእምውስተ፡ ሐፃናቱ፡፡[3] መቅዳሕተ፡ ውስተ፡
ኣዕይንቲሆሙ[4]፡ ለእለ፡ በዘንቱ፡ ዘመተ[5]፡ ገብ
ራ፡ ሙከናሆን፡ 5. ካልእ፡ ዕደው፡ ወአንከቱ፡
ይቀውሙ፡ ዕራቆሙ፡ መልዕልተ፡ ሠዮ፡ ወውሉዶ
ሙ፡ ይቀውሙ፡ ሠዮ፡ አንዳረ፡ ገጾሙ፡ ውስተ፡ መ
ካኑ፡ መሐውዝ[6]፡ 6. ወገዐር፡ ወይንሆኩ[7]፡ ወይገዕ
ሩ፡፡ ኀበ፡ እግዚአብሔር፡ በእንተ፡ አዘማዲ
ሆሙ፡ እለ፡ እሙንቱ፡ እለ፡ አስተቱ፡ ወረገሙ፡፡[8]

---

1. እለ፡ ክልኣሆን editor. እላ፡ ክልኤሆን PG; እለ፡ ክልኤሆን T.
2. ፡ PG; ' T.
3. ፡፡ T; :=: (occupies a space of one letter) P; ፡ G.
4. ኣዕይንቲሆሙ TG; ኣዕይንቲ፡ሆሙ P.
5. ለእለ፡ በዘንቱ፡ ዘመተ T; ለእለ∵ በዘንቱ፡ ዘመተ (with ፡ uncertain and a vertical pen stroke over the በ) P; ለእለ፡ በዘንቱ፡ ዘመቱ G.
6. መሐውዝ TG; መሖውዝ P.
7. ወይንሆኩ editor. ወይንኩ PT; ወይን[ሆ]ኩ G.
8. ፡፡ PT; ፡ G.

8:3-8:6

Literal Translation

the children whom they kept from living. [4]And they call out
to God and lightning comes [and] from among the infants (being) a drill in the eye of those who by this adultery have
brought about their destruction.

[5]"Other men and women are standing naked above there
and their children are standing there opposite them in a
place of delight. [6]And calling out, [and] they groan and
call out to God concerning their parents, 'These are they
who despised (us) and cursed (us)

Free Translation

live, those children which they kept from living. [4]When the
babies call out to God, lightning comes out from them, bor-
ing into the eyes of the women who managed their destruction
with this adultery.

[5]"Above there, other men and women are standing naked.
Their children stand facing them in a delightful place. [6]As
the children wail, they groan and call out to God against
their parents, 'They neglected us and cursed us,

ወተዐያዉ[1]: ተኽዛዛከ[2]: ወእሞቸ[3]: 7. ወረጋሙ:
መልእከ: ዘእሐኩ: ወሰቀጉ: ኪያነ: ወነንደዉ[4]::[5]
ብርሃነ: እዞኡ: መወሀበከ: 8. ሐጊበ: እማቲ
ሆነ: ያወሐዘ: እምእናገቲሆነ: ወያረጋዕ: መ
ያዷኸ: 9. እምወከቴቸ: እሪዌተ: በእዐያ
ኸ: ሠጋ: ወያወዐኸ: ወዐተመያጡ: ወያጼያንዋ
ሙ[6]: እንእያም:: [7]ያከስ: እምታቲሆነ: [8]እከሙ: ኸ
ያጉ: ተኽዛዛ: እጋዚ እብሔር: ወቀተስ: ውእቶ
ሙ: 10. ወእወጉቶሙስ[9]: ያሀብዎሙ: እመልእ
ከ[10]: ናያምግኩከ:: [11]ወእስ: ቀተልዎሙስ: ያያያንዋ

1. ወተዐያዉ T ; ወተጋያዉ PG.
2. ተኽዛዛከ T ; ተኽዛዛከ PG.
3. ወእሞቸ editor. ሞቸ PTG.
4. ወያንዷዉ T ; ወያንዷዉ PG.
5. :: PG; : T.
6. ወያጼያንዋሙ PT ; ወያያያንዋሙ G.
7. :: T ; : PG.
8. ያከስ: እምታቲሆነ: PG ; T omits.
9. ወእወጉቶሙስ PG ; ወእወጉቶሙ:ስ T.
10. እመልእከ PT ; እመልእከ G.
11. :: T ; : PG.

8:6-8:10

Literal Translation

and violated your commandment and put (us) to death. [7]And
they cursed the angel who formed (us) and they hung us up.
And they withheld the light, and to everyone you gave (it).'
[8]The milk of their mothers flows from their breasts and
congeals and rots. [9]From in it (are) flesh-eating animals
and they come out and return, and they are punished forever
with their husbands. For they forsook the commandment of
God and killed their children. [10]But their children will
be given to the angel Temlakos, but those who killed them
will be punished

Free Translation

and violating your commandment, they put us to death. [7]They
cursed the angel who formed us, and they hung us up. They
begrudged us the light which you gave to everybody.' [8]Their
mothers' milk runs from their breasts. It thickens and becomes putrid. [9]Meat-eating animals are in it, and they go
in and out of it, and they are punished forever, with their
husbands. For they abandoned the law of God when they
killed their children. [10]But the children will be given to
the angel Temlakos. Their killers will be punished

መ፡ልዓልም፡፡[1]እከመ፡ዘረቀደ[2]፡እግዚእብሔር፡
(9)1. ደመዱኅ፡መልእክ፡መዐቱ፡ዐዘሪኄል፡፡ዐየ፡
ወእንበተ[3]፡እበ፡ወዐደን፡መነረቀመ፡ወየወደደ
ቀመ[4]፡ውበተ፡መካነ፡ሕልመተ፡ዘገዛዓም[5]፡ዘዐደ[6]፡
2.ወመንረበ[7]፡መዐተ፡ደቀሠርመ[8]፡በዠኍ[9]፡መቀ
ሠናተ፡[10]ወዘኪደሳወም፡ዐየ፡ደበልየመ፡እጣ0
ተመ፡እመንቸ[11]፡ሰዓደያኄ ሀመ፡ወምግብእኒ ሀ
መ[12]፡ልዓደቃንየ፡3. ወኣቤሀመ፡እእበ፡ሀየ፡ካል
ኅን[13]፡ዐየ፡ወእንበተ፡፡[14]ወየሐደኁ፡ልሳዓመ፡ወ

---

1. :: T; : PG.
2. ዘረቀደ T; ዘረቋደ P; ዘ[ፀ]ረቋደ G.
3. ዐየ፡ወእንበተ PG; ዐየ፡ወእንበተ T.
4. ወየወደደቀመ PG; ወየወደደደቀመ T.
5. ዘገዛዓም PG; ዘገዛም T.
6. ዘዐደ editor. ዘእደ PTG.
7. ወመንረበ PT; ወመንረሰ G.
8. ደቀሠርመ T; ደቀሰርመ P; ደቀበርመ G.
9. በዠኍ G ; እዠኍ PT.
10. : PG; $\underline{\overline{I}}$ T.
11. እመንቸ PG; እማንቸ T.
12. ወምግብእኒ ሀመ editor. ወምግእኒ ሀመ PG; ወምግ ዓኄ ሀመ T.
13. ካልኅን editor. ካልኅኅ PTG.
14. :: T; : PG.

8:10-9:3

Literal Translation

forever, for (it is) God who has required it.

(9) [1]"The angel of his wrath, Ezrael, brings men and women who are half on fire. And they are put in a place of darkness which is the Gehenna of men. [2]And a spirit of wrath whips them with every whipping and a worm which never sleeps eats their bowels. They (are) the persecutors and betrayers of my righteous ones.

[3]"And near to those there (are) other men and women. And they chew their tongue. And

------

Free Translation

forever because God has required it.

(9) [1]"Ezrael, the angel of God's fury, brings men and women with half their bodies on fire. They are put in a place of gloom, human hell. [2]An enraged spirit whips them for every whipping and a never-sleeping worm eats their intestines. They persecuted and betrayed my righteous people.

[3]"Nearby, other men and women are chewing their tongues.

ያሬዕርፆሙ[1]፡በርሱን፡፡ጋዴን፡ወያወዕያፆ
ሙ፡ኸዕያንተ ሆሙ፡ኸ ጉ፡ ኸሙንቸ፡ፀፋፋኀ፡ወ
መያኗያኁ፡ስዶድቀዮ፡4. ስካልኸን፡ዕደ፡ወ
ኸንበተ፡ወምግገሩተ ሆሙ፡በተዕጋልተ፡ያመ
ተሩ፡ከኗሩዕ ሆሙ፡ወኸጋተ፡ያበወኽ፡ውበተ፡
ኸፄ ሆሙ፡ወኸማዐተሙ፡ኸስ፡ኸሞቸ፡ሰማዕተ።—።[2]
ሐሰተ፡5. ወኗቤ ሆሙ፡[ስኸስ፡ቀርቡ፡]መኸኀ፡በኸ
ብኀ፡ሐወልተ፡ዘኸጋተ፡ወያበልኁ፡ሐወልተ፡ኸ
መኗገሕተ፡6. ዕደ[3]፡ወኸንበተ፡ኸስ፡ያስብሱ፡መ
ጓሕግታተ[4]፡ወኸዕርቃተ፡ርሱሐ፡ወያወድያፆ
ሙ፡መበቴቸ፡ከመ፡ያተኁኁ፡ዠኀኜ፡ጓዕር፡ዘኁ

---

1. ወያሬዕርፆሙ PG; ወያሬዕርፆሙ T.
2. ።—። (occupies a space of two letters) P; ። ። (with a space of one letter between them) T; ። G.
3. ዕደ PG; ዕደ:ዕደ T.
4. መጓሕግታተ G; መከግሩሩተ PTGn.

9:3-9:6

Literal Translation

they are given pain with a fiery iron and their eyes are
burnt out. These are the blasphemers and betrayers of my
righteousness.

⁴"As for other men and women, their deeds (are done)
in fraud. Their lips are cut off and fire enters into their
mouth and their bowels, those who put to death the martyrs
(with) a lie.

⁵"And near them <to those who approached> (is) a place
(where is set) in stone a pillar of fire and its pillar is
sharper than a knife. ⁶(There are) men and women who are
dressed in rags and filthy tatters and they are set on it
that they might be punished (with) a punishment of pain
which does not

Free Translation

They are tortured with red-hot irons and their eyes are
burned out. These people are blasphemers and turn against
my righteousness.

⁴"There are other men and women who practice fraud.
Their lips are cut off and fire is put into their mouths
and intestines. These people used lies to put the martyrs
to death.

⁵"Close by is a place where a stake made of fire is
set in stone. It is sharper than any sword. ⁶Men and
women are dressed up in rags and filthy tatters and set on
the stake to be punished with relentless agony.

የኅልቍ፡[1][2] 7. እጓ፡እሙንቱ፡እለ፡ያትዔክቱ፡በብ
ዕሉ፡ወእቤር[3]፡ወብእሲተ፡እንጓ፡ማወታ፡ተዐ
ወፉ፡[ኮዕለ፡እ ጊዜእብዔር ፡](10)1.ወመካኒ፡ካል
እ፡ኅቤሆ፡ኍቱ፡፡ወጻጋግኑ፡ኮብ፡ወያወደያ ዋ
ሙ፡ወስቴቱ፡ዕ ፡ወእንክቱ፡እስከ፡ብረ ኪሆ
ሙ፡[4]እጓ፡እሙንቱ፡እ ለ፡ያዔ ቍሉ፡ወርደ፡ያሳሡ
ኡ፡2.ወካል ኍኅ[5]፡ዕ [6]ወእንከቱ፡እ ምኑ፡ሳዋሩ፡
ያ ዳ ርሙ፡ርእ ሶ ሙ፡[7]ወካዕበ፡ያ ግብእ፡ወያረ
ወ ፡ወያ ዓ ብርዋሙ፡እ ጋ ንትኑ፡[8][እጓ፡እሙንቱ፡
መ ዐ ፍ]3.ወያረ ክያ ዋሙ፡ወ ብተ[9]፡ኅነ ፡ሳ
እ ፡ወያ ዳ ድ ፉ ፡ወ ው እ ቱ፡ ከ መ ዝ፡ያ ግ ብ ፉ ፡፡ ወ

1. ዘኪ የኅልቍ TG; ዘኪ ያ ኅልቍ P.
2. ፡ PG; ' T.
3. ወኅ ቤC TG; ወኅ ቤC P.
4. ፡ PG; ' T.
5. ወካል ኍኅ T; ወካል ኑ P; ወካል[ኚ]ኑ G.
6. ዕ ፡ PG; ወ ፡ (with vowel marking of ዕ over the first hump of a ወ) T.
7. ፡ PG; 'T.
8. ፡ PG; ' T.
9. ወ ብተ TG; ወ ብተ P.
10. ሃ ኍ ና editor. ሕ ኒ ና PTG.

9:6-10:3

Literal Translation

end. ⁷These are they who have faith in their wealth, and
the widows and the women with orphans they neglected <con-
cerning God>.

(10) ¹"And (there is) another place near (it) to it
full of excrement. And men and women are put into it up to
their knees. These are they who lend (money) and accept
interest.

²"Other men and women from a height throw themselves
headlong. And again, they return and run and demons force
them. <These are idol worshippers.> ³And they force them
to the end of existence and they throw (themselves) over.
And this like this they do

Free Translation

⁷These people relied on their wealth but neglected the
widows and the orphaned families <with respect to God>.

(10) ¹"There is another place near it gorged with
diarrhea. Men and women are put into it up to their knees.
These people lend out money to draw interest on it.

²"Other men and women hurl themselves head first from
a height. They come back again, the demons making them run.
<They are idol worshippers.> ³The demons force them to the
end of existence, and they hurl themselves down. They do
this in the same way

ተረ፡ለጸለም፡ዖዖዖፉ፡4.ኽጕ፡ኽመንቶ፡ኽጕ፡ዖ
መተፉ፡ሥጋሆሙ፡ሐዎርዖፉ፡ብኽሲ፡ወኽንከ
ተ፡ኽጕ፡ሀለዎ፡ምከኔሆሙ፡ወወከቶቶ፡ኽጕ፡ከመ፡
ኽንከተ፡ብኽሲ፡በበዖናቲሆሙ፡ዖረ፡ዘለሱ፡5.ወ
ኮቤሆሙ፡፡ለኽጕ፡ሔል፡ወበታሕቴሆሙ፡ዖገብ
C፡መልኽኽ[1]፡ዐዘሪኬል[2]፡መኮነ፡ዘኽሳት፡በዘኑ፡[3]
ወዘሱ፡ግዖቶ፡ዘወርቅ፡ወብፉC፡ዠጕ፡ግዖቶ፡
ግብረ፡ኽዖ፡ኽጞጕ፡ኽመሕዖወ፡ወዘዖመከጐ፡
ኽምሳጕ፡ዷመቶ፡ወኽንበሳ፡ኽምሳጕ፡ዘዖተሐወ
ከ፡ወኽምሳጕ፡ኽረዌቶ፡[4]6.ወኽጕሂ፡ጋብርቀ
ሙ፡ምሳኄሆሙ[5]፡ዐዖ፡ወኽንከተ፡በለናከጕ፡ኽ

---

1. መልኽኽ G; መልኽከ PT.
2. ዐዘሪኬል G; ዘሪኬል PTGn.
3. ፡ PG; ፧ T.
4. ፡ PG; ፧ T.
5. ምሳኄሆሙ PG; ምከኔሆሙ T.

10:3-10:6

Literal Translation

continually. They are punished forever. [4]These are they who cut their flesh, sodomites and the women who were with them. And in it are those men who, like (with) women, defile one another.

[5]"And near them to these . . . (one unknown word) and beneath them the angel Ezrael makes a place of fire frequently [and] (with) every idol of gold and silver, every idol the work of human hands and which resembles the image of a cat and lion, the form of reptiles, and the form of animals. [6]But those men and women who made their images (are) in chains

---

Free Translation

continually. They are punished forever. [4]These people cut their own flesh (?). They are sodomites and the women who participated with them. Also in this pit are the men who defile each other as if they were with women.

[5]"Near them . . ., and beneath them the angel Ezrael often prepares a place of fire with every idol of gold and silver of human production, all the images of cats and lions and reptiles and other animals. [6]The people who made those images whip themselves with

ባት::ዘᎩተቀሠፉ[1]:በከሕተተሙ[2]:በቀይᎌሆ
ሙ::[3]ወከመዝ:ፀነኄሁ:ᎴᎰᎴም[4]:7.ወኄቤሆሙ:
ካልኸን:ዐይ:ወኸንከተ:ወᎩወዐይ:በᎴህበ:
ፀነኄ:ᎴᎰᎴም:ይዶዎሙ[5]:[6]ኸᎯ:ኸመንተ:ኸስ:
ይኸዶዝ:ተኸ ዛH:ኸጎዘኸብሔር[7]:ወተλᎡ:ፉ
ቆተ[8]:ኸጎንኸተ:[9](11)1.ወ ካᎴኸ[10]ወከን:ነዋጎ:
ኞቀ[11]:ምሀር:ወ ሔᎴ:ኸባተ:ወጠተ:ዘᎩነይይ:
ኸምጲንፍ:ወኸተ:ዘᎩነይይ:2.ዘᎩይጭፀ:
ዐይ:ወኸንከተ:ኸንH:ያንኩ፦ረ ዞር:ያወርይ:
ወጠተ:ዘሀ፦:ረᎩይ::ወካዐበ:ኸንH:ጎበር:
ያወ ሕH:ዖር ዝ:ወᎩወር ፉ:ወᎩይጎሙ::[12]ከ

---

1. ZᎩተ ቀሠፉ PG; ZᎩተ ቀስፉ T.
2. በከሕተተሙ PTG; των πλανων B.
3. :: T; : PG.
4. ወከመዝ: ፀነኄ:ᎴᎰᎴም PTG; και ανανα παυστως εξουσιν την κολασιν B.
5. ᎴᎰᎴም:ይዶዎሙ PTG; B omits.
6. : PG; Ī T.
7. ተኸዛH:ኸጎዘኸብሔር PTG; οδον του θεου B.
8. ወተλᎡ:ፉቆተ editor. ወተλወፉቆተ PT; ወተλወ:ፉቆተ G.
9. : PG; ' T.
10. ወካᎴኸ PTG. In P there has been an erasure at ኸ.
11. ኞቀ PG; ኞ:ቀ T.
12. :: T; : PG.

10:6-11:2

Literal Translation

of fire (with) which they beat themselves in their error
before them. And thus (is) his punishment forever.

[7]"And near them (are) other men and women and they
burn up in the heat of judgment. Their punishment (is)
forever. These are they who abandon the commandment of God
and followed harsh (?) demons.

(11) [1]"And another place, very high. . . . and . . .
(two unknown words) fire in which it burns over the edge,
this which burns. [2]Men and women who fall, rolling. They
go down into what was trembling (?). And again, when what
has been made flows, they go up and go down and repeat

Free Translation

chains of fire in front of the idols in their error.
Ezrael's punishment is like this forever.

[7]"Near them are other men and women burning up in the
heat of this punishment. Their sentence lasts forever.
These people abandon the commandment of God and have followed the way of life (?) of the demons.

(11) [1]"There is another very high place . . . (containing) fire that burns over the edge. [2]There are men and
women who slip and roll down to where the fear was. And
when the preparation (mountain?) flows, they repeatedly
climb up and go down

ማሀ፡ለአንኰርሡሮ፡ከማሀ፡ዖደየኑ፡ለዓለ
ም።[1] 3. እሉኬ፡እሙንቱ፡እለ፡ኢያከብሩ፡[2]አበ
ዊሆሙ፡ወእምሙ። ወበርእሶሙ፡ዖተዔገሠዎ
ሙ፡በእንተዝ፡ዖደየኑ፡ዘለዓለም[3]። 4. ወካዕ
በ፡ደቀ፡ወደናገለ፡ያመጽእ፡ዐዘራኤል[4]፡[5]መልአ
ክ[6]፡ከመ፡[7]ያርእዮሙ፡ለእለ፡[8]ዖደየኑ፡እሙንቱ፡
ዖተኬነኑ፡በሳዐር፡ወበከቀል፡ወበቍከል[9]፡በ
ዙሳ፡ዘያቈከሎሙ። ክዕዋሬ፡በገዐያኖ[10]፡ሠጋ፡
5. እለ፡እሙንቱ፡እለ፡የአምኑ፡በጌጋዮሙ፡በ
አዘማዲሆሙ፡ኢዖተኤዘዙ፡ወተምህርተ፡አበ
ዊሆሙ፡ኢዖተልዉ[11]፡ወዘዖልህቆሙ፡ኢያከብሩ፡

---

1. ። T; ፡ PG.
2. ኢያከብሩ GT; ኢያከ፡ብሩ P.
3. ዘለዓለም T; ዘለዓም P; ዘለዓ[ለ]ም G.
4. ዐዘራኤል PG; እዘራኤል T.
5. ፡ PG; ' T.
6. መልአክ TG; መልኣከ P.
7. ፡ TG; P omits.
8. ፡ PG; T omits.
9. ወበቍከል PG; ወበቈከል T.
10. በገዐያኖ T; በገዐኖ፡ በገዐ[ያ]ኖ G.
11. ኢዖተልዉ editor. ኢዖተልዎ PG; ኢዖተልዉ (ዉ ambiguous) T.

11:2-11:5

Literal Translation

like that, rolling. Thus they are punished forever.
[3]These, then,   are those who do not honor their fathers
and mother and by themselves abstain from them. On account
of this they will be punished eternally.

[4]"And again, Ezrael the angel brings children and
virgins that they might show them those who are being
punished. They will be punished with pain and with being
hung up and with many wounds which meat-eating birds cause.
[5]These are those who believe in their crime. Their parents
they do not obey and the teaching of their fathers they do
not follow and one who is older than they they do not honor.

Free Translation

rolling. They are punished like that forever. [3]These
people do not respect their parents but by their own will
stay away from them. For this they are punished forever.

[4]"Again, the angel Ezrael brings children and virgins
to show them those who are being punished. They will be
tortured in agony and will be hung up where meat-eating
brids inflict many wounds on them. [5]These children believe
in their mistake. They disobey their parents, disregard
the tradition of their ancestors, and show no respect for
grownups.

6.ምበሔሆሙ፡ Ī²ደፀፃልꛦ፡ወያለብሱ፡ሻልወ
ተ፡ኅልጋሰ፡ወእሙንቸ፡ያተ ኬናኑ፡ ፀናዬ፡ወሡ
ጋሆሙ³፡ያ ዘ2 ዘC⁴፡⁵7. ኡ ꛦ፡ኅሙንቸ፡ደንፃል
ናሆሙ⁶፡ኡ ꚝ ꛦ፡ ꚝ P0ꚍ ꚍ⁷፡ኅከከ፡ደከከ ꚍ ከብ ዋ
ን፡ወ ኅሙንቸ ꚍ፡ ያተ ኩ ናኑ⁸፡ ꛦያሁ።ፀናዬ፡ ꛦ
ንዘ፡ያተ0ወ ꚍ ን ።8. ወ ካ ዕበ፡ ካ ꚝ ኅ ን፡ዕደ፡
ወ ꛦ ን ከተ፡ ꚝ ꚍ ፡ P ሐ ያ ኩ፡ ꚝ ዓ ና ሙ፡ዘ ꛦ ን በ ꚝ ꚍ⁹፡
ዕ 2 ና ተ፡ ꛦ ን ዘ፡ያ ደ P ኑ፡በ ꛦ ዓ ተ፡ዘ ꚝ ዓ ꚝ ም።¹⁰
9. ꛦ ꚍ ꚍ ፡ ꛦ ፯ ብ ር ተ፡ ꚝ ꛦ ፳ ꛦ ዘ ተ ሆ ሙ፡ ꛦ ꚝ ꛦ
ያ ተ ꚍ ዘ ዘ ፡ ዘ ꚍ ፡ ወ ꛦ ተ፡ ፀ ና ꛦ ሆ ሙ፡ዘ ꚝ ዓ ꚝ ም፡¹¹

---

1. ፡ PG; Ī̱ T.

2. Ī PT; G omits. T has ፡ after Ī̱.

3. ወሡጋሆሙ TG; ወሡጋ፡Pሙ P.

4. ያዘ2ዘC TG; ያ Hꚍ HC (with ' on first C) P.

5. ፡ PG; ' T.

6. ደ ን ፃ ꚝ ና ሆ ሙ TG; ደ ን ፃ ꚝ ና ሆ ሙ P.

7. ꚝ P0ꚍ ꚍ TG; ꚝ ያ ꚍ ꚍ ꚍ P.

8. ያ ተ ኩ ና ኑ T; ያ ተ ኩ ና Ꚏ (with ambiguous vowel on ኩ and both ኩ and ā vowels on ኑ) P; ያ ተ ꚍ ና ꚍ G.

9. H ꚝ ን በ ꚍ T; H ꚝ ን ꚍ P; H ꚝ ን [ꛦ] ꚍ G.

10. ።T; ፡ PG.

11. ዘ ꚝ ዓ ꚝ ም T; ዘ ꚝ ዓ ም P; ዘ ꚝ ዓ [ꛦ] ም G.

11:6-11:9

Literal Translation

[6]"With them (are) ten virgins and they are dressed in darkness as clothing. And they will be punished severely and their flesh is torn apart. [7]These are they who do not keep their virginity until they were given in marriage. And they are punished with this same punishment while it is felt by them (or: while it is watched by them).

[8]"And again, other men and women who chew their tongue without rest while they are punished with eternal fire. [9]These, then, (are) slaves who did not obey their masters. This, then, is their eternal punishment.

Free Translation

[6]"With them are ten young women dressed in dark clothing. They are tormented extremely, and their body is torn into pieces. [7]These girls did not keep their virginity until they were married off. They are punished with this same punishment while they feel it.

[8]"Again, there are other men and women who are chewing their tongues without stopping while they are punished with fire forever. [9]These people are slaves who do not listen to their masters. So this is their punishment forever.

(12) 1. ወኀበ፡ ውእቱ፡ ደይን፡ ዐይ፡፡ ወአንከተ፡ ዕው
ራን፡ ወጸሙማን፡ ወአልገሲሆሙ፡ ጸዐዳ[1]፡፡[2] ወእ
ምዝ፡ ይትጋፍዑ፡ በበይናቲሆሙ፡ ወይወድቁ፡ ው
ስተ፡ አፍሓመ፡ እሳት፡ ዘኢይጠፍእ፡ 2. እሉ፡ እ
ሙንቱ፡ እለ፡ ይገብሩ፡ ምጽዋተ፡[3] ወይብሉ፡ ጻድ
ቃን፡ ንሕነ፡ ለእግዚአብሔር፡ ጽድቅ፡ ኢንሠሥ
ዎ፡ 3. ወያወፅእ፡ መልአክ፡ እግዚአብሔር፡[4] እዝ
ራኤል፡[5] እምነ፡ ውእቱ፡ ኅይ፡ ወያቀውም፡ ሽኅኔ፡
ደይን፡ ዘኬ፡ ሽኅኔሆሙ፡ 4. ወፈለግ፡ እሳት፡ ይው
ሕዝ፡ ወይወርድ[6]፡ ሽለ፡ ደይን፡ ማእከለ፡ ፈለግ፡
5. ወያቀውሞሙ[7]፡ ኡራኤል፡ ወመንኩራሽረ፡፡ ዘ

---

1. ጸዐዳ editor. ጸዓዳ P; ፀዓዳ T; ጸዓዳ G.
2. ፡፡ T; ፡ PG.
3. ፡ PG; | T.
4. ፡ PG; | T.
5. ፡ PG; | T.
6. ወይወርደ PG; ወይውርደ T.
7. ወያቀውሞሙ TG; ወያቀዎሞሙ (with both vowels ĕ and o on ወ) P.

12:1-12:5

Literal Translation

(12) [1]"And near this punishment (are) men and women blind and deaf and their clothing (is) white. And then they push one another and fall onto coals of fire which never goes out. [2]These are they who do a charitable deed and say, 'Righteous (are) we to God.' (And yet,) righteousness they have not sought [it]. [3]And the angel of God, Ezrael, brings them out from that flame and establishes the judgment of punishment. This, then, is their judgment.

[4]"And a river of fire flows and every punishment goes down into the river. [5]Uriel will make them stand and will give a wheel

---

Free Translation

(12) [1]"Near this punishment are men and women who are blind and who are deaf mutes. They are dressed in white. They push each other and fall down onto live coals that never go out. [2]These people do a kind deed and then say, 'We are just in God's eyes.' But they do not look for justice. [3]The angel of God, Ezrael, takes them out of the flames and confirms the truth of their sentence of punishment. So this is their sentence.

[4]"A river of fire will flow out and everyone in punishment will go down into the river. [5]Uriel will stand them up and produce a wheel

እሳት፡ዮሀብ፡ወዕደ፡ወእንከተ፡ከፀጓን፡ወከ
ቴቶ፡፡በኅዶስ፡እንኵርኵርተ፡6.ዘበጋብ፡ዮ
ወዕP፡²እሕኬ፡እሙንቶ፡መሠርያን፡ወመሠር
ያተ፡7.ወእከቶ፡መንኵሪኵር፡ወከተ፡ዠሎ፡ዶዓን፡
በእሳት፡እልቦ፡ኍልቈ³፡፡(13)1.ወእምዝ፡እምሶ
እዎ፡ስዓሩዮንP፡ወስዓዶቃንP፡ፉዱማን፡
በዝሎ፡ዶድቃ፡እንዘ፡ዮዶወርዎሙ፡መባእክተ፡
በእረዊሆሙ፡⁴እንዘ፡ዮስብሱ⁵፡እልገሰ፡ሕዶወ
ተ፡ዘገዕሎ፡2.ወዮሪእP፡ስዘ፡ዶእልዎ⁶፡እንዘ፡
ዮተቤቀሎሙ፡3.ዶዶን፡እዓልም፡እስ፡⁷b̄b̄⁸በከሙ፡
ገብሩ፡4.በእሐዱ፡ቃል፡⁹ወዮብሁ፡ከሎሙ፡እስ፡ወ

---

1. ወዕደ editor. ወኅደ P; ወእደ TG.
2. ፡ PG; ' T.
3. ኍልቈ T; ዓልቈ P; ኍልቈ G.
4. ፡ PG; ' T.
5. ዮስብሱ editor. ዮብሱ PTG.
6. ዶእልዎ፡ T; θልእልዎ PGn; θልእዎ G.
7. ፡ TG; P omits.
8. b̄b̄ PT; G omits. In T this is written over an erasure.
9. ፡ PG; ' T.

12:5-13:4

Literal Translation

of fire and men and women (will be) hanging in it by the power of its turning. [6]The one(s) in a pit are burned up. These, then, are the sorcerers and sorceresses. [7]This wheel (will be) in every punishment by fire without number.

(13) [1]"And then they (will) have brought my elect and my righteous ones, perfect in every righteousness, while the angels carry them in their hands while they don the clothing of the life of above. [2]And they will look at the one(s) who cursed it while he takes vengeance on them. [3]Punishment (is) forever for each one according to his deed. [4]With one voice [and] all of those

---

Free Translation

of fire. Men and women will be hanging inside it by its centrifugal force. [6]Those in the pits are burned up. These are the wizards and the witches. [7]The wheel will be in every punishment of fire numberless times.

(13) [1]"By that time the angels will have brought my chosen and my just people who are perfect in all justice, carrying them on their arms. They will be putting on the clothing of heavenly life [2]and they will see those who cursed that life receive vengeance. [3]Punishment is forever, each one punished appropriate to his action. [4]All those being tortured

ከተ፡ደዮን፡መሰረና፡ክበሙ፡ዖኽዚ፡ኽኽመርና፡
ዘነኔሁ፡ልኽግዚኽብሔር፡ዘኽቀደሙ፡ነጸር
ተነ፡ወኺ ኽመነ፡፡5. ወዶመጽኽ፡መልኽኽ፡ታጢ
ርኩበ፡ወዖጸሥዶሙ፡በደዮን፡ረደረደ፡፡ ወዶ
ቤሑሙ፡ዖኽዚ፡ተኔከሑ፡ኽሙ፡ኽልዖ፡ዘዚ፡ልኽ
ከቃ፡ወኺተረ ረ፡ሕዶወጥ፡፡7 6. ወዶብኡ፡ዘሉሙ፡ር
ተዐ፡ዙነኔሁ፡ልኽግዚኽብሔር፡ኽበሙ፡ሰማዕነ፡
ወኽኽመርና፡፡ ከሙ፡ሠናዶ፡ዙነኔሁ፡ኽበሙ፡ተረ
ደዮነ፡፡8 bb 9 በከሙ፡ምግገረነ፡፡ 10(14)1. ወኽማ ዮ
ኽሀሎሙ፡ልዓረ ዶን P፡ወለዓደ ቃን P፡ ነ ምቀተ፡

---

1. ኽበሙ TG; ኽበሙ፡ኽበሙ PGn.
2. ኽኽመር ነ editor. ኽኽ መረ P; ኽኽመረ T; ኽኽመር[ነ] G.
3. ልኽግዚኽብሔር T; ኸግዚኽብሔር PG.
4. መልኽኽ PT; መልኽኽ G.
5. ፡፡ T; ፡ PG.
6. ወኺተረ ረ PG; ወኺተርረ G.
7. ፡፡ T; ፡ PG.
8. ፡፡ T; ፡ PG.
9. bb P; bb or ልከ (ambiguous) T; G omits.
10. After ፡፡ T leaves a space of 2 or 3 letters (at the end of a line).
11. ወኽማዮ TG; ወኽ ማ ዮ P.
12. ወለዓደ ቃንP T; ልዓደ ቃን፡P P; ልዓደ ቃንP G; και
    εκλεκτοις (?) μου R.

13:4-14:1

Literal Translation

who are in punishment will say, 'Have mercy on us, for now
we have learned the judgment of God which he told us beforehand and we did not believe.' [5]And the angel Tatirokos will
come and rebuke them with punishment increasingly and he
said to them, 'Now you repent when there is no time for repentance and life did not remain.' [6]And all of them will
say, 'Righteous (is) the judgment of God, for we heard and
knew that his judgment (is) good. For we have been paid
back each one according to our deed.'

(14) [1]"And then I will give my elect and my righteous
ones the baptism

Free Translation

will say together, 'Show us mercy, because we have learned
God's judgment of which we were told before but did not believe.' [5]The angel Tatirokos will go to them and instruct
them even more with torture, saying, 'Now that it is too
late and life is past, you repent.' [6]They will all reply,
'God's decision is correct for we heard and learned about
the goodness of his decision and each of us has been paid
back matching what we have done.'

(14) [1]"Then I will give my chosen and my just people
the baptism

THE RAINER FRAGMENT

Apocalypse of Peter 14:1-4

The text of the Rainer fragment:

[1]<παρ>εξομαι τοις κλητοις μου και εκλεκτοις μου ον εαν αιτησωνται* με
εκ της κολασεως και δωσω αυτοις καλον βαπτισμα εν σωτηρια αχερουσιας
λιμνης ην καλουσιν εν τω ηλυσιω πεδιω μερος δικαιοσυνης μετα των
αγιων μου [2] και απελευσομαι εγω και οι εκλεκτοι μου αγαλλιωντες μετα
των πατριαρχων εις την αιωνιαν μου βασιλειαν [3] και ποιησω μετ αυτων τας
επαγγελιας μου ας επηγγειλαμην αυτοις εγω και πατηρ μου ο εν τοις
ουρανοις ιδου εδηλωσα σοι πετρε και εξεθεμην παντα [4] και πορευου εις
πολιν αρχουσαν δυσεως** και πιε το ποτηριον ο επηγγειλαμην σοι εν
χειροιν του υιου του εν αιδου ινα αρχην λαβη αυτου η αφανεια [5] και συ
δεκτος της επαγγελιας ...

* ον εαν αιτησωνται James; θν στεσωνται ms.

** δυσεως James; οπυσεως ms.

Translation of the Rainer fragment:

[1] I will gi<ve> to my called and my elect whoever they request of
me from out of punishment. And I will give them a beautiful baptism
in salvation from the Acherousian Lake which is said to be in the Elysian Field, a share in righteousness with my saints. [2] And I and my
elect will go rejoicing with the patriarchs into my eternal kingdom,
[3] and I will fulfill for them my promises which I and my heavenly
Father made to them. Behold, I have shown you, Peter, and I have
explained everything. [4] And go into a city ruling over the west, and
drink the cup which I have promised you at the hands of the son of
the One who is in Hades in order that his destruction might acquire
a beginning. [5] And you ... of the promise ...

ወመድኀኒት፡ ዘሰአልኩኒ፡ በኀበ፡ ሐቅል[1]፡ አክ
ሮስያ፡ እንተ፡ ያብልዋ፡ ኤኤስለሰልየ[2]፡ 2. ወእዴገ[3]፡
መክፈልተ፡ ጻድቃን፡[4] ወአሐውር[5]፡ [ያእዜ[6]] እትፌ
ሣሕ፡ ምስሌሆሙ፡ አበው፡ አሕዛብ[7]፡ ውስተ፡ መን
ግሥትየ፡ ዘለዓለም፡ 3. ወእገብር፡ ሎሙ፡ ዘአሰ
ፈውክዎሙ፡[8] አነ፡ ወአቡየ፡[9] ሰማያዊ፡ ነገርኩከ፡
ሴኖሮስ፡ ወአያዓዕኩከ፡ 4. ፃእ፡ እንከ፡[10] ወሖር[11]፡
እስከ[12]፡ ሀገረ፡ እንተ፡ ዐረብ፡ ወስተያ[13]፡ ወያን፡ ዘ

---

1. ሐቅል TG; ሐቀል P.
2. ኤኤስለሰልየ PT; ኤኤስለስልየ G.
3. ወእዴገ editor. ዴገየ PTG; δωσω R.
4. ፡ PG; । T.
5. ወአሐውር TG; ወአሖውር P.
6. ያዕዜ G; ማዕዜ PTGn; nothing corresponds to this in R.
7. አበው፡ አሕዛብ editor. አበውእ፡ አሕዛብ PTG; των πατριαρχων.
8. After ዘአሰፈውክዎሙ፡ PTG have ዘለዓለም፡፡ (፡ T); nothing corresponds to this in R.
9. ፡ PG; T uncertain.
10. ፡ PG; । T.
11. ወሖር PG; uncertain in T because of a shadow on the microfilm image.
12. እስከ editor. እንከ PTG; εις R.
13. ወስተያ editor. ውስተ PTG; και πιε R.

14:1-14:4

Literal Translation

and the salvation which they ask of me in the field of
Akeroseya which is called Aneslasaleya. ²And I will give
the portion of the righteous ones and I will go now rejoicing with the patriarchs into my eternal kingdom. ³And I
will do for them what I have promised them, I and my
heavenly father. I have told you, Peter, and I have informed you.

⁴"Go out, therefore, and go to the city which is (in)
the west and drink the wine

Free Translation

and salvation which they request, in the Acherusian field,
which is also called Elysium. ²I will give them their inheritance. Now I will go celebrating with the patriarchs
into my eternal kingdom, ³where I and my heavenly Father
will do everything we have promised them. I have told you
this, Peter, so that you know.

⁴"Leave, and go to the city of the west and drink the
wine

ኃቤእኅ፡ኃምኃደዊሁ፡ሕወልደP፡በዘኃንበ
ብ፡ኅቢኸት፡ክሞ፡ይ ቀደም፡ግብፉ፡ሞበ፡
5. ወኃንተሰ፡ሳፉይ፡በተበፉ፡ኃንተ፡ኃሰፈኩኅ፡
ወፈኑ፡ኃንኅ፡ወበተ፡ኸኡ፡ዓእም፡ዜ ፍP፡በሰበ
ም፡፡ 6.ኃበሞ፡ተፈሡሐ፡ፉቆO፡ቃልP፡ተበፉ፡ሐ
ይወተ፡ወግበተ፡ተሞሡጠ፡ዓእም፡፡(15)I.ወይቤስ
ኔ፡ኃግዚ ኃP፡ኢPሉበ፡ኅርበ ተበ፡ኃጉሡፉ፡ኃ
ሐር፡ወበተ፡ደብር፡ቆፉበ፡ወሞ ሸኩ፡ኅርፉ ኚ

---

1. ኃምኃደዊሁ editor. ኃምደ ፀሁ P; ኃምደ ፀሁ TG;
   εὐχεροιν R.
2. ሕወ ል ደP TG; ሕወ ል ደP P.
3. ሕ ዘ ኃንበሰ T; ከ ዘ ኃንበሰ (with uncertain first
   letter) P; ዘዘኃንበሰ G.
4. ይ ተ ቀ ደ ም editor. ይ ተ ቀ ደ በ P; ይ ተ ቀ ደ በ TG; ινα
   ᾶ ρ χ η ν R.
5. ግብ ፉ G; ግብ ረ PT; λ α β η α υ τ ο υ R.
6. ፡ PG; I T.
7. ኃሰፈ ኩ ኅ G; ኃሰፈ ኩ ኅ P; ኃሰ ፈ ወ ኩ ኅ T.
8. ፡ PG; I T.
9. ፡፡ T; ፡ PG.
10. ን ሐ ር PG; ን ሐ ር T.
11. ፡ PG; ፲ T.

14:4-15:1

Literal Translation

about which I have told you, from the hand of my son who is
without sin, that his work of destruction might begin. [5]But
you (s.) (are) chosen by the promise which I have pormised
you. And send out, therefore, into all the world my story
in peace. [6]For the Fountain of My Word has rejoiced at the
promise of life, and suddenly the world has been snatched
away."

(15) [1]And my Lord Jesus Christ our King said to me,
"Let us go to the Holy Mountain." And his disciples came

Free Translation

about which I informed you, the wine which comes from the
hand of my sinless son, so that he may begin his destructive
work. [5]You have been chosen because I made you my promise.
So tell my story in peace throughout the world. [6]For the
Source of my word has celebrated the promise of life and the
world has been snatched off unexpectedly."

(15) [1]My Lord Jesus Christ, our King, said, "Let us go
to the Holy Mountain." His disciples went

ሁ፡ምክሬሁ፡እንዘ፡ይቤልዮ፡፡²2.ወናሁ፡፪ሰብ

እ³፡ወከእነ፡ናፅርተ፡ገፆሙ፡፩እምወከቴቶሙ፡

እከሙ፡ይመሷእ፡ብርሃን፡፡ዘያበርህ፡እምፀሐ

ይ፡3.ወእልገሲሆሙኚ፡በሩሁ፡ወኢያትከሀል፡

ለሃዘC፡ወእልሰ፡ዘይካል፡ምክሬሆሙ⁴፡በዘን

ተ፡ዓእም፡፡⁵4.ወየወሁቶ፡እፍ⁶፡ዘኢይካል⁷፡ነዘ

ሬ፡ሥነ፡ልሐዮሙ፡እከሙ፡መፀምም፡⁸ሬእየሙ፡ወ

መንካC፡5.ወእልእ፡ዐበዮ፡እብል፡ያበርህ፡እ

ምበሬዳ፡በሬእዮ፡ሷ፪፡⁹ሬዳ፡እምሳእ፡ሐብሬ፡ሬ

---

1. እCዓእሁ PG;፪እCዓእሁ T.
2. ፡፡ T; ፡ PG.
3. ፪ዳብእ PG; ሰብእ T.
4. ምክሬሆሙ T;ምክሬሁ P;ምሳእሁ G.
5. ፡፡ PG; ፤ T.
6. እፍ PG; እፍ T.
7. ዘኢይካል PG; ዘኢይካል T.
8. ፡ PG; ፤ T.
9. ፡ TG; P omits.

234

15:1-15:5

Literal Translation

with him praying. ²And behold, (there were) two men. And
it was not possible for us to look at their face. For from
one of them comes a light which shines more than the sun.
³And their clothes (are) shining, and it is not possible to
tell, and there is nothing which prevails against them in
this world. ⁴There is no mouth which (in) its smoothness
is able to tell the beauty of their splendor (or: form),
for astonishing (is) their appearance,   and wonderful.

⁵And the second, large I say, shines more than hail
in his appearance (or: on his head). Rose flowers (are)
images of the color

Free Translation

with him praying. ²Suddenly two men were there. We could
not look at them, for from the first man streamed a light
brighter than the sun. ³Their clothing shone in a way impossible to describe. Nothing in this world can stand up
to them. ⁴No one is so eloquent that he can relate how
beautiful their form is. It is amazing and splendid.

⁵The second one was huge and gleamed more than crys-
tal. His face and his body resembled

ኣየ፡ ወሥጋሁ፡ 6. ወደምደማ[1]፡ ርእሱ፡ ወእምዲበ፡
መታክፍቲ፡ ወውስተ፡ ፍጻሜሁ፡ አክሊል[2]። ዘናር
ዶስ፡ ፀፍሮ፡ በጽጌ፡ ሠናይ፡ ከመ፡ ቀስተ፡ ደመና፡ ሠ
ዕርቱ፡ በውስተ፡ ሰማይ[3]፡ 7. ከማሁ፡ ሞገሰ፡ ገጹ፡ ወ
ከርግው፡ በሣሕ፡ ሰርጉ። ወሶበ፡ ርኢናሆሙ፡ ግ
ብተ፡ አንክርና፡ (16)1. ወቀረብኩ፡ ኀበ፡ እግዚአ
ብሔር፡ ኢየሱስ፡ ክርስቶስ።[4] ወእቤሎ፡ እግዚእ
የ፡ መኑ፡ ውእቱ። ወይቤለኒ፡ ዝውእቱ፡ ሙሴ፡ ወኤ
ልያስ።[5] ወእቤሎ፡ አብርሃም፡ ወይስሐቅ። ወያዕ
ቆብ፡[6] ወገዐዳንኒ[7]፡ አበው፡ ጻድቃን፡ 2. ወአርአ
የኒ፡ ገነተ፡ ርኅወ፡ ዐቢየ፡ ዕፀ፡ ሥሙር[8]፡ ወፍሬ፡ በ

---

1. ወደምደማ T; ወደምማ PG.
2. P has a sign ·~: in the left margine at this point.
3. ሰማይ editor. ማይ PTG.
4. ። T; ፡ PG.
5. ። T; ፡ PG.
6. ፡ PG; ፤ T.
7. ወገዐዳንኒ TG; ወገዐዳን፡ ኒ P.
8. ሥሙር editor. ከሙር PTG.

15:5-16:2

Literal Translation

of his appearance and his body. [6]And the hair of his head
and from his shoulders and on their forehead (is) a crown of
nard woven of a beautiful flower. Like the rainbow in the
sky (is) his hair. [7]Thus (is) the loveliness of his face,
and adorned with every ornament. And when we saw them
suddenly, we were amazed.

(16) [1]And I approached (to) God Jesus Christ and said
to him, "My Lord, who is (this)?"

And he said to me, "This is Moses and Elijah."

And I said to him, "(Where are) Abraham and Isaac and
Jacob and the other righteous fathers?"

[2]And he showed us a garden, open (and) large, a
pleasant (or: fruitful) tree (or: grove)

Free Translation

roses. [6]Resting on his hair and shoulders and forehead was
a crown with magnificent flowers; woven from nard, and it
made his hair look like the rainbow in the sky. [7]That is
what his face looked like, and he wore all kinds of jewelry.
When we saw them so unexpectedly we were astounded.

(16) [1]I went up to God Jesus Christ and said, "Lord,
who are these men?"

And he answered, "These are Moses and Elijah."

I asked, "But where are Abraham, Isaac, Jacob, and
all the other righteous ancestors?"

[2]He showed us a large open garden with a pleasant tree

ረካተ፡ምኡኽ። ቤ፡ኝ፡ኽረው፡ምኡኽ፡ቤኝሁ፡ው
ኝየ፡ 3. ወየመፄኽ፡ቤኝሁ፡ኅቤይ፡ወኽምወጠቱቱ፡
መንካረ፡ርኊኩ፡በዘን፡ኝረ። 4. ወየቤኅኒ፡ኽ
ግዘኽየ፡ወኽምልኪየ፡ኺየሱጠ፡ካርጠተጠ፡ወ
ርኊካሁ[1]፡ኽሐዛበ፡ኽበው። ወክማሁ፡ዘዐረኝተ
መ፡ 5. ወተረሣሐኩ፡ወኽመንኩ[2]።[3] ኽመዘ፡ካብር
መ፡ወጠብሐተመ፡ልኽኅ[4]፡የግኝዎመ፡ኽፄደቀየ፡
6. ወልበውኩ፡ዘኝተ፡ዘወጠተ፡መሾሐኝ። ዘተሾ
ሐረ[5]፡ዘኽግዘኽየ፡ኺየሱጠ[6]፡ካርጠተጠ።[7] 7. ወኽ
ቤሑ፡ኽግዘኽየ፡ተረቀደኑ፡ኽግበር።[8] 8. Ŧ ም
ሾጋለ፡ዘየ፡ኽሐተ[9]፡ለካ፡ወፑኅመሴ[10]፡ወፑለኬል

1. ወርኊካሁ PG; ወርኊኩሁ T.
2. ወኽመንኩ T; ወኽመንኩ፡ወኽመንኩ PG.
3. :: after the second ወኽመንኩ in P; Ŧ T.
4. ኅኽጠ T; ጠኅ P; ኅ[ኽ]ጠ G.
5. ሀተጰሐረ TG; ሀተጰሐረ P.
6. ኺየሱጠ TG; ኺየሱሱ P.
7. :: T ; : PG.
8. :: T ; : PG.
9. ኽሐተ G ; Ŧ (but in a space sufficient for two
   or three letters) T; ኽጰ PGn
10. ወፑኅመሴ T; ፑወኅመሴ PG.

16:2-16:7   Literal Translation

and full of the fruit of blessing, full of the smell of
fragrance. Its smell (was) beautiful. ³And its smell comes
to it, and from in it I saw a marvel: (there was) fruit
often (or: much fruit).

⁴And my Lord and my God Jesus Christ said to me,
"[And] you have seen the patriarchs, and like this (is)
that which is their rest."

⁵And I rejoiced and believed that this (will be) "the
honor and the glory of those who pursue my righteousness."
⁶And I understood what is written in the book of my Lord
Jesus Christ.

⁷And I said to him, "My Lord, do you wish that I make
three tabernacles here, one for you and one for Moses and
one for   _____

                    Free Translation

in which the fruit gave blessing and where the air was full
of perfume, a beautiful smell. ³The smell came to the
garden, and on the tree I saw a miracle happen: new fruit
was appearing constantly.

⁴My Lord and God Jesus Christ said, "Now you have
seen the patriarchs, and their reward is like that."

⁵I was full of joy and believed that this is "the
honor and glory of those who strive for my righteousness."
⁶So I understood the saying in the book of my Lord Jesus
Christ.

⁷Then I asked him, "Lord, do you want me to make three
tabernacles here, one for you and one for Moses and one for

ያበ፡ ፰ ወዳቤጋኢ፡ በመዐት፪፡ ሰያጣን፡ ያዳብኢ

ክ፡ ወጋልበበ፡ ሳቪፈክ፡ ወንብረተ፡ ዘንቸ፡ ዓል

ም፡ያመዉኢክ፡ ፱ ይታ ክሠተኬ፡ ኢዕይንተ ክ፡

ወይተረ ኑቃ፡ ኢዘሬ ክ፡ ክመ፡ ኢሰቲ፡ ምዳጋል፡ ኢ

ንተ፡ ኢ ጋበረ፡ ኢደ፡ ሰበክ፡ ኢንተ፡ ጋበረ፡ ኢቡየ፡

ሰማያዊ፡ ጊተ፡ ወስሃፈያን፡ ወርኢ ነ፡ ኢንዘ፡ ን

ተረ ሣሕ፫ ⁴(17) ፩ ወናሁ፡ መዱኢ፡ ቃል፡ ግበተ፡ ኢም

ሰማይ፡ ኢንዘ፡ ይብል፡ ዘንቸ፡ ውኢቸ፡ ወልደየ፡ ዘ

ኢፈቃር፡ ወሠመርኩ፡ ቦ፡ ተኢዘዘ⁵ ⁶ ፪ ወመዱኢ፡

፪ መና፡ በኢይ፡ ዘመጠኢ⁷ ፪በ፡ ርኢክበነ፡ ወጋዐ፞ ⁸

ኝቀ፡⁹ ወነሠኮመ፡ ኢኢጋዜ ኢነ⁰ ፡። ወለውሴ¹²፡ ወስኢ

1. ወ፮ጋኢልያበ PG: ወ፮በኢልያበ T.
2. በመዓተ G; በማዓተ P; በመዓ ተ T.
3. ንተረ4ሣሕ T; ንተ ሣ ሕ P; ንተ[ረ] ሣሕ G.
4. : PG; ' T.
5. ቦ፡ተኢዘዘ editor; ወ ቸኢ4ዘP PG; በ ቸኢ 4ዘP T.
6. : PG; ' T.
7. ዘመ ጠኢ4 TG; ዘመ መጠኢ4 P.
8. ወ ዓ94 PG; ወ ስ94 T.
9. : PG; ' T.
10. ጋኢጋዜኢነ PG; ኢጋዜኢነ T.
11. :: PG; : T.
12. ወለውሴ PG; ስ ውሴ T.

16:7-17:2   Literal Translation

Elijah?"

[8]And he said to me in wrath, "Satan wages war against you and has veiled your understanding and the manner of life (or: dwelling) of this world defeats you. [9]Your eyes will be uncovered and your ears will be opened up, that (there is) one tabernacle which the hand of men has not made, which my heavenly Father has made for me and for my elect."

And we saw (it), rejoicing.

(17) [1]And behold, a voice came suddenly from heaven saying, "This is my son whom I love, and I have been pleased with him. Obey him!"

[2]And a cloud large in size came over our head and (it was) very white and it lifted up our Lord and Moses and

---

Free Translation

Elijah?"

[8]He answered me angrily, "Satan is fighting you and has clouded your mind. The state of this world is defeating you. [9]Your eyes and ears will be opened up, so you may comprehend the One Tabernacle, not humanly made, but made for me and my chosen by my heavenly Father."

And when we saw it we were full of joy.

(17) [1]And suddenly a voice came unexpectedly from heaven, saying, "This is my beloved Son and I am pleased with him. Listen to him!"

[2]A large, very white cloud came above us and picked up our Lord and Moses and

ልያስ፡ወአነ፡ርዕይኩ[1]፡ወደንገፅኩ፡[2] 3. ወነጸ
ርነ፡ወተርኃወ[3]፡ውእቱ፡ሰማይ፡ወርኢነ[4]፡ሰብአ፡
እለ[5]፡በሥጋ፡[6]ወመጽኡ፡ወተቀበልዎ፡ለእግዚእ
ነ[7]፡ወለሙሴ፡፡ወለኤልያስ፡ወጾሩ፡ውስተ፡ካል
እ፡ሰማይ፡4. ወተፈጸመ፡ቃለ፡መጽሐፍ፡፡ዛቲ፡
ትውልድ፡ተኀሦ፡ሎቱ፡ወተኀሥሥ፡ገጾ፡ለአም
ላከ፡ያዕቆብ፡5. ወፍርሃት፡ዐቢይ፡ኮነ፡ወድን
ጋፄ፡ዐቢይ፡በሰማይ፡መላእክት፡ይትጋፍዑ፡ከ
መ፡ይትፈጸም፡ቃለ፡መጽሐፍ፡፡ዘይቤ፡አርኃዉ[8]፡
መኆኃተ[9]፡መኳንንት፡6. ወእምዘ፡ተዐጽወ፡ውእ
ቱ፡ሰማይ፡ዘተርኃወ፡7. ወጸለይነ፡ወወረድነ፡

---

1. ርዕይኩ T; ሬዓይኩ P; ረዓይኩ G.
2. ፡ PG; ። T.
3. ወተርኃወ TG; ወተረኃወ P.
4. ወርኢነ TG; ወርእነ P.
5. እለ TG; ኢለ P.
6. ፡ PG; ። T.
7. ለእግዚእነ T; ለግዚእነ P; ለ[እ]ግዚእነ G.
8. አርኃዉ T; አርኃው PG.
9. መኆኃተ PTGn; ኆኃተ G.

17:2-17:7

Literal Translation

Elijah, and I trembled and was astonished. ³And we watched and this heaven opened and we saw men who were in the flesh and they came and went to meet our Lord and Moses and Elijah and they went into the second heaven. ⁴And the word of scripture was fulfilled, "This generation seeks him and seeks the face of the God of Jacob."

⁵And there was great fear and great amazement in heaven. The angels flocked together that the word of scripture might be fulfilled which said, "Open the gates, princes." ⁶And then this heaven which had been opened was closed.

⁷And we prayed and went down

Free Translation

Elijah. I shook and was terrified. ³We watched as this heaven opened up and men with physical bodies came to welcome our Lord and Moses and Elijah. They went into the second heaven. ⁴The saying of scripture was fulfilled, "This generation looks for him; it looks for the face of the God of Jacob."

⁵There was great awe and amazement in heaven. The angels flocked together to fulfill the saying of scripture, "Open the gates, ye princes." ⁶Then this heaven, the one which had been opened, was closed.

⁷We prayed,

እምየብር ፡፡ እንዘ ፡ ንሴብሖ ፡ ለእግዚአብሔ
ር ፡ ዘጸሕፈ ፡ እከማቲሆሙ ፡ ስ ዳይቃን ፡ ወከተ ፡
መጽሕፈ ፡ ሕያወት ፡ በሰማያት ፡

17:7

Literal Translation

from the mountain praising God who wrote the names of the
righteous in the book of life in heaven.

Free Translation

and as we descended from the mountain we praised God who
has written the names of the righteous in the book of life
in heaven.

Index of Ethiopic Words

The numbers refer to the chapter and verse of the text. Variations given in the critical apparatus are included in the chapter and verse reference. All words are listed except the following:

the preposition and possession marker ለ ;

the preposition and possession marker በ ;

the conjunction ወ ;

the relative pronouns ዘ , እንተ , እለ .

Verbs are classified according to types using the system found in Thomas O. Lambdin, Introduction to Classical Ethiopic.

This is not intended to be a full glossary, only a thorough index.

ሀ

ሁ particle of interrogation: 16:4

ሂ enclitic particle: 7:7; 7:9; 10:6; 11:7; 16:1

ሀሎ existence: 10:3

ሀለወ verb in D, to be: 2:12; 3:6; 4:13; 5:5; 6:7; 7:8; 10:4; /11:2

ሄኖክ Enoch 2:12

ህየ adv., there: 7:3; 7:4; 8:5; 8:5; 9:3

ሃይማኖት faith: 5:1

ህየንተ prep., in place of: 2:6

ሀጕለ or ሀጐለ verb in Gt, to perish, die: 4:5; 6:7

ሀጕል destruction, end: 7:6

ሀገር city: 14:4

ለ

ልሀቀ verb in G, to grow up, grow old: 11:5

ለሀብ flame, heat: 8:1; 10:7

ለለ prep, to or for each: 2:3; 2:3; 4:7; 6:3; 6:3; 6:4; 6:6; /13:3

ለሊሁ himself: 3:3

ለሰሐ verb in G, to form, shape: 8:2; 8:7

ልሑኵት a formed thing: 3:6

ላሕይ brilliance, form, attractiveness: 15:4

ለምለመ verb in Q, to bloom, frow green: 2:1; 2:7; 2:11

ልሳን tongue: 7:2; 9:3; 11:8

አቀሐ verb in D, to lend: 10:1

ልብ heart: 3:2; 3:7

አልበሰ verb in G, to clothe, dress: 5:2; 11:6; 13:1
   in CG: 9:6

ልብስ clothes, a garment: 11:6; 12:1; 13:1; 15:3

አለቦ verb in D, to understand: 1:2; 1:3; 2:7; 16:6
   in CD: 1:2; 2:12

ግእክ servant: 2:6. or possibly verb in L, to send

መልአክ angel: 1:7; 3:3; 6:1; 6:6; 6:7; 7:4; 7:10; 8:7; 8:10;
   9:1; 10:5; 11:4; 12:3; 13:1; 13:5; 17:5

ልዑል high, lofty: 3:7 (here: Most High)

ላዕል adv., above, heavenly: 13:1

ላዕለ prep., on, over, about: 4:7; 9:7

መልዕልት prep., above: 8:5

ሌለየ verb in Q/Lt, to separate, divide: 3:2

መላልእት limb, joint: 4:8

ሊቅ elder: 2:4

ሰ

ሰሊብ milk: 8:8

ሰአየ verb in G, to sing, make music: prologue

ሰማም pain, illness: 7:9

ሰምህ venom, poison: 7:9

ሰመድ ash(es): 2:6

ሰለት a lie: 9:4

ሰነዊ adj., false: 2:7. subst., liar: 2:10

ሰቃል field: 14:1

ሰቀየ verb in G, to grind the teeth: 5:9

ሰበር color: 15:5

ሰውልት column, post: 9:5; 9:5

ሰረ verb in G, to go: 1:6; 5:5; 14:2; 14:3; 15:1; 17:3

ሰቀሬ:ብእሲ sodomite: 10:4

ሰሰ verb in CG, to move, shake

   ዘየተሰመን reptile(s): 10:5

ሰውH pleasure, delight   መሰውH (unattested form): 8:5

ሐዘብ people, nation: 6:2; 6:2; 14:2; 16:4

ሐዘነ verb in G, to be sad: 3:7

ሐዘን sadness, sorrow, gloom: 3:3

ሐየ unattested word: 10:5; 11:1

ሐየከ verb in G, to chew: 9:3, 11:8

ሐየወ verb in G, to live, revive, recover: 4:10; 4:11

ሐይወት life, lifetime: 2:13; 4:11; 13:1; 13:5; 14:6; 17:7

ሕያው adj., living: 1:7; 4:2; 8:3

ሕፃን infant, baby: 8:4

መ

ምህር unattested word: 11:1

ተምህርት teaching: 11:5

ምሉእ adj., full: 7:3; 7:9; 16:2; 16:2

መለከ verb in CG, to worship: 1:4

እግዚእ a god, the Lord: 1:4; 6:8; 16:4; 17:4

ምሕረ verb in G, to have mercy: 3:6; 13:4

መሓሪ (one who is) merciful: prologue

ምሕረት mercy: prologue

መሐፀነ verb in CQ/L, to entrust: 4:11

ማሕፀንት pledge, custody: 4:11

መሠጠ verb in CG, to seize, grab: 7:2; in Gt: 14:6

ምሥጢር mystery: prologue

መሪር adj., bitter: 5:4

ሙሴ Moses: 16:1; 16:7; 17:2; 17:3

መሰለ verb in G, to be like, resemble: 10:5; in Gt: 5:6

ምስለ prep., with: 1:6; 1:7; 2:13; 4:5; 4:13; 6:1; 6:9; 7:7; 7:9; 8:9; 10:4; 11:6; 14:2; 15:1; 15:3; see 10:6

እምሳል image: 2:1; 2:3; 3:1; 10:5; 10:5; 10:5; 15:5; see 15:4

ምሳሌ parable, proverb, image: 10:6

መሲሕ messiah: 2:7

ማሰነ verb in CL, to corrupt, wipe out: 8:2

ሙስና corruption, destruction: 8:4, 14:4

መሰወ verb in Gt, to melt: 5:4; 5:6

ምት husband: 8:9

መተረ verb in G, to cut, cut off: 9:4; 10:4

መተን   nerve, tendon: 4:8

መኑ   interrogative particle, who?: 16:1

ምንት   interrogative particle, what?: 1:2; 2:3; 4:8

ለምንት   interrogative particle, why?: 3:5

መንገለ   prep., to, toward: 5:7; 5:7

ማእስ   skin, hide: 4:8

ማእከለ   prep., in the midst of: 6:5; 12:4; see 6:2

ማዕዜ   interrogative adv., when?: 14:2

ሞተ   verb in G, to die: prologue; 2:11; 2:13; 4:11; 6:4
in CG: 8:6; 9:4

ሞት   death: 6:4

ምዉት   adj., dead: prologue; 1:7; 4:9

ማውት   see እንተ : ማውት   corpse, the dead: 9:7

ምህ   verb in G, to conquer, defeat: 16:8

መዋዕት   day: 2:3; 3:7; 4:1; 4:6

መዐት   wrath: 5:4; 5:8; 5:8; 9:1; 9:2; 16:8

እማዐት   intestines, bowels: 9:2; 9:4

ማይ   water: 2:6; 5:3; 5:5; 15:6

መጠ   verb in Gt, to turn: 5:3; 8:9

መያጢ   vacillator: 9:3

ምድር   land, soil, earth: 2:5; 4:10; 4:10; 4:11; 4:11; 4:13

መጠን   size, measure: 17:2

መጽአ   verb in G, to come: 1:2; 1:5; 1:6; 1:7; 1:7; 2:7;
2:8; 2:12; 4:1; 6:1; 6:4; 7:1; 7:8; 7:11; 8:4; 13:5;
15:1; 15:2; 16:3; 17:1; 17:2; 17:3

in CG: 3:6; 5:8; 6:6; 6:7; 7:10; 8:2; 9:1; 11:4; 13:1

ምጽአት   coming: prologue; 1:2; 1:2; 1:3; 1:6

ምጽዋት   alms, act of charity: 12:2

ሠ

ሠመረ   verb in G, to be pleased: 17:1; in CG: 2:13

ሠሙC   adj., pleasing, pleasant: 16:2

ሠርቅ   the east: 5:7; 5:7

ሠረወ   verb in G, remove, uproot: 2:5; in Gt: 3:2

ሥርው   root, nerve, muscle, tendon: 2:6; 4:8

ሠርዐ   verb in G, to put into order, establish, set up: 4:9

ⲇⲱⳙ wizard: 12:6; 12:6

ⲱⳙ verb in G, to sprout: 2:3

ⲱⳙ sprout: 2:1

ⲙ beauty: 15:4

ⲱ adj., beautiful, good: 6:4; 7:6; 13:6; 15:6; 16:2

ⲙ imitation, copy: 6:7

ⲙ hair: 4:8; 7:5; 15:6

ⲱ verb in G, put, place, set: 1:3

ⲙ meat, flesh, body: 4:4; 4:8; 8:9; 10:4; 11:4; 11:6; 15:5; /17:3

ⲱ verb in CG, to cast nets: 7:6

ⳑ

ⲗ adj., dirty, filthy: 9:6

ⲗ adj., fiery, red-hot: 9:3

ⳑ verb in D, put, place, set: 10:3

ⳑ exorcism: 5:5

ⳑ uprightness, justice: 7:11

ⳑ adj., upright: 3:2; 13:6

ⳑ verb in CG, to open: 4:3; 17:5
in Gt: 5:2; 16:9; 17:3; 17:6

ⳑ adj., open: 16:2

ⳑ head: 1:7; 6:2; 10:2; 11:3; 15:6; 17:2

ⳑ verb in G, to see: 2:8; 3:3; 3:3; 3:7; 4:1; 4:10; 6:1;
6:2; 6:4; 7:10; 13:2; 15:7; 16:3; 16:4; 16:9; 17:3
in CG: 3:1; 3:7; 11:4;16:2
in CGt: 1:6; 4:4

ⲇ vision, appearance: 15:4; 15:5; 15:5

ⳑ verb in CG, to pollute, defile: 10:4

ⳑ verb in G, to find: 2:5; 4:1; 5:8

ⳑ verb in G, to run: 10:2

ⳑ verb in G, to tremble: 17:2

ⳑ tremor: 11:2

ⳑ rose: 15:5

ⳑ disciple: 15:1

ⳑ interest (monetary): 10:1

ⳑ verb in G, to curse, execrate: 8:6; 8:7

ረገዐ verb in G, to congeal: 8:8

ሰ

ሰ emphatic particle, also: 1:6; 2:1; 2:10; 3:4; 3:7; 5:9; 6:4;
6:5; 6:5; 6:5; 8:10; 8:10; 14:5

ሰላም peace: 14:5

ስሕተ verb in CG, to err: 1:4; 2:12

መስሕት imposter, seducer: 2:12

ስሕተት error, sin: 10:6

መስሕን rags, cheap clothes: 9:6

ሰሙር adj., fruitful: 16:2

ሰሜን the south: 5:7; 5:7

ሰምዐ verb in G, to hear: 1:3; 7:11; 13:6

ሰማዕት martyr: 2:10; 2:11; 2:11; 2:13; 2:13; 9:4

ሰመየ verb in G, to name, call: 6:8

ስም name: 1:5; 17:7

ሰማይ heaven, sky: 1:6; 4:13; 5:4; 5:5; 5:5; 15:6; 17:1; 17:3;

ሰማያይ adj., heavenly: 6:1; 14:3; 16:9 /17:3; 17:5; 17:6; 17:7

ሰርኁ ornament: 15:7

ስርጉው adj., adorned, made beautiful: 15:7

ሰለሰ verb in CD, to remove: 2:6

ሰቀለ verb in G, to hang up, to crucify: 2:9; 7:2; 7:5; 7:7;
/8:7; 11:4; 12:5

መስቀል cross: 1:6

ሰቆ ቆር abomination: 8:1

ሰቆቀው lamentation: 3:7

ሰቀየ verb in G, to water, to wet: 2:6

ሶበ conj., when: 2:7; 2:8; 2:10; 3:4; 3:7; 15:7

ሰብሐ verb in D, to praise: 17:7

ስብሕት 1:6; 1:7; 1:7; 2:9; 6:1; 16:5

ሰበከ verb in G, to preach: 1:3

ስቡክ poured metal-work, statue: 6:7

ምስብዕት seven times: 1:7

(አ)ስተት verb in CG, to despise, reject, scorn: 8:6

ሰትየ verb in G, to drink: 14:4

ስን tooth: 5:9

ሰንሰለ chain: 10:6

ሰአለ   verb in G, to ask for: 1:2; 14:1; in Dt: 3:4

ስእነ   verb in G, to be unable: 15:2; in Gt: 4:5

ሰከበ   verb in G, to lie down: 7:7

ሰዓት   hour: 2:6

ሰይጣን   Satan: 16:8

ሰደደ   verb in G, to drive out, persecute: 5:8

ሰዳዲ   persecutor: 9:2

ሰገደ   verb in G, to bow down: 1:1

ሰረወ   verb in CD, to promise: 14:3; 14:5; in Dt: 2:8

ተስፋ   promise, hope: 14:5; 14:6

ቀ

ቃል   word, saying: 1:3; 3:4; 13:4; 14:6; 17:1; 17:4; 17:5

ቀሠፈ   verb in G, to beat, whip: 9:2; in Gt: 10:6

መቅሠፍት   beating, whipping: 9:2

ቀርበ   verb in G, to approach: 1:1; 1:5; 9:5; 16:1

ቈስለ   verb in CG, to be wounded, be injured: 11:4

ቍስል   wound, sore: 11:4

ቀስት   a bow, rainbow: 15:6

ተቀበለ   verb in Dt, to welcome: 17:3

ቀተለ   verb in G, to kill: 2:10; 7:11; 8:9; 8:10; in Gt: 7:10

ቀታሊ   murderer: 7:9

ቀመ   verb in G, to stand: 6:3; 6:5; 8:5; 8:5; in CG: 12:3; /12:5; in Glt: 3:5

ቀደሰ   see ደቀሰ

ቀደመ   verb in CG, to be first: 13:4; in Gt: 14:4

ቀድመ   prep., before: 1:6; 4:2; 6:3; 10:6

ቀዳሚ   first: 2:9

ቀደሰ   verb in Dt, to sanctify: 14:4

ቅዱስ   adj., holy: 1:7; 15:1

በ

በህለ   verb in G, to say: 1:2; 1:4; 1:5; 2:2; 2:4; 2:5; 2:6; 2:7; 2:9; 3:4; 3:5; 3:5; 4:5; 4:7; 4:8; 7:8; 7:11; 12:2; 13:1; 13:4; 13:5; 13:6; 14:1; 14:4; 15:1; 15:5; 16:1; 16:1; 16:1; 16:4; 16:7; 16:8; 17:1; 17:5

በእኘ   verb in G, to be sharp: 9:5

በለስ   fig, fig tree: 2:1; 2:2; 2:3; 2:3; 2:5; 2:5; 2:11

ዕፀ:በለስ   fig tree: 2:4; 2:7

በልዐ   verb in G, to eat, devour: 4:4; 9:2

በላኢ   one who devours: 6:4; 8:9; 11:4

ባሕር   ocean, sea: 5:3

መንገሕበሕት   cataract, waterfall: 5:2

ባሕትት   adj., only: 1:1; 2:11

በርህ   verb in G, to shine, be bright: 15:5; in CG: 1:7;

በርሃን   light: 8:7; 15:2   /15:2

በፁህ   adj., bright, shining: 6:1; 15:3

በፁር   silver: 10:5

መብረቅ   lightning: 1:6; 5:5; 8:4

በረከት   blessing: 16:2

በርክ   a knee: 10:1

በረድ   hail: 15:5

(ተ)በቀለ   verb in Dt, to be avenging: 13:2

ኣስተበቀዐ   verb in CGt, to plead: 1:1

በበይናት   prep., among, between: 7:8; 7:11; 10:4; 12:1

በእሲ   a man: 2:5; 4:4; 4:11; 7:6; 10:4; 15:2; 16:9; 17:3

በእሲት   a woman: 9:7

በእንት   prep., about, because of: prologue; 2:2; 2:13;

በእንተ H   thus, therefore: 11:3 /3:4; 3:7; 4:12; 8:6; 11:3

በከየ   verb in G, to weep: 3:3; 3:3; 6:2

ኣብሰ,ኣበሰለ   verb in CG, to permit: 3:4

ቦኣ   verb in G, to enter: 9:4; in CG: 14:3

በዕል   wealth, riches: 9:7

ባዕድ   adj., other, different: 1:4; 16:1

በዝኀ   verb in G, to be many/much: 7:10

ብዙኀ   adj., many, much: 1:5; 1:6; 2:10; 2:11; 5:9; 11:4

ብዙኀ   adv., much, often: 10:5; 16:3

ቤት:ክርስቲያን   church: 1:3

ቤት:እስራኤል   House of Israel: 2:4; 2:7; 2:11

በድን   corpse: 5:6

ተ

ተለወ   verb in G, to follow, accompany: 10:7; 11:5

 በታሕት prep., under: 2:6; 10:5

እምታሕት prep., from under: 5:4

ተረፈ verb in G, to be left over, remain: 13:5

ተከለ verb in G, to plant: 2:5; 2:6

መትከፍት or መትከፍ shoulder: 15:6

ጠርጣሮስ Tatirokos (=ταρταρουχοσ): 13:5

ነ

ነጸፈ verb in G, to come to an end: 6:9; 9:6

ነጸፍት end: 1:2; 2:1

ኈለቈ verb in Dt, to count: 2:13

ኈልቈ number, limit: 12:7

ነፍስ understanding, mind: 16:8; see 10:3

ነለየ verb in G, to think: prologue

ነለፈ verb in G, to pass: 6:2

ነወወ verb in G, to look for, seek: 2:5; 12:2; 17:4; 17:4

ኄር adj., good: 2:13

ኅሩይ adj., chosen, selected, elect: 4:12; 6:4; 13:1; 14:1

ነበ prep., by, with, to: 1:1; 3:6; 4:8; 6:4; /14:5; 16:9
    6:6; 6:9; 7:9; 8:1; 8:3; 8:4; 8:6; 9:3; 9:5; 10:1; 10:5;

በነበ prep., by, with, to: 14:1   /10:7; 12:1; 16:1; 16:3

ነበረ verb in G, to be associated: 7:9

ኅቡረ adv., together, at the same time: 4:13

ኆኅት gate: 17:5

ነያል power, host: 1:6; 12:5

ነየሰ verb in G, to be better: 3:4; 3:5

ነደገ verb in G, to leave, abandon: 8:9; 10:7

ነጢኅት sin: prologue; 5:1; 6:6; 14:4

ጎጢኅ sinful, sinner: 3:2; 3:3; 3:4; 3:7; 6:5; 6:7

ነጢኅ want, lack, failure: 5:5

ኃጺን iron tool, instrument, weapon: 9:3

ሀ

ሁ particle of interrogation: 2:4; 2:7; 16:7

ሂ enclitic particle, even, the very: 4:4; 4:4; 4:13; 5:3; 5:3;

ሀሉ introductory particle, behold!: 15:2; 17:1   /5:4; 15:3

ነህበ verb in G, to sigh, groan, lament: 8:6

ንሕነ we: 1:1; 12:2

ነሠአ verb in G, to lift, raise: 10:1; 17:2; in CG: 4:12

ተንሣኤ resurrection: prologue; 4:9

መንሡግ bar, bolt: 4:3

ናርዶስ nard: 15:6

ነስሐ verb in D, to repent: 13:5

ንስሐ repentance: 13:5

መንቀዐት thigh: 7:7

ነቅዐ fountain, source, spring: 14:6

ነበረ verb in G, to sit, stay, live: 1:1; 6:1; 6:8; 6:9;

መንበር throne, chair: 6:1   /8:3; in CG: 1:7; 6:1; 6:2

ንብረት sitting down, dwelling, manner of life: 16:8

ነበበ verb in G, to speak, tell: 3:4

ነበየ verb in Dt, to prophesy: 4:7

አንከረ verb in CG, to marvel, be amazed: 15:7

መንከር marvel, wonder: 2:12; 16:3

መንከር adj., wonderful, marvelous: 15:4

አንኰርኰረ verb in CQ/N, to roll: 11:2; 11:2; 12:5

ናሁ particle, behold!: 7:3

ኖመ verb in G, to sleep: 9:2

ነዋኅ adj., high, lofty: 10:2; 11:1

ሥንዓብ affliction, torment: 3:3

ነደደ verb in G, to flame: 5:8; 7:7; 11:1; 11:1; in CG: 7:4

ነደ flame: 5:4; 5:8; 12:3

መንግሥት kingdom, kingship: 14:2

ንጉሥ king: 15:1

ነገረ verb in G, to say: prologue; 1:2; 13:4; 14:3; 15:3;

ነጸረ verb in D, to look at: 15:2; 17:3; in CG: 7:2/15:4

ነፀረ verb in CG, to break in pieces: 7:2

ነፍስ soul: 3:1; 4:9; 4:10; 6:7; 7:6; 7:9; 7:10

መንፈስ spirit: 4:9; 5:6; 9:2

መንፈቅ half: 9:1

ተፋቀ adj., hesitant, doubtful: 1:4

ሓ

ሖ interjection, O: 3:5

ኢ particle of negation: prologue, 1:4; 1:4; 1:4; 1:5;1:5;
1:6; 2:3; 2:4; 2:5; 2:5; 2:5; 2:6; 2:7; 2:10; 3:4; 3:5;
3:6; 3:6; 5:4; 5:4; 5:5; 5:5; 5:8; 5:8; 6:5; 7:2; 7:8; 7:11;
9:2; 9:6; 11:3; 11:5; 11:5; 11:5; 11:7; 11:9; 12:1; 12:2;
13:4; 13:5; 15:3; 15:4; 16:9

እላ these: 3:4; 7:6; 8:2; 8:3; 8:6 9:3; 9:7 10:1 10:2; 10:4;
10:5; 10:7; 11:3; 11:5; 11:7; 11:9; 12:2; 12:6

እላ conj., but: 1:6; 7:6; see 8:3; 17:3

እለኡሁ his own: 1:1

እልቦ there is/are not: 4:10; 12:7; 13:5

እልቦ:ዘ no, none: 4:5; 4:5; 6:4; 15:3

እልያስ Elijah: 2:12; 16:1; 16:7; 17:2; 17:3

እሐዱ one: 13:4; 16:7; 16:9

እም prep., conj., adv., when: 1:7; 4:1; 4:9; 4:12; 4:13;

እም and እምነ prep., from: 1:6; 1:7; 2:1; 3:6; /5:1; 13:5
4:2; 6:3; 8:8; 9:5; 10:2; 11:1; 12:3; 14:4; 15:2; 15:5;
/17:1; 17:7

ለእም conj., if: 2:6

እሞ either . . . or: 3:3; 3:3

እም mother: 8:8; 11:3

እምዝ adv., then: 2:1; 2:11; 6:2; 14:1

እእምረ verb in CG, to know: prologue, 1:2; 2:1; 2:2; 2:3;
2:4; 4:10; 7:8; 13:4; 13:6

ተእምርት sign, miracle: 1:2; 2:12

እምነ verb in G, to believe: 4:12; 7:11; 11:5; 13:4; 16:5;

እሙንቱ they: 1:3; 7:6; 8:2; 8:6; 9:2; 9:3; 16:5; in Gt: 1:5
9:7; 10:1; 10:2; 10:4; 10:7; 11:3; 11:4; 11:5;
11:6; 11:7; 11:7; 12:2; 12:6

እምዘ adv., then, next: 5:6; 7:1; 12:1; 13:1; 17:6

እርስ palm, hand: 3:1

ኡርአል Uriel: 4:9; 6:7; 12:5

እርዌ animal: 4:4; 7:9; 8:9; 10:5

እስመ conj., for: prologue, 1:6; 2:3; 2:12; 3:4; 3:5;
3:6; 4:5; 4:5; 4:7; 4:9; 4:13; 7:11; 8:9; 8:10;
13:4; 13:6; 13:6; 14:6; 15:2; 15:4

አሳት fire: 5:2; 5:3; 5:3; 5:4; 5:4; 5:6; 5:8; 5:8; 5:8;
6:2; 6:4; 6:5; 6:9; 7:4; 7:9; 9:4; 9:5; 10:5; 10:6;
11:1; 11:8; 12:1; 12:4; 12:5; 12:7

እስከ prep., until, up to: 1:6; 3:3; 8:2; 10:1; 11:7; 14:3

አብ father: 1:7; 2:9; 4:2; 6:1; 11:3; 11:5; 14:2; 14:3;
16:1; 16:4; 16:7; 16:9

እብC widow, unmarried woman: 9:7

አብርሃም Abraham: 16:1

አበሰ verb in D, to sin: 3:7

አበሰ crime, guilt: 6:6

አበን stone: 6:8; 9:5

አበየ verb in G, to refuse, be unwilling, to reject: 2:10

አሐ I: 1:5; 2:2; 2:8; 3:4; 14:3; 17:2

አኤሊስዮስ Elysium: 14:1

አንስት women: 7:1; 7:5; 8:2; 8:5; 9:1; 9:3; 9:4; 9:6; 10:1;
10:2; 10:4; 10:4; 10:6; 10:7; 11:2; 11:8; 12:1; 12:5

ዘእንበለ prep., without, except for: 7:9; 11:8; 14:4

እንተ prep., via, by way of: 4:2; 7:10

እንተ፡ማእከለ prep., among, through: 6:2

አንተ you (s.): 3:5; 3:6; 14:5

አንተሙ you (pl.): 2:1

እንክ particle, so, then, therefore: 14:4; 14:4; 14:5

እንዘ conj., while: 1:1; 1:2; 1:4; 1:5; 1:6; 1:7; 4:4; 5:8;
5:8; 5:9; 6:1; 6:4; 7:9; 11:2; 11:2; 11:7; 11:8; 13:1;
13:1; 13:2; 15:1; 16:9; 17:1; 17:7

እንጊዘ prep., opposite, facing: 8:3; 8:5

አኮ particle of negation, no, not, it is not: 7:6

አኬሮስያ Acherusia: 14:1

እኩይ evil, wickedness: 2:8

እዘን ear: 16:9

አዘዘ verb in D, to command: 4:3; 4:4; 4:6; 6:2; in Dt: 11:5;

ተአዘዘ commandment: prologue; 4:9; 5:6; 8:6; 8:9; 11:9; 17:1
/10:7; 17:1

አየሱስ Jesus: 15:1; 16:1; 16:4; 16:6

በአይቴ interrogative adv., where?: 2:2

አይኅ the Great Flood, the Deluge: 6:7

እድ hand, power: 2:11; 2:13; 10:5; 13:1; 14:4; 16:9

አድማስ adamant: 4:3

ኽ ፇ ኢ : ኽ መ ሕ ዖ መ offspring of the mother of the living = human beings: 4:2; 5:7; 5:9; 10:5; see 4:7

ኽ ፇ ኢ : ማ መ ት offspring of the dead = orphans: 9:7

ኽ ፇ ሐ ኽ the Lord, master: 1:4; 2:3; 3:4; 11:9; 15:1; 16:1; 16:4; 16:6; 16:7; 17:2; 17:3

ኽ ፇ ሐ ኽ ብ ሴ ር God: prologue; prologue; 1:6; 2:6; 2:13; 3:6; 4:1; 4:2; 4:5; 4:5; 4:7; 4:9; 4:9; 4:12; 5:1; 5:6; 6:1; 6:7; 7:11; 8:2; 8:4; 8:6; 8:9; 8:10; 9:7; 10:7; 12:2; 12:3; 13:4; 13:6; 16:1; 17:7

ኽ ሬ interrogative adv., how?: 4:12

ኽ ፍ mouth: 9:4; 15:4

ኽ ዺ መ pleasant odor, perfume: 16:2

ከ

ከ enclitic particle of conclusion, so, then, therefore: 2:11; 4:6; 4:7; 8:2; 11:3; 11:9; 11:9; 12:3; 12:6; 16:9

ከ ሀ ለ verb in G, to be possible: 15:3; 15:4; in Gt: 4:7; 15:3

ኩ ለ quantifier, all, each, every: 1:7; 1:8; 3:1; 3:3; 4:2; 4:3; 4:4; 4:5; 4:5; 4:6; 4:6; 4:7; 4:13; 5:2; 5:3; 5:6; 6:1; 6:7; 6:7; 6:7; 6:8; 6:9; 8:1; 8:7 9:2; 10:5; 10:5; 12:4; 12:7; 13:1; 13:4; 13:6; 14:5; 15:7

ኩ ሎ adv., completely: 4:4; 5:2

በ ኩ ለ ሄ adv., everywhere, wherever: 5:8

ኽ ም ኩ ለ ሄ adv., from all sides: 8:1

ኽ ከ ሊ ል crown: 1:7; 6:2; 15:6

ከ ል ኽ verb in G, to prevent, withhold: 8:3

ከ ል ኽ other, another: 2:6; 7:5; 8:3; 8:5; 9:3; 9:4; 10:1; 10:2; 10:7; 11:1; 11:8; 15:5; 17:3

ከ ል ኽ ት two: 7:5

ከ ል ኽ two: 8:3

ከ ሕ ደ verb in G, to deny: 2:9; 7:3

ከ መ prep., like, as; conj., that; conj., according as, as: with subjunctive: prologue, 1:2; 1:3; 2:5; 2:12; 3:4; 4:3; 4:4; 7:2; 7:6; 9:6; 14:4; 17:5 with imperfect: 1:3; 1:7; 7:8; 7:11; 11:4 other: 1:6; 2:4; 2:7; 2:8; 2:12; 4:5; 4:10; 5:4; 5:5; 7:10; 10:4; 13:6; 15:6; 16:9

ከማሁ prep., thus: 1:6; 4:6; 4:7; 11:2; 11:2; 15:7; 16:4

በከመ prep., according to: 1:8; 2:5; 4:6; 4:11; 6:3; 6:6; 13:3; /13:6

እግብከመ conj., as soon as, when: 2:1

ሐከመ conj., how: 3:2; 3:2; 3:2; 3:3 (with dittograph)

ከመዝ prep., thus: 3:5; 10:3; 10:6; 16:5

ከሠተ verb in Gt, to open, reveal: 16:9

ክርስቶስ Christ: prologue, 1:5; 2:8; 2:9; 2:10; 15:1; 16:1; 16:4; 16:6

መንኰራኲር wheel: 12:5; 12:7

ከረየ verb in G, to dig: 2:6

ክሳድ neck: 7:5; 8:2

ከበረ verb in CG, to make glorious: 11:3; 11:5

ክብር honor, glory: 16:5

ኰነነ verb in D, to judge: 1:7; in Dt: 4:13; 9:6; 11:4; 11:6; /11:7

ኵነኔ judgment, trial, justice: 4:2; 4:5; 4:9; 5:1; 5:4; 5:8; 7:11; 8:1; 9:6; 10:6; 10:7; 11:6; 11:7; 11:9; 12:3; 12:3; 13:4; 13:6; 13:6

መኰንን judge, ruler: 17:5

ምኵናን place of punishment: 7:11

ከንፈር lip: 9:4

ኮነ verb in G, to be, become: 1:4; 2:1; 2:10; 2:10; 2:11; 2:11; 2:13; 3:6; 3:7; 4:6; 4:6; 5:1; 5:2; 5:3; 5:5; 5:6; 5:9; 17:5

መካን place: 6:6; 6:9; 7:1; 7:3; 7:7; 8:3; 8:5; 9:1; 9:5; 10:1; 10:5; 11:1

ኮከብ star: 5:4

ካዕብ adj., second, other: 7:3

ካዕበ adv., again, moreover: 7:5; 10:2; 11:2; 11:4; 11:8

ኪያሁ him: 4:9; 11:7

ኪያነ us: 8:7

መክፈልት portion, share: 14:2

ወ

ወሀበ verb in G, to give: 4:9; 8:7; 8:10; 12:5; 14:1; in Gt: 4:11; 5:3

ወልድ son: prologue; 1:6; 8:2; 8:3; 8:5; 8:9; 8:10; 14:4; 17:1

ተወልድ generation: 17:4

ወልደ፡እጓለ፡እመሕያው son of the offspring of the mother of the living = son of man: 4:7

ውሕዘ verb in G, to flow: 5:4; 5:8; 8:1; 8:8; 11:2; 12:4

ወሐየ verb in L, to go around: 7:4

አውሥአ verb in CG, to answer: 1:4; 2:2; 2:4; 3:5

ወርቅ gold: 10:5

ወረደ verb in G, to go down: 11:2; 11:2; 12:4; 17:7

አውሰበ verb in CGlt, to give someone in marriage: 11:7

ውስተ prep., in, into, to: 1:1; 1:3; 2:5; 2:8; 2:12; 3:1; 3:1; 4:2; 4:3; 4:6; 4:7; 4:8; 4:8; 4:10; 4:10; 4:11; 5:3; 5:7; 5:7; 5:7; 5:7; 5:7; 5:8; 6:7; 6:7; 6:7; 6:7; 6:8; 6:8; 7:1; 7:3; 7:4; 7:5; 7:7; 7:7; 7:8; 7:9; 7:9; 7:11; 8:1; 8:4; 8:5; 9:1; 9:4; 9:6; 10:1; 10:3; 10:4; 11:1; 11:2; 12:1; 12:5; 12:7; 13:4; 14:2; 14:3; 14:4; 14:5; 15:1; 15:6; 16:6; 17:3; 17:7

እምውስተ prep., from in: 2:6; 8:4; 8:9; 15:2; 16:3

በውስተ prep., in, into, to: 15:6

ወትረ adv., always, continuously: 10:3

ውኁጥ verbal adj., swallowed: 8:2

ወንጌል gospel: 1:3

ውእቱ he, that: 1:5; 2:3; 2:4; 2:7; 2:8; 2:11; 2:12; 3:6; 4:11; 7:7; 10:3; 11:1; 11:9; 12:1; 12:3; 12:7; 16:1; 16:1; 17:1; 17:3; 17:6

ተወከለ verb in Dt, to trust, have faith: 9:7

ውዕየ verb in G, to be burned up: 5:3; 10:7; 12:6; in CG 6:9; /9:3

ውዑይ adj., hot, burning: 9:1

ወይን wine, vineyard: 14:4

ወድቀ verb in G, to fall: 12:1

ወደየ verb in G, to put, place, set: 7:5; 7:9; 9:1; 9:6; 10:1

ወፅአ verb in G, to go/come forth: 2:1; 8:9; 14:4; in CG: 12:3

ወግር heap, mound, hill: 6:8

ሞገስ favor, loveliness: 15:7

ሞገድ wave: 5:9

O

ዓለም world: 1:2; 2:1; 2:8; 2:12; 4:6; 5:2; 5:5; 14:5; 14:6; 15:3; 16:8

ለዓለም forever: 3:2 (እስከ፡ ዓለም); 6:6; 6:9; 8:9; 8:10; 10:3; 10:6; 10:7; 11:2; 13:3

ዘለዓለም eternal: 4:2; 6:1; 6:9; 7:8; 7:11; 11:3; 11:8; 11:9; 14:2

ዕለት day: 3:1; 4:1; 4:2; 4:5; 4:5; 4:9; 4:12; 4:13; 5:1

ዐለወ verb in G, to pervert, rebel: 5:1

ማዕምቅ or ማዕምቅት the deep, abyss: 6:5

ዕሙቅ adj., deep: 8:1

ዐማፂ adj., unjust, wicked, criminal: 3:2; 6:5

ዓመት year: 2:3; 2:5

ዕራቅ— adj., naked, alone: 8:5

ምዕራብ the west: 1:6; 4:2

ዐረብ the west: 5:7; 14:4

ዐርገ verb in G, to go up: 11:2

ዕረፍት rest: 7:9; 11:8; 16:4

ዐቀበ verb in G, to keep: prologue; 11:7; in Gt: 1:3

ዐቃቢ guardian, keeper: 2:5; 2:6

ዐቢይ adj., large, great: 3:3; 4:9; 7:3; 8:1; 8:2; 15:5; 16:2; /17:2; 17:5; 17:5

ዐንበሳ lion: 10:5

ተዐወረ verb in Dt, to neglect, despise: 9:7

ዕውር adj., blind: 12:1

ዐቀ verb in G, to be aware of: 1:4; in Gt: 1:6; 7:9; 11:7

ዐ verb in G, to go around, tour: 7:6

ዐ bird: 4:4; 11:4

ዕዝራኤል Ezrael: 7:10; 9:1; 10:5; 11:4; 12:3

ዐይን eye: 3:3; 8:4; 9:3; 16:9

ዕድ men, menfolk, males: 7:1; 7:7; 8:5; 9:1; 9:1; 9:3; 9:4; 9:6; 10:1; 10:2; 10:6; 10:7; 11:2; 11:8; 12:1; 12:5

ዓዲ adv., besides, even, still, yet: 3:3

ዐደወ verb in Gt, to transgress: 8:6

ተዐግለት fraud: 9:4

ዐፀወ verb in Dt, to be patient: 11:3
ዐስቅ branch: 2:1; 2:7; 2:11
ዐጸወ verb in Gt: to close: 17:6
ዐፀ tree, grove: 16:2; see 2:4; 2:7
ዐፀም bone: 4:7; 4:8; 4:8; 4:8
ዐፅ worm: 7:10; 9:2

H

H and ዝኣ this, these: 11:3; 11:9; 12:3; 16:1
ሀለ adv., continuously: 7:2
ዝሙት adultery, harlotry: 7:6; 7:7; 8:4
ዝሙድ parents: 8:6; 11:5
ዘርእ verb in G, to sow, seed: 4:10; Gt: 4:10; 4:11
ዘርእ seed, progeny: 4:10; 4:11
ዘርዘረ verb in Q, to scatter, dash to pieces: 11:6
ዝንቱ and ዝቲ this: prologue; 2:5; 2:6; 2:10; 4:11; 7:11; 8:1;
ዜና story, pronouncement: 14:5   /8:4; 15:3; 16:8; 17:1; 17:4
ዚኣሁ his: 2:11; 2:13; 3:6; 4:5
ዝየ here: 16:7

P

የማን the right (side, etc.): 3:1; 3:1; 6:1
ይስሐቅ Isaac: 16:1
ይቡስ adj., dry, arid: 4:10
ይእዜ adv., now: 4:1; 13:4; 13:5; 14:2
የውሀት gentleness, mildness: 15:4
ያዕቆብ Jacob: 16:1; 17:4
አየደዐ verb in CG, to inform, tell: 14:3

ደ

ደለወ verb in G, to be suitable: 7:1; in CGlt: 6:6
መደለወ hypocrite: 6:5
ድምን see ድምድም : 15:6
መደምም adj., astonishing: 15:4
ደመት cat: 10:5
ደመና cloud(s): 1:6; 6:1; 7:10; 15:6; 17:2

ዸ ግዸ ጻ hair: 15:6

ዸ ቅ children: 11:4

 መዸ ቀ ጠ or መ ቀ ዸ ጠ drill: 8:4

ዺ ጠ prep., on, upon: 1:7; 6:2; 17:2

እ ግ ዺ ጠ prep., from on, from upon: 15:6

ዸ ጠ ር mountain: 15:1; 17:7

ዸ ጠ ረ : ዘ ዮ ት Mt. of Olives: 1:1

ዸ ሰ ጠ the north: 5:7

ዸ ጻ ፈ what comes after, the last: 2:7; 3:1; 3:7; 4:1; 4:6

ዸ ሐ ፈ prep., behind, last: 2:8

እ ግ ዸ ሐ ፈ conj., after, last: 1:2; 6:9

መ ዸ ሐ ን savior: 3:5

መ ዸ ሐ ን ት salvation: 14:1

ዸ ሐ ዐ verb in G, to fall, slip, trip: 11:2

ዸ ን ጰ ወ verb in Q, to be envious: 8:7

ዸ ን ግ ለ a virgin, maiden: 11:4; 11:6

ዸ ን ግ ለ ና virginity: 11:7

ዸ ን ገ ዐ verb in Q, to be astonished: 17:2; in CQ: 5:5

ዸ ን ገ ዮ terror, amazement: 17:5

ዸ ዮ sickness: 14:4

ዸ ፈ ነ verb in D, to judge, punish: 6:9; in Dt: 8:2; in CD:
8:9; in G: 8:10; in Gt: 6:6; 7:9; 10:3; 11:2; 11:3;
/11:4; 11:8

ዸ ዮ ነ judgment, punishment: 4:2; 4:5; 4:12; 4:13;
6:5; 7:4; 7:4; 7:8; 7:10; 10:7; 12:1; 12:3; 12:4;
12:7; 13:3; 13:4; 13:5

ዮ ነ ፈ verb in Q/L, to pursue, chase: 16:5

ዸ ገ መ verb in G, to do again: 11:2

ፈ ግ ግ second: prologue

ገ

ገ ሀ ነ ም or ገ ነ ህ ም Gehenna, Hades, hell: 4:3; 9:1

ገ ለ ሰ ሰ verb in Q, to veil, cover: 16:8; in Qt: 5:2

ገ መ ረ verb in Gt, to promise, confirm: 3:1

ገ ወ ረ verb in D, to reproach: 13:5

ገ ሩ ም adj., awesome, terrible

ገ ጠ hole, cave, lair: 7:3; 7:5; 8:1; 12:6

ገብረ verb in G, to do, make: 2:12; 3:2; 4:12; 5:1; 6:4; 8:4;
      10:3; 10:5; 10:6; 12:2; 14:3; 16:7; 16:9; 16:9;
      in CD: 10:2
ኀገበር see ገብረ : 1:2
ምግባር work: 1:8; 2:8; 3:7; 6:3; 6:3; 9:4; 13:6
ገበር work: 8:2; 10:5; 13:3; 14:4
ግብር a thing made, preparation: 11:2
ገብር servant: 11:9
ግብት adv., suddenly: 14:6; 15:7; 17:1
ገብአ verb in G, to return: 2:8; 10:2;   in CG: 2:3; 4:3;
      4:4; 4:11; 4:13;   in Glt: 4:2
ምግብአ returning, converting, betraying: 9:2
ገነት garden: 2:5; 2:5; 2:6; 2:6; 16:2
ጋኔን demon: 10:2; 10:7
ተጋነየ delayed: 2:5
ጸውዐ verb in G, to call, cry out: 8:4; 8:6; 8:6
ጊዜ time: 1:2; 1:3; 13:5
ጐየ verb in G, to flee: 5:7; 5:7; 5:7
ጐጐየ verb in Q/L, to err, go astray: 2:9
ጌጋይ error, sin, guilt: 11:5
ገጽ face: 1:6; 8:3; 8:5; 15:2; 15:7; 17:4
ገፍዐ verb in Glt, to push/press: 12:1; 17:5

ጠ

ጠምልኮስ Temlakos (= τημελουχοσ): 8:10
ጥምቀት baptism: 14:1
ጥቀ adv., very: 8:1; 11:1; 17:2
ጽጋ gloominess, darkness, fog: 5:2
ጥብ breast, teat: 8:8
መጥባሕት knife, sword: 2:10; 9:5
ጣዖት heathen idol(s): 6:7; 10:5; 10:5
ዐማዖ worshipper of idols: 10:2
ጠፍአ verb in G, to go out, perish: 5:4; 5:8; 5:8; 6:5;
                                    /7:2; 12:1

ጴ

ጴጥሮስ Peter: prologue; 2:2; 3:5; 14:3

ጸ

ግጽላ a shady place, arbor: 16:7; 16:9

ጸልመት darkness: 5:2; 6:5; 7:10; 9:1; 11:6

ጸልኸ verb in G, to hate: 13:2

ጸለዮ verb in D, to pray: 15:1; 17:7

ጓሐጸጸ verb in Q, to weed, thin out: 2:6

ጸሐፈ verb in G, to write: 17:7; in Gt: 16:6

መጽሐፍ writing, book, scripture: 4:7; 16:6; 17:4; 17:5; 17:7

ጸሙም adj., deaf and/or dumb: 12:1

ጸገሐ the east: 1:6; 4:2

ጸበኸ verb in G, to wage war: 16:8

ጼና odor, smell: 16:2; 16:2; 16:3

ጸንዐ verb in G, to be strong, harsh: 2:5

ምጽናዕ a firm base, firmament: 5:5

ጸንፍ edge, end: 10:3; 11:1

ጸረ verb in G, to carry, bear: 13:1

ጸበ ? adj.?, excretory?: 8:1; 10:1

ጸዐለ verb in G, to curse, revile: 13:2

ጸዐረ verb in CD, to inflict grief: 9:3

ጻዐር pain: 8:2; 9:6; 11:4

ጻዕዳ white: 12:1; 17:2

ጼኸ verb in G, to rot, decay: 8:8

ጸድቅ righteousness, truth: 7:2; 7:3; 7:11; 9:3; 12:2; 13:1;
ጸዲ᎓ adj., righteous: 2:13; 3:2; 3:3; 9:2; 12:2; 13:1;/16:5
14:1; 14:2; 16:1; 17:7

ጸደረ verb in G, to rush headlong: 10:3; in CG: 10:2

ጸገበ adj., full, sated: 10:1

ጸገወ verb in D, to show grace or favor, give gifts: 14:2

ጸገየ verb in G, to flower: 14:2

ጸገ flower, blossom: 15:5; 15:6

θ

θሐይ sun: 1:7; 15:2

θርቅ rag, tatter: 9:6

ኸθርዐ verb in CG, to cease, leave a space, be unfruitful: 2:5

θረፈ verb in G, to blaspheme: 7:2

ፀፍፍ adj., blasphemous, wicked: 9:3
ፀፈፈ verb in G, to weave, plait: 7:6
ፀፍር a plaited work: 7:6; 15:6

ፈ

ፈጠሰ verb in G, to bubble, boil, rage: 5:9
ፈሃ7 river: 5:8; 6:2; 12:4; 12:4
ፈሃም verb in CGlt: to be made to separate: 5:9
ፍምሦ a live coal: 5:3; 12:1
ፈውጠ verb in Dt, to rejoice: 14:2; 14:6; 16:5; 16:9
ፍርሀተ fear, dread: 17:5
ፈፈየ verb in G, to bear fruit: 2:5; 2:6; 4:10
ፍፈ fruit: 2:3; 2:5; 16:2; 16:3
ከፍፀፈ verb in CG, to love: 17:1
ፍፀር love (?): 6:7
ሞፍፀሪ lover: prologue
ፍፀተ ????: 10:7
ፈፀየ verb in G, to wish, want, require: 4:4; 8:10; 16:7
ፈ4ጠ verb in D, to send: 14:5; in Dt: 2:12
ፍፍተ road, way: 6:8; 7:2
ፈሀፈ verb in D, to interpret, explain: 2:2
ፈፀየ verb in G, to pay back: 1:8; in Gt: 13:6
ፈፈፈፈ adv., exceedingly: 2:9; 4:12; 13:5
ፈምፈ verb in G, to create: 3:6; 4:6; in Gt: 3:4; 3:5; 5:4; /5:5
ፈሃሪ creator: prologue
ፍፍፈተ creation: 5:6; 7:6
ፈሃሞ verb in Dt, to be completed: 17:4; 17:5
ፍሀሦ adj., done, completed, perfect: 13:1
ፍሃሦ forehead: 15:6

NUMERALS

Ϩ one: 6:3; 6:3; 6:6; 15:2; 16:7; 16:7
ϨϨ each one: 12:3; 13:6
Ϩ two: 15:2; see 15:1
Γ three: 16:7
Ι ten: 11:6

CHAPTER FOUR

NOTES ON THE ETHIOPIC TEXT

The Prologue

I have understood the singular relative pronoun of ህ
ነገር 'which he told' to refer to the whole preceding
clause while the verb must harken back to ክርስቶስ 'Christ.'
The plural relative pronoun እለ 'who' has ሙታን 'the
dead' for its antecedent. Further on, we have to assume
that ሐለየ 'he pondered' describes what Peter did. Thus we
have a shift in subject with each of the verbs, ነገረ, ሞተ,
ሐለየ, but the subject is not immediately obvious for any
of them.

Upon whose mystery is Peter thinking? All translators
of this text have taken ምሥጢሮሙ፡ ለወልደ፡ እግዚአብሔር
to be the mystery of the Son of God. Literally the Ethiopic
reads "their mystery of the Son of God" where we would expect "his mystery of the Son of God." The tension is between the plural suffix on mystery and its singular execu-
tion in Son of God. The scribe of T or some later reader
apparently felt this tension and relieved it by erasing the
ሙ. This leaves the grammatically correct singular suffix.
But this also means that both manuscripts witness to the
plural suffix in the tradition.

266

This tension between the plural and the singular may
be insignificant, since such a state of affairs is not uncommon in Ethiopic literature. What is at stake is whether
the author intended to say "his mystery," i.e., the mystery
of the Son of God, or "their mystery," i.e., the mystery of
those who die on account of their sin. The issue cannot be
decided with any certainty. But this Prologue was intended
to be descriptive of the whole following Pseudo-Clementine
composition. The theme of the latter is the mystery of salvation for sinners rather than the mystery of the Son of
God, though the distinction may not be clearly drawn since
it is by the mercy of the Son of God that sinners are saved.
In the translations I have given full weight to the plural
suffix. Peter ponders the fate of sinnners. Then the remaining phrase I take to be a dedication, "to the Son of
God, the merciful and the lover of mercy." This phrase is
similar in form and perhaps in function to the dedication
which opens each sura of the Qur'ān save one, "In the name
of Allah, the Merciful, the Compassionate." To this should
also be compared the dedication in Rev. 1:5b-6: τω αγαπωντι
ημας και λυσαντι ημας εκ των αμαρτιων ημων.

Chapter One

V. 1. The Apocalypse of Peter begins like the Little
Apocalypse of the synoptic gospels (Mt. 24:3ff; Mk. 13:3ff;
Lk. 21:7ff). This should be compared to Jn. 7:53-8:2. It
is not our intention to present in this dissertation a

complete study of the relationship of the <u>Apocalypse of
Peter</u> to the New Testament and other Early Christian literature. We will, however, in the course of this chapter point
out enough detail to demonstrate that the <u>Apocalypse of
Peter</u> is not simply dependent upon any one of the canonical
gospels.

   This is an exact translation of Mt. 24:3 with the following exceptions: 1) οι μαθηται 'the disciples' is translated by ℏλℏℓ 'his own, his followers' (cf. Jn. 13:1:
having loved his own); 2) κατ' ιδιαν 'privately' is mis-
translated by ∩∩ : ∩ℏ±†ℎ 'each alone'; 3) the words
"and we bowed down and besought him" have nothing corresponding to them in Matthew. These last words could possibly
mean "and we worshipped him and prayed to him,"[1] but this is
not always so. (Cp. Mt. 20:20 προσκυνουσα και αιτουσα when
the mother of the sons of Zebedee approaches Jesus with her
request; but see also Mt. 28:17.)

   The use of the first person plural, however, is a
claim by the author to be one of those making the request.
Leaving aside the Prologue, only in 2:2 does the author
identify himself as Peter. Peter did not, of course, write
this apocalypse. It is pseudonymous.

---

[1] The cultic overtones of προσερχομαι in Matthew 24:1
and 24:3 are here made explicit. For Matthew's use see J.
Schneider, ερχομαι, TDNT 2, 683-684; Fred. W. Burnett, <u>The
Testament of Jesus Sophia. A Redaction-Critical Study of
the Eschatological Discourse in Matthew</u> (Lanham, MD: University Press of America, 1981), 215-218.

Vv. 2-3. መ ሰ ከ ዳ ፄ ቦ : ኅ ኀ ሂ : ኀ ቦ ጠ 'and we asked
him, saying to him' reflects επηρωτησαν δε αυτον λεγοντες of
Lk. 21:7 (rather than the form in Matthew or Mark).

Though both manuscripts have ኀ ፖ ሰ ር this is very
difficult. An independent subjunctive carrying a jussive
force, ኀ ፖ ሰ ር would have to mean 'Let us do (make/act)'.
But this makes no sense in the context. Hugo Duensing attributed the problem to a faulty Arabic forerunner.[1] Both
he and Grébaut[2] indicate in their translations that ኀ ፖ ሰ ር
must mean 'inform us'. Surely this must be a translation of
the Greek ειπε as we find it in Matthew 24:30 (or ειπον Mk.
13:4). The most natural explanation is that the word was
literally translated into Ge'ez as 'tell (us)'. During the
course of its transmission in Ethiopic a ሰ was inadvertently
inserted and that error was passed along so that it appears
in P T. It was probably allowed to stand because the initial ኀ from the root could now be read as a first person
plural prefix, which in some sense fit the context. I have
therefore restored ኀ ፖ ር to the text.

The question "what (will be) the signs of your coming
and of the end of the world" is an exact translation from
Mt. 24:3 τι το σημειον της σης παρουσιας και συντελειας του

---

[1]Hugo Duensing, "Ein Stücke der urchristlichen Petrus-
apokalypse enthaltender Traktat der äthiopischen Pseudoklementinischen Literatur," Zeitschrift für die neutestamentliche
Wissenschaft und die Kunde der älteren Kirche 14 (1913):66.

[2]Sylvain Grébaut, ibid., p. 208.

αιωνος except the Ethiopic has the plural "signs" where the
Greek has the singular.[1] This should be compared to John
7:31: When the Christ appears, will he do more signs than
this man has done? For the phrase "that we might know and
understand" we can compare ινα γνωτε και γινωσκητε in John
10:38. The remainder of vv. 2-3 has no direct parallels in
the gospels. But these verses should be compared to Akhmim
2:5:

> And we, the twelve disciples, went with him and en-
> treated him to show us one of our righteous brethren
> who had departed from the world that we might see in
> what form they are, and taking courage might encourage
> the men who should hear us.

Throughout P there is ambiguity concerning those verbs
ending in final ም or ዉ. Both of these appear as ም in P.
On ያስበዉ P has ም but T has no ዉ at all. These phenom-
ena can be explained if both P and T had ም in whatever

---

[1]The words ποτε ταυτα εσται 'when will these things
be?' are missing here in the Apocalypse of Peter. In the
synoptic gospels this question ties the destruction of the
temple (and of Jerusalem) with the sign of the end. (Cf.
Fred W. Burnett, ibid., 198-225.) This connection, which
is related to the theology of this apocalypse, is also
found in Gospel of Peter 7:25, "Woe on our sins, the judgment and the end of Jerusalem is drawn nigh"; and to the
variant reading at Luke 23:48, vae nobis quae facta sunt
hodie propter peccata nostra; appropinquavit enim desolatio
Hierusalem, "Woe unto us (for) the things which have been
done today on account of our sins; for the destruction of
Jerusalem has come near."
    Burnett believes that the strong connection of the
destruction of Jerusalem with the predictions of the end in
Mark is cut in Matthew, so that the predictions in Mt. 24-5
are only of the end. The opposite appears to be the case in
Luke, where the predictions may refer entirely to the destruction of Jerusalem. In the Apocalypse of Peter the
material from the synoptic apocalypse is not connected with
the destruction of Jerusalem or the temple. But this theme
is taken up in ch. 2 in connection with the fig tree parable.

manuscripts they used. P always retained ዐ . But T usually
has corrected it to ዐ when the plural is required. Here at
the end of v. 3 he has not done so even though the plural is
needed. Rather he has written the more common shortened
form of the singular ያለት where ነዐ is shortened to ት.
It is likely that he has failed to correct to the plural
because this is the first occurence of this problem in our
text. I have restored the correct plural form to the text.

In vv. 2-3 the disciples are not expecting that the
parousia will occur during their lifetime, for they wish to
pass the information on to their successors. But perhaps
the phrase "that they might be aware of your coming" indicates that the parousia was expected by this writer before
that generation immediately following the disciples passed
away.

V. 4. The warning against apostasy (Mt. 24:4par.) is
here expanded with warnings against doubt and idolatry. The
reasons for these additions are not clear. Idolatry is a
major theme in the Apocalypse of Peter. Idols will be
destroyed and the spirits which inhabited them will be punished (6:7-9). Idol makers and idol worshippers will also
be punished (10:5-7 and the probably misplaced sentence in
10:2). Compare Jn. 7:12 where Jesus is accused of leading
people astray--a false messiah. The final apostasy is
described in 2:7-13. Doubt, however, is not mentioned

elsewhere in this apocalypse,[1] though some of its teachings
are aimed at those who doubt them. This is true, for example, of the teachings about the restoration of physical
bodies at the resurrection (chapter 4).

V. 5. The irregular vowels which P has on ብህጎዖ
'in my name' most likely came about because he at first mistakenly read ብህወ 'in heaven'. Realizing his mistake
before he wrote ዖ for ዖ , he corrected the ወ by simply
adding the correct vowel, leaving it with both vowels.

The first part of this verse reflects Mark 13:6 in
that there is no conjunction (γαρ in Mt. and Lk.) in the
Ethiopic. However, the form of the saying is "I am the
Christ" as in Matthew, where Mark and Luke have εγω ειμι.
But then the continuation "Do not believe them and do not go
near them" is similar to Luke's continuation "Do not go
after them." Matthew and Mark both have "And they will lead
many astray," but "do not believe" is from Mt. 24:26. In
John 7:41 others make the claim about Jesus, "This is the
Christ."

V. 6a. The saying likening the parousia to lightning
has parallels in Mt. 24:27 and Lk. 17:24 (cf. Jn. 11:27,
14:18, 1 Jn. 5:20). The first noticeable difference is
that Ap. Pt. has "Son of God" for the synoptic "Son of man."[2]

---

[1]To have faith and never doubt is related to the curs-
ing of the fig tree in Matthew 21:21, but not to the parable
of the fig tree in Apoc. Pt. 2 or Luke 13.

[2]The history of the application of both titles is much
disputed. For Son of man see H. E. Tödt, The Son of Man in

Given this difference in title, the saying here follows the
form in Matthew quite closely with one exception. That exception lies in the words "the coming . . . will not be revealed." This is in all likelihood from the same tradition
as a saying of Jesus found in Luke 17:20, where, however, it
is applied to the kingdom of God rather than to the parousia
of Jesus: The kingdom of God is not coming with signs to be
observed. The emphasis here in v. 6a is clearly upon the
suddenness and unexpectedness of the parousia. Cf. Jn. 7:
4, 27, 31.

Vv. 6b-7. Here are three sayings which are each ex-
pansions of "I will come in my glory."

> 6b Thus I will come in a cloud of heaven with great
> power in my glory while my cross goes before
> my face. (Compare 6:1)

> 7a I will come in my glory while giving out light
> seven times brighter than the sun.

---

the Synoptic Tradition (Philadelphia: Westminster Pr., 1965);
P. Vielhauer, "Gottesreich und Menschensohn," Festschrift
für Günther Dehn, ed. W. Schneemelcher (Neukirchen: Moers,
1957), 51-79; Eduard Schweizer, "Der Menschensohn," Zeitschrift für die neutestamentliche Wissenschaft 50 (1959),
185-210; J. Fitzmyer, "The New Testament Title "Son of Man"
Philologically Considered," A Wandering Aramean (Missoula:
Scholars Pr., 1979), 143-160; H. Gese, "Wisdom, Son of Man,
and the Origins of Christology: The Consistent Development
of Biblical Theology," Horizons in Biblical Theology 3
(1981), 23-57; Barnabas Lindars, "The New Look on the Son of
Man," Bulletin of the John Rylands University Library of
Manchester 63 (1981), 437-462. For Son of God see Eduard
Schweizer, "υιος," TDNT 8, 363-392; F. Hahn, Christologische
Hoheitstitel, 2nd. ed. (Göttingen: Vandenhoeck und Ruprecht,
1964), 280-333; Martin Hengel, The Son of God (Philadelphia:
Fortress Pr., 1976). See also Helmut Merklein, "Die Aufer-
weckung Jesu und die Anfänge der Christologie (Messias bzw.
Sohn Gottes und Menschensohn)," Zeitschrift für die neutes-
tamentliche Wissenschaft 72 (1981), 1-26.

7b <u>I will come in my glory</u> with all my holy angels
        when my father will set a crown upon my head
        that I might judge the living and the dead.

The first of these three sayings is paralleled by Son
of man sayings in the synoptic apocalypse:

    Mt. 24:30 and they will see the Son of man coming on
            the clouds of heaven with power and great glory.

    Mk. 13:26 and then they will see the Son of man coming
            in clouds with great power and glory.

    Lk. 21:27 and then they will see the Son of man coming
            in a cloud with power and great glory.

In our apocalypse "cloud" is singular[1] as in Luke, but it is
modified by "of heaven" as in Matthew. In 6:1 the cloud is
shining. For the clouds at the parousia see also Mt. 26:64
par., 1 Th. 4:17, Rev. 1:7, 14:14-16; cf. 10:1. The adjective "great" modifies power as in Mark; in Mt. and Lk. it
modifies "glory." <u>Ap. Pt.</u> differs from all the synoptics in
reading "in my glory" for "and glory." For the glory of the
Son of man cf. Lk. 9:26 where Luke adds "his glory" to "the
glory of his Father" found in the parallels Mt. 16:27, Mk.
8:38.

The last half of 6b, "while my cross goes before my
face," is very likely the sign of the Son of man which is
expected to appear in heaven, Mt. 24:30. This must be the
same cross which follows Jesus out of the sepulchre and
speaks in <u>Gospel of Peter</u> 10:39, 42. The mention of the
cross here in 1:6 and the crucifixion in 2:9 are the only

---

[1] ℓⲟϭ 'cloud' may be used collectively to mean
'clouds'.

signs of Jesus' death in the Apocalypse of Peter. Jesus'
death does not play an important role in this document.

The saying in 7a concerning the shining Jesus is paralleled in 6:1 by the shining, eternal cloud. In Rev. 21:
23-26 the heavenly city has no need for the sun because "the
glory of God is its light and its lamp is the lamb." See
also Rev. 10:1 where the mighty angel's face is like the
sun. In the New Testament Jesus shines in appearance stories
(Acts 9:3-5; 22:6-8; 26:13-15; Rev. 1:16) and at the transfiguration (Mk. 9:2-3, Mt. 17:2, Lk. 9:29-32).[1] The conception may have arisen from Isaiah 30:26 (LXX): και εσται το
φως της σεληνης ως το φως του ηλιου και το φως του ηλιου
εσται επταπλασιον εν τη ημερα οταν ιασηται κυριος το
συντριμμα του λαου αυτου και την οδυνην της πληγης σου
ιασεται "And the light of the moon will be like the light of
the sun and the light of the sun will be sevenfold in the
day when the Lord will restore the destruction of his people
and he will heal the pain of your wound."

The third saying, 7b, concerns in its first part the
angels which will accompany Jesus at the parousia. See 6:1.
Matthew has almost these exact words at 25:31: "When the Son
of man comes in his glory, and all his [v.l. holy] angels
with him. . . ." The angels also play a role in the Son of
man sayings connected with Peter's confession (Mk, 8:38 par.;

---

[1]The trajectories of luminous appearances are traced
by James M. Robinson, "Jesus: From Easter to Valentinus (or
to the Apostles' Creed)," Journal of Biblical Literature 101
(1982), esp. 7-17.

cf. Lk. 12:8-9). See 2 Th. 1:7; Mt. 13:41; Mk. 13:27 par.; Jn. 1:51; 1 Pt. 3:22; Rev. 3:5; 14:10.

The second part of the saying in 7b concerns the crowning of Jesus which is also described at 6:1-2. (See Heb. 2:9; Rev. 6:2; 14:14; 11:15-17; 19:6; 1 Cor. 15:25.) In the gospels Jesus is crowned during his passion (Mt. 27: 29; Mk. 15:17; Jn 19:2-5; cf. Gospel of Peter 3:7-8). The purpose of the coronation makes up the last section of the saying in 7b: that Jesus might judge the living and the dead. This is a common motif (Acts 10:42; 1 Pt. 4:5; 2 Tim. 4:1; cf. 1 Cor. 14:9) but not found in the gospels in exactly this form.

V. 8. This is in reality the theme of the Apocalypse of Peter (1:8; 6:3, 6; 13:3, 6). The punishments in chapters 7-12 are each made to fit the crime in accordance with such passages as Wis. 11:16: one is punished by the very things with which he sins. Originally this wisdom teaching (Ps. 62:12, Pr. 24:12, Ps. 28:4, Jer. 17:10, Ps. Sol. 17:10) meant that reward or punishment would be in proportion to the deed. It is found with that meaning throughout the New Testament (Heb. 2:2, 1 Cor. 4:5, Mt. 16:27, Rom. 2:6, 2 Tim. 4:14, Rev. 2:23, 20:12-13, 22:12; cf. 2 Th. 1:6, Jn. 5:29, 1 Cl. 34:3, 2 Cl. 11:6).

Chapter Two

In chapter two Jesus continues speaking as in chapter one and indeed he continues with another saying from the synoptic apocalypse. But this apocalypse form is overlain in this chapter by that of a parable and its interpretation, or, rather, the figure of the fig tree in the synoptic apocalypse is explained by that from Luke 13:6-9 and this combination is in turn given a further apocalyptic explanation.[1] This latter apocalyptic interpretation (2:7-13) uses some standard costuming from the apocalyptic wardrobe but it also for the most part tells of a specific historical event --the Bar Kochba rebellion of 132-135 CE. I will bring forward the evidence for this in my last chapter. But for now a short explanation should be given to facilitate the commentary on specific verses.

When an apocalyptic chronicle of coming events is part of an apocalypse, there is usually some reference to historical happenings described ex eventu. It is not always easy or even possible to untangle the costuming from the historical event itself. But in this instance I believe it is relatively simple. The clue is detectable in v. 8 where we find a sudden shift from the plural (numerous false christs) to the singular "his deed." The words "they will

---

[1]This reflects a two-level interpretation of scripture: Jesus speaks first a parable and then openly an interpretation. The resemblance to a three-level interpretation is superficial. It is not that one enigmatic saying of Jesus has been taught again as a parable and then yet a third time explained clearly, but that two originally separate parables have been associated and then this new combination has been interpreted. For a discussion of two-level interpretation and its relationship to the developing genres of gospel and dialogue of the resurrected Christ with his disciples (which latter is the genre of Apocalypse of Peter) see James M. Robinson, ibid., 20-37.

follow after them" still mean that some people will follow the false christs. But everything from then on to the end of the chapter indicates that the author had in mind one particular false christ. I understand the scenario as follows: Some Christians (probably Jewish Christians) will be impressed by what a messianic pretender has done and they will accept him as messiah or at least join his cause (v. 8). This will constitute a denial of Jesus as Christ (v. 9). But these same people will discover that he is only a messianic pretender and they will reject him, whereupon he will in turn persecute and kill some of them (v. 10). Then Enoch and Elijah will come and inform people that this is the end-time Deceiver who had to enter the world and lead people astray (v. 12). Therefore, these people will be counted as martyrs even though they had gone astray (v. 13).

In this apocalyptic prediction, I take the messianic pretender to be Bar Kochba and his evil deed to be some act which was part of his early success against the Romans. Early Christians joined his cause, which in the eyes of other early Christians was a denial of the messiahship of Jesus, and then later deserted the cause. Bar Kochba then persecuted them, most likely to convince them to join his rebellion again (as happens in guerilla warfare). Probably the coming of Enoch and Elijah was expected to be soon after this was written, and with them the apocalyptic costuming returns.

In chapter one the disciples have asked for the signs of Jesus' return and of the end of the world. Apparently the author has understood these as two separate questions. 1:4-8 deals with the signs of Jesus' return and will be especially helpful to distinguish it from the claims of the false christs. Chapter two answers the second question, that about the end of the world, with the parable of the fig tree. While this chapter also is concerned about false messiahs, it focuses especially on one such claimant from the House of Israel and upon the martyrs which will result from this historical occasion.

To put the contrast more sharply, the signs of Christ's return are his sudden appearance in glory with a heavenly army and with his cross, his brilliant emission of light, and his coronation preparing him for judgment. The signs of the end of the world are the 'sprouting' of Israel, the appearance of false christs including one in particular who succeeds at first in leading many Christians astray before they reject him, the martyrdom of many Christians, and the sending of Enoch and Elijah to teach.

V. 1. The parallels in the synoptic apocalypse (Mk. 13:28 par.) have "Then you will know that summer is near" for "Then will be the end of the world."

Vv. 2-4. The question-and-answer session continues. Peter's appeal for an explanation is like that of the request of the disciples in Mt. 13:36: Explain to us the parable of the weeds of the field. Even closer is Mt. 15:

15-16 where Peter says "Explain the parable to us." In this latter passage Jesus answers Peter, "Are you (pl.) also still without understanding?" This resembles Jesus' answer here in 2:4: Did you not know. . .? In Ap. Pt. this request for an explanation is followed by the parable of the unfruitful fig tree (Lk. 13:6-9) which is to be rooted up. In Matthew the request has just been preceded (Mt. 15:13) by Jesus' saying "Every plant which my heavenly Father has not planted will be rooted up."

Here for the first time in the apocalypse Peter is mentioned. He asks for this explanation only for himself: ኣተ 'to me' and Jesus addresses Peter in the singular. Is this intended to be a teaching known only to Peter until he writes this document for us? In P v. 4 Jesus answers 'me' and says to 'me'. But in T he answers 'us' and says to 'us'. I have retained the ኒ (singular) endings in the text because they agree with ኣተ in v. 2 and with the second person singular used in Jesus' answer. But it is not clear that this is original, for Peter also says in v. 3 ኒ ያአክ ዐCኒ '"we" have not known it' and earlier ወ ኣ ኽ ዩ ት ፡ ፍ ኽ ጓC 'where are we to learn it?'. The question of Peter reflects puzzlement in the early Christian communities at Jesus' mention of the fig tree in the synoptic apocalypse (Mt. 24:32).

The word ኣ ፵ 'elder, chief' in this context means teacher. It translates διδάσκαλος in the Ethiopic of Lk. 12: 13; 11:45; Mt. 12:38; 19:16. Teacher is a common address to Jesus in the gospels and he is often spoken of as the

teacher. This is, however, always on somebody's lips, never
as part of the narrative as here. Rabbi might also be a
good translation. Cf. Jn. 1:38; 20:16; Mt. 23:8.

Vv. 5-6. This parable of the fig tree is obviously
related to the one in Luke 13:6-9. This is of some help in
restoring the text of ከመ : ኢታፅንዕ : ለነ : ምድርነ. P has
(apparently inadvertently, as happens frequently in P)
omitted a letter. Grébaut restored a C, and his restoration is based on one textual tradition of the Ge'ez New
Testament which reads ከመ : ኢታዐcን : ምድረነ 'that it
might not make our land unproductive'. But T has ከመ : ኢ
ታፅንዕ : ለነ : ምድረ ነ 'that it might not make our land harsh
for us'. This reading of ኢታፅንዕ must be favored as the
more likely, since there almost certainly would have been
some tendency to make the reading conform to the scripture
but no reason to make it different if it had been ኢታዐcዐ.
P has ምድር in the nominative case, T in the accusative.
The accusative would be the easier reading and T has probably corrected an original nominative to an accusative. T
shows a tendency to correct grammar in that fashion. I
therefore favor ከመ : ኢታፅንዕ : ለነ : ምድርነ 'that our land
might not make (our life) harsh for us'. But at the suggestion of W. Leslau I have retained Grébaut's reading, ኢ ታ
ዐcዐ , in which case ምድር is better in the accusative
case.

ለእግዚኢብሔc: እንከ 'to God, a servant' is a difficult reading. Grébaut translates "(nous, tes) serviteurs"

'(we, your) servants' which is also favored by W. Leslau. I
have followed a suggestion of Duensing, emending ䷀䷀䷀ to
䷀䷀䷀ 'send'.[1] Then it becomes the first word of the
speech of the gardener,'Send (us)'. It is strange that the
owner is called "a man" in v. 5 and God in v. 6.

The chief differences between the account of this
parable in Luke 13:6-9 and here are 1) in Luke the fig tree
is in a vineyard, in Apoc. Pt. in a garden; 2) in Luke the
man has sought three years for fruit, in Apoc. Pt. he has
sought fruit for many years; 3) the Ethiopic mentions God
while Luke does not (but the Ethiopic text may be corrupt
here); 4) the vinedresser in Luke is ordered to cut down
(Mt. 3:10=Lk. 3:9; Mt. 7:15-20; cf. Jn. 15:6) the tree while
the gardener in Apoc. Pt. is ordered to uproot it (Mt. 13:29,
15:13; Lk. 17:6; Jude 12); 5) in Apoc. Pt. the parable ends
with "we will plant another in its place." No such words
are in Luke.

It is not clear how this fig tree material is related
to the other fig tree material in the New Testament: Mt.
21:18-22; Mk. 11:12-14, 20-25; Jn. 1:43-51. The fig tree
does have eschatological connotations, however, and is
closely connected with an anti-temple theology.[2]

---

[1]S. Grébaut, ibid., p. 209; H. Duensing, ibid., p. 67.

[2]William R. Telford, The Barren Temple and the
Withered Tree (Sheffield: JSOT Press, 1980), esp. 224-250.

V. 7. What is the House of Israel? (See also vv. 4, 11.) There is some agreement that in Luke the fig tree is Israel or the Jewish people.[1] And certainly here the House of Israel could mean the Jewish nation which had not born fruit. Another possibility is that the House of Israel is Jerusalem or the temple in Jerusalem. The word "house" could mean "temple" and was also used of the city of Jerusalem in apocalyptic imagery.[2] It is not always possible to distinguish whether the word means temple or Jerusalem or both. Since the Apocalypse of Peter shows no interest in Jerusalem but a great interest in the temple or tabernacle (16:7-9; cf. 15:1), I believe the choice is between the nation or the temple unless it can really mean both here (cf. 2 Sam. 7:5-17 where "house" is used both for the temple and for the dynasty of David). It is the nation which

---

[1]G. B. Caird, Saint Luke, The Pelican Gospel Commentaries (Baltimore: Penguin Books, 1963), 169-170; Frederick W. Danker, Jesus and the New Age According to St. Luke (St. Louis: Clayton, 1972), 156-158; I. Howard Marshall, The Gospel of Luke: A Commentary on the Greek Text, The New International Greek Testament Commentary (Grand Rapids: Eerdmans, 1978), 554-556; Telford, ibid., 226-7.

[2]See Mt. 23:37-39; En. 89:50; 90:27-36; Test. Levi 10: 5; 2 Bar. 4:2-7; Sib. Or. 5:414-433; Marcel Simon, "Retour du Christ et reconstruction du Temple dans la pensée chrétienne primitive," Aux sources de la tradition chrétienne: Mélanges offerts à M. Maurice Goguel à l'occasion de son soixiante-dixième anniversaire (Newchatel: Delachaux & Niestle, 1950), 247-257; Paul Volz, Die Eschatologie der jüdischen Gemeinde im neutestamentlichen Zeitalter (Hildesheim: Georg Olms, 1966; reprint of ed. of 1934), 373; Christopher Rowland, The Open Heaven (New York: Crossroad, 1982), 162-163; Otto Michel, οικος, TDNT 5, 119-159, esp. 121-129; Telford, ibid., 227-233 believes that in the pre-Lukan tradition of the parable the fig tree referred to the nation but that in Luke it means Jerusalem and its temple.

revolts under Bar Kochba, but in the explanation which describes the revolt (2:7-13) it is the sprouting fig tree (2:1, 3, 11) which is interpreted by the revolt, not the fig tree in the garden. What function does the parable of the fig tree in the garden have? The words "we will plant another in its place" may give us the answer. Before, during, or after the revolt the site of the temple which had been destroyed in CE 70 became the site of another temple built for the worship of Jupiter Capitolina. This latter temple could be the other planted in the place of the Jewish temple. There is another possible explanation. In the Apocalypse of Peter there is mentioned a tabernacle made without hands by the Father (16:9). It may be that our author was expecting this heavenly tabernacle to replace the Jewish temple (not literally on the same site). This means that in the sprouting fig tree saying the House of Israel is the nation Israel; in the parable of the fig tree in the garden it is the temple of Israel. The coming of false christs is found in Mt. 24:24 par., but see also 1 Jn. 2:18, Did. 16:3-4, 2 Pt. 2:1, Mt. 24:11, 7:15, Acts 13:6, Rev. 16: 3. Cf. Akmim Apoc. Pt. 1:1-2.

The reading ወ ሰ is difficult. Duensing[1] brands it 'sinnlos' and suggests በእ ማን 'truly'. He translates ወሰ: እ ብ አ ክ with 'Wahrlich, ich sage dir' and everyone since has followed suit. But the standard translation of 'truly I

---

[1] Hugo Duensing, ibid., p. 67.

say unto you' in Geʿez is እግን : እኔእክ , e.g., Mt. 5:26.
The Ethiopic verb is present tense, as in the Greek. I
believe this effort to conform the Ethiopic of our apocalypse to the gospels is unnecessary. በ can and often does
mean 'by means of'. With the third person singular suffix
ወበ is 'and by its means', that is, by means of the parable
Jesus is saying something about the end of the world (v. 7
with v. 1), the ደኃ 'the last time'.

V. 8. Is ይበልዎ singular or plural, given the ambiguity I have discussed in 1:3 above? ስብውደኅ is plural
and T most likely was influenced by that to interpret the
ambiguous text in front of him as plural. But in this same
sentence the quotation is in the singular and the singular
verb is regularly used of this false messiah in what follows. Therefore I have kept the singular in the text. The
description of the historical event begins here, then, and
is a specific application of the predicted 'false messiahs'
of v. 7.

But if ይበልዎ is singular and everything else agrees
with it in number (እኅ,እርበተበ,ዘሙሽኅኅ,እከP :ም
ጎገፈ), why does ይኅልዎሙ have a plural suffix rather
than a singular? The nearest possible plural antecedent is
the 'false christs' in v. 7. If we reverse our judgment
above and read ይበልዎ as a plural verb, then it does not
agree in number with እከP : ምጎገፈ. Moreover, ይኅልዎሙ
does not agree with the use of the singular in v. 10. I do
not believe these differences can be reconciled, and it is

not easy to see why an original $\mathcal{R} \mathcal{H} \mathcal{L} \mathcal{U}$ would have been
changed to $\mathcal{R} \mathcal{H} \mathcal{L} \mathcal{U} \sigma$. We must simply let the text stand
as it is.

There is yet another problem with $\mathcal{L} \mathcal{B} \mathcal{L} \sigma$. Its form
is passive, meaning 'he will hope for'. Yet clearly its
meaning must be active 'he will promise' in this context.
Perhaps the passive here means "they will be promised" with
the subject "the people" being understood.

"I am the Christ who has come into the world" can be
either a claim to be the one expected messiah or a claim to
be Jesus returned. Perhaps historically the claim of Bar
Kochba seemed to be the former to other Jews but the latter
to Jewish Christians. Then while Gentile Christians saw
that they were denying the 'first Christ' (v. 9) by joining
Bar Kochba, the Jewish Christians thought the fulfillment of
their hopes had arrived in Jesus' return. The warning in
1:4-6 also seems to be intended for those who might make a
mistake about Jesus' return rather than those who would
desert him for a new messiah.

"The Christ who has come into the world" has its
closest New Testament parallels in the Gospel of John: "I
believe that you are the Christ, the Son of God, he who is
coming into the world" (Jn. 11:27). Also Jn. 16:28. Cf.
Jn. 4:25-6, Jn. 12:13 par., 2 Jn. 7. Similarly the statement that the people followed the false christs, having seen
their (his) wicked deed (who would join a cause because of
its wickedness?) can be understood in the light of Jn. 3:19:

men loved darkness more than light, because their deeds were evil.

v. 9. ᑢᎤᎬ : ᏁᏁᎯᎿ : ᎻᎵᏒᎯ is difficult and is said by Duensing to be 'sicher falsch'.[1] He understands it to mean 'to whom our fathers gave praise'. It could also mean "who is called 'the Glory (or praise) of our fathers.'" (Cf. "God of our fathers," Acts 3:13.) The verb is imperfect, not perfect as Duensing translates. Since the reference is to Jesus, 'our fathers' must refer to the generation of the first Christians as seen from the perspective of the writer. It does not make sense put into the mouth of Jesus as it is here. Similarly, the following words "whom they crucified, the first Christ, and sinned exceedingly" are at least awkward in the mouth of Christ. We may conclude that either the writer forgot for a moment from what perspective he was writing or that some of this verse was added later. Perhaps all that was originally here was "and they denied the first Christ who was crucified."

V. 10. "This liar was not the Christ" should be understood in relationship to 1 Jn. 2:22 "Who is the liar but he who denies that Jesus is the Christ? This is the antichrist. . . ." and Jn. 8:44 "[the devil] is a liar and the father of [the liar]." He is a liar who claims to be the messiah because by that claim he denies that Jesus is the messiah.

---

[1]Hugo Duensing, ibid., p. 67.

ፕ ቴ ፞ 'was not' (in the perfect) may indicate that this whole historical incident is past. How do we know that he is not the messiah? Because he has been defeated.

ይ ቀ ተ ፞ 'he will kill' (P) is to be preferred to the reading of T ይ ቀ ተ ፞ ፞ 'they will kill him'. If they had killed him, he could not have martyred them (v. 11). Cf. Jn. 16:2-3.

Vv. 11-13. Here martyrdom is associated with the leaving of the fig tree. ባ ፞ ት ት 'only' seems intended to prevent the reader from interpreting the fig tree of something other than the House of Israel. Perhaps it means that the end of the world is not to be expected when other martyrdoms occur, but only those at the hands of this false christ.

The two teachers apparently arrive after the apostasy has taken place, even after the messiah has been rejected and has caused many martyrdoms. It is not clear how the 'signs and wonders' relate to the historical figure of Bar Kochba. But v. 13 reveals the real importance of this to the author. These deaths will not be discredited by the apostasy which has happened. These dead will still be counted as martyrs just as if they had never been unfaithful. Why? Because the deception is among those events that must occur before the End. Compare the early Christian hymn in 2 Tim. 2:11-13:

> If we have died with him, we shall also live with him;
> if we endure, we shall also reign with him;

if we deny him, he also will deny us;
if we are faithless, he remains faithful.

The two teachers are Enoch and Elijah (cf. 16:1). The two witnesses in Rev. 11:3-13 have the traits of Moses and Elijah. There were eschatological expectations associated with each of the three. "Deceiver" was also, like liar (v. 10), a title for the devil (Rev. 12:9) or for one who denies "the coming of Jesus Christ in the flesh" (2 Jn. 7). The term, like liar, is here applied to the false christ. Doing signs and wonders in order to deceive is part of the standard early Christian apocalyptic script for end-time villains. See Did. 16:3-4, 2 Th. 2:9-10, Mt. 24:24 par., Rev. 18:23, 13:13-14, 19:20.

Chapter Three

V. 1. Apparently Jesus' hand served somewhat like a television screen to show a picture of the events of the last day. Compare the Jesus of Rev. 1:16 who held seven stars in his right hand. See also Dt. 32:20 (LXX) "I will show what will happen to them in the last day," Jn. 4:25 "when [the Messiah] comes he will announce to us all things," and Jn. 16:13 "he [the Spirit of truth] will declare to you the things that are to come."

V. 2. Here are listed the events of the last day: 1) the righteous are separated from the wicked (cf. Mt. 25:32); 2) the upright of heart apparently receive some sort of reward (cf. Mt. 5:6); 3) the offenders are "rooted out."

This last may be destruction of some kind or maybe annihilation (cf. 2 Th. 1:9-10).

It remains mysterious why T leaves a gap at the end of v. 2. When he continues he begins with a superfluous ⲱHⲧⲟⲟ just as P has. Perhaps this is an indication that something has dropped out here, a continuation of this series of ⲱHⲧⲟⲟs.

V. 3. Sinners weeping in punishment at the end time is a common theme (Mt. 8:12; 13:42,50; 22:13; 24:51; 25:30; Lk. 13:28; cf. Lk. 6:21,25), but not the weeping of others.

V. 4. Peter's question introduces what is known to be a saying of the Lord concerning the punishment of sinners-- it would be better for them if they had not been born (here, created). Nowhere except here is this applied to all those in punishment. In Mk. 14:21 = Mt. 26:24 it is applied to Judas for his betrayal. In I Cl. 46:7-8 it is applied to those who "divide and tear asunder the members of Christ." Hermas Vis., 4, 2, 6 reads "Woe to those who hear these words and disobey; it were better for them not to have been born." Other variations include the saying about the millstone (Mk. 9:42 par.; cf. 1 Cl. 46:8), the saying in 2 Pt. 2:21 that it would have been better for those who have left the way of righteousness never to have known it, and Gospel of Peter 11:48 where the people who try to cover up the report of the resurrection say "For it is better for us to make ourselves guilty of the greatest sin before God than to fall into the hands of the people of the Jews and be stoned."

V. 5. In vv. 4-6 P has omitted letters five times and once put three different vowels on the same letter. P makes many such omissions and corrections, but I am at a loss to explain why there are so many in such a short text. One of the omissions deserves mention because T has also omitted this letter--the ⳑ (sign of negation) on +ⲇ ⳑⲤ (v. 5). The negative particle must be included for the sense of the passage. Besides, the saying including ⳑ+ⲇⳑⲤ is only a reworked form of Peter's question (v. 4) where the negative particle is present. The absence of the negative form in both manuscripts is an indication that it was missing in the common ancestor of P and T. The failure of either P or T to correct this obvious error and also their retention of Ⲱ Ⲏ ⳑ ⲟⲟ at the beginning of v. 3 indicate how slavishly the scribes copied what was before them.

The speech of Jesus which begins in v. 5 is very long and comes to an end only with the end of chapter 14. It begins with Jesus' rebuke of Peter much on the line of Mk. 8: 33 par., but see also our own Apoc. Pt. 16:8. Peter's question in v. 4 is taken by Jesus to be an affront to the mercy of God.

Vv. 6-7. Jesus gives two different answers to this question about God's mercy. First, in v. 6 he says that no one whom God has created could show more mercy towards God's creation than God himself. Therefore the challenge by a human being to God's mercy is inappropriate. In v. 6 ⳑⲙⳑ+: Ⲏ ⳑ ⳙ 'his formation' may be the predicate of ⳑⳑ .

In that case "his formation" would equal "you" (Peter). But it is a greater distance than normal from the verb. It could also be understood as attached to Ħ ̵ ̵ ̵ ̵ ̵ ̵ 'who has had mercy on them' in which case "his formation" would refer to the sinners which have just been seen in torment.

The second answer Jesus gives to Peter is in v. 7. Peter weeps for the sinners only because he has not taken into account what they have done. Jesus will show Peter (and the other disciples) their evil works. After that Peter should be approving rather than sympathizing.

6b, "For he created them and brought them forth where they had not been," is an expression of creatio ex nihilo of the type found in early Christian literature in Herm. Man. 1:1, 2 Cl. 1:8, cf. Rom. 4:17, 1 Cor. 1:28, Heb. 11:3.

Chapter Four

V. 1. In this chapter we have a graphic description of a very physical resurrection of the dead which should be compared to the "spiritual body" resurrection in 1 Cor. 15: 42-57 and 1 Th. 4:13-18. The closest parallel to the physical resurrection in Apoc. Pt. is in the Gospel of John 5: 28-29 (cf. Jn. 11:38-44; 6:40, 44, 54).

The present verse is an introduction for this chapter. Does the word "see" indicate that the vision in 3:1-3 continues in this chapter? Surely "them" must mean the sinners who have done wrong (3:7), but in what follows in chapter four we have a description of the general resurrection of the dead. This is indicated not only by the repetition of all (vv. 2-6) but also by the assurance to the believers and elect that they will also be raised (v. 12). This introduction should be compared to the one in 5:1 which specifically mentions sinners and which is appropriate for that chapter. The expression "day of God" refers to the day of judgment[1] (as in v. 2, 5:1; cf. Akhmim 1:2 "God will come").

V. 2. መዕአተ፡ የዓጎ is difficult. It must mean 'on' the day of punishment, and perhaps መ has replaced በ here somehow. Or perhaps we should take the entire phrase መዕአተ : የዓጎ : እንተ : ዘሰ : እንዘ እብሔር to be conjoined with the preceding verse, as James does, and translate "when the day of God and the day of the decision of the judgement of God cometh."[2] But the verb is in the singular, and the sentence remains awkward.

For the gathering of all people at the judgment see Mt. 25:32 and 13:30, 41-43. But "gather" is also used only of the elect (Mt. 24:31 par.). "East and west" is a comprehensive phrase indicating "everywhere" (cf. 1:6; Mt. 8:11, Lk. 7:29). For the Father "who lives forever" see Rev. 4: 9-10, 10:6.

V. 3. Gehenna = Hades, the realm of the dead. For Hades giving up its dead see Rev. 20:13.

---

[1]Gerhard Delling, "ημερα," TDNT 2, 947-953.

[2]M. R. James, The Apocryphal New Testament, ibid., p. 512.

ኵሎ፡ ዘሎቱ፡ ውስቴታ must mean more than 'everything in it' as it is usually translated. ውስቴታ certainly means 'in it' but also reveals that the author understood Gehenna to be feminine. ዘሎቱ, rather than a masculine repetition of the same thought as ውስቴታ, is better understood in its possessive sense 'what belongs to him'. Thus it is not Gehenna which gives back everything in it, but God who takes back everyone in it who is his. (Cf. Jn. 6:39.)

V. 4. Are these dead beasts and birds waiting in Gehenna precisely for this purpose? Or is the author thinking only of live animals? It is a difficult conception that the creatures will be able to give back what they have digested. In v. 5 the author must fall back on the premise that nothing is impossible for God. His concern is that all people without exception must appear for the judgment. For resurrection of the <u>flesh</u> see 2 Cl. 9:1, Herm. Sim. 7:1-4.

Vv. 5-6. The connection of the resurrection with the creative power of God is evident in the liturgical formula which Paul uses in Rom. 4:17: [God] who gives life to the dead and calls into existence the things that do not exist.[1] That nothing was impossible for God was a common theme (Mt. 19:26 par., Lk. 1:37, 1 Cl. 17:2), as was creation by the word (Ps. 33:9, 148:5; Rom. 4:17, 2 Pt. 6:5-7, 1 Cl. 17:4).

---

[1]Ernst Käsemann, "The Faith of Abraham in Romans 4," <u>Perspectives on Paul</u> (Philadelphia: Fortress, 90-95); <u>Commentary on Romans</u> (Grand Rapids: Eerdmans, 1980), 121-124.

These themes became connected with the resurrection probably under the principle that the last shall be like the first: thus [like the command at the beginning] it will be in the last days (v. 6; cf. the famous words in Barn. 6:13: the Lord says "See, I make the last things as the first.").

ዠአ:ከመ:ዚኩ 'all is as his' must mean 'everything is his' as it is usually understood. But why ከመ before ዚኩ? It is unlikely the author intended 'as if it were his'. Perhaps this was originally ከመ 'even, also' and the text read 'even everything is his,' but ከመ has no manuscript support. Therefore ከመ should be retained.

Because the verb in ከመ:ይፈጥር is imperfect I believe it means 'in the way he does his creating'. Then ዓለም:ወኵሎ:ዘውስቴታ must be the object of አዘዘ, 'he commanded the world and everything in it (to be)'.

Vv. 7-9. The scripture quotation is based on Ezekiel 37:1-14. There God speaks to Ezekiel, calling him son of man and ordering him to prophesy upon the bones (37:1-6). In accordance with what God has told him, Ezekiel prophesies and the bones receive their body parts (37:7-8) but do not live. Finally he is told to prophesy to the spirit (or wind). When he does this the bodies live (37:9-10). The two stages of the resurrection in this Ezekiel passage are reflected here in the Apocalypse of Peter, where the Angel Uriel is in charge of giving life to the dead bodies. Uriel ("Fire of God") is a prominent angel in 1 Enoch (20:1; 21: 5, 9; 27:2, 33:3-4; cf. 2 Esd. 4:1 and Rev. 14:18) where he

is in charge of punishments, etc., in material obviously related to the Apocalypse of Peter. "Son of man" here does
not seem to go beyond the meaning "human being."

This is clearly intended to be a quotation of scripture. As it is introduced, Grébaut has emended ✝ᛃᑎᑭ 'he
prophesied' to ✝ᛃᑎᛃ 'prophesy' (imperative) and has
translated ᗯ✝ᒐᎮ 'and you said to it' as if it were an
imperfect rather than a perfect.[1] According to this understanding, the quotation begins with ᗯᗩᒪ. This is in accord with Ezekiel 37:4 "Prophesy to these bones and say to
them." But the peculiar punctuation marks in T after ᛃᗝ
ᎧᎮ✝ and ᛃᎰᒿ ᛃᎰᛰᏟ probably indicate the extent
of the quotation, at least as it was understood in the tradition of T. How far back this understanding goes is uncertain, but these marks occur only here in T. Perhaps the
quotation was not taken directly from Ezekiel but from an
apocryphal work based on Ezekiel, a work wherein Uriel the
Angel was in charge of the resurrection. Supporting this is
the second person singular perfect ᗯ✝ᒐᎮ 'and you said to
it'. For it is not easy to see how this error could have
occurred unless it was no error but part of the quotation.

ᗯᛃᎦᎰ :ᗯᗰᛃᗰᎰ (v. 9) could be a continuation of
the list of body parts in v. 8, but then there is no object
for the verb ᛃᑌᎰ. They are more likely intended to be
the object of that verb. The return of life is a separate

---

[1]Sylvain Grébaut, ibid., pp. 201, 210.

action here, just as in Ezekiel 37 Ezekiel must prophesy twice, once to bring together the bones, etc., and once to bring life to the restored corpses.

ᎯᏛᎵᎻᏖᏬ ᏔᏉ᎑ᏚᏴ is another awkward expression. It must be 'over his resurrection of the dead' where ᏔᏉᎻᏖᏖ is in construct in spite of the suffix Ꮗ, which latter probably refers to God.

Vv. 10-13. The illustration of the seed sown in the earth is used by Paul in 1 Cor. 15:36-44 (cf. Jer. 31:27-30; 1 Cl. 14:4-5), but the closest parallel is in Jn. 12:24: unless a grain of wheat falls into the earth and dies, it remains alone; but if it dies, it bears much fruit. In both Apoc. Pt. and John the seed "bears fruit." To the illustration of the seed is added the argument that if God does so much for seed surely he will do even more for his believers and the elect. It was for the elect that God made the earth (cf. 2 Esd. 7:10-11 where the world was created for Israel's sake). And finally, the dead human body put into the ground is said to be only given to the earth as a pledge (v. 11), and the earth will be held accountable for it on the day of judgment (v. 13). Compare the judgment of heaven with the judgment of heavenly things, Ig. Sm. 6:1.

In v. 12 ᏛᎾᏟ 'earth' must be understood as the object of the verb ᏔᏁᏝ 'he made'. It is the earth which was made for the sake of believers and God's elect.

ᏅᏖ 'in it' in v. 13 must have its referent in ᏬᏁᏖ 'day'.

Chapter Five

V. 1. This verse is an introduction to chapters five through twelve. It closely resembles 4:1, but this time we are not disappointed but are actually told what will happen to the sinners on judgment day. Two classes of transgressor are mentioned here--the heretics (those who have perverted the faith) and the offenders against morals (those who have committed sin). Cf. 2 Th. 1:8 "Those who do not know God and those who do not obey the gospel."

The conflagration of the universe depicted in this chapter is based in large part on Isaiah 13:6-13. 2 Pt. 3: 5-7, 10-13 is the only place in the New Testament where the dissolution of the world by fire is expressed (cf. Rev. 20: 9). But in 2 Peter the first creation was through water in order to have it ready, it seems, to be destroyed by fire. Cf. Heb. 10:27, Rom. 2:5, Acts 2:19-20 (Jl. 2:30-31), 2 Th. 2:7-8, Heb. 12:29, James 5:3, Rev. 16:8-9, 17:16, 18:8. This devouring fire is a fire which gathers and should be distinguished from the river of fire which is a test of one's works (6:2) and the fire which punishes (chs. 7-12). It should also be distinguished from a cleansing fire, which does not appear in the Apocalypse of Peter. (But see 14:1 where the baptism in the Acherusian Lake may be a cleansing fire, though it is not described that way there.)

Vv. 2-3. The fire which gathers the sinners before the seat of judgment is consistently described in terms of flowing water, but having flames. For "cataracts of fire"

cf. "columns of fire," 1 En. 18:11, 21:7, 90:24. The "opening up" of the cataracts indicates that the fire was conceived to be kept in the heavenly storehouses. This fire
does not give light but brings darkness (cf. Mt. 8:12).
Compare the darkness over the whole land at Jesus' death
(Mk. 15:33 par.). Among the things which have been changed
into fire or burned the earth is not mentioned.

Vv. 4-5. The calamities in vv. 4-5 are brought about
by the "bitter" fire which apparently reaches the sky from
the earth. This "fire which does not go out" is the unquenchable fire with which we are familiar from the New
Testament (Mt. 3:12; Mk. 9:43, 48; Lk. 3:17; cf. Is. 24:66,
and "eternal fire" in Mt. 18:8, Jude 7). There seems to be
a problem with the text when the firmaments of heaven are
said to lack water. I believe the problem lies with the
translation from Greek. If the translator had the Greek
word αυχμηρος before him he probably knew only its more
usual meaning "dry." Therefore he translated "in lack of
water." But in some instances it had come to mean "dark"
as in 2 Pt. 1:19 and Akhmim 6:21. In the context of vv. 4-
5 we may conclude that the original Apocalypse of Peter read
"The firmaments of heaven became dark." Compare the "going"
and "becoming like what were not created" with Rev. 20:11
"From his presence earth and sky fled away, and no place was
found for them." For the demise of the heavenly powers cf.
Mt. 24:29 par.

The stars, the firmaments, and the lightnings are dissolved by the bitter fire. Originally the heaven itself may have been dissolved. As Duensing already noted[1] ዐኅያየዳ፡ : መᓂᲪቅተ : ሰዏዩ 'the lightnings of heaven will go out of existence' is possibly corrupt for 'the heaven will become lightnings'. Continuing in this vein, ዐᲪᲪቅቦተሙ 'and their exorcism' may be corrupt for መᓂᲪቅተሙ 'their lightnings (or flashes)'. With these changes we would have 'The heaven will turn into lightnings and their flashes will frighten the world'. This would be very appropriate following the disappearance of the firmaments.

It is probably in relation to vv. 4-5 that we are to think of the quote from the <u>Apocalypse of Peter</u> in Macarius Magnes 4.7, "Moreover, he also asserts a saying full of impiety, 'And every power of heaven will melt and the heaven will be rolled up like a book and all the stars will fall like the leaves from the grapevine and like the leaves from the fig tree.'"[2] This is an exact quotation from LXX of Isaiah 34:4, and it may be that the heathen writer who Macarius is quoting had this passage from Isaiah in his text, though it is not in ours. If so, it may not have been original to the Greek <u>Apocalypse of Peter</u>, but added later to give scriptural support to the document.

---

[1] Hugo Duensing, ibid., p. 69.

[2] See the Greek text in Erich Klostermann, ibid., p. 13.

V. 6. What is the መንፈሰ፡ በድን 'spirit of the corpse'? Are all the spirits of the dead sinners changed into fire after release from Gehenna? Would this fiery spirit, trapped in the resuscitated body, burn and cause pain? Or is this a deterioration of the bodies? With this the dissolution has reached its climax. "Then all creation has been dissolved." The verb is perfect, but the adverb እምዝ carries a future sense. We can understand "Then all creation will have been dissolved." For the melting of heaven and earth, see 2 Cl. 16:3.

Vv. 7-9. People are being chased by the fire. The chase is described in an abbreviated form, but probably nothing is missing from the Ethiopic text. The fire always finds them and drives them out of hiding.

V. 8 contains a large dittograph which can be translated "And it will bring them to judgment and wrath in the river of fire which never goes out." This dittograph can be explained by the two occurrences of ኀበ ይመፅእ in the text. Some scribe, having written everything through the second ኀበ ይመፅእ , brought his eyes back to the first one and went on from there. In the course of transmission the "judgment of wrath" became "judgment and wrath, or vice versa, and ወያመጽኦሙ was changed to the imperfect, the latter in T's tradition only.

The result of this fiery roundup is given in v. 9. The sinners, herded into the river of fire, gnash their teeth in the boiling flames. This would seem like their

punishment. But in this context, it is only a means of
bringing unwilling participants to the judgment which does
not actually take place until 6:2. In comparison with the
heat of hell, this is just the warmup. We are to understand
that the sinners are not yet actually in the river of fire
but are brought up to its edge and behold its seething. For
gnashing of teeth see Mt. 8:12; 13:42, 50; 22:13; 24:51;
25:30; Lk. 13:28; but unlike the usage in the gospels, here
it is used without accompanying "weeping" (κλαυθμος).

Chapter Six

V. 1. Compare "all of them will see" with "every eye
will see him," Rev. 1:6. For the clouds and the angels see
the notes at 1:6b-7. The Ethiopic manuscripts read "The
angels of God who are with me will sit upon the throne of
my glory. . . ."[1] Since we would expect Jesus, however, and
not the angels to sit on the throne, and since it is Jesus
who is crowned in v. 2, for whom the throne is present, I
believe the Ethiopic text may have originally read ይኅንፉ
'they placed'. This very same mistake has been made at 1:7.
For the placing of thrones see Dn. 7:9; with "the
throne of my glory" compare "the throne of his glory"
in Mt. 19:28, 25:31; and for the throne at the right
hand of God see Pol. 2:1, but this is part of the common

I do not believe that Apoc. Pt. 6:1-2 has any connection with Lk. 12:8-9 where the angels may have the function
of judgment. See Willi Marxsen, The Beginnings of Christology (Philadelphia: Fortress, 1979), 45.

conception of Jesus sitting or standing at God's right hand
(Mt. 26:64, Acts 7:55, Heb. 8:1, and often).

V. 2. The judgment follows a coronation as in 1:7-8.
Each "nation" is judged by itself, apparently, for each
weeps alone (cf. Mt. 24:30, 25:32; Rev. 1:7). It appears as
if individuals enter the river of fire only in these same
groups. Yet, according to the chapters which follow, this
is a very individualistic judgment. For a fire which tests,
as the river of fire here may do, see 1 Cor. 3:13-15. But
if this river is for testing, do any pass the test? See
v. 4.

V. 3. The numbers in the text are found in P but not
in T. They are written in the left margin before the line
in which they belong and a space is left for them in the
line. See the discussion of numbers in these manuscripts in
the introduction to manuscripts. Since the tendency would
be to eliminate them, especially since they are really
superfluous in these instances, I judge them to be original
to the Ethiopic.

The works of the sinners are almost hypostatized and
are able to stand before the sinners as evidence of their
guilt. See Ps. 51:3, 44:15. See also 1:8, etc.

V. 4. The elect are also those who have done good
deeds. Their fate is somewhat obscured by problems in the
text. It is certain that they will come to Jesus, ሰዐደኩ:
ኅበቦየ 'they will come to me'. But what are the words which
follow this? Duensing calls these words "unübersetzbar" and

omits the rest of this verse from his translation.[1] Grébaut
has "ils viendront vers moi, alors qu'aucun d'eux ne verra
la mort, ni le feu déverant."[2]   (They will come to me when
none of them will see death, nor the devouring fire.) But
there is nothing in the Ethiopic corresponding to "nor" and
the translation like the original does not make sense.
Weinel has followed Grébaut.[3] Finally, James translates
"they shall come unto me and not see death by the devouring
fire,"[4] and the edition in Hennecke-Schneemelcher based on
Duensing follows James here.[5]

The first problem is that እንዘ 'while' is here followed by a noun ሞት 'death'. It belongs with a verb or
adjective, but there are no adjectives and the nearest verb
is ያሰኅፎሙ 'he/it will see them' which is determined by
እልቦ:ህ 'no one/nothing'. I believe the problem is easily
alleviated. ሞት after እንዘ should be ሞቱ 'they have
died', a simple scribal error, and this should be taken with
the previous phrase so that we have 'they will come to me
when they have died'. The elect will go directly to Jesus
at death. See Jn. 5:24: he does not come into judgment but
has passed from death to life.

[1]Hugo Duensing, ibid., p. 69.

[2]Sylvain Grébaut, ibid., p. 211.

[3]Heinrich Weinel, ibid., p. 320.

[4]M. R. James, ibid., p. 514.

[5]Ch. Maurer, ibid., 672.

A second problem is the subject of 𝒴𝒵𝓀𝛤𝜎 'he/it will see them'. If we understand fire as subject rather than object (it is not in the accusative case), then we can read 'the devouring fire will see none of them'. The point is an important one. It is only the sinners (5:1) who are driven to the judgment in the first place. The elect are already with Jesus, supposedly in heaven.

V. 5. The 𝜎𝟫𝟫𝜙𝜏 : 𝑓𝑎𝜎𝜏 'abysses of darkness' must be underground caves or pits of some sort, patterned no doubt on Tartarus. See 2 Pt. 2:17, Jd. 7, and "outer darkness" in Mt. 8:12, 22:13, 25:30. The "darkness which does not go out" follows the pattern of the light which does not go out, but here means that light never enters these chambers. For fire as punishment see Mt. 3:10-12 par., 5:22, 7:19, 13:36-43, 18:7-9 par, 25:41; Jn. 15:6; Jm. 5:3; Jude 7; Rev. 8:7-8, 9:17-18, 14:10-18, 16:8, 17:6, 18:8, 19:20, 20:9-10, 20:14-15, 21:8.

V. 6. As in v. 3, the sins seems to have an existence of their own. Here they are brought by the angels to be used as a model for making a place of punishment that is appropriate to the offense. This principle is very important--the punishment of each one must correspond in kind to his vice.

Vv. 7-9. For the angel Uriel, see the notes at 4:7-9. The judgment for people does not begin until 7:1. The "spirits of those sinners destroyed in the flood" is a reference to the spirits of the dead giants born to the

Watchers and women, as in Enoch 15-16. Punished along with
them are those spirits which are falsely worshipped as gods
and which inhabit idols, etc., leading people into all sorts
of idolatry. The fire from the burning idols serves as a
fit punishment for them.

ϛϕ⊂ 'love' in v. 7 can only mean 'object of love'
but a more precise explanation is not available. The word
ⲙⲟⲇ 'imitation' may refer to painted pictures, but these
terms are general and we cannot be precise about them.

The burning of the idols and of the spirits means that
they "have come to an end," but this is not the end of their
torment. They are still punished forever. This principle,
that the divine punishment does not destroy so thoroughly
that it cannot continue forever, is also found throughout
the punishments in chapters 7-12.

Chapter Seven

Chapters 7-12 relate the punishments of the wicked in
"hell." This is the most notorious section of the Apocalypse of Peter, and it makes such an impression on the
reader that often the rest of the writing is forgotten. The
vivid descriptions of the punishments are primitive and in
poor taste. But this should not keep us from analyzing them
as best we can. I have prepared a table in which I outline
these chapters. (See below.) This is not easy to do because in some places the text is corrupt, and it is not
always clear when we are moving from one punishment or place

to another. I believe there are more punishments than
places because related punishments are described together
as in the same place. There seems to be some organization
in grouping crimes of the same kind together, but this is
not consistent. The author has made no attempt to clarify
these things for us. There does not appear to be a direct
relationship to the ten commandments.

This series of descriptions of other-world punishments
is often called an inferno, and this term will do so long as
we remember that there is no descent beneath the surface in
the Apocalypse of Peter and that there is no interest in the
geography of this inferno but only concern with the punishments themselves.

This inferno is a series of descriptions of specific
punishments which are representative for their class. A
murderer is depicted receiving the sort of punishment that
all murderers will receive. The function then is that of
moral teaching or admonishment. It is parenetic in nature
and as such is related to the New Testament catalogues of
vices (Gal. 5:19-21; 1 Cor. 6:9-11; 2 Cor. 12:20; Rom. 13:
13; 1 Pt. 4:3) and even to the Haustafeln (Col. 3:18-4:1;
Eph. 5:22-6:9; 1 Pt. 2:13-3:7; Did. 4; cf. Apoc. Pt. 11).
The moral teaching of the Apocalypse of Peter is concentrated in this inferno. It is the inferno which more or
less serves the same function in this apocalypse as the
earthly life of Jesus serves in gospel literature.

The Places of Punishment

Place	Punishment No.	Type	Passage	Crime	Commandment
I a place	1	hanging by tongue, tongues torn to pieces	7:1-2	blaspheming the way of righteousness	3(?): taking name in vain
II a place,			7:3-11		
a pit	2	fire	7:3-4	denying righteousness	
	3	women: hanging by hair; men: hanging by thighs, burning	7:5-8	adultery	7: no adultery
	4	fire, poisonous animals, worm, their victims watch, they must admit God's justice	7:9-11	murder	6: no killing
III a pit			8:1-10		
	5	swallowed in discharge, pain, lightning from the aborted drills the eyes	8:1-4	abortion	

The Places of Punishment--Continued

Place	Punishment No. Type	Passage	Crime	Commandment
	6 nakedness, children witness against them, rotting milk, flesh-eating animals, stench	8:5-10	exposing children	6: no killing
IV Gehenna= place of darkness		9:1-4		
	7 darkness, whipping, worm eats bowels	9:1-2	persecuting and betraying the righteous	6(?): no killing
	8 chewing tongues, pain, burning eyes out	9:3	blaspheming and betraying the righteous	3(?): taking name in vain
	9 lips cut off, fire in mouth and bowels	9:4	using lies to put martyrs to death	9: no false witness
V a place	10 dressed in rags and tatters, impalement on a pillar of fire, pain	9:5-7	faith in wealth, neglecting widows and orphaned families	

The Places of Punishment--Continued

Place	Punishment No.	Type	Passage	Crime	Commandment
VI a place of excrement			10:1-4		
	11	stand in excrement up to knees	10:1	usury	8(?): no stealing
	12	throw themselves from a cliff again and again with demons chasing them	10:2-4	sodomy, homosexual practices	
VII a place of fire			10:5-7		
	13	beating themselves with chains of iron	10:5-6	idol making (cf. 10:2)	2: no images
	14	burning in heat	10:7	abandoning the commandment of God and following demons	1: no other gods
VIII a very high place			11:1-9		

The Places of Punishment--Continued

Place	Punishment No.	Type	Passage	Crime	Commandment
	15	rolling up and down a burning mountain? fear?	11:1-3	neglected parents (?)	5: obey parents
	16	children and virgins watch, pain, hanging up, wounds from meat-eating birds	11:4-5	did not believe crime, disobey parents, left the ancestral teaching, disobey elders	5: obey parents
	17	dressed in dark clothing, flesh torn apart, watched	11:6-7	loss of virginity	
	18	chew tongues without rest, eternal fire	11:8-9	disobedience by slaves	
IX(?)	19	blind and deaf, white clothing, push one another onto coals of fire	12:1-3	hypocrisy in giving?	
X a river of fire, a pit? all the punishments by fire?	20	hanging in a wheel of fire, burning up	12:4-7	wizardry and witchcraft	1(?): no other gods

At 7:2 we begin to have parallels with the Akhmim Fragment. We will compare our Ethiopic text to the Akhmim when it is helpful.

V. 1.   After the punishment of the spirits, human beings receive their punishment. The description which begins here continues through chapter twelve. ይ ረ ፀ ⶖ ሙ in this verse has often been translated 'prepared for them', but 'proper for them' is the correct meaning.

The Akhmim Fragment has nothing like this, but it has an introduction of its own: "And I also saw another place opposite that one. And it was a place of torment. And those being tormented there and the tormenting angels had their clothes dark, being dressed according to the air of the place" (6:21).

V. 2.   The particular places of punishment begin here. The first punishment is introduced abruptly. ይ ⶃ ⶄ C ፀ ⶖ : ⶆ ⶖ ፦ H ⶇ ይ ⶆ Ⴠ ⶇ 'they will shatter them for them which does not perish/go out' is emended by Duensing to read ይ ⶇ ⶈ ⶉ ፀ ⶖ : ⶆ ⶖ ፦ ⶇ ⶊ ⶋ : H ⶇ ይ ⶆ Ⴠ ⶇ 'they will spread out for them fire which does not go out'.[1] H ⶇ ይ ⶆ Ⴠ ⶇ is often used with fire in this writing. And 'to spread out fire' would agree with the Akhmim text which mentions at this point "fire flaming and tormenting them." But the value of the latter in restoring the Ethiopic text is doubtful. Moreover, these changes make the remainder of v. 2

---

[1]Hugo Duensing, ibid., p. 70.

completely incomprehensible. I believe the verse should be translated in accord with the Ethiopic. The tongues are 'shattered', but they are not destroyed, the relative pronoun ሕ having its antecedent in ልሳን 'tongue'. The reason the tongues are not destroyed is so that they can be seized again, taking the causative of ሰውም in its basic stem meaning. ይቀብርሙ 'they will shatter them' could also be ይኅብርሙ 'they will watch them'[1] but the following ሎሙ would make this senseless.

Akhmim reads: "And some there were hung up by the tongue. And these were those blaspheming the way of righteousness. And fire was placed underneath them, burning and punishing them" (7:22).

Vv. 3-4. After the blasphemers come 'those who denied righteousness'. It probably means unbelievers, both those who refuse to accept the faith and those who leave it. The exact nature of their punishment is uncertain. We would expect ምሉእ 'full of' to have an object but none is given.

Akhmim has: "And there was a certain lake, large, full of burning mud in which were some men who had turned away from righteousness. And torturing angels were urgent upon them" (8:23). The offense is the same as in the Ethiopic and both have angels. The Akhmim has "lake" where Ethiopic has "pit," but they both agree that it is "full." Cf. 2 Pt. 2:21; Lk. 12:9; Acts 3:13-14; 2 Tim. 2:12-13; Rev. 2:13,

---

[1]Sylvain Grébaut, ibid., p. 211.

3:8, 19:20, 20:14. The only lake in the Ethiopic text is the Acherusian Lake in 14:1, except that, in the Ethiopic text as we have it, Acherusia is a field!

Vv. 5-8. For these adulterers Akhmim reads: "And there were also others: women having been hung by the braids over that boiling mud. These (f.) are they who adorned themselves for adultery. And those (m.) who had united with them for the defilement of adultery were hung by the feet and had their heads in the mud. And with a loud voice they said "We did not believe that we would come into this place."

This corresponds tolerably well with the Ethiopic, though of course the mud which was earlier introduced in Akhmim is missing in the latter. The Ethiopic is more specific about why the women are hung by the hair--because they wove braids to seduce the men (cf. 1 Pt. 3:3). The men, on the other hand, are hung by the feet (Akhmim) or the thighs (Ethiopic). Since both were used as euphemisms for "penis" I suspect that is what the author intended.

In 8:5, 9:3, 9:4, 10:2, 10:7, 11:8 we have the formula "other men and women." Here in 7:5 the Ethiopic manuscripts read "two women." This appears to me to be an inner Ethiopic corruption. I have therefore restored ካልእት 'other' to the text where PT have ክልኤት 'two'. Akhmim supports this.

Vv. 9-11. The Akhmim reads: "And I saw the murderers and their accomplices cast into a compressed place full of poisonous snakes. And they were being struck by those

animals and thus writhing there in that punishment, and
there were laid upon them worms like dark clouds. And as
the souls of the murdered stand and gaze at the punishment
of those murderers they said, 'O God, your judgment is righteous'" (10:25). This is again fairly close to the Ethiopic.

The murderers are bitten by poisonous snakes, made to
feel pain as their victims have felt pain. They will then
have to tell the victims, who are watching, how just their
punishment is. The worms may be just compensation for the
worms which the victims have experienced in the grave.

The last part of v. 10 beginning with ወርእ ዩ ፆሙ and
the first word in v. 11 are usually taken together and
translated 'and they shall see the torment <of those who>
killed <them>'.[1] But this necessitates the addition of
'those who'[2] and it means that the victims speak in v. 11,
whereas surely it is the punished who must say this, as in
other passages. The verb ርእ ዩ ፆሙ is in the perfect,
which is unusual in this forecast from the mouth of Jesus
and is a problem in any case. The Ethiopic seems most understandable if we mentally supply a verb "receive" between
ርእ ዩ ፆሙ and ዸ ዩ ፆሙ and then leave ቀተልዎሙ 'they
killed them' as the start of a new sentence. Then we have
'and they saw them (get) their punishment. They killed
them, and they will say to them together', etc.

---

[1]Ch. Maurer, ibid., p. 673.

[2]As Hugo Duensing does, ibid., p. 70.

For the pain cf. Ps. 38:17 "my pain is ever with me."
Is Ezrael the angel Sariel of 1 En. 20:7? Otherwise we know
nothing of him. For justice and righteousness as attributes
of God's judgment, see Ps. 19:9, 1QS 1, 19; Rev. 16:7, 19:2.

Chapter Eight

Here punishments are meted out to those who abort
their children (vv. 1-4) and to those who expose their
children (vv. 5-10). The first group includes only women,
the second men also. There may have been some confusion
between these two groups with readers among the church
fathers, for both Clement of Alexandria and Methodius of
Olympus have the aborted children rather than the exposed
children given to the guardian angel.[1] But they may have
understood the conclusion of this section (v. 10) to apply
to both groups of children.

Vv. 1-2. ⵯⵏⵜⵜ 'in it' almost certainly goes with
ⵯⵔⵯⵑⵟ 'and it flows' and not with the previous clause.
Perhaps the ⵯ translates the enclitic particle δε and is
in this position for that reason. I have understood ⵑⵏ
(found also at 10:1) to be a corrupt form of the more common noun ⵑⵏ (also written ⵑⵯⵑ). ⵑⵏ is any bodily
discharge such as excrement, menstruation, or a runny

---

[1]The Greek texts of the quotations in Clement and
Methodius with translations and the Akhmim text with a
translation are included in the introductory chapter above
under Clement and Methodius. There also a comparison of
the Ethiopic and Akhmim of this section is found.

abscess. In the context of this punishment it must refer to
the aborted fetus and related matter.

The women are buried up to their necks in this flow,
and it apparently causes them great pain. From what does
the pain come? Perhaps the stream is hot. The evil is that
they were undoing what God had done. This is one of the
earliest anti-abortion statements in Christian literature.[1]
The verb in ". . . which he had formed" is from the same
root as "[God's] formation" in 3:6.

V. 3. ዖኅበቍ can mean either they sit or they
dwell. It is usually translated 'sit', but I do not believe
this is only a place for them to sit. They live there. It
is a home taking the place of the home of which they were
deprived. Are these children also given to the angel in
v. 10?

ኽአ፡ከኗኽ𝘝ኅ ፡ ሕያሙ 'who withheld life' is a con-
jectural emendation. P has ኽኗ፡ከኗኮ𝘝ኅ 'but two of
them' while T has ኽኗ፡ከኗኽ𝘝ኅ 'who (were) two of them'.
This makes no sense in this context, and it is easy to see
how the word ከኗኽ𝘝ኅ 'they withheld from them' could have
been corrupted. This corruption probably took place in connection with ከኗኽተ/ከኗኽተ in 7:5. After a corruption
took place in one or the other of these passages and introduced the number two, the other was changed to conform to

[1]For a discussion of abortion in early Christianity,
including the Apoc. Pt., see Michael J. Gorman, Abortion and
the Early Church (New York: Paulist Pr., 1982), 49-53.

this. Duensing already noted the connection.[1] The connection between these passages was easily made because of the
reference to adultery in both (7:6-7 and 8:4). We cannot
say which change took place first.

V. 4. There is apparently in the mind of the author a
connection between light and life. The aborted children
were never allowed to see light, therefore it is the eyes of
the women through which the women are punished. This equa-
tion of life with light is seen again in v. 7.

መቅጋሕት must derive from መድቀሕ by transposition
of letters. The meaning 'drill/borer' is clear. በዝኅት :
ዝሙት 'with this adultery' perhaps does not refer to real
adultery but rather to the insertion of something into the
vagina to cause an abortion. It does not seem that this
punishment was only for abortions of children conceived in
adultery, although Methodius of Olympus may already have
understood it that way.[2] The editors of the Akhmim text
have restored αγαμως 'without being married' in the lacuna
at the end of this section. This has been done because of

---

[1]Hugo Duensing, ibid., p. 70, notes 4 and 8.

[2]See the text under Methodius in chapter one. Abortions were frequently performed in antiquity by inserting
some sharp instrument into the womb, but I can find no specific instance where this is called adultery. See Werner A.
Krenkel, Erotica I. Der Abortus in der Antike., Wissenschaftliche Zeitschrift der Universität Rostock 20 (1971)
443-452; and Sheila K. Dickinson, "Abortion in Antiquity,"
Arethusa 6 (1973), 159-166. Since abortion was often understood as contraception, see also Keith Hopkins, "Contraception in the Roman Empire," Comparative Studies in Society
and History 8 (1965), 124-151.

the reference to adultery in Clement, but is probably incorrect. On the photographic plate in von Gebhard's edition
the top of a θ can clearly be seen where a γ would have to
be if αγαμως were the reading.

Vv. 5-7. The nakedness of the men and women is fitting as part of the punishment for those who exposed infants. Textually speaking, several problems are present in
these verses. መስዐ-ዝ in v. 5 is a hapax legomenon in
Ethiopic literature, but there can be no doubt about its
meaning. It derives from ስዐዝ 'to please, delight, be
pleasing to' and it means 'delight'. But the word immediately following it ወገዐር (v. 6) is difficult. Duensing
began the usual practice of leaving it untranslated.[1]
Grébaut seems to have thought መስዐ-ዝ to be in parallel
with ገዐር 'cries', and so he translated it 'cris'.[2] "And
calling out, [and] they groan and call out to God" is still
awkward, but the entire text is understandable.

The reading ወሞቱ 'and they died' in both manuscripts
cannot be correct. The idea expressed is not that the
parents died because they violated God's law, but that they
caused their children to die and in doing so violated God's
commandment. ሞቱ 'they died' originally read አሞቱ 'they
caused to die'. Cf. ቀተሉ:ወሰ ደቆሙ 'they killed their
children', v. 9.

---

[1] Hugo Duensing, ibid., p. 70, note 13.

[2] Sylvain Grébaut, ibid., p. 212.

In v. 7 ሰቀልነ፡ኪያነ means 'they hung us up' or 'they
crucified us'. We do not know more exactly what this means,
but it may refer to some particular custom involved with
exposing babies, such as tying them to a tree or stake.[1]

The plea which the babies make to God must end with
ወሀብከ 'and you gave'; what follows is involved in the
further description of the parents' punishment. The position
of the ወ may again reflect the postpositive particle δε,
for surely ለኩሉ 'for all' must be the object of ወሀብከ.
Thus the last four words in v. 7 can be translated 'they
begrudged (us) light, but you gave (it) to everyone'.

Vv. 8-9. The flow of milk from the breasts is the
problem nursing women have when children are withdrawn, but
amplified to fit this situation. The children should be
receiving the milk. ወያቤሕንዎሙ is the reading of both
manuscripts and means 'they make them stink'. W. Leslau has
suggested we read ወያልይንዎሙ with Grébaut.

Were the husbands originally included in this punishment or not? ምስለ : ኅምታቲሆን 'with their husbands' is
present in P but not in T. The expression 'other men and
women' (v. 5) is the one commonly used to introduce these
punishments. If it was used here just because it was the
pattern of introduction, 'with their husbands' could have

---

[1]A. Cameron, "The Exposure of Children and Greek
Ethics," Classical Review 46 (1932), 105-114, traces the
changing customs and attitudes concerning child exposure
from the early Greeks through Orphic eschatology into Christian times. The condemnation of child exposure seems to be
closely tied with the sort of eschatology expressed in the

been added to make the punishment in v. 9 fit the introduction in v. 5. The punishment does seem to apply well only
to women. But exposure is a crime of which either sex or
more likely both together could be guilty. When in 8:1-4
the punishment is intended only for women, only women appear
in the introductory formula (8:1). Moreover, in those
verses (8:1-4) the suffixes referring to the punished are
consistently feminine, whereas here they are just as consistently masculine, indicating that both sexes are intended.
For these reasons I conclude that ⵯⵏⵉ : ⵃⵯⵜⵜ ⵓⵊ was
original and that it was later omitted by one strand of the
manuscript tradition. This happened probably because it was
thought that the punishment was not appropriate for men.

V. 10. ⵜⵯⵉⵔⵏ is understood to be an angel's
name. It is a transliteration of τημελουχος 'care-taking'.
"This adjective τημελουχος," says James, "occurs nowhere
else in Greek literature." And he thinks that it is "an un-
mistakable sign of the presence of pseudo-Peter" at some
point of ancestry whenever it later appears.[1] By pseudo-
Peter James means the Apocalypse of Peter itself. For
intercessory angels for "little ones" see Mt. 18:10.

Apocalypse of Peter. The normal method of exposure at least
in some periods of time was to put the newborn into clay
pots which were also used for those children who had died a
natural death.

[1]M. R. James, "The Recovery of the Apocalypse of
Peter," Church Quarterly Review 80 (1915):33.

⊾ φℓ 'he has required' is a reading preferable to 𝓎⊿Ꝓℓ 'he will require' because 𝓎 is missing in both manuscripts. But the reading is far from certain. A 𝓎 inadvertently omitted in their common ancestor would explain why P has the incomprehensible mix ⊿Ꝓℓ. T has a tendency to correct and may have changed ⊿Ꝓℓ to ⊿φℓ. In addition, it might be said that the future 'God will require it' (at the final judgment) is more in keeping with the style of this text than is the past 'God has required it' (determined from the beginning).

Chapter Nine

Vv. 1-2. The persecutors and betrayers are treated like those who have been persecuted and betrayed. The suffix on 𝓂𝓸Ⴕ 'his wrath' probably has its referent in God (8:10).

What can 𝟩𝒴𝟦𝒮 : Ⴖ𝓸ℓ 'human hell' be? If only this one 'place' is hell, what are all the others? But perhaps there is an important distinction intended here. Since this is a different 'place' from that in chapter eight and we do not move to another 'place' until 9:5, vv. 1-4 contain three different categories of offenders who seem consigned together in Gehenna because they act unjustly against Christians. A more severe punishment might seem appropriate for them. They are the persecutors and betrayers of Jesus' righteous ones (vv. 1-2), the blasphemers and

betrayers of Jesus' righteousness (v. 3), and those who used
lies to put the martyrs to death (v. 4).

The furious spirit whips these men and women 'with
every whipping', that is, they are whipped with every kind
of whipping suffered by those they persecuted. If አዘኘ in
PT is correct, this may mean 'for every whipping', that is,
for every whipping the persecuted received. It is not clear
how the devouring worm is an appropriate punishment (cf.
7:10). Even though በ is lacking in both P and T, there is
no doubt that it must be restored to ምንኣለቦሙ as Duensing
also saw.[1]

V. 3. Here we meet the blasphemers again (cf. 7:2).
But these people have not only blasphemed, they have also
been መያናያነ ፡ ኣቦደቀቀ 'betrayers of my righteousness.'
A መይጢ is one who changes his mind, vacillates, or is
fickle. The root is ሜጢ 'to turn away, divert; to turn;
to convert, transform'. The usual translation 'doubter'
does not carry strongly enough the intention of the author.
መያናያነ ፡ ኣቦደቀቀ probably should be translated 'those
who turn away from my righteousness' or even 'those who turn
against my righteousness'. It refers to those people who
become Christians and then abandon the faith or even join in
opposing it. Their blasphemy is punished with perpetual
gnawing of their own tongue, and their eyes are burnt out
probably because they were unable to see the true way.

V. 4. Those who witness falsely and by their testimony

---

[1] Hugo Duensing, ibid., p. 71.

cause the death of Christians have their lips cut off for
their false testimony and then have fire put into their
mouths and intestines to suffer what their victims have
suffered. Cf. 2:10-13.

The ለ on ከልኽን is to be taken with the መ on
ምግባፈተሆሙ to indicate 'as for the others . . . their
deeds . . .' etc. ተዐጋል 'fraud' is a word usually
associated with robbery. ሕሰት 'lie' must be understood
to mean 'with a lie', and perhaps originally was ሰሐት.

The Akhmim Fragment varies some in details. It reads
"And other men and women were burning up to half of them and
they were thrown into a dark place and whipped by evil
spirits and were having their bowels eaten by worms which
never tired. These were those who had persecuted the righteous ones and betrayed them.

"And near those again (were) women and men biting
through their lips and being punished and receiving burning
iron in their eyes. And these are they who blasphemed and
spoke evil of the way of righteousness.

"And opposite these, others again, men and women
(were) biting through their tongues and having flaming fire
in the mouth. These were false witnesses" (12:27-14:29).

It should be said that usually (9:1) in translating
both the Greek and the Ethiopic the words "half of their
bodies" or something similar is used for lack of a better
expression, but neither the Greek nor the Ethiopic has any
word here for body. It is the souls also which are being

punished. There is no appearance of the angel Ezrael (cf.
7:10) in the Akhmim. While I believe the Ethiopic has these
three punishments separated from the other punishments and
calls their place "the Gehenna of men," there is no such
place in Akhmim and these punishments are treated like any
other. In the Ethiopic these crimes are related to Jesus
who is speaking and who uses the word "my," as in the betrayers of <u>my</u> righteous ones, the betrayers of <u>my</u> righteousness. In other words, the Ethiopic tradition views these
three as offenses specifically against Christians, while the
Akhmim tradition sees them more generally, as it sees all
the others.

Vv. 5-7. አኀአ : ቀርቡ 'to those who had approached'
is probably an intrusion. In any case it makes no sense in
this context for there is no one mentioned who can be approaching. The stake set in stone would be familiar to the
ancients as the instrument for impaling. The rags and tatters are proper punishment for the rich, and the sword
piercing the lower body may have been thought fitting for
lack of compassion. The rich ought to have been more gener-
ous with their money, not necessarily with their knowledge
of God, so we may conclude that ኀበአ : አግዚአብሔር 'concerning God' is an intrusion. Yet we do find in Lk. 12:21
the expression "rich toward God." Cf. Pr. 11:28; James 1:
27.

The expression "women with orphans" is not abnormal
for that time period. A child was considered an orphan upon

the death of his father. Both parents need not have died.
Among documents found in the Cave of Letters near the Dead
Sea are personal and legal papers of a woman follower of
Bar Kochba whose name was Babata. Some of these fascinating
documents concern Babata's son Yeshua who is often called
"Orphan Yeshua son of Yeshua" even though Babata was still
alive and had even remarried. See Yigael Yadin, Bar Kochba
(Jerusalem: Weidenfeld and Nicolson, 1972), 233-253.

The account varies considerably in Akhmim 15:30, "And
in a certain other place were fiery hot stones sharper than
swords and any skewer. And women and men dressed in dirty
rags were rolling themselves upon them, being punished. And
these were the rich and those trusting in their riches and
not showing mercy to the orphans and widows, but neglecting
the commandment of God."

The punishment of rolling on fiery sharp stones does
not seem related to the crime of trusting in wealth, unless
perhaps it may have something to do with the gems which the
wealthy might own. For rolling, see the Ethiopic text at
11:2 and 12:5.

Riches were a big problem for the early Christians.
See 1 Tim. 6:6-10; Lk. 12:15-21; 16:19-31; 6:24; Mt. 19:23-
30 par., James 5:1-6 (where moth-eaten clothes are mentioned), Mt. 13:22 par. For the phrase "those who trust in
riches," see the ancient addition to Mk. 10:24 and 1 En.
94:8. Also see the usurers in Ethiopic Apoc. Pt. 10:1.

Chapter Ten

V. 1. The punishment for usury seems lighter than that of other crimes. The excrement was probably thought to be appropriate for those who participated in such filthy business. For the word ብጎ see the discussion in the notes at 8:1.

The Akhmim (16:31) reads, "And in another great lake full of pus and blood and boiling mud stood men and women up to (their) knees. And these were the moneylenders and those demanding compound interest." Here again we see the preference in Akhmim for lakes (Akhmim 8:23, 11:26; cf. Eth. 7:2, 8:1).

Vv. 2-4. If this punishment takes place in the same place as the previous one, then it is into the excrement that the offenders dive to escape the demons.

The words now found at the end of v. 2 ክጎ: ክሙንተ: ሰሞዕፏኝ 'these are idol worshippers' are without doubt intrusive, for they interrupt the description of the punishment and form a doublet for v. 4 where we are told who these really are. They are also lacking in the Akhmim text (see translation below). There are two places where these words might actually belong. First, they might have been in v. 5 in place of or near the unknown word ሐበ. In that case the idols would be burned beneath their worshippers. Secondly, these words may have followed the word ክፏኝኝተ 'demons' in v. 7 rather than here. In that case, having been omitted, they may have been inserted after the wrong occurrence of ክ፤ሃሃ፞ት in the text. Neither of these explanations is without its problems, but punishment of the idol worshippers would be appropriate with the burning of the idols, the punishment of the idol makers, and the punishment of those in some way associated with demons found in vv. 5-7.

The word now standing in the text as ሀአ፞ሃ 'existence' is quite uncertain. The manuscripts read ሕአ፞ሃ 'mind' (see 16:8), but 'they drive them to the end of (their) mind' is not very good (but cf. Rom. 1:26-28). 'They drive them to the end of existence' is not much better, but at least conveys the idea that physically they had nowhere else to go but off the cliff. This seems to be the intention of the author, for I doubt that he had in mind some sort of insanity. The association of these sexual acts with mental illness is probably anachronistic in this text.

ይ፞ሰ፞ት፞ቈ : ሠ፤ሀፆ 'they cut their flesh' is uncertain in meaning. Weinel, realizing that it did not mean 'they were circumcised', thought it might refer to self-mutilation and was therefore an intrusion from sometime after Origin.[1] But it seems more likely that it was synonymous with the following words ሕፇርፆክ : ፈክስ with which they are in apposition. This latter phrase is not 'apostles of a man' as it has usually been translated but 'sodomites'.[2] In v.4,

---

[1]Heinrich Weinel, ibid., p. 317.

[2]Sylvain Grébaut, Supplement au Lexicon Linguae Aethiopicae de August Dillmann (1865) et Edition du Lexique de Juste d'Urbin (1850-1855), (Paris: Imprimerie Nationale, 1942), p. 56

then, sodomy of both heterosexual and homosexual types is condemned in contrast to the Akhmim text where it is homosexuality of both sexes which is condemned.

The Akhmim text reads, "Other men and women who had thrown themselves down from a large cliff came down and again were driven by those pressing upon them to go up on the cliff and they were thrown down from there, and they had no rest from this punishment. And these were those who had defiled their own bodies, behaving like women. And the women with them were those who had slept with one another as if man with woman" (17:32).

As I have already mentioned, in Akhmim the crime seems to be homosexuality, both male and female, while in the Ethiopic the crime is sodomy, both heterosexual and homosexual. The reference to idol worshippers is not found here. Finally, "they had no rest from their punishment" in Akhmim appears in Ethiopic as "And this like this they do continually. They are punished forever." (See the comparison on Manuscript B, the Akhmim, and the Ethiopic of 10:6-7 in Chapter Two under Manuscript B.)

Vv. 5-6. Here we meet again the burning of idols and images which we first saw in chapter six. But there it was associated with the punishment of the demons who had inhabited them. Here human beings are punished--those who made the idols and, if my conjecture concerning ኸአ:ኸሞነተ: ሞታ ዐየኸ in v. 2 is correct, those who worship the idols.

The word 𝑛𝑏𝑎, if it is a word and not an abbreviation, is unknown. We find it again in 11:1 where it is
conjoined with another unknown word. No one has offered any
clue to its meaning. Grébaut's translation 'brasier (?)'[1]
has nothing to commend it and it does not fit the context.
Perhaps 𝑛𝑏𝑎 is only an indication by a later scribe that
something is wrong with the text in these places. As for
the restoration of the name 𝑜𝐻𝑑𝑘𝑎, this is more likely
than that another angel name 𝐻𝑑𝑘𝑎 is freshly introduced
here (cf. 7:10, 9:1, 11:4, 12:3). But why has neither P nor
T restored it? Perhaps they hesitated to restore even the
obvious in a text which is in places so corrupt. 𝑛𝐻𝑡 is
probably not a mistake for the adjective 𝑛𝐻𝑡 'much, many'
but is the adverb 'frequently, often' and indicates the
repetition of the punishment.

The corresponding Greek of Akhmim is found in 18
-19:33. It reads, "And beside that cliff there was a place
full of the greatest fire. And there stood men who with
their own hands made images for themselves in place of God.
And beside those, other men and women having rods of fire.
And they were beating one another and never resting from such
punishment. . . ."

In v. 5 (Ethiopic) there is found a list of animal
shapes into which idols were made. Cf. Rom. 1:22-3. This
is lacking in the Akhmim. For a comparison of v. 6 with the

---

[1]Sylvain Grébaut, "Litterature Ethiopienne pseudo-
clémentine," ibid., p. 213.

Akhmim and Manuscript B, see Chapter Two under Manuscript B.

V. 7. Neither manuscript has a word divider in ዐ
+ኣመ⁻ፈ፬ት , but we can make sense of መ+ኣዑ 'and they
followed'. ፈ፬ት is another matter. It is not in construct with ኽ፯ኽኽት as most of the translations imply.
Neither is ፈ፬ት nor ኽ፯ኽኽት in the accusative case,
though the importance of this is blunted by the fact that
many objects of verbs are not accusative in this document.
Thus ፈ፬ት is most likely an adjective modifying 'demons'
or a noun in apposition with it. No satisfactory explanation has been found, but I have translated ፈ፬ት as if it
were an adjective of the pattern q̄atel[1] derived by transposition of letters from ፬ፈት 'hardness, severity'. In this
interpretation 'harsh demons' is the object of the verb
'followed'. The subject of that verb is 'those who have
abandoned the commandment of God'. In another possible interpretation, ፈ፬ት:ኽ፯ኽኽት may be related to a more
common expression ፯ኽኽ : ፬ትC 'demon of midday' which
appears several times in the Ethiopic scriptures.[2] Such
demons were considered to be hot or burning demons. In this
passage 'burning demons' would be the subject of the verb,
so that 'burning demons followed (them)' would be a possible
translation. The demons here, then, would not be those who

---

[1]Thomas O. Lambdin, Introduction to Classical Ethiopic
(Ge'ez) (Missoula, MT: Scholars Pr., 1978), 68.

[2]August Dillmann, Lexicon Linguae Aethiopicae, ibid.,
col. 1177.

originally led people astray but those who were carrying out
the punishments, similar to the demons in v. 2. However,
with all of this said, it is best to conclude that we do not
know what 𝟺 𝟽 𝟷 means. For a comparison of v. 7 with the
Akhmim and Manuscript B see Chapter Two under Manuscript B.
The text of the Akhmim Fragment ends at this point.

Chapter Eleven

This chapter deals with those who have been negligent
in their duties to their superiors. Vv. 1-3 concern men
and women who neglect their parents. Vv. 4-5 concern children who are disobedient, while vv. 6-7 treat the specific
violation of loss of virginity. In v. 8 those slaves are
punished who will not execute their masters' orders. These
three categories belong together, and the punishments seem
to occur in the same 'place', even though the punishment of
the first class takes place on a height which does not appear in the others.

Vv. 1-3. These verses are among the most corrupt in
this document. V. 1 is especially problematic, for not
only are the words 𝕊𝕍ℂ and 𝕓𝕒 unknown but the remainder of the verse does not make sense. V. 2 is better grammatically, but we have still a mysterious 'terror' which is
at the bottom of the slope apparently, and some kind of
mysterious "what has been made" which flows. We can glean
from this fragmentary remnant (1) that the punishment took
place on a high elevation; (2) that fire was involved; (3)

that there was some 'edge' or 'end' over which the fire poured or flamed; and (4) that people try to climb up in order to escape something at the bottom but slide back down again. What is happening here? Grébaut saw here a furnace and a brazier with fire coming from their ends,[1] but I cannot see how this fits the context. M. R. James says this about verses 1-2: "This suggests a narrow bridge over a stream of fire which they keep trying to cross."[2] He must have in mind the famous bridge of the Zoroastrians which everyone must cross at the judgment.

A more happy suggestion has been made by William H. Brownlee.[3] He believes that $7 \Lambda C$ 'preparation' is an inner Ethiopic corruption for $\text{\textit{L}} \Lambda C$ 'mountain' and that the whole image is that of a volcano, a mountain which 'flows'. This explains all the data except the 'terror' at the bottom of the mountain. The word $\angle 9 \text{\textit{L}}$ which is translated 'trembling' normally refers to the emotion of fear. Yet here it might also be related to the earthquake which so often accompanies a volcanic eruption. Is the rolling presumed to take place in the hot magma as it flows down the slope?

$\text{\textit{f}} \text{\textit{V}} C$ has the form of an infinitive and could mean 'to teach'. But that makes no sense in this context. Its

---

[1] Sylvain Grébaut, ibid., p. 213.

[2] M. R. James, The Apocryphal New Testament, ibid., p. 517.

[3] In a private conversation with the author.

meaning is completely unknown. ሔል has been discussed above in connection with 10:5.

Against whom is this punishment directed? It is for those who dishonor their parents, but the offenders are men and women, not children as in vv. 4-7. These adults have 'abstained from' or 'withdrawn from' their parents. The word ተዐገሠ is unusual in this sense and is more normally used of those things from which one abstains, for example during a fast or when conforming to monastic rules. Here it means that these adults would not take care of their parents in their old age. በርእሶሙ 'by themselves' signifies free will, that is, 'on their own inclination' and is a release clause for those who are unable to care for their parents.

Just how the punishment on the mountain fits the crime is uncertain.

Vv. 4-5. The text here is much more clear. The children and the virgins who are brought in to watch this punishment must be those who have been good. Vv. 6-7 are tied together with these verses by their presence here and by the fact that they are still watching in v. 7.

በሰቀል 'with hanging up' is not a separate punishment but what is done to expose these children to the birds. እለ፡የአምኑ፡በጌጋዮሙ 'those who have faith in their sin' alludes to the confidence which children have, that they know better than their parents. Three ways are listed in which the children have disobeyed: (1) they do not obey

their own parents; (2) they do not conform to the traditions
which they are taught; and (3) they do not show respect for
other adults. Cf. 1 Tim. 5:3-8. The pains which the birds
inflict upon the children reflect the pains parents feel
when their children are disobedient.

Vv. 6-7. Here we have the 'virgins' who did not keep
their virginity. Both manuscripts have the number 10 before
the word ᎓Ꮝ7ᕲ. Surely by this number 10 a superficial
connnection with the Parable of the Ten Virgins (Mt. 25:
1-13) is intended. How did these virgins become connected
with the ten virgins? It is not easy to say, but it must
certainly not have been in the original Greek Apocalypse of
Peter. This connection may have been present already in the
Greek text which was translated into Geez. We cannot be
certain. But in a Latin tradition of the fourth century at
least, the Apocalypse of Peter was connected to the Parable
of the Ten Virgins by the image of the river of fire. In a
sermon found in a manuscript at Epinal the following is
written: "The closed door is the river of fire by which the
ungodly will be kept out of the kingdom of God, as it is
written in Daniel and by Peter in his Apocalypse."[1] The
river of fire appears in 5:8; 6:1; and in the section immediately following this one, 12:4. While this does not show,

---

[1]English translation from Ch. Maurer, ibid., p. 678,
note 1. The complete Latin text of the sermon is in André
Wilmart, "Un anonyme ancien de X Virginibus," Bulletin
d'ancienne litterature et archéologie chrétienne I (1910):
35-49, 88-102. See the short discussion by M. R. James in
"A New Text of the Apocalypse of Peter," ibid., p. 383.

of course, that any connection between the Parable of the
Ten Virgins and the virgins here in the Apocalypse of Peter
was present in a Greek text, it does illustrate the ease
with which that connection could be made, even if all ten
virgins are here punished.

The loss of virginity is a special case of disobedi-
ence to parents. Our author thought that wearing dark
clothing and having their bodies torn to pieces would be
appropriate for these young women.

Vv. 8-9. Disobedient slaves are not overlooked. They
chew their tongues, a punishment we have met before in connection with blasphemers (9:3). The punishment implies that
the slaves were sassy. The punishment with fire is not precisely described and its propriety is not evident. ሐጸ፞ጸ፞ም
'eternal' does not refer to the quality of the fire but its
duration and is synonymous with 'forever'.

Chapter Twelve

Vv. 1-3. Though no new 'place' is mentioned here, we
assume a change of scene. The people believe they are just
but they are not, because justice is not attained with a
simple kind deed. The depth of this perception places this
punishment in a different class from those which have preceded it. For this is no violation of a specific law, nor
even a call for mercy, but a demand that justice be established. The white clothing (cf. the dark clothing of those
who had lost their virginity, 11:6) suggests the

righteousness which the people thought they had, while their
blindness and lack of speech and hearing illustrates their
failure to sense justice or to speak out for it. Compare
Peter's blindness and deafness in 16:8.

ዩተጋፉ ዐ ፡ ቦቦይ ፍተ ሀ ሶ 'they push one another' may
refer to the rush of such people to do charity. We have met
the coals of fire previously in 5:3 where water becomes live
coals. ሥ ሰ ዋ ተ 'kind deed' is the usual term for alms
giving. Because these people are unable to comprehend that
they have done any wrong, they are taken from the fire and
their sentence is pronounced just.

Vv. 4-7. These verses form a conclusion to the section on punishments which began in 6:7 (or, for human
beings, in 7:1). It seems to combine punishments inflicted
on every sinner with those suffered by a particular category
of sinner, the magicians. This combination causes some ambiguity, but the section is well written and not fragmentary
or corrupt. I interpret the text in the following way:
first, a river of fire rises like a flood and washes all the
punished out into the center of the river; then a wheel of
fire begins rolling, and inside this wheel are male and
female magicians, so that the whirling of the wheel is their
punishment; finally, this wheel rolls from pit to pit (the
pits separating the classes of sinners have not been destroyed by the flood) and burns up those in each one, though
I do not think that by this latter development we are to
assume that their punishments are in any way to cease.

ሐበፀበ 'the one in the pit' (v. 6) must go with
ያወዐፕ 'they are burned up'. The singular is to be understood in a general sense, 'whoever is in a pit will be
burned up'. ባእ ሰተ 'by fire' (v. 7) may mean that the
wheel goes to every pit in which there is fire or that it
puts fire into every pit.

Chapter Thirteen

Those who have been punished and those who have been
saved from punishment are brought together in this chapter
in bold contrast. The righteous are wearing their heavenly
bodies (clothing) and watch the sinners first plead for
mercy and then, being punished even more severely, confess
that they are receiving their just desserts. Here is the
answer to the puzzle posed in chapter three. How is such
great torment possible from a merciful God? Even the
punished themselves in their agony know and proclaim that
this is as it should be. It is an oblique answer: Is God
merciful? Yes, but he is also just. And what more can be
said when we are caught on the horns of that dilemma? But
the author of the EC Apocalypse of Peter did indeed have
more to say, though it is lacking in our Ethiopic translation. That will be discussed with chapter fourteen below.

It should be noticed that these same chapters (3-13)
with their theme that each person will be recompensed
according to his work (see also 1:8) form a certain interpretation of the wisdom saying in Psalm 61:12-13 (LXX):

απαξ ελαλησεν ο θεος, δυο ταυτα ηκουσα, οτι το ηρατος
του θεου, και σοι, κυριε, το ελεος, οτι συ αποδωσεις
εκαστω κατα τα εργα αυτου 'God has spoken once, twice I
have heard these things, that the power is God's; and
yours, O Lord, is the mercy, for you will reward each
person according to his deeds.'[1] In this short passage not
only is the dilemma of God's mercy and power presented, but
there is a suggestion of an eschatological solution, though
the latter was not originally intended.[2]

Vv. 1-2. Are two groups of saved in mind here, the
elect and those who are perfect in righteousness? More
likely the second defines the first, that is, the elect
are those who are perfect in every righteousness.

The manuscripts have እነ H: ይብሉ 'while they say'
as if ክዕሰ : ሕይወት: ሕገሰት 'the clothing of celestial
life' were the words of the angels or of the righteous. In
this case we should need to add a verb such as 'Receive'
or, as Grébaut does,[3] 'Let us put on'. This saying would
then correspond to those of the punished, which follow.

---

[1]The Ethiopic transposes 'power' and 'mercy' in the
psalm thus: ምዕረ:ሰበበ:እንዘእበልሕር: ወኀንተ : ከመ:ሰግ
ዕኩ:: እበመ:ሕእንዘእበበሕር:ሣሀሰ::ወሕእክ ክ:እንዘፍ : ሀ
ይሰ:: እበመ:እነተ:ተፈድይ:እስተ:በከመ:ምግባሬ::

[2]Cf. Rom. 2:6; Mt. 16:27; Rev. 20:12-13; Pr. 24:12;
Sir. 35:22 (LXX).

[3]Sylvain Grébaut, ibid., p. 214.

However, as Duensing has already noted, there is an inner
Ethiopic corruption here.[1] He suggests that we read ይ
ተለብሱ 'they were dressed' for ይበሱ. More likely the
text read ይለብሱ 'they put on' (active rather than passive). If ሱ was inadvertently omitted, the remains ይለ ብ
were converted to ይበሱ , influenced by the fact that the
punished speak shortly hereafter. I have therefore restored ይለብሱ to the text.

What is this 'clothing of celestial life'? It could
be a new spiritual body given in place of or in addition to
the physical body which has been resuscitated. Such a body
is frequently called clothing, e.g., 1 Cor. 15:53-54;
2 Cor. 5:4; Asc. Is 8-11. If the description of Moses and
Elijah from chapter fifteen can be admitted as evidence, it
may also have included some sort of heavenly 'clothing'
worn over the heavenly body and even suitable bodily orna-
mentation.

Under the influence of Ps. 53:9 and 58:11 (LXX) the
obvious scribal error ዐደከደዎ in P was taken by everyone
to be ዐደኸዎ '(the one who) hated it/him' and the singular
suffix was usually interpreted as plural '(those who) hated
them'. While the singular relative pronoun is often used
for the plural, the singular suffix is seldom so used.
Meanwhile, T clearly has the correct reading በኸደዎ '(who)
cursed it/him'. This must refer to those who were

---

[1] Hugo Duensing, ibid., p. 72.

contemptuous of <u>eternal life</u>, not those who hated or reviled
<u>the righteous</u>. Here we see a new reading in the making.
The scribe P made an error and omitted ሽ in ፀሽ ፈ ፐ but
immediately realized his mistake and corrected it by simply
continuing with the correct letters (P almost never erases).
Modern scholars erroneously corrected this to ፀ ፈ ሽ ፐ by
harmonizing it with the scriptures.

The elect and righteous (cf. 1 En. 60: 8) look on
those who spurned eternal life 'while he takes vengeance on
them'. Who is taking this vengeance? A subject for the
verb is not supplied and no suitable antecedent is at hand.
We must assume an angel or perhaps even God himself. It
could go back so far as 12:5 where the angel Uriel is involved with the punishment of wizards and witches.

V. 3. This short verse simply serves to remind us
that the punishment is not over yet. It will last forever.

Vv. 4-6. From these verses it is clear that no
amount of pleading on the part of sinners in torment will
have any effect after they have been condemned. The plea
only brings punishment more harsh. Cf. 2 Cl. 8:3.

Grébaut's suggested reading ሽ ሽ ሞ ር ሽ 'we learned'
for ሽ ሽ ሞ ር (not a correct form) in P or ሽ ሽ ሞ ረ 'he
learned' in T is almost certainly correct. Lacking ሽ in
the ancestor of both, T corrected ር to ረ which at least
made a word, though that word in context made no sense.

The parallel verb ኢኸጦኅ shows us what has dropped out here.

The sinners learn now the punishment of God about which they were skeptical when they were told previously. When were they told previously about this? It must refer to the preaching activity directed at non-apocalyptic people. It is a κηρυγμα which includes knowledge of God's punishments upon sinners following the judgment. Cf. 7:8 where the adulterers claim not to have known ahead of time about their coming punishment.

The angel Tatirokos is the angel in charge of Tartarus. The verb ይቤሎሙ 'he said to them' is perfect in form, but it is governed by the two previous imperfects. ኢተረፈ ፡ ሕይወት 'there is no more life' means that death is the boundary line for repentance. Whatever kind of existence these sinners now have it is not life. This is in stark contrast to the reward of the elect and righteous which is an elevated, celestial life.

For the tormented admitting the justice of God, see 7:11, Ps. 19:9, Rev. 16:7, 19:2; cf. Jn. 5:30; 1 En. 63:8.

Chapter Fourteen

This chapter is the most corrupt portion of the Ethiopic text, at least to our knowledge. But we are very fortunate to have most of it preserved for us in a Greek text, the Rainer fragment described above in the section on manuscripts. This Greek text allows us to reconstruct the

Ethiopic text in many places where it is corrupt. That is what I have done. But each restoration must be justified, particularly since some restorations are more certain than others. Because a detailed comparison must be made between the Greek text and the text of the Ethiopic manuscript tradition, I have presented these texts with accompanying translations in Supplement I. Some progress has already been made in such a comparison by James in the article from which the Greek text was taken, and by Prümm.[1] But I believe that neither has seen through the corruption of the Ethiopic text to recognize the extent to which the texts actually correspond.

The following Greek words have nothing obvious in Ethiopic corresponding to them: εκ της κολασεως; και δωσω αυτοις καλον; μετα των αγιων μου; εγω και οι εκλεκτοι μου; των πατριαρχων; ιδου; παντα. These Ethiopic words have no such correspondence in the Greek: ሰገዩ ; ይእዜ (or ማዕዜ); ኢበውኢ፡ኢሐሣብ ; ዘለዓለም (its second occurrence).

However, the following listing shows the obvious textual agreements, using the order of the Greek:

---

[1]K. Prümm, "De genuino apocalypsio Petri textu examen testium iam notorum et novi fragmenti Raineriani," Biblica 10 (1929): 62-80.

Supplement I

A. The text of the Rainer fragment:[1]

<παρ>εξομαι τοις κλητοις μου και εκλεκτοις μου ον εαν αιτησωνται* με
εκ της κολασεως και δωσω αυτοις καλον βαπτισμα εν σωτηρια αχερουσιας
λιμνης ην καλουσιν εν τω ηλυσιω πεδιω μερος δικαιοσυνης μετα των
αγιων μου και απελευσομαι εγω και οι εκλεκτοι μου αγαλλιωντες μετα
των πατριαρχων εις την αιωνιαν μου βασιλειαν και ποιησω μετ αυτων τας
επαγγελιας μου ας επηγγειλαμην αυτοις εγω και πατηρ μου ο εν τοις
ουρανοις ιδου εδηλωσα σοι πετρε και εξεθεμην παντα και πορευου εις
πολιν αρχουσαν δυσεως** και πιε το ποτηριον ο επηγγειλαμην σοι εν
χειροιν του υιου του εν αιδου ινα αρχην λαβη αυτου η αφανεια και συ
δεκτος της επαγγελιας ...

* ον εαν αιτησωνται James; θν στεσωνται ms.

** δυσεως James; οπυσεως ms.

B. The Ethiopic manuscript tradition:[2]

ወኩሜሃ፡ኣ ሀሮሙ፡እ ሣሩያኑ፡እ ጸ ደቃኑ ፡ ጛ ም ቀ ተ ፡ ወ መ ደ
ኍኂተ ፡ ዘሰኩ ኍ ፡ በ ኍ ብ ፡ ሐ ቆ ኵ ፡ ኩ ክ ር ኬ ያ ፡ ኩ ኍ ተ ፡ ያ ብ ዋ ቀ ፡ ኩ
ኴ ሀ ኵ በ ል ያ ፡ ይ 7 ዮ ፡ መ ኩ ፈ ፟ ብ ተ ፡ ያ ደ ቃ ኍ ፡ ወ ኩ ሐ ወ ር ፡ ያ ዕ ዘ *፡
ኩ ተ ፟ ሣ ሔ ፡ ም ብ ኬ ሀ ሙ ፡ ክ በ ዉ ኩ ፡ ኩ ሐ ዛ በ ፡ ወ በ ተ ፡ መ ኍ ግ ሡ
ተ ዮ ፡ ዘ በ ዓ በ ዮ ፡ ወ ኩ 7 በ ር ፡ ሕ ሙ ፡ ዘ ኩ ኍ ፈ ወ ከ ዎ ሙ ፡ ዘ በ ዓ
እ ዮ ፡፡ ኩ ኍ ፡ ወ ኩ በ በ ዮ ፡ ሰ ግ ያ ዌ ፡ ኍ ግ ር ኩ ኩ ፡ ዬ ኍ ር በ ፡ ወ ኩ ደ ዓ ኩ
ኩ ኩ ፡ ቀ ኩ ፡ ኩ ኍ ኩ ፡ ወ ጦ ር ፡ ኩ ኍ ኩ ፡ ሀ 7 ፈ ፡ ኩ ኍ ተ ፡ ዐ ፈ በ ፡ ወ በ
ተ ፡ ወ ዮ ኍ ፡ ዘ ኩ ኬ እ ኩ ፡ ኩ ም ያ ዌ ሁ ፡ እ ወ ብ ደ ዮ ፡ ዘ ዘ ኩ ኍ በ ብ ፡ ኍ
ጠ ኩ ተ ፡ ኩ በ ፡ ያ ተ ቀ ደ በ ፡ ግ በ ፈ ፡ መ በ ና ፡ ወ ኩ ኍ ተ ለ ፡ ቋ ፈ ዮ ፡ በ
ተ በ ፈ ፡ ...

* ይ ዕ ዘ Grebaut; ማ ዕ ዘ mss.

---

[1]From M. R. James, "The Rainer Fragment of the Apocalypse of
Peter," ibid., p. 271.

[2]As printed in Grébaut, ibid., p. 208.

Supplement I

A. Translation of the Rainer fragment:

I will gi<ve> to my called and my elect whomever they request of me from out of punishment. And I will give them a beautiful baptism in salvation from the Acherousian Lake which is said to be in the Elysian Field, a share in righteousness with my saints. And I and my elect will go rejoicing with the patriarchs into my eternal kingdom, and I will fulfill for them my promises which I and my heavenly Father made to them. Behold, I have shown you, Peter, and I have explained everything. And go into a city ruling over the west, and drink the cup which I have promised you at the hands of the son of the One who is in Hades in order that his destruction might acquire a beginning. And you . . . of the promise . . .

B. Translation of the Ethiopic manuscript tradition:

And then I will give my elect, my righteous, the baptism and salvation which they requested of me. In the field of Akerosya which is called Aneslasleya a portion of the righteous have flowered, and I will go there now. I will rejoice with them. I will lead the peoples into my eternal kingdom and I will make for them what I have promised them, that which is eternal, I and my heavenly Father. I have told you, Peter, and informed you. Leave, therefore, and go therefore, (to) the city which is in the west, to the vineyard (or: wine) (about) which I have told you, that his work of destruction might be made holy from the sickness of my Son who is without sin. But you (are) chosen by the promise which I have made you. And send out my story into the whole world in peace. For the Fountain of my Word has rejoiced at the promise of life, and the world has been snatched away unexpectedly.

παρεξομαι τοις κλητοις μου και εκλεκτοις μου	እሁቦሙ፡ለኅሩያንየ፡ለጻድ ቃንየ (ወለጻድቃንየ T)
I will give to my called and elect	I will give to my elect, my righteous (and my righteous, T)
ον εαν αιτησωνται με	ዘሰአሉኒ
whoever they will ask of me	what (or: who) they have asked of me
βαπτισμα εν σωτηρια	ጥምቀተ፡ወመድኀኒተ
baptism in salvation	baptism and salvation
αχερουσιας λιμνης ην καλουσιν εν τω ηλυσιω πεδιω	በኀበ፡ሐቅል፡አክሮስያ፡እንተ፡ ይብልዋ፡አኔስለስልየ
the Acherousian Lake which is said (to be) in the Elysian Field	in the field of Akerosia which is called Aneslasleya
μερος δικαιοσυνης	መክፈልተ፡ጻድቃን
a portion of righteousness	a portion of the righteous
και απελευσομαι	ወእሐውር
and I will go	and I will go
αγαλλιωντες μετα	እትፌሣሕ፡ምስሌሆሙ
rejoicing with...	I will rejoice with them
εις την αιωνιαν μου βασιλειαν	ውስተ፡መንግሥትየ፡ዘለዓለም
into my eternal kingdom	into my eternal kingdom

και ποιησω μετ αυτον τας επαγγελιας μου ας επηγγειλαμην αυτοις	ወእገብር፡ሎሙ፡ዘአሰፈው ክዎሙ
and I will do for them my promises which I have promised them	and I will do for them what I have promised them
εγω και πατηρ μου ο εν τοις ουρανοις	አነ፡ወአቡየ፡ሰማያዊ
I and my Father who is in heaven	I and my heavenly Father
εδηλωσα σοι πετρε και εξεθεμην	ነገርኩከ፡ጴጥሮስ፡ወአይዓዕኩከ
I have showed you, Peter, and I have explained	I have told you, Peter, and I have explained to you
και πορευου εις πολιν αρχουσαν δυσεως	ፃእ፡እንከ፡ወሑር፡እንከ፡ሀገረ፡ እንተ፡ዐረብ
and go into the city ruling (over) the west	leave, therefore, and go, therefore, to the city which is (in) the west
και πιε το ποτηριον ο επηγγειλαμην σοι	ውስተ፡ወይን፡ዘእቤለከ
and drink the cup which I have promised you	to the vineyard (or: wine) (about) which I have told you
εν χειροιν (read χερσιν) του υιου του εν αιδου	እምደዌሁ፡ለወልድየ፡ዘዘእንበለ፡ (ለዘእንበለ PT) ኃጢአት
at the hands of the son of the one in Hades	from the sickness of my son who is without sin (my sinless son PT)

ινα αρχην λαβη αυτου

η αφανεια

in order that his destruction might acquire a beginning	that his work of destruction might be sanctified

---

και συ δεκτος της επαγγελιας

and you acceptable? of the promise	and you (are) chosen by the promise

---

Let us begin with a group of related difficulties in vv. 1-2. The Greek text clearly teaches a form of universal salvation, that is, if any who are saved request pardon for any wicked, condemned person the latter will be released from punishment. It is possible that this could refer only to the relatives and friends of the saved, but I believe it is implied that no saved person could be happy as long as any are being punished, and therefore that all will receive salvation. This is a curious doctrine, but it appears also in Sib. Orac. 2:330-338; the Coptic Apocalypse of Elias; and the Epistula Apostolorum 40.[1] It is a doctrine which would not be accepted by many people, and there can be no doubt that the references to it were removed from our text because someone had theological objections to it.

---

[1]M. R. James, ibid., pp. 272-273. James had already before the discovery of the Rainer fragment seen from these passages that the doctrine must be here, in his Apocryphal New Testament, ibid., p. 521. See Chapter One where these writings are discussed.

This transformation meant that all references here to salvation had to refer only to the righteous, and any trace of the condemned and the righteous had to be erased. εκ της κολασεως 'from out of punishment' was dropped. μετα των αγιων μου 'with the saints' also had to go because it implied that others besides the saints were receiving an inheritance. The 'portion in righteousness' μερος δικαιοσυνης (here righteousness = salvation) was changed to 'a portion of the righteous ones'. By this change the baptism in the Acherusian Lake which was a purification of sinners became instead a special reward for some of the righteous. Indeed, the word 'lake' λιμνη may also have been expunged at this time, though I am inclined to think rather that the strange use of the verb καλειν which usually means 'to call' but which here must mean 'which is said (to be)' had led the translator to eliminate 'lake' because he understood Acherusia to be called a lake when it was really a field, the Elysian Field.

The removal of 'from out of punishment' was not enough if the author wished to retain in the text a reference to the request of the righteous, which apparently he did. So the future tense 'they will ask me for' was put into the past 'they have asked me for', and the phrase 'baptism of salvation' now changed to 'baptism and salvation' (because the former was still tainted by the idea of final universal salvation) was moved (with its modifiers) upward to become the object of παρεξομαι rather than δωσω. The move was

facilitated by the fact that δωσω has two objects in the
Greek text, 'the baptism in salvation' and 'the portion of
righteousness'. With this move the relative pronoun H no
longer referred to the sinners in punishment but to the
baptism and salvation, that is, the righteous will no longer
ask after the judgment for the salvation of the wicked, but
they will receive the baptism they had already requested for
themselves. If all this seems complicated expressed on
paper, it is easy to see when comparing the Greek and Ethiopic texts.

A few more details can be cleared up. While at first
sight the Greek has two different verbs meaning 'to give'
and the Ethiopic only has one, ኽቡ ፡ ሰም, this discrepancy
has been caused by a corruption of the Ethiopic text during
its transmission. The Ethiopic word ወኽ7ፆ 'and they have
flowered', which is so awkward, even incomprehensible in
this context, was ወኽሽ7 'and I will give', a literal
translation of καὶ δωσω. In Geʿez ወኽሽ7፡ ሰኽፈዕተ፡ ፆየቃኽ
could mean either 'I will grant (it) (to) some of the righteous' or 'I will distribute the inheritance of the righteous (to them)'. Returning from this to the beginning,
τοις κλητους μου και εκλεκτοις μου is translated by
ኽሕፈፆኽፆ ፡ ኽፆፆቃኽፆ 'my elect, my righteous ones'.
Leaving aside the question if the ወ was originally present
before ኽፆፆፆኽፆ , there is a possibility that 'righteous
ones' is present here because of someone's theological bias,
that is, the saved are not the 'called and chosen' so much

as they are the righteous, those who have done good. In
support of this it might be said that εκλεκτοις, the second
element of this phrase in Greek, would ordinarily be translated by λዛሩ ደዛP , the first element of the phrase in
Geᵉz. This might be some indication that the literal translation of the first Greek element κλητοις was dropped in
order to permit (for theological reasons) the 'righteous'
to appear here, even to permit the righteous to be identified with the chosen if the ⊕ has been added by the tradition of T. But the evidence is not conclusive. Perhaps
the translator used λዛሩ ደዛP to translate τοις κλητοις
μου and then when searching for a synonym put λሩ ደ ፆ ዛ P .
(Cf. 1 En. 60:8.) Finally, it should be said that it is
not obvious why the adjective καλον dropped out.

When did these changes take place? I do not believe
it is possible to say. It may have happened during the
course of transmission in Ethiopic. Or the translator may
have made these changes. Or, finally, this transformation
may already have taken place in the original Greek, for we
cannot assume that the text in front of the scribe who made
the translation was identical to R. I cannot see any evidence one way or another. Therefore I have not inserted
any of the missing phrases into the Ethiopic text.

From this point on we find no further displacement of
the text. The words εγω και οι εκλεκτοι μου 'I and my

---

[1]In my edition of the text I have retained   because
there is a και in R.

elect' have nothing in Ethiopic to correspond to them, but
it is not clear why these should have been eliminated for
the theological reasons given above. I can offer no explanation. But we can best reconstruct the original Ethiopic
text if we assume for the remainder of the text a literal
word-for-word translation.

Let us consider the words μετα των πατριαρχων 'with
the patriarchs'. μετα clearly is translated by ᎃ᎐ᎆᎁᎂᎀ
'with them'. And των πατριαρχων must have something to do
with ᎄᎅᎆᎇ 'nations' as James and Prümm both saw.[1] But
from where does the Ethiopic ᎄᎇᎈᎄ 'I will cause to go'
come? It is, I believe, an inner Ethiopic corruption for
ᎄᎇᎈ 'fathers'. The phrase ᎄᎇᎈ:ᎄᎅᎆᎇ which is
literally 'fathers of the nations' must mean 'patriarchs'.
This is not a common expression for 'patriarchs', but when
in chapter 16 Peter asks about Abraham, Isaac, and Jacob,
Jesus says (v. 4), "You have seen the ᎄᎅᎆᎇ:ᎄᎇᎈ ."
The words ᎄᎅᎆᎇ and ᎄᎇᎈ when put together in construct
in either order must mean 'patriarchs', at least in this
document. For this reason I have restored ᎄᎇᎈ:ᎄᎅᎆᎇ
to the text.

The next disagreement between the Greek and Ethiopic
occurs when the Ethiopic inserts ᎃᎄᎉᎄᎊ 'eternal' after
'what I have promised'. It is, I believe, a simple scribal
error made when ᎃᎄᎉᎄᎊ at the beginning of a line was

---

[1]M. R. James, ibid., p. 273; and K. Prümm, ibid.,
p. 78.

repeated accidentally by a copyist before the mistake was noticed, and then he continued with the correct text. The line length of that copyist's original must have been twenty letters per line (ሀአጓአፆ through ሀኽብⷈዎኽጰጮ), which is about right for an Ethiopic text with one column per page. For this reason I have omitted the second occurrence of ሀአጓአፆ from my edition.

There is nothing in the Ethiopic text translating the Greek word ιδου. εδηλωσα σοι πετρε και εξεθεμην παντα 'I have showed you, Peter, and explained everything' is translated by ኣጎⷭኹኽ : ብ፣ⷭጠ : ⷈኽዷጓኽⷉኽ 'I have told you, Peter, and informed you'. The notion which the Greek carries of a vision and a detailed explanation (a very apocalyptic notion) is lost in the Ethiopic translation which uses two synonymous verbs of oral communication. παντα was probably understood by the translator to mean 'to everyone' rather than 'everything'. Since Jesus did not tell everyone, but only his disciples, and since only Peter is here addressed by Jesus, 'everyone' was corrected to 'you' (s.).

'And go into a city ruling (over) the west' και πορευου εις πολιν αρχουσαν δυσεως is translated by ፱ኽ : ኽጓኽ : ⷈብC : ኽጓኽ : ሀጘ : ኽጓ፥ : ዐ፩ⷍ 'go out, therefore, and go, therefore (to) a city which is (in) the west'. I believe this came about when the translator read ερχου ουν 'go, therefore' in the text where we now read αρχουσαν 'ruling'. The translator in an attempt to make sense of

this transferred this ερχου ουν to before και and wrote
ፃኅ፡ኅጎጠ፡ወሐር 'go out therefore and go'. It is also
likely that he translated εις πολιν with ኅጠኅ፡ ሀጎረ 'to
the city' but that ኅጠጠ 'to' was corrupted to ኅጎጠ
'therefore' during the course of Ethiopic transmission by
the influence of the ኅጎጠ which was already there.

What are we to make of the correspondence of και πιε
το ποτηριον ο επηγγειλαμην σοι 'and drink the cup which I
have promised you' and ወጠተ፡ወይጎ፡Hኅብላጠ 'into the
vineyeard of which I have told you'? It is really no problem that ο επηγγειλαμην σοι is translated Hኅብላጠ. I believe the present corrupted Ethiopic text arose because the
translator chose to translate το ποτηριον 'the cup' with
ወይጎ. In Geʹez ወይጎ can mean either 'wine' or 'vineyard'. The translator wrote ወጠተይ፡ ወይጎ 'and drink the
wine'. Later a scribe understood ወይጎ to mean 'vineyard'
and put ወጠተ 'into' for ወጠተይ 'and drink'. Perhaps
this change was facilitated by the omission of ይ, in the
same way that so many single letters are omitted in manuscript P.

Again, what relationship does εν χερσιν (read this
for χειροιν) του υιου του εν αιδου 'at the hands of the son
of the one in Hades' have with ኅምይβሀ፡ኢወጎ ደP ፡ H
Hኅጎ ∩ ጓ ፡ጎጠኅተ 'from the sickness of my son who is
without sin', beyond the use of the word 'son'? Again I
believe that an inner Ethiopic corruption resulted from the
translation, but this time because the translator either

misread the Greek or had a different Greek text before him.
For τou υιou τou εν αιδou he read τou υιou μou αναιτιou 'my
sinless son'. Thus a reference to the son of Satan became
a reference to the son of God, something which could have
taken place already in the transmission of the Greek. The
appearance of the word 'son' would naturally trigger an
image of Jesus, as we see when both Wessely and Prümm attempt to interpret this of Jesus' descent into Hades.[1] This
means that the ሳ of the manuscript T preceding ዘእንበለ
is original (because it reflects an adjective in the Greek)
compared with the ዘዘእንበለ which Grébaut reads (reflecting a relative pronoun) from the ambiguous mark in P. It is
also clear that the translator put እምእደዊሁ for εν
χερσιν 'by his hands', rendering it very literally. But
this meant that Peter was about to suffer at the hands of
Jesus. A later scribe probably found this unacceptable and
altered እምእደዊሁ 'from his hands' to እምደዌሁ 'from
his sickness/weakness' by which he intended a reference to
Jesus' crucifixion. Peter also would have to drink the wine
(undergo martyrdom) which flows from Jesus' death. Since
ለወልዱ ፡ እዘእንበለ ፡ ኃጢአት was apparently in the
original Ethiopic text I have retained that reading. But
እምደዌሁ has been restored to እምእደዊሁ.

---

[1]Charles Wessely, "Les plus anciens monuments du
Christianisme: Ecrits sur Papyrus II," Patrologia Orien-
talis 18 (1924):258-259; K. Prümm, ibid, pp. 79-80; cf.
M. R. James, ibid., pp. 273-274.

Finally, how does ινα αρχην λαβη αυτου η αφανεια 'that his destruction might acquire a beginning' compare with **ከሙ፡ይትቀደስ ፡ግብረ ፡ሙኃኑ** 'that his work of destruction might be made holy'? It appears that the author understood αρχην to be the verb. Then λαβη was a noun modified by αυτου. He then translated the whole as **ከሙ፡ ይትቀደሥ ፡ግብረ ፡ሙኃኑ** 'that his work of destruction might begin'. I cannot explain how λαβη 'handle' or 'acceptance' was translated with 'work' or why the translator would put **ግብረ** 'work' in the construct state with **ሙኃኑ** 'destruction' which translates αφανεια. In the course of transmission **ይትቀደሥ** 'it might begin' was changed to **ይትቀደስ** 'he might sanctify', probably because it was understood that Jesus was sanctifying Peter's work in Rome, rather than that Peter was beginning the destruction of Satan. The final words in Greek και συ δεκτος της επαγγελιας 'and you acceptable of the promise' do not really make any sense, but the Ethiopic translator read εκλεκτος 'elect' for δεκτος 'acceptable' and this makes perfect sense: **ወአንተ ፡ኅሩይ፡ በተስፋ** 'but you (are) chosen by the promise'.

By a thorough comparison of the Ethiopic text with the Rainer fragment I believe we have succeeded in restoring it substantially. From this comparison the following conclusions may be drawn. (1) The Ethiopic text has many corruptions which took place during its transmission. This is an indication that it is an old text with a lengthy transmission period. (2) At some time either before, during or

after the Apocalypse of Peter was translated into Geʿez, the
text was subjected to changes because of theological objections to some of its doctrines. (3) The translator attempted a wooden but accurate translation. He did not,
however, always understand the text he had before him.
(4) It is very likely that the translator had before him a
Greek text similar to the one in R. I find no evidence in
this section that this is a translation from the Arabic as
was so long assumed. (5) The Greek text of the Apocalypse
of Peter which was translated into Geʿez probably was already
corrupt in many places, similar to what we can see in R.
Thus it is not always possible to know whether the translator misunderstood his Greek text or whether he understood
well enough a Greek text which was corrupt.

The Ethiopic text of chapter 14 which appears in this
edition is the earliest form of the text in the Ethiopic
language which we can discern. However, it still reflects
the problems of theological restructuring, translation in-
accuracies, and copyists' mistakes. Since we have the
earlier text of R before us I will discuss both texts together.

V. 1. God honors the request of Jesus' followers.
See Jn. 14:14, "If you ask anything in my name I will do
it." (Cf. Jn. 13:37, 14:29, 15:7, 15:16, 16:23-4.) Also
compare 1 Jn. 5:15-17, "If any one sees his brother commit-
ting what is not a mortal sin, he will ask, and God will
give him life for those whose sin is not mortal." Cf. Sib.

Or. 2:330-338. Cf. also Jesus' claim that he has come not to condemn the world but to save it (Jn. 3:17, 12:47-8. Cf. also Jn. 13:9, Col. 1:13). In 1 En. 39:3-7 those in the resting places pray for the children of men.

The Ethiopic translator has not understood that Acherousia is a lake, not a field. The connection of baptism with the waters of Acherusia is thus lost. The translator was not familiar with the geography of the Greek otherworld. The purification of sinners by some sort of afterlife baptism may be older than Christianity.[1]

v. 2. ኸ ቤ ? : ሠ ኸ ∠ ፅ ተ : ፃ ድ ቀ ነ means 'I will bestow the share (= inheritance) of the righteous'. Cf. Col. 3:24.

The word ያ ኸ ሀ has not been discussed above. Both Ethiopic manuscripts have ማ ዐ ሀ while there is nothing at all which could correspond to this in R. At first sight ማ ዐ ሀ must be ማ ኸ ሀ, the interrogative adverb 'when?'. But that makes no sense whatever here. In many ways ማ ዐ ሀ remains a mystery. It is the only word in this entire section which cannot somehow be explained by reference to the Greek text. Perhaps it is related to the verb ፆ ዐ ሀ 'to smell good, be fragrant' and was added after ኸ ቤ ? had been corrupted to ቤ 7 ፅ , that is, the righteous were not only made to bloom but they were also made to smell nice. But then, what grammatical form would ማ ዐ ሀ be? More likely,

---

[1] Erik Peterson, "Die Taufe im acherusischen See," ibid., 310-330. But Peterson opts for a Jewish background. The evidence is not conclusive, but even the use of the terms Acherusian Lake and Elysian Field make a Greek back-

it is corrupt for 𝒴ℎ𝒽ℍ𝒷 'now', and I have put 𝒴ℎ𝒽ℍ𝒷 in the text. This makes perfect sense in the context, but I am unable to find a good explanation for this change. It is important for the understanding of this passage. Is Jesus going to take the patriarchs into his kingdom now or will he do so after the judgment? As the texts read now, the Ethiopic would favor the former, R the latter. We cannot decide between them with any assurance. For the kingdom, see Mt. 25:34, 46; Jn. 18:36, 14:2-5. Cf. also 2 Cl. 19:4, "he shall live again with the fathers above."

V. 3. The promises are to be fulfilled, but no details are given. 'I and my heavenly Father' link Jesus and God together as those who execute the promises. For the eschatological promises see Heb. 4:1, 6:12, 8:6, 12:26; 2 Pt. 1:4, 3:13.

As I have already pointed out, the Greek text εδηλωσα σοι πετρε και εξεθεμην παντα 'I have showed you, Peter, and explained everything' is a reference to the apocalyptic vision which Jesus has just given his disciples and to his exposition of it. But the Ethiopic ነገርኩከ፡ አቶስጰ : ወአያድዕኩከ 'I have told you, Peter, and informed you' was probably understood by later readers, possibly even the translator, to refer to Jesus' prediction of Peter's death

---

ground more likely. Dieterich, ibid., argues persuasively for an Orphic background for at least the inferno, Akhmim 6:21-20:34 (= Eth. ch. 7-12).

(v. 4). Cf. 2 Pt. 1:13-15, Jn. 21:18-19; also Mk. 13:23,
Mt. 24:25, Jn. 13:19, 14:29, 16:4.

V. 4. This is possibly the oldest known unambiguous
allusion to Peter's death in Rome.[1] It witnesses to the
idea that Peter's death must occur before Satan's destruction can begin, or to the idea that Peter's death must occur
before Satan can really begin his (final) work of destruction (cf. 2 Th. 2:6-8). Either way, Peter's death is seen
as a sign of the End, and surely this must be a very early
idea, one which would not have arisen too long after Peter's
(assumed?) death in Rome and one which would not be incor-
porated into new works at a date too far removed from that
period of time. A command of Jesus telling Peter to go to
Rome, however, is anachronistic.

The phrase "drink the cup" was a common one associated
with impending death: Jn. 18:11, Mk. 10:38-9 par., 14:36
par. "The son of the One who is in Hades" is in this context most likely Nero. Cf. Jn. 17:12, Akhmim 1:2.

V. 5. Here unfortunately R breaks off. 'The promise
which I have promised you' alludes to what Jesus had told
Peter, probably something about a heavenly reward or possibly to his leadership role in the church. In this verse
the commission to spread the message is given to Peter
alone. It is important that the gospel be spread 'peace-
fully' ሰላም.

---

[1]Erik Peterson, "Das Martyrium des hl. Petrus nach
der Petrus-Apokalypse," ibid., 88-91.

V. 6. This verse is not easy to comprehend and is possibly corrupt. But here we have no Greek text to help us. It is part of these last verses which Duensing called 'unverständlich' and did not translate.[1] Grébaut has "En effet, (les hommes) se réjouiront; mes paroles seront la source de l'espérance et de la vie et soudain le monde sera ravi."[2] James gives us "Verily men shall rejoice: my words shall be the source of hope and of life, and suddenly shall the world be ravished,"[3] which is a good translation of Grébaut. But the verb +ⷀⷅⷆ is neither imperfect nor plural as they imply, and since +ⷍⷎ⷏ 'has been snatched off' is also perfect we should be wary of supplying an imperfect verb between them. In fact the last verb to appear in the imperfect is in v. 3. The sense of the perfect should therefore be retained. In addition, these translations make it appear as if ⷐⷑ 'source/fountain' is in construct with +ⷒⷓ 'promise/hope' and ⷔⷕⷖ 'life' when actually it is in construct with ⷗ⷘⷙ 'my word' (singular, not plural). Finally, +ⷒⷓ and ⷔⷕⷖ are not joined by a conjunction, but +ⷒⷓ is in construct with ⷔⷕⷖ. For these reasons I have translated 'For the Fountain of My Word has rejoiced at the promise of life, and suddenly the world has been snatched away'. 'Fountain

---

[1] Hugo Duensing, ibid., p. 73.

[2] Sylvain Grébaut, ibid., p. 214.

[3] M. R. James, The Apocryphal New Testament, ibid., p. 518.

of My Word' I believe to be a divine epithet, indicating
that Jesus' words have their source in the Father. Compare
Jn. 4:14. God has rejoiced that Jesus has proven to be a
promise of life.

The expression 'suddenly the world has been snatched
away' is not at all clear. How has it been snatched? Who
has done the snatching? When did this take place? I do
not think we can be certain of any answers, but the impression is that the snatching has already been done by Jesus
and that the world is no longer in the hands of evil or the
devil. It is this fact which makes possible the spread of
the story commissioned in v. 5.

Chapter Fifteen

V. 1. With this verse we change scenes. The next
chapters (15-17) are related closely to the transfiguration
setting known to us from the synoptic gospels and in 2 Pt.
1:16-18, though here the events occur just prior to the ascension. We can again compare the Ethiopic with the Akhmim
Fragment as we proceed with the discussion. The latter
reads

> And continuing, the Lord said "Let us go to the
> mountain (and) pray." And we the twelve disciples,
> going with him, asked that he show us one of our
> righteous brothers who had departed from the world
> in order that we might see what sort of form they
> have and, taking courage (from that), might encourage
> also those men who hear us. And while we were pray-
> ing. . . .

The association of the transfiguration scene with
praying is also found in Luke (9:28-9). In Luke Jesus goes

up the mountain to pray and the transfiguration occurs as he is praying. In Akhmim, Jesus suggests that the twelve disciples go with him to the mountain and pray. The appearance of the two men takes place while the disciples are praying, but only after they request it. Here in the Ethiopic the disciples simply pray as they go (cf. 17:7).

They go to the "holy mountain." This agrees with the account in 2 Pt. 1:18. What mountain is this? If we take seriously the setting in 1:1 where Jesus is seated on the Mt. of Olives, the holy mountain may be the temple mount (cf. Mk. 13:3). Otherwise we do not know which mountain is meant.

In "My Lord Jesus Christ our King' a number of different titles have been amalgamated. We meet the same phenomenon in 16:1 and 16:4, which makes it characteristic of this "holy mountain" section of the apocalypse. These titles are evidence of a high christology. They would suit the transfiguration of Jesus, but in the Apocalypse of Peter Jesus is not transformed. By their very form these titles must be under suspicion, but the Akhmim is also different and may preserve the more original titles. In that case "Jesus Christ our King" is an addition. I believe also that in a similar way the words "(to) God Jesus Christ" at 16:1 and "and my God Jesus Christ" have been added to the original text, probably after the apocalypse had been translated into Ethiopic.

Vv. 2-7. These verses are difficult and may be slightly corrupted. We may attribute some of the awkwardness to the subject matter, that is, according to the account itself it is attempting to describe what cannot be expressed in words. Here the Akhmim is similar but reads smoother.

(3) 6. And while we were praying, suddenly two men appeared standing before the Lord, at whom we were not able to look. 7. For there came out from their face a ray like the sun and their clothing was shining, of a sort the eye of man has never seen. For no mouth was able to describe nor the heart to contemplate the glory which they wore and the beauty of their face. 8. Having seen them, we were amazed. For their bodies were whiter than any snow and redder than any rose. But their red was mixed with the white and I am simply not able to describe their beauty. 10. For their hair was curly and flowery and becoming to their face and to their shoulders, like a crown of woven nard-flower and many-colored blossoms or like a rainbow in the air. Such was their fine appearance. (4) 11. Having seen, therefore, their beauty, we became astonished at them, for they appeared suddenly.

The most important difference between the Ethiopic and the Akhmim in this chapter is in the way the description is applied to the two figures. In the Akhmim all of what is said about the men applies to both of them. In the Ethiopic first one man ("from one of them," 2b) and then the other ("and the second, large I say," 5a) is described, using however approximately the same words as the Akhmim. Is the smoother text of the Akhmim more original in this regard? Put together, the two descriptions of the Ethiopic do not duplicate, so that we may have a description originally applied to both (as in Akhmim) now divided between the two

figures. On the other hand I am inclined to believe that
each of the men was described individually from the beginning. There are two expressions of amazement (4b, 7b) which
may express the response to each heavenly figure. But the
issue cannot be decided. The description of the men is very
similar to that of the newborn Noah in 1 En. 106:2, 11.

The position of ሕበሙ (v. 2) possibly indicates the
postpositive Greek conjunction γαρ, for ፩ ሕምውንተፈሙ
'one of them' preceding ሕበሙ must go with what follows
ሕበሙ, not what goes before it.

In v. 3 P has omitted the final ሙ on ምበኁሆሙ 'with
them', causing Grébaut to misread the text as ምለኁሁ 'its
image'. ሕሀλ : ምበλ is an idiom meaning 'to prevail
against'.[1] λ ሐዩ in v. 4 can be either 'brilliance' or
'form' since either of these meanings of that word fit well
in this context.

The phrase ዐኒዩ : ሕበä 'large, I say' in v. 5 is
intrusive and awkward, though a reference to the large size
of these figures should not surprise us in this context.
It is just possible, though I do not think it likely, that
we should read ሕኒዩ: ሕበä 'I speak reluctantly' interpreting ሕኒዩ as an infinitive from ሕበጶ 'to refuse, be
unwilling'. In that case this phrase would carry on the
theme found in vv. 3-4 of the inability to describe these
figures. ዶ ሕጶ :ዐሥጁ 'his appearance and his flesh' is

---

[1] Grébaut reads ምለኁሁ 'its image" in his text but
translates it with "à cela" as if he read ምበኁሁ 'to it'.

most likely the skin of his face and the rest of his body.
In v. 6 ⳋⳞ Ⳙⲟⳟ 'their forehead' has a plural suffix which
is out of place. It is not clear why this is so.

Chapter Sixteen

V. 1. The Akhmim reads

> And approaching the Lord I said, "Who are these?" He
> said to me, "These are our righteous brothers whose
> form you (pl.) wished to see." And I said to him,
> "And where are all the righteous or of what sort is
> the world in which they are who have this glory?"
> (Akh. 4:12-14)

For the titles in the address to Jesus, see the notes
at 15:1.

The dialogue between Peter and Jesus is intended to
give an explanation of the vision, however short the explanation may be. Peter's question about the patriarchs is
incomplete and we must assume an interrogative particle such
as ⳛ ⳉ ⳁ 'where?'. Is he asking about where Moses and
Elijah have come, or are they in another category? I believe that Moses and Elijah appear as heavenly figures
(assuming they both ascended into heaven and did not suffer
death), and that Abraham, etc., are not yet in heaven but
are kept at 'rest' in paradise (a garden) of which the disciples catch a glimpse in the next verses. But see the "men
in the flesh" who come to meet Jesus in 17:3.

Moses and Elijah were commonly associated with the
eschaton.[1] See 2:12 where Enoch and Elijah are sent. It

---

[1]Paul Volz, ibid., pp. 194-197.

is Moses and Elijah who also appear in the synoptic transfiguration account (Mk. 9:4 par.). Does this tradition reflect the gathering of three eschatological figures--the
prophet (like) Moses, Elijah, and the messiah? In Jn. 1:19-
28 it is about these three figures which John the Baptist is
asked. The Akhmim does not mention Moses and Elijah but
calls the two men "righteous brothers" in accord with their
previous question about righteous brothers (Akh. 2:5).

Vv. 2-3. The text here is awkward and probably corrupted. It is not clear whether the adjective ዐቢይ
'large' modifies ገነት 'garden' or ዖም 'grove' or 'tree',
though usually ዐቢይ precedes the noun it modifies. Nor
is it clear whether the disciples see one tree or many
trees. ፍሬ፡በረከት 'fruit of blessing' means probably
'the fruit which gives blessing'. What does the phrase
ይመጽእ፡ሽታ፡ኀቤሁ 'its smell comes to it' mean? Duensing has suggested that the text be emended to ኀቤነ 'to
us' and he may be correct.[1] But when he says that 'miracle'
is untranslatable[2] I must disagree. Peter has seen a miracle, and that miracle is the frequent appearance of fruit.
ብዙኀ may be understood as an adverb meaning 'often' (cf.
Ezk. 47:12, Rev. 22:2).

This description of the garden (paradise) is very
close to some which are found in Enoch (1 En. 24:4, the tree

---

[1] Hugo Duensing, ibid., p. 73, note 11.

[2] Ibid., note 12.

of life; 32:3-6, many trees including the tree of wisdom;
cf. 22:2). In the Akhmim Fragment the description is much
longer, the only place where we find a significantly greater
amount of material in Akhmim than in the Ethiopic. Akhmim
reads

> And the Lord showed me a very large place outside
> this world, very bright with light and the air there
> was lighted with the rays of the sun, and the soil it-
> self (was) blooming with unfading flowers and (was)
> full of spices and plants beautifully blooming and
> imperishable and bearing blessed fruit. So strong
> was the fragrance of the flowers that it carried from
> there to us. And the inhabitants of that place wore
> the shining clothes of angels. And their clothes
> were similar to their land. And angels walked around
> among them there. And the glory of the inhabitants
> was equal, and with one voice they praised the Lord
> God, rejoicing in that place.

The points of contact between the Ethiopic and Akhmim
are: (1) the blessed fruit; (2) the fragrance born to (it or
us). The Ethiopic is much closer to the descriptions in
Enoch. This could mean that the Ethiopic text of Enoch has
influenced the Ethiopic of this section of the Apocalypse of
Peter. But I am inclined to believe that an originally
short account based on a tradition similar to those in Enoch
has been expanded in the Akhmim tradition by material found
in other descriptions of paradise, such as the tradition
found in Theophilus of Antioch, Ad Autolycum 2, 19: "God
chose for Adam as paradise a place in the eastern region,
marked out by light, illumined by shining air, with plants
of wondrous beauty." See chapter one under Theophilus.
This expansion may have served the purpose of those who were
interested in more information on paradise and found the

account in the EC <u>Apocalypse of Peter</u> too brief.

V. 4. For the titles of Jesus, see the notes at 15:1.
ርእ ከሁ: ኸሕ ሃ ፡ ኸ ፡ ኸ ፡ 'You have seen it, the patriarchs'
is difficult. I have already shown above, in the discussion
of 14:2 where the text is reconstructed, that ኸ ሕ ሃ ፡ ኸ ፡ ኸ ፡
means 'patriarchs', for R has πατριαρχων there. In spite of
the fact that ሁ is singular, I understand it as a third
person singular suffix in apposition with patriarchs. This
is slightly awkward, but the sentence then is a statement of
explanation such as we would expect. It has usually been
understood and translated as if it were ርእ ከሁ 'have you
seen?' where ሁ is the sign of interrogation. But a question is not really appropriate from Jesus at this point. It
further complicates matters that T has ርእ ከ ሁ 'have I
seen?'. This latter reading is senseless in its present
context and only serves to point out how uncertain we are
about what we should read here. The Akhmim, which goes into
the inferno immediately following this (5:20), has, "The
Lord said to us, 'This is the place of your brothers, the
righteous men.'" However, the word αδελφων 'brothers' has
been conjectured from the difficult manuscript reading
αρχερω̄. I believe that on the basis of the reading πατριαρχων in ms. R and the use of "patriarchs" here in the Ethiopic we can safely say that αρχερω̄ is corrupt for πατριαρχων.
We may then translate "This is the place of your patriarchs,
the righteous men" or "This is the place of the patriarchs,
your righteous men." (Cf. 2 Cl. 19:4.) For "rest" as a

designation of the coming reward see 2 Th. 1:7, Heb. 3:11,
3:18, 4:1-11.

How does v. 4 relate to vv. 2-3? In the Ethiopic v. 4
reads "You have seen the patriarchs" while in vv. 2-3 no
people are present. Perhaps "You have seen the patriarchs,
and like this (is) that which is their rest" refers in its
two parts to the appearance of Moses and Elijah and to the
vision of the garden respectively. Or the mention of the
inhabitants of the garden (as in Akhmim) has fallen out of
the Ethiopic.

Vv. 5-6. አጽድቅP 'for my righteousness' at the
very end of v. 5 would seem to indicate that Jesus was
speaking through the whole verse, for surely 'my' refers to
Jesus. For this reason Duensing has removed ወተፈሣሕኩ:
ወኣመንኩ 'and I rejoiced and I believed' (which Peter
says) from this place in the text and inserted it after
አጽድቅP .[1] I do not believe it is necessary or desirable
to do so. አጽድቅP does indeed refer to Christ's righteousness, but it is, I believe, inside a quotation which
begins with ከመዝ 'such' and ends with አጽድቅP . When
the author in v. 6 says 'I understood what is written in the
book of my Lord Jesus Christ' he refers to what he has just
quoted. Perhaps by 'the book of my Lord Jesus Christ' he
means the Gospel of Matthew, and a specific reference to Mt.

---

[1]Hugo Duensing, ibid., p. 74, notes 1 and 2.

5:10. The same idea appears in 1 Pt. 3:14. Cf. 1 En. 95:7;
Ep. Diog. 10:7-8; Pol. 2:3.

Vv. 7-9. Peter's question is closer to that in the
transfiguration story of Matthew (17:4) than to the parallels in the other gospels in that it addresses Jesus as Lord
and uses the word "wish," but in Matthew Peter's words are
not in the form of a question but an offer. The word
"arbor, booth" is the word ordinarily used for the booths at
the Feast of Tabernacles and is a good translation of
σκηνη.[1]

In v. 8 we have the tradition of the rebuke of Peter
which occurs in the synoptics (Mt. 16:23 par.) in connection
with Peter's confession but always preceding the transfiguration (cf. Jn. 6:70). In the gospels Peter is rebuked because he is against Jesus' approaching death. Here he is
rebuked because he is interested in a worldly tabernacle.
The "dwelling of this world" apparently refers to the tabernacles which Peter wished to build. This is in contrast to
to the heavenly tabernacle which is seen in v. 9.

In Isaiah 6:9-10 the obstinacy of the people in their
failure to listen to the prophet is described as shutting
the eyes and ears. In the synoptic gospels the saying of
Isaiah is applied to lack of understanding of Jesus' parables (Mt. 13:13-14 par.) and in the Gospel of John to

---

[1]The edition of the Ethiopic New Testament which I
have uses the word ዓኅ ደ C 'dwelling' at Mt. 17:4. Cf.
the use of ኅብደ ተ 'dwelling' in v. 8.

unbelief in the signs which Jesus performed. In Acts 28:25-29 it is applied to the refusal of the Jews of Rome to accept the teaching of Paul. Cf. Rom. 11:8. Already Is. 32:3 had predicted the time when this would be reversed (cf. Is. 35:5), that is, people would see and hear. The fulfillment of that prediction is here (v. 9) applied to the removal of Satan's veil from Peter's mind. Cf. Jn. 9:39.

This uncovering of the eyes is accomplished by a vision from heaven (v. 9c) and the opening of the ears is accomplished by a voice from heaven (17:1). Thus 17:1 belongs together in form with 16:9. This same form is to be found in 4 Ezra 10:55-56 where Ezra is first invited to go in and see as much of the heavenly city as his eyes can see and told that afterwards he will hear as much as his ears can hear.

The tabernacle made without human hands is a variation of the temple saying found in Mk. 14:58. See also Heb. 8:2, 9:11, 24; Acts 7:48-50, 17:24. Cf. Mk. 13:2, 15:29; Mt. 23:38, 26:61, 12:6, 27:40; Jn. 2:19, 4:20-25; 2 Cor. 5:1, Eph. 2:11, Heb. 9:8, 11:10, 13:10.

The vision of the heavenly tabernacle and the accompanying voice should be understood as the climax of the writing. This is what all the faithful look forward to seeing.

Chapter Seventeen

V. 1. The saying of the heavenly voice is familiar to

us from the synoptic transfiguration accounts (Mk. 9:7 par.),
the account of the transfiguration in 2 Peter 1:17, and the
synoptic account of the baptism of Jesus (Mk. 1:11 par.).
The voice comes from heaven as in 2 Pt. 1:18, not from the
cloud as in Mk. 9:7 par. But the form of the saying is
closer to that in Mt. 17:5. The command "Obey him!" is not
clearly present. P reads ወፐሕዘዘየ 'and my commandment'
while T has በፐሕዘዘየ 'in (or with) my commandment'. It
would be possible then to read "This is my son whom I love
and I am pleased with my commandment." It seems more
likely, however, that the text is slightly corrupted here.
If we read የ: ፐሕዘዘ for በፐሕዘዘየ we have the words of
the synoptic tradition "listen to (obey) him." I think this
is highly likely, and I have placed this reading into the
text. Cf. Jn. 1:49, 3:35-6, 8:28-9, 8:54, 10:36, 11:27,
1 Jn. 5:9, Lk. 20:36; Acts 13:33; Heb. 7:28.

V. 2. The cloud is the source of the voice in the
synoptic gospels (Mk. 9:7 par.). The cloud is here the
vehicle of transportation into heaven for Jesus, Moses, and
Elijah. Or so it is in P. In T where there is no ል before
ሕ7ዘሕነ or ወ before ልሙቤ it is our Lord who picks up
Moses and Elijah! This, then, is here the cloud of ascension as in Acts 1:9. Cf. Lk. 24:51; Rev. 11:12. The motif
of fear is found not in the ascension story of Acts but in
the synoptic transfiguration account (Mk. 9:6 par.).

V. 3. It is hard to decide if ሕ፞ል 'who' or ሕል 'but'
is correct in the phrase ሰበ፞ሕ:ሕል:በሙጋ 'men who are in

the flesh'. ኸՈ makes more sense in Ethiopic, but ኸՈ may
translate the Greek αλλα 'but, yet' expressing surprise that
people who came from heaven would have physical bodies. Who
are these men? William H. Brownlee has suggested in private
conversation that they might be the dead who rose from the
graves when Jesus gave up the ghost on the cross (Mt. 27:52-
53). But I believe they might be all the righteous dead who
are kept in the first heaven awaiting this moment. In any
case we might expect that at some time or even right now
they would be given bodies similar to those of Moses and
Elijah described above. Cf. Heb. 4:14; 7:26; Jn. 6:62.

Vv. 4-5. Both scripture quotes are from Psalm 23
(LXX). The first is interpreted of the disciples who look
into the second heaven trying to catch a glimpse of God.
Cf. Jn. 7:34, 36; 8:21. The second is interpreted of the
angels in heaven, heavenly rulers, who are apparently sur-
prised at this turn of events. They are in some consternation. Quite probably this is a remnant of the ancient
soteriology where Jesus surprises the angels by his trium-
phal ascent through the heavens.[1] I believe that መዓጹት
is simply an unattested variant plural of ጻጹት 'door'.

Vv. 6-7. The closing of the second heaven draws the
scene on the mountain sharply to an end. We have been given
no clue to the exact number of heavens, but there may be

___

[1] See Ernst Kähler, Studien zum te Deum und zur
Geschichte des 24. Psalms in der Alten Kirche (Göttingen:
Vandenhoeck and Ruprecht, 1958), 53-55.

more than two. The book closes with the descent from the mountain and a reference to the book of life which records the names of the righteous. Cf. Rev. 17:8, 20:12.

The ascension of Jesus into heaven is conclusive in the discussion about the time when this is supposed to take place, in spite of James's opinion to the contrary[1]: the Apocalypse of Peter is set after the resurrection of Jesus. We cannot expect to see him again until his return in glory as prophesied in chapters one and six.

---

[1]M. R. James, "The Recovery of the Apocalypse of Peter," ibid., pp. 14-16.

CHAPTER FIVE

THE RELIABILITY OF THE ETHIOPIC TEXT

In this final chapter we will deal with those problems
concerning the reliability of the Ethiopic text. In no
sense can this text be "proven" to reflect faithfully in
every detail the original Apocalypse of Peter. That sort of
evidence is just not available. But yet there are many reasons to support its accuracy in general, and I believe the
preponderance of evidence is in favor of this view.

I. The Pseudo-Clementine Writing

The faithfulness of the Ethiopic text is brought into
question first of all because it is embedded in another
document. We must ask whether it has not been transformed
significantly to conform to this larger work. The question
may be put more radically: do we have before us the Apocalypse of Peter at all? Do we not rather have a Pseudo-
Clementine composition which perhaps used this apocalypse
as a source? Is this Ethiopic text, then a genuine translation of the Apocalypse of Peter or is it instead only
another witness to its use in the early church?

Comparisons of the available Greek fragments with the
Ethiopic are given elsewhere in this dissertation. We can
see from them the reasons why I believe the Ethiopic is a

376

translation from our oldest Greek texts. But what are the connections between this translation and the Pseudo-Clementine work? Has material from this latter writing or from elsewhere entered this translation? Has the translation been altered in style of language or detail to conform to the larger writing? It is this relationship which we here investigate.

The Apocalypse of Peter is marked off at the outset by indications in the Ethiopic text. The first sentence of the Ethiopic is a title descriptive of the whole Pseudo-Clementine writing. It is a long, descriptive sentence, but nevertheless a single sentence set off by Ethiopic punctuation. This sentence has its own style, using several relative clauses in contrast with the style of that which follows (Apoc. Pt. 1-17). We have labelled it a Prologue because of its length. It is clearly distinguished from the narrative which begins in Apocalypse of Peter chapter 1. This prologue is connected to the Pseudo-Clementine work at that point where Peter is told to meditate on the exposition which Jesus has made for him (Ps.-Cl. 142ra).[1]

---

[1]Since the Pseudo-Clementine work has never been divided into chapter and verse, we refer to it by folio number, side of folio, and column designation as given by Grébaut in his edition of this text. Fortunately in both his Ethiopic text and his French translation Grébaut has inserted these numbers at approximately the correct points. Thus 142ra means folio 142, recto side, first column. Sylvain Grébaut, "Littérature Ethiopienne pseudo-clementine," Revue de l'orient chrétien 15 (1910), 198-214, 307-323, 425-439.

The end of the Apocalypse of Peter in the Ethiopic
text is also easily distinguishable. It ends with the
sentence where the disciples descend from the mountain
(Apoc. Pt. 17:7; Ps.-Cl. 137rb), and the material following
this is "very evidently of later date" as James has said.[1]
But James did not set forth his case, with the result that
doubts about this point have been raised by those less familiar with the Ethiopic text and with apocalyptic materials.[2]
The distinction actually comes in the Ethiopic text itself,
and we will here set out the case for that viewpoint.

The opening sentence of the Pseudo-Clementine work,
following the Apocalypse of Peter, reads, "He opened his
mouth and said to me, 'Hear, O my son Clement'" (137rb). It
is a complete change of scene from the preceding narrative.
Clement is introduced for the first time, indicating the
supposed course of the transmission of this tradition and by
this name adding a second generation of authority to it.
"Me," which up to this time has always been Peter, now
refers to Clement. At the same time the "we" often used in
the apocalypse to refer to the disciples never appears again.
The expression "he opened his mouth" is never used in the
Apocalypse of Peter, and it indicates that something new is
beginning here. The story told by Peter has become an

---

[1]M. R. James, The Apocryphal New Testament, ibid.,
520.

[2]See G. H. Boobyer, St. Mark and the Transfiguration
Story, ibid., 30-40.

exposition from Clement. The transfiguration scene is now described in the third person with Peter, James and John mentioned by name as if this had happened to someone other than the supposed writer (Ps.-Cl. 138vb-139ra). It is true that quite unexpectedly and without indication the dialogue between Jesus and Peter resumes with Peter relating it in the first person (Ps.-Cl. 139rb-145rb; cf. also the very end, 146va). This latter dialogue, however, contains an explicit reference to a "first revelation" which Jesus has already given to Peter (Ps.-Cl. 140ra). Here the text itself explicitly distinguishes between the first revelation (the Apocalypse of Peter) and the second (the Pseudo-Clementine work).

There is also following the Apocalypse of Peter a noticeable change in style. The narrative setting so important in the apocalypse in missing in the Pseudo-Clementine. In the latter the style is more philosophical and explanatory. The sentences tend to be longer and there are numerous lists of various sorts (Ps.-Cl. 137va, 138va, 139ra-139rb, 139vb, 142ra-142rb, 144va). There is a change in the use of vocabulary so that now, for example, ꞑꞑ Ꭓꞇ which in the Apocalypse of Peter has always stood for eternal light-glory now also carries the meaning of the ceaseless heavenly praises and singing of the various orders of creation (Ps.-Cl. 136rb-138rb). This latter again shows that we have landed in a wholly different atmosphere. In the apocalypse the end of the world is expected momentarily. In the Ps.-Cl. work

God has divided the universe into various regions, ordaining kings, governors, princes, prophets, apostles, etc., for the longer range governance of his world.

These differences are also seen in a change of content. We may facilitate the discussion of this point by analyzing the superstructure of Ps.-Cl. in the following way:

I. Report of Peter's speech to Clement concerning the glory of God in all creation. 137rb-139rb (mid.).

II. Report (unintroduced) of a dialogue between Peter and Jesus concerning the salvation of sinners. 139rb (mid.)-144rb (beg.).

  A. Request of Peter for explanation on the fate of sinners at the last day: Peter's consternation at the thought of the second death. 139rb (mid.)-140ra (beg.).

  B. Report of Jesus' answer: Sinners will not repent if they understand. 140ra.

  C. Report of Peter's plea to Jesus: He is the chief of sinners because of his three-fold denial. 140ra (end)-140rb (mid.).

  D. Report of Jesus' answer: As scripture shows (Mt. 5:45; Mk. 2:5-7; Jn. 10:37-38), mercy is the work of the Father. 140rb (mid.)-140vb (beg.).

  E. Report of Peter's plea: Speak plainly, not in parables. 140vb.

  F. Report of Jesus' answer: When he comes he will destroy the devil and punish sinners severely. 140vb (end)-141vb (beg.).

  G. Report of Peter's fear of the second death (the punishments). 141vb (beg.).

  H. Report of Jesus' answer. 141vb (beg.)-143vb (mid.).

1. The Lord will have pity on them and will give to everyone "the life, the glory, and the kingdom without end" because Jesus will plead for them, but this must be kept a secret so as not to encourage sin. 141vb-142vb (end).

2. The parable of the Potter. 142vb (end)-143ra (end).

3. Scriptural proof from the Psalms. 143ra (end)-143vb (mid.).

I. Report of Peter's response: Gratitude for the clear explanation upon which he can meditate, with the statement that now he can believe and not doubt. 143vb (mid.)-144ra (beg.).

J. Report of Jesus' final explanation: Description of the ranks of the saved. 144ra (beg.) -144vb (beg.).

III. Further report of Peter's speech to Clement: A summary of what has been said with a warning to keep this mystery locked in a box, and a short ecclesiastical calendar. 144vb (beg.)-146va (end of the document).

The concern of both Apoc. Pt. and Ps.-Cl. is the salvation of sinners. But while sinners are saved in the Apoc. Pt. by the prayers of the righteous directed toward Jesus (14:1-2), in Ps.-Cl. sinners are saved by the plea of Jesus to the Father (142va, beg.). In the original apocalypse this salvation is openly expressed, but in Ps.-Cl. the author is at least as concerned to keep this teaching a secret, for if ordinary people found out about it they would no longer have a reason to keep from sinning (142vb, beg.). Indeed, the whole form of the Ps.-Cl. document comes from a desire to show how difficult it was even for Peter to get this knowledge.

In line with this, the author of the <u>Apocalypse of
Peter</u> may have chosen Peter for his pseudonym because
Peter's eyes had been uncovered and his ears unstopped (16:
9). For the author of the Ps.-Cl. work it was more important that Peter was chief of sinners because he had denied
Christ (140rb). Peter's fate also was at stake because he
was a sinner himself. None of our sources in the early
church witness to the content of the Ps.-Cl. work. It was
intended to be read only by the mature Christians who would
not be led into sin through the knowledge that even sinners
have hope.

Having said this much, we must still ask, why is the
<u>Apocalypse of Peter</u> embedded in this Pseudo-Clementine writ-
ing? To say "embedded" is probably too much. For it is not
embedded in the Ps.-Cl. work but it stands just before it,
after the title but before anything about Clement has
properly begun. The <u>Apocalypse of Peter</u> serves the Pseudo-
Clementine work as text for commentary. The entire work
(<u>Apoc. Pt.</u> and Ps.-Cl.) can be called a midrash. We demonstrate this relation with the following table.

What this table shows is that the author of Ps.-Cl.
was not afraid to use <u>Apoc. Pt.</u> creatively in his own work.
He did not go back into the material of the apocalypse and
harmonize it with his own later ideas. He had a text before
him upon which he commented by taking ideas from it and
changing them or expanding them as he saw fit. We may say,
then, that the work as a whole (<u>Apoc. Pt.</u> and Ps.-Cl.) is a

Ps.-Cl.	Apoc. Pt.	Ps.-Cl. Use of Apoc. Pt.
137rb (mid.)	17:9 (cf. 15:1)	the elect will inherit the mountain of God's temple, and interpretation of the temple made without hands
138va (beg.)	1:7; 15:2-7	the resurrected just are described with the same characteristics as the glory bodies of Moses and Elijah and even Christ himself
138vb (end)	15:2-7	the glory of the angels is described as that of Moses and Elijah but with an additional reference to the fuller of Mk. 9:3
138vb (end)- 139ra (beg.)	16:7-17:2	the transfiguration is mentioned by name, and elements of the synoptic account are brought in--it is assumed that Jesus has been transfigured; it is said that upon that mountain the Lord showed his second coming. (In Apoc. Pt. Jesus is not transformed and there is a change of mountain between the prediction of the coming and the appearance of Moses and Elijah.)
139ra (beg.)	1:7; 6:1-2	the Father will not himself judge but will turn judgment over to the Son
139rb (mid.)	3:4-7	Peter reminds Jesus not to forget his earlier question about the mercy of God to sinners (he quotes the saying). Cf. Ps.-Cl. 139vb (beg.).
139vb (beg.)	6:7-9; 10:5-6	list of forms of idolatry
139vb (mid.)	1:8, etc.	quote of "they will be paid back according to their sins"

Ps.-Cl.	Apoc. Pt.	Ps.-Cl. Use of Apoc. Pt.
139vb (end)	4:1-4	God will raise up the dead bodies for judgment, interprets this as the second judgment for the second death
140rb (end)- 140va	14:1 (?)	God has mercy on the just and unjust
141ra (end)- 141rb (beg.)	2:8-2:10; (14:4)	the liar who is the son of perdition who has said I am Christ and then made martyrs of those who refused to believe in him is followed by the sending of many evil spirits on the earth
141rb (end)	4:3	the dead resurrect at Jesus' word rather than that of the Father
141rb (end)- 141va (beg.)	1:7; 6:1-2	the Father will place the crown on Jesus' head at Jerusalem
141va (beg.)	2:12; 16:1	Moses and Elijah come to Mt. Tabor after Jesus' parousia
141va (beg.)	6:1-2	Jesus' throne is in the middle of the river of fire
141va (end)	3:1-3	the heart of the just and of the angels is troubled at the arrows of pain which shoot through the heart of sinners
142va (end)	14:1	at the word of those who have believed in Jesus, he will have pity
142vb (end)	ch. 6-12	exhort sinners with the punishment by flames of fire so that they do not do injustice to one another

Ps.-Cl.	Apoc. Pt.	Ps.-Cl. Use of Apoc. Pt.
143va (mid.)	6:4	those who believe in Jesus will not come to the fiery punishments because they have received the body and blood of Christ and have become his children

midrash, for it attempts to make an older text relevant to its own age.[1] At the same time it has preserved for us relatively intact that earlier text.

Now we have not shown by this that the author of the Pseudo-Clementine work did not alter the text of the Apocalypse of Peter. We have shown that he was free enough in his use of its text that he need not have changed anything at all. But did he make changes? We can detect two or three places where changes in the text have been made, and these may very well be traced to the author of the Pseudo-Clementine work, though we are not able to prove it. First

---

[1]"The word midrash designates a composition which seeks to make a text of Scripture from the past understandable, useful and relevant for the religious needs of a later generation." Addison G. Wright, The Literary Genre Midrash (New York: Alba House, 1967), 143. The debate about the genre "midrash" has been long and complicated and is not yet finished. See William H. Brownlee, "Biblical Interpretation Among the Sectaries of the Dead Sea Scrolls," Biblical Archaeologist 14 (1951), 54-76; idem, "The Habakkuk Midrash and the Targum of Jonathan," Journal of Jewish Studies 7 (1956), 169-186; idem, The Midrash Pesher of Habakkuk (Missoula, MT: Scholars Pr., 1979); Renée Bloch, "Midrash," Dictionnaire de la Bible Supplement v. 5 (Paris: Librairie Letouzey et Ane, 1957), col. 1263-1281; M. Gertner, "Midrashim in the New Testament," Journal of Semitic Studies 7 (1962), 267-292; John Bowker, The Targums and Rabbinic Literature (Cambridge: University Pr., 1969), 45-46; Roger

and most importantly, the elimination of the rescue of the tortured (14:1) from the Ethiopic text may have been done by the Ps.-Cl. author. We can guess that his motives were to hold back the salvation of sinners until he was ready to introduce it later in his own work, and then to transform the teaching from a plea by the righteous to Christ into a plea from Christ to the Father. Secondly, the string of divine names found at 15:1, 16:1 and 16:4 may have been added by the Ps.-Cl. author to bolster the divinity of Jesus, which may not have been evident in the Apocalypse of Peter and with which he was concerned (144vb, mid.). Thirdly, he may be responsible if references to the eternity of punishment have been added to the text (as it seemed when we compared the Ethiopic with ms. B at 10:6-7; see chapter two under Manuscript B), for he wanted the punishments to put fear into the hearts of sinners (142vb, end). The extent of the Ps.-Cl. author's intrusion into the text of the Apoc. Pt. must not have been extensive, however, since the style, the vocabulary, the content, the form, and the ultimate concerns of both writings are still so recognizably different.[1]

Le Déaut, "Apropos a Definition of Midrash," Interpretation 25 (1971), 259-282; Merrill P. Miller, "Targum, Midrash, and the Use of the Old Testament in the New Testament," Journal for the Study of Judaism in the Persian, Hellenistic and Roman Period 2 (1971), 29-82; idem, "Midrash," Interpreter's Dictionary of the Bible, Supplementary Volume, 593-597.

[1]It is not acceptable in any case to quote from the Ps.-Cl. work as if it were the Apocalypse of Peter or to read the ideas of its author into the apocalypse. J. T.

II. The Unity of the Apocalypse of Peter

Past research has concentrated on the many sources
which the author of the Apocalypse of Peter has used in his
work. I have found no place in the literature which has
taken this apocalypse seriously as a unified work. The
primitive characteristics of the punishments of the inferno
have contributed to the idea that the author was primitive
and lacked the ability to write a really unified account.
The point of view is summed up well by Philipp Vielhauer
when he says that the interest of the Apoc. Pt. lies wholly
in the description of the other-world.[1] The very profusion
of the sources has contributed to the idea that this work
lacks unity of thought or even of authorship.

Let us begin with what I believe to be the climax of
the story, the vision of the heavenly tabernacle and the
accompanying heavenly voice (16:9c-17:1). The voice, speaking in the third person, tells the disciples that this man
is God's Son. Now this announcement takes us back to 1:6,
"For the Coming of the Son of God will not be revealed but
like lightning which appears from the east to the west."
There the one who is Son of God is the one who will come in
glory, and this one is identified with the speaker Jesus
(1:6-7).

Milik (The Books of Enoch, ibid., 107) and G. H. Boobyer
(St. Mark and the Transfiguration Story, ibid., 35-38) are
guilty of this.

[1]Philipp Vielhauer, Geschichte der urchristlichen Literatur (Berlin: Walter de Gruyter, 1975), 512.

When this Son of God comes in his glory <u>his Father</u>
<u>will place a crown on his head</u> "that I might judge the
living and the dead." The same motif is found in the final
trial scene at 6:1-2. There the angels first place a throne
at the right hand of the Father, and then the Father places
the crown on the head of the Son. In this case, however,
the purpose of this is not for judgment, since it is the
Father who orders the nations to pass through the river of
fire. Rather, the purpose of the throne and the crown in
6:1-2 is to show this publicly to the nations who weep when
they see it. There can be no doubt that this is a coronation scene. The Son of God is made king. And what is then
his proper title? I believe it is Messiah or Christ. The
Son of God becomes the Messiah (= king) when he comes in
glory. The kingdom is totally eschatological (14:2).

How is the title "Christ" used in the Apocalypse of
Peter? The title appears six times: 1:5, 2:8-9, 15:1, 16:1,
16:4, 16:6. In 1:5 the false christs are said to come "in
my name." This refers to an eschatological claim. In 2:
8-9 it is said that the "first christ" was crucified, but
this also is part of the eschatological debate about who is
really messiah when false messiahs appear. The title Christ
in 15:1, 16:1, and 16:4 is part of those additions to the
text which were suspect on stylistic grounds and were shown
to be additions by comparison with the Akhmim. It is only
16:6, "the book of my Lord Jesus Christ," which may be an
oblique reference to Jesus' messiahship during his lifetime,

that is, before his parousia. We might suspect an addition
here also, but we have no evidence for it since we have no
other text with which to compare it. The subject of discussion in 16:5-6 is the coming honor and glory of the
Christian martyrs. Perhaps this led the author to use the
title proleptically of the one for whose sake the martyrs
were suffering. He could be called messiah only because he
would become messiah. The coronation scene demonstrates so
clearly what the author understood messiahship to be that I
believe the title could not be applied by this author to
Jesus in its full sense prior to the parousia. The author
of the Apocalypse of Peter, then, did not consider Jesus to
be messiah during his lifetime. He would become messiah at
his return in glory. What is really important about Jesus
is his eschatological role.

I believe this also explains three more things.
First, the resurrection of Jesus plays no role in this apocalypse. Indeed, it is not even mentioned. It is true that
the Jesus who is sitting on the Mt. of Olives at the beginning of this document (1:1) must be the resurrected Jesus,
but his resurrection in itself did not seem important to our
author. Secondly, the crucifixion of Jesus is also not important to the author. The salvation for sinners through
Jesus is not brought about by Jesus' death on the cross or
his resurrection. Salvation of sinners occurs when they are
taken from torment and dipped in the Acherusian Lake (14:1),
and it is with this in mind that Jesus is called Savior in

3:5 where the fate of sinners is discussed. It is doubtful
if Jesus' salvation has anything to do with the righteous at
all, since they receive their reward but are not in need of
salvation. (Cf. Mk. 2:17, "I came not to call the righteous
but sinners.") The only two references to the crucifixion
of Jesus are in 2:9 and (obliquely) in 1:6. In 2:9 the crucifixion is brought in, I believe, as an example of martyrdom for those whom the false messiah is persecuting. And in
1:6 the cross of Jesus goes before him at his coming in
glory perhaps as the symbol of what qualifies him to be the
messiah. For this purpose his crucifixion is essential in
that it qualifies him to be Messiah. In its own right, the
passion is not a subject for reflection. Thirdly, the
earthly life of Jesus, his teaching and miracle working
which play such a large role in the gospels, does not even
come into view. In the face of the coming judge, what importance could it have? Only the saying which Peter quotes
in 3:4 is perhaps an acknowledgment of earlier teaching of
Jesus, but if this is so the saying also assumes the eschatological character of the earlier teaching. That is, if
Jesus taught earlier, his teaching then was also what he
taught now. Here he must correct a misunderstanding.

Let us stop for a moment and sum up what we have
covered so far. Jesus' main role is yet to be accomplished.
He will come as Son of God in glory. At that time he will
become messiah and serve as judge of all people. It is this
consistent christology which permeates the entire writing

and which gives the Apocalypse of Peter its unity.

If now we return to the heavenly voice which announces that Jesus is Son of God let us consider whether for the author this is true of Jesus before the announcement or if it only becomes true at the time of the announcement. The title most often used of Jesus is Lord. It appears in 1:4, 3:4, 16:7 (twice), 17:2-3 (twice) and the suspect verses 15:1 and 16:4 where it may be original (cf. Akhmim). The second instance in 16:7 is a special case where Peter refers to "the book of my Lord Jesus Christ," and I do not think we can gain much information from its use there. In 1:4, 3:4, 15:1, 16:6, and 16:7 we see the title used in addressing Jesus or in contexts where Jesus is about to address his disciples. These are all occasions for teaching, and I believe the title Lord is here equivalent to Rabbi or Teacher. In 2:4 Jesus is called ኦ ̀ 'teacher, master'. Since the teaching is always eschatological we may say that Jesus is understood to be the eschatological prophet. But by "eschatological prophet" we mean not the prophet expected at the end time (though this meaning cannot be dismissed), rather the teacher who makes eschatological predictions and reveals to his disciples visions of the heavenly world. Nowhere here does the title Lord mean that Jesus is a heavenly being.

The last two uses of Lord, however, are otherwise. In 17:2-3 Jesus is put on the same level with Moses and Elijah when all three ascend into heaven. We must remember that in

this account of the "transfiguration" Jesus has not been
transfigured. It is Moses and Elijah who have bodies of
glory. This is an account of Jesus' ascension. And I believe he ascends to receive his glory. This may also be the
meaning of 2 Pt. 1:17, the voice was born to him as he received honor and glory. Thus we have come back to the
heavenly voice which announced that Jesus was God's Son.
But I believe it was more than an announcement. It was the
declaration which made him God's Son in order that he might
at this time ascend and receive his glory, and then return
for his coronation as Messiah. This is why Jesus calls God
his Father only in those contexts where he has already received his sonship (1:7, 4:2, 6:1, 14:3, 16:9). It is the
Son who inherits the throne.[1]

To summarize briefly here, the christology of the
Apocalypse of Peter is what we might call a low christology.
An extraordinary man has been martyred.[2] Then he is (resur-
rected and) taken up into heaven at the time he is declared
to be God's Son. As God's Son he will return, become the
Messiah, and begin his reign in an eternal kingdom with the

---

[1]In the account of the ascension (17:2-6), Psalm 23
(LXX) is quoted twice. There are words from that psalm that
are not quoted but which surely would come to mind, namely
"that the King of glory may come in." I believe these words
may have been omitted precisely because the newly appointed
Son was not yet King.

[2]For the persecution and exaltation of the Righteous
Man, see George W. Nickelsburg, Resurrection, Immortality,
and Eternal Life in Intertestamental Judaism, Harvard Theological Studies 25 (Cambridge: Harvard U. Pr., 1972).

Father. (At no time does he in any sense become equal with the Father, and in 3:5-7 the Creator is kept distinct from Jesus.) This christology is related to that in Rom. 1:3 and Acts 3:18-23, and we recognize it as the pattern of one of the earliest christologies, perhaps even the earliest of all.[1] By saying this I am not suggesting that the apocalypse was written very early, only that it reflects an early christology.

Now let us return to the climax of the Apocalypse of Peter, the vision of the heavenly tabernacle and the voice from heaven. We have discussed at some length how this second element, the voice, relates to the christology of the writing and its unity. What about the first element, the vision of the heavenly tabernacle? Here we are on less firm ground. Certainly this vision and the saying of Jesus which

---

[1]We cannot attempt here to sort through the amazing amount of literature on early christology. But there is a general agreement that the pattern of the Apocalypse of Peter is early. See Helmut Koester, "The Structure and Criteria of Early Christian Beliefs" in James M. Robinson and Helmut Koester, Trajectories through Early Christianity (Philadelphia: Fortress, 1976), 57-66; J. A. T. Robinson, "The Most Primitive Christology of All," Journal of Theological Studies 7 (1956), 177-189; H. Merklein, ibid.; F. Hahn, ibid., 67-132; Oscar Cullmann, The Christology of the New Testament (Philadelphia: Westminster, 1963); Reginald H. Fuller, The Foundations of New Testament Christology (New York: Charles Scribner's Sons, 1965); C. F. D. Moule, The Origin of Christology (Cambridge: University Pr., 1977); Willi Marxsen, ibid.; Richard N. Longenecker, The Christology of Early Jewish Christianity (Grand Rapids: Baker, 1970); Werner Kramer, Christ, Lord, Son of God (Naperville, IL: Alec R. Allenson, 1966); John J. Collins, "The Apocalyptic Context of Christian Origins," Michigan Quarterly Review 22 (1983), 250-264. Cf. Hans Bietenhard, Die himmlische Welt im Urchristentum und Spätjudentum (Tübingen: J. C. B. Mohr (Paul Siebeck), 1951), 63-71.

immediately precedes it ("There is one tabernacle which the
hand of man has not made, which my heavenly Father has made
for me and for the elect.") have some connection with the
temple saying recorded in Mk. 14:58 par. and in Jn. 2:19 as
well as the christology of Hebrews (9:11, 24) and that of
the Hellenists (Acts 6:14). That some form of the temple
saying may even go back to Jesus is possible. However, we
know less about this particular christology. There existed
at the time of Jesus a hope that the messiah would bring a
new temple when he came.[1] And here Jesus may have been understood as the one who would bring the new tabernacle. At
least it seems as if Jesus is telling Peter not to expect or
desire any sort of earthly tabernacle (temple) but to wait
for a heavenly one made without hands by the Father himself.
If the fig tree parable in 2:4-6 is a parable about the temple (= house of Israel), then the words "we will plant
another in its place" (v. 6) may refer to the replacement of
the temple in Jerusalem by this heavenly tabernacle. The
earthly temple is replaced by the spiritual. If that is so,
then the heavenly tabernacle is another theme which shows
unity between different sections of the apocalypse.

---

[1] Marcel Simon, "Retour du Christ et reconstruction du
temple dans la pensée chrétienne primitive" in Mélanges offerts à M. Maurice Goguel à l'occasion de son soixiante-
dixième anniversaire (Neuchâtel: Delachaux and Niestlé,
1950), 247-257, esp. pp. 250-251. See also R. G. Hamerton-
Kelly, "The Temple and the Origins of Jewish Apocalyptic,"
Vetus Testamentum 20 (1970), 1-15; A. M. Dubarle, "Le signe
du temple," Revue Biblique 46 (1939), 21-44; A. Feuillet,
"Le discours de Jésus sur la ruine du temple," Revue Biblique 56 (1949), 61-92; R. J. McKelvey, The New Temple

Perhaps the unity of the work can be seen most clearly
in the teaching on the resurrection of the dead. In chapter
four there is a description of the general resurrection. It
is a very physical resurrection. Hades (Gehenna) holds the
dead but gives them up at the command of God (4:3). The
animals and birds give back all the human flesh they have
eaten (4:4). The flesh and bones, etc., are brought together (4:8) and then the soul and spirit are restored to
them (4:9). What follows this is not quite so clear. The
resurrected sinners are apparently driven by fire to the
river of fire where they will be judged (5:1, 8) and during
this process their spirits may also be turned to fire (5:6).
Then follow their punishments (ch. 7-12). On the other
hand, the righteous dead have already been with Jesus before
being reunited with their bodies (6:4 but possibly corrupt;
cf. also 16:2-4). After the resurrection they will put on
the "clothing of celestial life" (13:1) and then view the
punishments of the wicked (13:2). This "clothing of celestial life" (cf. Mt. 22:11-13; 2 Cor. 5:1-10) must be the
light/glory bodies which are described in 15:2-7, but why
do Moses and Elijah already have their glory bodies? I believe it is because they were thought to have never died and
so their bodies are not in Hades and would not participate

(London: Oxford, 1969); B. Gärtner, The Temple and the Community in Qumran and the New Testament (Cambridge: University Pr., 1965); Daniel R. Schwartz, "The Three Temples of
4Q Florilegium," Revue de Qumran 10 (1978), 83-91; Werner
Georg Kümmel, Promise and Fulfillment, Studies in Biblical
Theology 23 (London: SCM Pr., 1961), 79-82, 99-102.

in the general resurrection. They have already in their
bodies ascended into heaven. In any case we see throughout
the writing an interest in the resurrection of the flesh
coupled with an interest in the glorious body of heaven.
This shows unity of authorship and the author's purpose in
taking up his pen. He was involved in the debate over the
believer's resurrection bodies. He insists on a very
physical, future resurrection for believers.

The body of the resurrected believers must also be
like that of the resurrected Jesus since he is their supreme
example of resurrection. Nothing is said about the appearance of the resurrected Jesus in the Apocalypse of Peter
other than that he had a prophetic right hand (3:1).[1] Indeed he must have had something like an ordinary body of
flesh since the disciples are so amazed at the glory bodies
of Moses and Elijah (15:4, 7). I believe this explains the
author's use of the transfiguration tradition.[2] The story

---

[1]This right hand which here is only used to show a
vision was later interpreted as that in which he held the
entire universe. Cf. Arabic Book of the Rolls [Arabic Apocalypse of Peter], v. 14, pp. 213-214 in the edition of
Mingana.

[2]The literature on the transfiguration is massive and
there is little consensus on any point. I hold the point of
view that the transfiguration was originally a post-
resurrection appearance of Jesus. But there is much debate
on that score. In addition to the references given in chapter one where the history of research is discussed, see Benjamin Bacon, "The Tranfiguration Story: A Study of the
Problem of the Sources of our Synoptic Gospels," American
Journal of Theology 6 (1902), 236-265; Georg Bertram, "Die
Himmelfahrt Jesu von Kreuz aus und der Glaube an seine Auferstehung," Festgabe für Adolf Deissmann zum 60. Geburtstag
(Tübingen: J. C. B. Mohr (Paul Siebeck), 1927), 187-217;

was originally a story of the appearance of the already glorified resurrected Christ to Peter and it may have been known to our author in that form. But here Jesus is not transfigured. The author has "untransfigured" the Jesus of that tradition to conform with his low christology (Jesus becomes Son of God only at his ascension) and with his concern that resurrection bodies be bodies of flesh (only at the parousia will Jesus appear in glory).[1] Thus two themes, the low christology of the author and the fleshly bodies of the resurrected including Jesus, before they receive their glory bodies, which in themselves show unity of thought

Ernst Lohmeyer, "Die Verklärung Jesu nach dem Markus-Evangelium," Zeitschrift für die neutestamentlichen Wissenschaft 21 (1922), 185-215; Joseph B. Bernardin, "The Transfiguration," Journal of Biblical Literature 52 (1933), 181-189; G. B. Caird, "The Transfiguration," Expository Times 67 (1954), 184-203; A. Feuillet, "Les perspectives propres à chaque évangéliste dans les récits de la transfiguration," Biblica 39 (1958), 281-301; Hans-Peter Müller, "Die Verklärung Jesu: Eine motivgeschichtliche Studie," Zeitschrift für die neutestamentliche Wissenschaft 50-51 (1960-61), 56-64; Maurice Sabbe, "La rédaction du récit de la transfiguration," Recherches bibliques 6 (Louvain: Descalés de Brouwer, 1962), 65-100; Howard Clark Kee, "The Transfiguration in Mark: Epiphany or Apocalyptic Vision?," in J. Reumann, ed., Understanding the Sacred Text (Valley Forge: Judson Pr., 1972), 135-152; B. D. Chilton, "The Transfiguration: Dominical Assurance and Apostolic Vision," New Testament Studies 27 (1980), 115-124.

[1] In a brief analysis George J. Brooke has reached the same conclusion: "The Ethiopic Apocalypse of Peter 15-17 and Mark 9:2-13," unpublished research paper for William H. Brownlee, Claremont Graduate School, 1977. He concludes, "In sum, therefore, the Ethiopic Apocalypse of Peter 15-17 is an early non-canonical attestation of the rejection of transfiguration resurrection appearances; and yet, as it stands, it has the same intention, derivable from its structure, as the synoptic transfiguration story, especially as present in Mark, that Jesus is Messiah and that he is the guarantor and the guarantee of the resurrection of the dead."

throughout the writing, are intimately interwound. Little

material can be considered unoriginal and disentangled with-

out unravelling the whole cloth. I believe it was the ori-

ginal author who wrote so purposefully, for the issue he

addresses was being debated at the very time the Apocalypse

of Peter was written according to its traditional dating.[1]

III. The Date of the Apocalypse of Peter

A. Trajectories

Let us begin the dating of the apocalypse by glancing

briefly at some of the sources its author used. The method

is treacherous at best, but we may gain some information

from it. The use of the synoptic apocalypse dominates the

first section of the apocalypse.[2] There are traces of all

three synoptic gospels in Apoc. Pt. 1-2 but the form of the

sayings is often so close to Matthew's that we must believe

he had this part of the Gospel of Matthew before him in

written form or was very familiar with its oral reading.

He also knew a form of the transfiguration story and a form

of the parable of the fig tree. These are obvious. What

are less obvious but also very important are the connections

---

[1]A surface structure analysis also points to the unity of the work, but such analyses cannot be conclusive. I am including my own analysis (certainly not filled out in detail in all parts) in the appendix.

[2]The synoptic apocalypse is another area on which there is no scholarly consensus. See V. Taylor, ibid., 636-644; W. G. Kummel, ibid., 95-104; T. F. Glasson, The Second Advent (London: Epworth Pr., 1963), 71-75, 194-203; G. R. Beasley-Murray, Jesus and the Future (New York: St. Martin's Pr., 1954).

with the Johannine literature. The saying about the seed
sown into the ground (4:10) has the same form as that in
Jn. 12:24; the idea of physical resurrection for judgment
in Apoc. Pt. 4-5 has its closest New Testament parallel in
Jn. 5:28-29; the saying about the Liar in Apoc. Pt. 2:10 is
related to 1 Jn. 2:22; the christ who has come (or is coming
into the world) in Apoc. Pt. 2:8 (cf. 1:6-7) has its closest
New Testament parallels in Jn. 11:27, 4:25 (cf. 2 Jn. 7);
the request of the righteous in Apoc. Pt. 14:1 for anyone
whom they wish out of torment is paralleled by John's doctrine of prayer in general (Jn. 14:14, etc.) and by prayer
for sinners (1 Jn. 5:15-17); both predict Peter's death
(Apoc. Pt. 14:4, Jn. 21:18-19). Now these connections are
surprising because the Apocalypse of Peter has such a heavy
emphasis on end-time eschatology and the Johannine literature is oriented so strongly to realized eschatology. The
interests, concepts and ideas show some connection, but the
Gospel of John uses these very differently than the Apocalypse of Peter.

Now Raymond Brown has analyzed the trajectory of the
Johannine community from its origins until it dissolved in
the second century.[1] In phase one of the community, the
time period before the Gospel of John was written, Brown believes that three groups of people contributed to the community makeup--first the originating group of Jewish

---

[1]Raymond E. Brown, The Community of the Beloved Disciples (New York: Paulist Pr., 1979).

Christians which had a background relatively similar to the
background of the synoptic tradition but with a lower christology; secondly a mixed group of Jewish Christians and
Samaritans with an anti-temple bias and a higher christology
who later entered the community; and thirdly a group of
Gentiles who came in even later. Brown may have distinguished these groups more clearly than the evidence allows,
but nevertheless he has done a valuable service in pointing
out the mix of theological expression present in that pre-
gospel setting. The most important factors involve: 1) a
low christology based on the titles Christ and Son of God;
2) an anti-Jerusalem temple bias similar to that of the Hellenists of Acts 7:48-50, but with a christology not based on
the Davidic Messiah, rather associated with the title Savior;
3) lack of an ecclesiastical structure; 4) a future-oriented
eschatology;[1] 5) the superiority of the Beloved Disciple
over Peter; 6) a connection with John the baptist; 7) some
connection with Galilee.[2]

These factors may be related to the Apocalypse of
Peter in the following ways. First, the low christology of
the apocalypse is based, like that of the early Johannine
community, on the titles Christ and Son of God. Secondly,
the anti-temple bias of the Johannine community is based on
the concept of spiritual worship; in the apocalypse Jesus

---

[1]Brown does not relate this to the Johannine Apocalypse of John, but the connection is possible.

[2]Raymond E. Brown, ibid., 25-58.

rebukes Peter for desiring to build earthly tabernacles when there is only one heavenly (spiritual) temple. Thirdly, there is no hint in the apocalypse of an ecclesiological structure.[1] Fourthly, the future-oriented eschatology of the early Johannine community may have been very similar to that of the Apocalypse of Peter. Not only are there similarities with the small amount of material believed to be earlier than the gospel, but the realized eschatology of the gospel is often expressed in a similar manner. For example, the very physical resurrection of the body is seen in the resurrection of Lazarus (Jn. 11:38-44) but is used there as an example for Jesus' gift of eternal life during his earthly ministry. Fifthly, since the Apocalypse of Peter derives much of its authority from the figure of Peter, the advocates of the present-oriented eschatology may have used the theme of the superiority of the Beloved Disciple over Peter to show the superiority of their present-oriented eschatology over the future-oriented eschatology associated with the Peter tradition. The final two elements, connections with John the Baptist and Galilee, cannot be directly related to the Apocalypse of Peter.[2]

---

[1]The Ethiopic translator has probably understood the successors of the disciples (1:2-3) to be church officials. But I believe the original author had only converts in mind. We may mention here that the apocalypse has the tradition of calling Jesus' disciples "his own" (1:1) just as does the Johannine community (Jn. 13:1).

[2]It cannot be pressed very far, but George W. E. Nickelsburg finds Galilee connections in the Peter and Enoch traditions which may be associated with the Apocalypse of

The theological mix of the early Johannine community
coupled with a view of a very active Holy Spirit caused the
community to undergo great changes during which the christology was elevated and the eschatology brought forward to
result in the theology which appears in the Gospel of John.
Many of the older elements have been preserved in the gospel
in radically changed form, and others have simply been
placed alongside the newer interpretation. For example,
Jn. 5:25-27 is a present-oriented spiritual eschatology, but
placed beside it is 5:28-29, the older future-oriented physical eschatology. Later on, Brown says, the Johannine community divided. The letters of John reveal this division,
and their author (not the same one who wrote the gospel) was
able to reach back to utilize the older apocalyptic traditions of an earlier time in the history of his own community
(1 Jn. 2:18-22; 4:1-3).

I am suggesting that the Apocalypse of Peter, from a
later time, is reflecting many of the elements found in the
early Johannine community. These elements may have also un-
dergone change. The eschatological elements in particular
may have been radicalized and made more physical in a reaction against the developing higher christology of the Johannine community. Be that as it may, in matters of eschatology in particular the earlier traditions reflected in the

Peter. See his article, "Enoch, Levi, and Peter: Recipients
of Revelation in Upper Galilee," Journal of Biblical Literature 100 (1981), 575-600, esp. 599-600.

Apocalypse of Peter may have found as time went on a close-
ness to some of the more radical apocalyptic elements of the
synoptic tradition (such as the little apocalypse and the
transfiguration account) after these had already been highly
developed, and the author of the Apocalypse of Peter was
able to utilize those elements for his own purpose in his
writing. I am suggesting, then, a trajectory of which the
origin lies close to that of the origin of the Johannine
community. It developed in opposition to the higher christology and realized eschatology of the Johannine community,
became even more apocalyptically radical, and using apocalyptic elements from the synoptic tradition welded together
these pieces into the theology we find in the Apocalypse of
Peter. It is possible (but certainly the evidence is incon-
clusive) that the group which broke away from the Johannine
community just prior to the composition of the Johannine
letters (1 Jn. 1:19) may be the radically conservative eschatological group in which our apocalypse was composed. It
is this conservative position which may have given the writing its initial popularity. By the time the Apocalypse of
Peter began to lose its early respected and popular position, the christology of the Johannine community had become
orthodox. But by then so had the apocalyptic eschatology of
the Apocalypse of Peter, though it was never declared offi-
cially to be orthodox in the same way that the christology
of pre-existence was declared to be orthodox at Nicaea.

Having found what we believe to be the trajectory of
the tradition found in our apocalypse, we shall now see
where that trajectory intersects the more general trajectories which stretch from Jesus to Valentinus and to the
Apostles' Creed as they have been surveyed by James M.
Robinson.[1] The original luminous resurrection appearances
of Jesus were favored by those with gnostic leanings because
they could be easily interpreted as inner religious experi-
ences. The reaction against this was to downplay the luminous and emphasize the physical nature of Jesus' resurrection,
resulting in the empty tomb stories and the identification
of Jesus' physical body before his resurrection with his
post-resurrection appearance. In a similar manner, the
resurrection of the believer into a spiritual body of glory
(as we find it in Paul) carried with it the possibility of
easy adaptation into the present accomplished resurrection
of the believer as a religious experience. The tendency to
orthodoxy countered with an insistence on the futurity of a
resurrection which was assured by its physicality. These
two trajectories manifested themselves in different genres
of literature. The gnostic tendency was to place authority
more and more in new interpretations from continuing experi-
ences of the resurrected Lord. The genre of dialogue of the
resurrected Christ with his disciples was appropriate to
express this. On the other hand, the orthodox trajectory

---

[1] James M. Robinson, "Jesus: From Easter to Valentinus
(or the Apostles' Creed)," ibid.

was travelled by those who more and more insisted that Jesus
had already disclosed himself fully before the resurrection.
The canonical gospel genre was suitable for this.

Where on these trajectories does the _Apocalypse of
Peter_ lie? It is a dialogue of the resurrected "Christ"
with his disciples such as the gnostics preferred. Jesus is
the teacher who gives authoritative teaching in answer to
his disciples' queries. But there are some important differences. Jesus does not "appear" as he commonly does in
the gnostic dialogues. He does not appear from heaven apparently because he has not gone there yet. This is not,
therefore, a revelation made by a heavenly being. And the
dialogue is not left open-ended, that is, it is not repeat-
able. When Jesus appears from heaven the eschaton will have
arrived. There will be no more such dialogues, and so this
dialogue becomes the last and final word of Jesus before a
scene of departure, that is, the dialogue has become a testament. In fact it is Jesus' testament and Peter's also.
The review of the life of the departing one which is often
found in a testament is totally missing here, but the inferno serves in place of the normal ethical exhortation. But
unlike the departing Jesus in the gospels, there is no doctrine of the Holy Spirit. The finality adds to the authority of the words, filling the role of supplying authority, a
role usually given to the _heavenly_ nature of the teacher in
the gnostic dialogues. Yet certainly this writing is also
an apocalypse, revealing both the eschatological salvation

and the supernatural world.[1] For the life of the believer
the apocalyptic knowledge is all that is deemed necessary.

The Apocalypse of Peter ignores the earthly life of

Jesus. The author knew of a "book of my Lord Jesus Christ"
which may be the Gospel of Matthew, since he may also have
known the little apocalypse from Matthew, or perhaps he
knew these only in oral form, since there is considerable
variation from the synoptics. In any case he chose not to
write a gospel. If he actually knew the Gospel of John, he
may have viewed it as an example of how christology could
become distorted in that genre. Perhaps he was imitating
the genre of his opponents, who by his time might be fully
gnostic. But regardless of his reason, it was the genre
"dialogue of the resurrected Christ with his disciples"
which he found congenial to his purpose.[2] In this genre
Jesus could deliver his final word on these eschatological

<hr>

[1]Technically, if my analysis is correct, Jesus, though
resurrected, is not yet the Christ nor an otherworldly being.
Therefore the Apocalypse of Peter would not technically be
an apocalypse but a prophecy or some such thing. But I
think to deny the term apocalypse to this text would border
on the absurd. Cf. Adela Yarbro Collins, ibid.

[2]For the gnostic examples of this genre, see Kurt Ru-
dolph, "Der gnostische 'Dialog' als literarische Genus" in
Peter Nagel, ed., Probleme der koptischen Literatur (Halle:
Wissenschaftliche Beiträge der Martin-Luther Universität
Halle-Wittenberg 1968/1 (k2), 1968), 85-107; Stephen Emmel,
"Post-Resurrection Dialogues Between Jesus Christ and His
Disciples or Apostles as a Literary Genre," unpublished re-
search paper for B. Layton, 1980; Pheme Perkins, The Gnostic
Dialogue: The Early Church and the Crisis of Gnosticism (New
York: Paulist Pr., 1980; cf. Manfred Hoffmann, Der Dialog
bei den christlichen Schriftstellern der ersten vier Jahr-
hundarte (Berlin: Akademie-Verlag, 1966).

matters by elaborating clearly on the more enigmatic earlier
sayings (the saying of the fig tree, 2:1; the "better to
have never been" saying, 3:4; the saying concerning the
glorious reward for loyalty to Christianity under persecution, 16:5). Into the second of these he was able to place
a description of the physical resurrection with apologies
for it (ch. 4). He was able to use the synoptic apocalypse
material to reinforce his low christology by inserting into
it the description of Jesus' coronation. And more importantly for our discussion of Robinson's trajectories, he
adapted the transfiguration material in such a way that the
glory bodies of Moses and Elijah actually served as a contrast to the physical (but not described) body of Jesus
after the resurrection but before his ascent. The disciples
are amazed to see such bodies (ch. 15). Thus the resurrected body of Jesus has been made to conform to the resurrected body of the believer.

We see here an advanced stage of the trajectories
toward orthodoxy. The resurrection body of the believer is
entirely physical. The resurrection body of Jesus is
equally physical. These concepts are expressed in polemical
fashion using a genre which may also have been well advanced
but which was more usually used by the author's gnostic opponents.[1] At this point Robinson's trajectories intersect

---

[1]A trajectory for the genre Dialogue of the Resurrected Christ with his Disciples has been proposed by Emmel,
ibid., 23-24. He sees three stages: 1) dialogues without
narrative; 2) dialogues with a narrative serving only as a

with the trajectory of the Apocalypse of Peter which I have drawn. These trajectories are extremely imprecise as a tool for dating a writing. But on this basis we may eliminate a first century dating for the Apocalypse of Peter. It clearly lies in the milieu of the second century and participates in the debates with gnosticism which occurred at that time.

B. Bar Kochba

Now let us turn to the evidence which indicates that the Apocalypse of Peter was written about the time of the Bar Kochba revolt. It is meager enough, to be sure. But I think it is convincing.

All of the evidence is from chapter two. There we find the chronicle of events leading to the end. I have explained some of this summarily in chapter four, the notes to Apoc. Pt. chapter two. The relevant passage (2:7-13) runs:

> [7]Did you not understand that the fig tree is the House of Israel? And by its means I have told you: when its branches have sprouted at the last (time) false christs will come. [8]They will promise that "I am the Christ who has come into the world." And when they have seen the wickedness of his deed they will follow after them. [9]And they will deny him whom they call the Glory of our Fathers (or: they will deny him to whom our fathers gave praise), whom they crucified (or: who was crucified), the first Christ, and sinned exceedingly.

---

framework for the dialogue; 3) dialogues in which the narrative framework intrudes into the dialogue. This is a logical development, but we must await corroboration as we become able to date the various documents by other means. The Apocalypse of Peter would belong to stage 3 of this trajectory.

[10]But this liar was not Christ. And when they have rejected him he will kill with the sword and many will become martyrs. [11]Therefore, then the branches of the fig tree have sprouted. This is the House of Israel only. There will be martyrs by his hand. Many will die and become martyrs. [12]For Enoch and Elijah will be sent that they might teach them that this (is) the deceiver who must come into the world and do signs and wonders to deceive. [13]And on account of this those who die by his hand will be martyrs and will be reckoned with the good and righteous martyrs who have pleased God in their life.

The predicted events as I can reconstruct them from this terse account are: 1) a particular false christ arises who does an evil deed (v. 8); 2) some Christians (specifically Jewish Christians perhaps, "the House of Israel only" in v. 11) will join the cause of this man (v. 8); 3) this will be considered a denial of the crucified one (v. 9); 4) when they realize that he is not the messiah, they will desert his cause (v. 10); 5) the false messiah will persecute and kill many of his former followers; 6) Enoch and Elijah will come to let people know that this is the end-time deceiver who had to come.

Heinrich Weinel had already seen that this must refer to Bar Kochba.[1] The revolt may in complete fairness be described as follows[2]: 1) soon after the revolt began Simeon

---

[1]Heinrich Weinel, "Offenbarung des Petrus," ibid., 317.

[2]Peter Schäfer, Der Bar Kokhba-Aufstand: Studien zum zweiten jüdischen Krieg gegen Rom (Tübingen: J. C. B. Mohr (Paul Siebeck), 1981); Yigael Yadin, Bar Kokhba, ibid.; idem, "Bar Kochba," Interpreters Dictionary of the Bible, Supplementary Volume, ed. Keith Crim (Nashville: Abingdon, 1976), 89-92. Schäfer does not accept this section of the Apocalypse of Peter as evidence in his review of sources pertaining to the revolt. He believes this passage to be

bar Kosibah assumed leadership of the rebels; 2) soon after
he became leader, while he was enjoying his initial vic-
tories, Rabbi Akiba declared him to be the Messiah; from
this declaration he became known as Bar Kochba, "Son of a
Star;" 3) there were Jewish Christians in the territory con-
trolled by the rebels, and when they refused to take part in
the war against Rome, Bar Kochba dealt harshly with them;[1]
4) Bar Kochba became known as Bar Koziba, "son of a liar
(= liar)." To this we should add that at the beginning of
the revolt there may have been a number of "messiahs" vying
for the leadership of the revolt, but historians do not
agree on the matter.[2]

The description of the end-time events in the apocalypse and the historical situation at the time of the revolt
match precisely if we assume that a group of Jewish Christians supported the revolt at first and then turned against
him. They may have deserted him precisely over the issue

full of stock apocalyptic images. He also places a dichot-
omy between Jews and Christians, claiming it is very imag-
inative to find Jewish Christians here.

[1]Two short passages are important here, and I will
quote the English translations found in Yadin, Bar Kockba,
ibid., 258. From Justin Martyr, a contemporary of Bar-
Kochba:
"For in the present Jewish war it was only Christians
whom Bar Chocheba, the leader of the rebellion of the
Jews, commanded to be punished severely, if they did
not deny Jesus as the Messiah and blaspheme him."
From Eusebius, Chronicle, Hadrian's Year 17 (AD 133):
"Cochebas, duke of the Jewish sect, killed the Christians with all kinds of persecutions, (when) they refused to help him against the Roman troops."

[2]Yigael Yadin, "Bar Kochba," ibid., 90.

about whether or not he was messiah. This is not stereo-
typed apocalyptic imagery, and we find nothing else quite
like it anywhere except the undatable Ethiopic Apocalypse
in the Tübingen Manuscript which I have described in chapter
one. This ms. is probably a distant descendant of our Apocalypse of Peter. In v. 10 we read "this liar was not Christ
(or: the christ)." Now it is true that the term "liar" was
available in an antichrist context (1 Jn. 2:22; cf. Jn. 8:
44), but this is the first time we find the term Liar
applied to a specific historical individual of the past who
was Liar because he had claimed to be the messiah.[1] It indicates, I believe, that the term Bar Kozibah "Son of a
Liar" may have been applied to Bar Kochba that early. There
is one more possible connection of Apoc. Pt. 2 to the Bar
Kochba revolt, but it lies outside those verses we have so
far been considering. If as I have suggested, the words
"House of Israel" may mean "temple of Israel" in the parable
of the fig tree (vv. 4-6), then "we will plant another in
its place" (v. 6) may be a reference to the new temple to
Jupiter which was erected on the old temple site following
the war.

This is the evidence, and I believe the parallels are
striking enough for us to accept a date during or shortly

---

[1]There is a trajectory here from the Johannine tradition. In Jn. 8:44 the Liar is the devil. In 1 Jn. 2:22
the Liar is anyone who denies that Jesus is the Christ, and
there are many of these "antichrists" (v. 18). Here there
is one Liar, the end-time false messiah.

after this war. Since the war lasted from 132-135 CE we can safely date it, I believe, between 132 and 140 CE. This is well within the time period of 125-150 or so CE which is the usual date given based on its use by Clement of Alexandria. But perhaps we can be even more specific yet. The author gives us no indication that the false messiah has been put out of the way completely. Rather, he seems to expect Enoch and Elijah to come, and unless he saw two people in his own community who fulfilled that role, he must have been expecting them to come before the war was finished. Therefore, a date during the war, 132-135 CE is very likely.

C. External Evidence

The date and the unity of the Apocalypse of Peter must be discussed together. If the document is a unity (though we of course must take into account the use of older traditions), then we have one author and one date. If there have been significant additions to the apocalypse, then we must contend with a disunity and with various dates each depending on its own section. Except for the inferno (and then not the whole of that) and the descriptions of Moses and Elijah (ch. 15) every part of the document has been put into question by somebody. It is not enough to do as I have done in chapter one to list the places where the apocalypse may be attested. Since it is put into question by sections we must see which sections of the apocalypse are attested.

This external evidence will carry us some way in corroborating or questioning a date arrived at on another basis.

The following is a table of attestation by sections. This table is a useful summary of the use of the Apocalypse of Peter in the early church, material which we examined in chapter one. It shows which sections of the apocalypse were useful to later writers. In the late fourth century the author of the Apocalypse of Paul found use for much material from chapters 3-17. Already a century earlier the Coptic Apocalypse of Elijah used chs. 1, 2, 6, 9, 12, 13, and 14. The Sibylline Oracles Book 2 uses not only the inferno but also chs. 2, 4, 13, 14. So, too, the Apocalypse of Thomas shows acquaintance with chs. 1, 4-6, 13-17. It is highly likely that the Epistula Apostolorum knew chs. 1, 14, 17. These works show acquaintance with many sections of the Apocalypse of Peter. This shows that the authors were not merely acquainted with some of the same traditions or with a section travelling about independently. Little of the text as we have it in the Ethiopic could be a late addition, since virtually all of what we have in the Ethiopic was already known in its context at an early stage.

IV. The Ethiopic Apocalypse of Peter and the Akhmim Fragment

Up until now the greatest challenge to the reliability of the Ethiopic text has been the existence of the Akhmim Fragment. The two are obviously two different rescensions of the same original work. The differences between them I

TABLE 2

ATTESTATION BY SECTIONS

Section	Topic	Place of Attestation
Chapter One	the signs of the parousia	1:6-7 Ep. Apost. (160-170) 1:5-7 Coptic Apoc. Elij. (3rd cent.) 1:6-7 Apoc. Th. (c. 450)
Chapter Two	the fig tree and its interpretation	2:7-13 Sib. Or. (c. 150) 2:7-13 Coptic Apoc. Elij. (3rd cent.) Tübingen Ms. (uncertain)
Chapter Three	"It were better . . ." saying	3:4-6 Apoc. Pl. (late 4th cent.)
Chapters Four-Six	resurrection of dead bodies, dissolving fire, final judgment	Chs. 4-6 Apoc. Th. (c. 450) Chs. 4-5 Porphyry (c. 270) Chs. 4-6 Ephriam Syrus (4th cent.) Chs. 4-5 Celsus (178?) 4:2-4:3 Sib. Or. (c. 150) 5:4-5 Porphyry (c. 270) 5:8 Apoc. Pl. (late 4th cent.) 5:8-6:5 Homily on Ten Virgins? (?) 6:1-2 Cyril of Jerusalem (c. 350) 6:3, 6:2-5 Apoc. Pl. (late 4th cent.) 6:3, 6:4 Coptic Apoc. Elij. (3rd cent.)
Chapters Seven-Twelve	the inferno	Chs. 7-12 Sib. Or. (c. 150) Chs. 7-12 Apoc. Pl. (late 4th cent.) Chs. 7-12 Ps.-Titus (5th cent.?) Chs. 7-10 Akhmim Fragment (6th-9th cent.)

TABLE 2--Continued

Section	Topic	Place of Attestation
Chapters Seven-Twelve (cont'd)		Chs. 7-10 Acts. Th. (c. 200)
		7:11 Apoc. Pl. (late 4th cent.)
		7:8 Theophilus (180?)
		Ch. 8 Clement of Alexandria (c. 200)
		8:5-7 Methodius (c. 300)
		8:10 Apoc. Pl. (late 4th cent.)
		9:1-2 Coptic Apoc. Elij. (3rd cent.)
		10:6-7 Bodleian Fr.(3rd or 4th cent.)
		10:2-4, 6 De laudi martyrii (3rd cent.?)
		11:6 Homily on Ten Virgins? (?)
		12:1, 4-6 De laudi martyrii (3rd cent.?)
		12:4-7 Apoc. Pl. (late 4th cent.)
		12:4-7 Homily on Ten Virgins? (?)
		12:5-6 Coptic Apoc. Elij.(3rd cent.)
		12:5-7 Acts of Th. (c. 200)
Chapter Thirteen	the rewards of the righteous	Chs. 13-17 Apoc. Th. (c. 450)
		13:1-14:3 Sib. Or. (c. 150)
		13:5-6 Apoc. Pl. (late 4th cent.)
		13:5 Hippolytus (c. 230?)
		13:1-2 Coptic Apoc. Elij. (3rd cent.)
Chapter Fourteen	salvation out of torment	14:1-3 Ep. Apost. (c. 160-170)
		14:1-3 Coptic Apoc. Elij. (3rd cent.)
	Peter's commission	14:1 Apoc. Pl. (late 4th cent.)
		14:1-5 Rainer Fr. (3rd or 4th cent.)

TABLE 2--Continued

Section	Topic	Place of Attestation
Chapters Fifteen- Seventeen		15:1-16:4 Akhmim Fr. (6th-9th cent.) 15:2-16:6 Apoc. Pl. (late 4th cent.) 15:2-3, 5 De laudi martyrii (3rd cent.?) 16:2-3 Apoc. Pl. (late 4th cent.) 17:2-6 Ep. Apost. (c. 160-170?)

have described in chapter two in my discussion of the Akhmim manuscript. For the sake of the discussion I will repeat the most significant differences here.

1. The Ethiopic is much longer and has a long section on the Second Coming and the Final Judgment (chapters 1-6) and a shorter one on Jesus' ascension (chapter 17) which are not present in the Akhmim text, though the former is hinted at in Akhmim 1-3. Nor is there anything comparable in the Greek to chapters 13-14 of the Ethiopic.

2. In the Ethiopic the description of the punishments in hell (chapters 5-12) precedes that of the blessedness of the saved (chapters 15-16). In the Akhmim text, on the other hand, the order is reversed with the punishments appearing in vv. 21-34 and the blessings in vv. 4-20.

3. The description of hell is fuller and longer in the Ethiopic while the description of the garden of blessing is fuller and longer in the Greek.

4. In the Akhmim text both descriptions, those of hell and of blessedness, are in the form of a vision and are told in the past tense. In the Ethiopic this is true of the latter also, but the punishments are part of a longer prophecy of Jesus in the imperfect (future) and appear only after the description of the Judgment.

Now I have not been secretive about the fact that I believe the Ethiopic text to reflect on the whole the original writing. The Akhmim is a drastically altered text. But surely the burden of proof must rest on the one who

makes that claim. After all, the Ethiopic is a version when
in Akhmim we have the text in its original language. Moreover, the earliest of the Ethiopic manuscripts is possibly
to be dated to the sixteenth century, and the Akhmim manuscript has been dated by various authors to the period from
the sixth to the ninth centuries. The respective dates of
the individual manuscripts, however, should play little role
in the discussion, since none of the differences can be explained by the age of the manuscripts alone.

We have, then, a text preserved in its original language and one preserved in a version. At least that is the
way these two texts are usually pitted against each other.
But the problem cannot be stated fairly that way. We do not
just have the two texts, Ethiopic and Akhmim. We have the
earlier Greek text (third or fourth century) of manuscripts
B and R. The first step must be to compare the Greek of the
Akhmim with that of B and R. This we have done in chapter
two where we demonstrated that the Akhmim text could not be
used to edit the Ethiopic. There it was also demonstrated
that the Akhmim was a different recension from B, and that
the Ethiopic (at that point at least) was a translation of
B. This means that we are now pitting two Greek texts
against each other and that the Ethiopic is the same recension as that contained in the earlier of the two Greek
texts. This point has not been given its due in past discussions. Yet it has a limited force because unfortunately

the amount of text where we can compare all three, Akhmim,
B, and the Ethiopic, is small.

The arguments of James and Maurer are still relevant.[1]
The Ethiopic is about the right length according to the
stichometries. The Akhmim contains only one of the quotes
found in the early church fathers, while the Ethiopic contains all of them with the exception of the quote from LXX
of Is. 34:4 found in Macarius Magnes. The quotes from the
church fathers together with the Bodleian and Rainer fragments prove that the inferno was originally written in the
future tense. To these should be added what I have demonstrated above, that the greater bulk of the text which we
find in the Ethiopic was known to several writers of early
Christian literature, and, very importantly I believe, that
the Ethiopic text shows unity of thought and purpose. This
latter point in particular shows us that the writer was not
only interested in describing heaven and hell, something
which is often said about him more as an accusation than a
statement of fact. He was participating in the orthodox-
gnostic debate of his time.

Some objections to the Ethiopic text have been raised
on the basis of the Akhmim text.[2] In both texts Jesus and

---

[1]M. R. James, "A New Text of the Apocalypse of Peter,"
ibid., 573-577; idem, "The Rainer Fragment of the Apocalypse
of Peter," ibid., 270-274; Ch. Maurer, "Apocalypse of
Peter," ibid., 664-667.

[2]Philipp Vielhauer, Geschichte der urchristlichen
Literatur, ibid., 508-511.

the disciples go to the mountain. In Akhmim this occurs immediately after Jesus' eschatological predictions, so that the vision upon the mountain contains both the "paradise" and the inferno. In the Ethiopic text, on the other hand, the inferno is in the form of a prediction, then there is a trip to the holy mountain followed by a description of "paradise." The argument is that the order in Akhmim must be earlier because the descriptions of heaven and hell which correspond with each other are not there interrupted by the trip to the mountain. In addition to this, the command given to Peter (Eth. 14:4-6) is a concluding remark, beyond which one would expect no new revelation. This conclusion must have been at the end of the original, not before the vision of paradise where we find it in the Ethiopic. Thus the Akhmim, in spite of other deficiencies, is said to preserve the order of events of the original--the paradise preceded the hell.

Now it should be kept in mind that the future-form of the inferno has been established as original.[1] I believe the connection between this future form and the question of the order of events has not been noticed. First of all, it is not simply a matter of prophecy-form in the Ethiopic versus the report-form in Akhmim. Both texts agree that the description of paradise was in the report-form (past tense). It is only the inferno which was originally described in the

_____

[1]Vielhauer, ibid., accepts this in spite of his other objections.

prophecy-form (future tense). This means that in the original the two descriptions were not in the same tense. Why?
There must have been something between them to make this
difference. The Akhmim has nothing between them. The trip
to the mountain is not a later intrusion misplaced from an
earlier position in the text, but the sort of change in setting we might expect to account for the change in tense. It
is likely to be in its correct place between the two descriptions. Furthermore, both texts also agree that the
vision of paradise immediately follows the trip to the mountain. If this trip and the vision of paradise came first,
then we lack an explanation for the change of tense, in this
case it would have to be a change of tense from past to
future, a change of form from report to prophecy. I cannot
see a reasonable explanation for it, particularly since in
Akhmim Jesus' prophecies have ceased before the trip to the
mountain. The correct explanation for all this is found in
the order of events in the Ethiopic text. With the firm
establishment of the prophetic-form of the inferno of the
original text we have also established that the Ethiopic
order, inferno then paradise, is the original order. And
with this established we have removed the basis of the case
for assuming that neither the Ethiopic nor Akhmim reflect
the original Greek but that both are later recensions.[1] The

---

[1]Vielhauer, ibid., 511.

Akhmim can have no claim to reflect the original in any instance where there is a major deviation from the Ethiopic.

But let us return for a moment to that part of the
objection we have been treating which says that the command
given to Peter (14:4-6) is a conclusion beyond which we
should expect no new revelation. The argument has a certain
force. Jesus' speech here is a commission of the type we
would expect to be a final, to precede a departure. But it
is Jesus' departure which is just what we find in the Ethiopic text. The trip to the holy mountain is for the sake of
the ascension of Jesus with which the apocalypse closes.
The form is similar to Luke 24:44-53. In Luke Jesus teaches
his disciples, leads them to Bethany, ascends into heaven,
and then the disciples return to Jerusalem with joy. In the
Apocalypse of Peter Jesus teaches his disciples (chs. 1-14),
leads them to the holy mountain (15:1), ascends into heaven
(17:2-6), and then the disciples descend from the mountain
in joy (17:7). The appearance of Moses and Elijah and the
vision of paradise are subordinated to this form, that is,
they not only tell about the believer's future body of glory
and his reward, but they also show the reader what Jesus
will soon be like and where he is going.

One last word needs to be said about the Akhmim Fragment. Having concluded that it is a rescension of the apocalypse which shows great changes from the original, can we
say anything more about it? The earlier studies, described
in chapter one under the history of research, found many

similarities of vocabulary between Akhmim and 2 Peter as
well as the Gospel of Peter. The language of the apocalypse
was made to conform to that of the latter two. But much
more striking is the absence of all the end-time material
from the Akhmim. I do not see how this can be accidental.
What remains is almost entirely the descriptions of heaven
and hell, oriented to present-time punishments and rewards.[1]
Thus Vielhauer's statement, mentioned above, that the interest of the author lies wholly in the description of the
other-world, is true for the Akhmim Fragment. The prophecy
made by Jesus has been reduced to predictions about heretics
who persecute true Christians.

The purpose of this author (editor?) was very different from that of the original author. I believe the request
of the disciples (missing in the Ethiopic) in v. 5 is revealing. "We . . . asked that he show us one of our righteous brothers who had departed from the world in order that
we might see what sort of form they have. . . ." This concern with "righteous brothers" may be the concern of a monk.
It was in the grave of an Egyptian monk that Akhmim was
found. This would explain why the names Moses and Elijah do
not appear. The Old Testament figures were no longer of
concern, but there was concern about the fellow monks who
had passed away. This may also be why there is special

---

[1]As Vielhauer has observed, these descriptions are
closer to the vision-form found in later Christian apocalypses than to the prophecy of the original apocalypse.
Ibid., 511.

mention (v. 19) of the equality of glory. All the righteous brethren (= non-heretical monks) would receive equal reward. The author of Akhmim had more interest in the fate of the blessed than in the punishments of the wicked. It is this interest which may have caused him to eliminate the end-time material, reverse the order of the descriptions of hell and paradise so that paradise would be viewed first, and expand slightly the vision of paradise. But with this guess we have only been speculating, and there is much about the Akhmim Fragment which we are yet unable to explain. What is important for our purposes is that there is in it nothing which is likely to be more reliable than the Ethiopic text. The original text of the Apocalypse of Peter is closely re-flected by the Ethiopic text. This is supported by the weight of a considerable amount of evidence, and the existence of the Akhmim is no longer able to call this into question as it once so effectively did.

V. Summary

With this dissertation the research on the Early Christian Apocalypse of Peter has been greatly advanced in the following ways.

We have presented a new edition of the Ethiopic text. This text takes into account the recently discovered Ethiopic manuscript which we have designated T. Some errors in the edition of Grébaut have been corrected. We have also been able to use the Bodleian and Rainer Fragments to aid

in restoring some material which had become corrupt in the
Ethiopic. This is especially true of the Rainer Fragment.
A detailed analysis (found in the notes to ch. 14) has
enabled us to make several significant corrections to the
Ethiopic text of 14:1-4. The addition of verse numbers to
the text has made citation of the text easier and more accurate. We have made an index to the Ethiopic which will
assist further research on the document.

We have given two new translations based upon the new
edition. They reflect the changes we were able to make in
the Ethiopic text. Besides this, the language of the literal translation points more clearly than previous translations to the often extremely close parallels with certain
New Testament traditions. Finally, both translations, but
particularly the free translation, are modern translations
reflecting current English style and vocabulary and thus
serve to update the access of non-Ethiopic readers to the
text.

In chapter two of this dissertation we have given a
more thorough discussion of the manuscripts than was previously available.

The analysis of the Rainer Fragment (found in the
notes to ch. 14) has shown that the Ethiopic has apparently
had a long history of transmission in that language. This
may mean that it was translated into Ethiopic at a relatively early date. We have also shown by this analysis that
at this point the text was subjected to certain changes

probably because the reviser had theological objections to universal salvation. These changes were limited and did not prevent scholars from recognizing the original intention even before the Rainer Fragment was discovered. The Ethiopic translator was attempting a fairly wooden but accurate translation, but perhaps there are instances where either he did not understand the text before him or where that text may have been slightly corrupt. Yet with the Rainer and Ethiopic texts both before us we are able to see a close correspondence between them and to see how any discrepancies arose. The analysis has also made it more likely that the Apocalypse of Peter has been translated directly from the Greek, since another intervening translation appears completely unnecessary to account for their differences.

We have also included in the discussion of the manuscripts (chapter two) a study of that section where we have preserved for us the Akhmim, the Ethiopic and the Bodleian Fragment. This comparison allowed us to see that the Ethiopic is a translation virtually word-for-word from the earlier Greek tradition of B (which is also that of R) while the Akhmim is another rescension differing considerably from the earlier Greek manuscripts. This is a strong endorsement of the reliability of the Ethiopic text.

In a study analyzing the Pseudo-Clementine work in which the Apocalypse of Peter is found, we discovered that the apocalypse is not embedded in that writing but stands at its beginning, immediately following the title sentence.

The Pseudo-Clementine writing is a commentary on the apocalypse. It treats the material from the apocalypse very
freely and the author did not feel it necessary to revise
the text of the apocalypse in order to harmonize it with his
commentary. The style, vocabulary, content, and ultimate
concerns of the author of the Pseudo-Clementine work are
easily distinguished from those of the author of the apocalypse, and thus much of the suspicion that the text of the
apocalypse has been tampered with has been removed. It is
possible that the noticeable changes in the text, discussed
in the analysis of the Rainer Fragment, are attributable to
the author of the Pseudo-Clementine writing. This Pseudo-
Clementine writing bears no known relationship to other
extant Pseudo-Clementine literature.

We have presented the evidence for the use of the
Apocalypse of Peter in the Early Church more thoroughly than
has previously been done. First in chapter one, thirty possible witnesses were discussed and twenty-seven of them were
found to be acquainted with the apocalypse. Then in chapter
five this evidence was listed by section of the apocalypse,
showing clearly to what extent a significant portion of the
apocalypse was known and used. This external evidence indicates the early date of the apocalypse in a form much as
we have it in Ethiopic.

Chapter four is the first commentary to be written on
this apocalypse. It is short, but offers the first detailed
discussion of the difficulties encountered in the Ethiopic

text. Connections with other literature, particularly with the New Testament, are pointed out when helpful. I believe it is generally helpful in preventing misunderstandings of the text.

Perhaps the most important research has been done on the unity of the apocalypse. The Apocalypse of Peter has been found to be an example of the genre Dialogue of the Resurrected Christ with his Disciples. The climax of the document is the vision of the heavenly temple and the accompanying voice (16:9-17:1). There is a consistent low christology and a consistent eschatology with an emphasis on the physicality of the resurrection. These themes reveal the purpose of the document, which was written to defend orthodoxy against gnosticism on these points. This places the document in the polemical discussions of the first half of the second century. The various "seams" and other signs of disunity of the writing are found to be imaginary. This also means that it is incorrect to say that the author was mainly interested in describing hell and paradise. He was interested in supporting his low christology and a very physical resurrection.

The dating of the document has been made more certain. A first century date has been eliminated by analyzing the probably trajectories. The Apocalypse of Peter seems to have come from a community with an origin in or close to the Johannine community of the New Testament literature. It comes from a group which opposed the high christology developing in that Johannine community and relies for its basis on a very future-oriented, physical eschatology against the Johannine realized, spiritual eschatology. This trajectory fits well the trajectories from Jesus to Valentinus or the Apostles' Creed described by James M. Robinson. The internal evidence from ch. 2 which indicates a date for the apocalypse sometime during the Bar Kochba rebellion, 132-135 CE, is reenforced by using the theme of the eschatological Liar, already found in the Johannine trajectory, and applying it to Bar Kochba as the false messiah.

Finally, we have shown that the Akhmim Fragment can no longer be considered a rival claim to represent the original Greek. The last substantial argument in support of the Akhmim Fragment's originality was that the Akhmim provided us with the original order of the descriptions, paradise first and then the inferno. I have shown that conclusion to be very unlikely, and have presented reasons to believe that the order of events was just as we have it in the Ethiopic. Thus the most important objection to my thesis that the Ethiopic reflects the original apocalypse has fallen.

My hope is that a new era of research on the Apocalypse of Peter can now begin. Many of the doubts and obscurities which have shrouded the document have now been cleared. There are many intriguing connections with other early Christian literature. I believe that the Apocalypse of Peter can be a valuable asset for study of the New

Testament and the Early Church History. The <u>Apocalypse of Peter</u> no longer need be limited in use by an approach of extreme caution and hesitation.

APPENDIX

Jacques de Vitry, Bishop of Acra, written in a letter
to Honorius III, pope around the year 1219 A.D., in
Dacherius Tom. VIII, spicilegii veterum scriptorum page 382,
has this:

> In the present year, the Syrians who were with us in
> the army, showed us a very ancient book from their
> library-chest written in the Saracen language. Its in-
> scription (title) reads: The Revelations of the Blessed
> Apostle Peter, published in one volume by his disciple
> Clement. Whoever was the author of this book, he pro-
> phesied (praenuntiavit) openly and plainly on the con-
> dition of the church of God from the beginning up to the
> time of the Anti-christ and the end of the world. His
> purpose is to make the faith of future (people? things?)
> firm by means of what has happened in the past. He pro-
> phesied, among other things, about the consummation and
> completion of the treacherous law of the Agarenes (Mos-
> lems, Agarenorum), and how, with the destruction (of,
> by?) the pagans imminent and almost at the door, the
> Christian people was about to subdue the verdant and
> well-watered city (which they called Damiata = Damascus?).
> After this, he added (material) on two new kings. The
> one is to come from the West and the other from the East
> against the aforementioned King (God?) in the Holy City.
> He also prophesied that by the hands of these kings, the
> Lord was about to exterminate the abominable law of im-
> pious men. He would put some to the sword, and convert
> others to Christ so that all the Gentiles might enter and
> all Israel might be saved, and after that, the son of
> perdition, and then the judgment and the end.

> Vitry added that he (Vitry?) preached the Apocalyptic
> book to all the people in the sand in front of Damiatam,
> gathered for the word of God - for their consolation and
> refreshment. And (Vitry) noted that the Apocalyptic
> prophecy applies to the eastern king David and the
> western Emperor Frederic. However, these men did not
> abolish the Mohammedan law, so the interpretation is
> false.

431

Moreover, from Jacques Vitry's words concerning the length of the entire Apocalypse of Peter, one can conjecture that it wasn't such a small book. According to the stichometry of Cotelerius it was 2070 lines but others claim it was 270 lines. No doubt this error arose from a scribal confusion of the two numbers. If the first reading is genuine, the Apocalypse of Peter would be almost twice the size of John's Apocalypse, which runs 1200 lines. If the second is correct, it would be larger than First Peter, which is said to run 200 lines. But nothing certain can be said about this.

FROM THE LETTER OF JAMES DE VITRY TO POPE HONORIUS III, C. 1219 CE.

Text in Johann Ernst Grabe, Spicilegium ss. patrum ut et haereticum (Oxoniae: theatro Shedoniano, 1689-90) Vol. 1, 76-77.

Translated by Fr. Terrence G. Kardong, OSB.

APPENDIX

TRANSLATION OF PP. 152-157 OF THE TÜBINGEN MANUSCRIPT
(from Dillmann's German translation, Bratke, ibid., 481-484)[1]

[1]Hear, my son Clement, what our Lord Jesus Christ has
told me, the King of heaven and earth, the creator of the
whole world, that in the last days many of their believers
will fall away, and love will grow cold among the brethren,
and many false prophets and false messias will come and will
corrupt the people through the wickedness of their deeds and
through their impure faith. [2]For the nearness of his coming
and the increasing age of the world cause evil things to
appear which do not originate from the holy churches. And
they will cause corruption through their impure writings,
and they will seek (find) protection with the kings and the
powerful, and their way (is) perverse, even more than that
of the idolaters. [3]At that time Satan will find in them an
opportunity to corrupt the people through them, because he
has found the way of their words. And therefore they will
become more wicked, for the others will be seduced through

---

[1]The words enclosed in parentheses are either other
equivalents of the Ethiopic expressions or are glosses inserted by Dillmann. I have divided the translation into
verses for easy reference. This translation is rather
wooden in order to stay as close as possible to Dillmann's
German. Apparently he has also stayed quite close to the
Ethiopic style.

their deceit. ⁴In those days the shepherds will treat their flock violently and not accept their penance. Woe to such on the day of judgment when they will stand before the judgment seat of God, for he will punish them first, and after them the lay people who did not keep God's word and commandment will be dragged in and brought into damnation (the judgment). ⁵In those days will come a king with evil mind and evil deeds, and the sun will be allowed to rise in the west and the moon toward Aelam [sic]. In those days Zebulon will rise and Naphtali stretch its neck high and Capernaum boast, Zebulon and Naphtali exult, Chorazin and Bethsaida, for they will hold that man to be Christ. ⁶And when they see his doings, they will (not!) [sic] be ashamed, for he does not seek justice, but all his doings are done to flatter people. ⁷In those days the Lord (God) will stop the rain from heaven, and there will be a house of winter (sic!; perhaps: wintry), and the earth will remain without dew and fog, and the rain of earth will become [sic] to clouds of darkness and storm winds, and the springs of water will give no flowing water, and the sea will be dried up. ⁸And those evil days will be shortened, as it says in the gospel: if those days were not shortened none of the living would be saved, but on account of the elect those days will be shortened. The sun will be darkened and the moon will become blood, even the stars will fall from heaven before the greatness of the wrath of God (the Lord) at the children of men and at the messiahs [sic]. ⁹For he will bring corruption

upon those who live upon earth, for they will corrupt their
thoughts (their understanding) out of fear for him and will
keep his commandments. And his image will stand[1] in the
churches, especially will it stand[1] in Jerusalem, the holy
city of the great kings. And then on every so-called (?)
altar[2] he will say: fall down before my image! [10]But I
have given you another order previously: Don't do it! And
many will say in that hour: Why did you not tell it to us,
our Lord, that he would abolish the gospel and Paul and Acts
and all the writings of the law! He did not tell us that he
would (wished to) destroy the heritage of his writings which
he had previously decreed. We do not hear of this utterance.
[11]And others will leave their relatives (parents), women and
children, and will flee to the hills, caves, and ravines and
hide themselves, as the prophet Isaiah said: Go, my people
into your house and hide yourself a little while until the
wrath of the Lord (of God) will be past. [12]But those who
are not afraid of the terror of that king will step before
him and revile him, and they will be beheaded and become
martyrs. In those days will be fulfilled what is said in
the gospel: When the branches of the fig tree become sappy,
then know that the time of the harvest has come near.
[13]Those good people will be called Sprouts of the Fig Tree,
who become martyrs through his (the king's) hand, and the

---

[1]If jeqaum has not been mistakenly written for jâqaum
'he will set up.'

[2]Possibly: on every altar the man referred to will
say.

angels will go to meet them with joy, and not a hair of
their heads will perish (be lost). [14]After that Enoch and
Elijah will come down, will preach, and will put that tyr-
annical (rebellious) enemy of righteousness, the son of
lies, to shame. Immediately they will be beheaded, and
Michael and Gabriel will raise them and bring them into the
garden of joy, and no drop of his [sic] blood will fall to
the ground. [15]And as the last enemy he will annihilate
death. And our Lord will come from heaven in order to set
up the covenant (the promise) of his kingdom with his elect.
And the trumpet will be sounded three times by the mouth of
the archangel Michael. [16]At the first blast of the trumpet
the bodies which have become like dust will come together.
And at the second blast of the trumpet the houses in which
the souls are kept will be opened, and they will return into
the bodies through the dew of mercy which comes down upon
them from the Lord (God), as Isaiah says (26:19): For the
dew from you here is their life. [17]And at the third blast
of the trumpet the dead will rise in an instant and will be
placed before his face, when he will put the sheep at his
right hand and the goats at his left and will say to them:
Enter, you accursed, you who have not kept the commandment
of the Lord! and they will be brought into weeping and
gnashing of teeth and outermost darkness. [18]But the righteous who are at his right hand will enter into eternal life
where there is no illness or suffering, where they do not
die, and afterwards once more to the garden of delight and

joy, and their joy will never cease for eternity, and their
souls will not die again for eternity. [19]And when these
things come to pass, on that accursed day of weeping and
fear and trembling, then the righteous will weep over the
sinners, and the sinners will weep over their sins, and the
angels of heaven will weep over the sinners. [20]In those
days everyone will come into their inheritance: those who
have done good to the dwelling of life, but those who have
done evil to eternal damnation.

APPENDIX

ANALYSIS OF THE SURFACE STRUCTURE OF THE TEXT

[with the use of traditional material]

The Apocalypse of Peter

I.   Narrative Concerning the Teaching of Christ to His
     Disciples on the Mount of Olives. 1-14.
     [synoptic little apocalypse]

   A. Narrative Relating the Dialogue Between Jesus and
       His Disciples Concerning the Signs of Jesus' Par-
       ousia. 1-2.

       1. Introduction relating how Jesus' disciples came
           to him while he was seated on the Mount of
           Olives. 1:1.

       2. The dialogue between Jesus and his disciples.
           1:2-2:13.

           a. Introduction + report of the request from
               the disciples to be taught the signs of the
               Parousia and of the end of the world for
               their use in instructing the Church's next
               generation of leaders. 1:2-3.

           b. Report of Jesus' answer. 1:4-2:1.

               1) Introduction. 1:4a.

               2) Exhortation concerning heresy, doubt,
                   and idolatry. 1:4b.

               3) Prediction of false Christs + Exhorta-
                   tion not to believe them or go near
                   them. 1:5.

               4) Predictive report of the Parousia of
                   the Son of God. 1:6-8.

                   a) Simile on the suddenness of the
                       Parousia. 1:6a.

438

> b) Three predictions in the form of "I will come" statements describing Jesus' appearance at his Parousia and his coronation for judgment. 1:6b-7.
>
> c) Statement of the principle by which judgment will be given. 1:8.

5) The giving of the parable of the fig tree. 2:1.

> a) Exhortation to receive. 2:1a.
>
> b) The parable proper: the end of the world will come when the shoots are out and the boughs sprouted. 2:1b.

c. Report of Peter's request for an explanation of the parable. 2:2-3.

1) Introduction. 2:2a.

2) Request proper + expression of puzzlement. 2:2b-3.

d. Report of Jesus' answer. 2:4-13.

1) Introduction. 2:4a.

2) Question indicating Jesus' puzzlement at Peter's question. 2:4b.

3) The parable of the fig tree given in full: the unfertile tree will be uprooted. 2:5-6. [Lk. 13:6-9]

4) Repetition of Jesus' question. 2:7a.

5) Explanation of the parable in terms of the coming of false christs and associated events. 2:7b-13.

> a) Explanation of the sprouting of the branches: a prediction that deceiving christs will come (with quotation of their claim). 2:7b-8a.
>
> b) Predictive report of the results of the coming of the false christs. 2:8b-13.

(1) Predictive report of the apostasy: many will follow these
false christs and in doing so
will deny the first Christ.
2:8b-9.

(2) Predictive report of the rejection of a particular false
christ and associated events.
2:10-13.

(aa) Predictive report of the
rejection and its results:
many martyrs. 2:10.

(bb) Further explanation of
the parable: the branches
of the fig tree are the
martyrs and they are con-
nected with Israel only.
2:11.

(cc) Predictive report of the
coming of Enoch and Eli-
jah to teach the people
about this false christ.
2:12. [tradition of the
two witnesses]

(dd) Explanation concerning
the standing of these
martyrs. 2:13.

B. Narrative Relating the Dialogue Between Jesus and
Peter Concerning the Last Days. 3-14.

1. Vision introducing the fate of the righteous and
of the sinners in the last day. 3:1-3.

a. Introductory report of circumstances of the
vision. 3:1.

b. The vision report proper. 3:2-3a.

1) The scene of the separation of the righteous from the sinners. 3:2a.

2) The scene of the fate of the righteous
and of the sinners. 3:2b.

3) The scene of the weeping of the sinners.
3:3a.

c. Report of the response to the sinners' weeping by those seeing it: they themselves weep. 3:3b.

2. Report of Peter's response to the vision: Peter quotes a saying of Jesus. 3:4. [a saying of the Lord]

3. Report of Jesus' answer to Peter. 3:5-14:6.

   a. Narrative introduction. 3:5a.

   b. Rebuke of Peter by Jesus: Peter opposes God while Jesus defends God by appeals to the compassion of the Creator and to the works of the sinners. 3:5b-7.

   c. Jesus' predictive report of the Last Days. 4:1-14:6.

      1) Predictive report of the physical resurrection of the dead from Hades with an explanation of how this is possible by the word of God. 4:1-13. [Ezekiel 37]

      2) Predictive report of the gathering of the nations for judgment: the dissolution of the creation into fire and how the fire drives people to the river of fire for judgment. 5:1-9.

      3) Predictive report of the final trial: the Parousia of Christ, his coronation, the trial of the nations in the river of fire, and the recompense given to the elect, the sinners, and the inhabitants of the heathen idols. 6:1-9.

      4) Predictive report of the punishments given sinners to match their sin. 7:1-12:7. [See table of places of punishment in ch. 4, notes on ch. 7] [orphic myths]

      5) Predictive report of the rewards given the elect and righteous, including the sight of the punishments of the sinners. 13:1-3.

      6) Predictive report of the dialogue between the punished and the angel Tatirokos. 13:4-6.

        a) Predictive report of plea for mercy by the punished. 13:4.

        b) Predictive report of the response of Tatirokos: increased punishment. 13:5.

        c) Predictive report of the response of the punished: an acknowledgment of the justice of God. 13:6.

    7) Predictive report of the fulfillment of the requests of the elect and righteous including salvation for those in torment. 14:1-3a.

    8) Jesus speaks to Peter. 14:3b-6.

        a) Introduction. 14:3b.

        b) Jesus' command to Peter to go to Rome. 14:4-5a.

        c) Jesus' commission to spread the gospel. 14:5b.

    9) Concluding statement (corrupt). 14:6.

II. Narrative of the Subsequent Events which Occurred on the Holy Mountain. 15:1-17:7. [transfiguration]

    A. Introduction Relating a Change of Setting. 15:1.

        1. Introductory words + hortatory words of Christ. 15:1a.

        2. Compliance report with description: while praying. 15:1b.

    B. Narrative of Events on the Mountain including Moses and Elijah. 15:2-17:6.

        1. Report of the glorious appearance of Moses and Elijah. 15:2-7.

        2. Report of the dialogue between Peter and Jesus concerning the men. 16:1-17:1.

           a. Introductory words + Peter's question: Who is this? 16:1a.

           b. Introductory words + Jesus' answer: Moses and Elijah. 16:1b.

c. Introductory words + Peter's question concerning righteous fathers. 16:1c.

d. Report of Jesus' response. 16:2-4.

   1) A vision report in which Jesus causes his disciples to see the fruitful garden. 16:2-3.

   2) Report of a statement by Jesus concerning whom the garden is for. 16:4.

      a) Introduction. 16:4a.

      b) Statement proper: the patriarchs rest there. 16:4b.

e. A report of Peter's response to the vision (in first person). 16:5-7.

   1) A report concerning Peter's rejoicing because of the vision of glory with a quote from Matthew on the persecuted. 16:5.

   2) A report concerning Peter's understanding of the book of his Lord. 16:6.

   3) A report of Peter's suggestion to build three tabernacles. 16:7.

f. Report of Jesus' answer: a rebuke + a vision. 16:8-9.

   1) Introductory words describing Jesus' anger. 16:8a.

   2) Rebuke concerning Satan. 16:8b. [Jesus' rebuke of Peter]

   3) Vision and audition report with explanation for its necessity. 16:9-17:1.

      a) Explanation of the need for a vision: Satan has covered Peter's eyes and stopped Peter's ears but they will be opened. 16:9a.

      b) The vision report: the temple. 16:9b.

      c) The audition report: the voice from heaven. 17:1.

3. Report of the ascension of Jesus. 17:2-6
   [ascension]

   a. Report of the coming of the cloud. 17:2.

      1) Report of the action of the cloud.
         17:2a.

      2) Report of the reaction of Peter. 17:2b.

   b. Report of what the disciples saw. 17:3-6.

      1) Introduction. 17:3aa.

      2) Report of the opening of the heavens.
         17:3ab.

      3) Report of what was seen while the
         heavens were opened. 17:3b-5.

         a) Report of the men in the flesh +
            their greeting of the Lord, Moses,
            and Elijah. 17:3b.

         b) Report of the ascension of these
            into the second heaven. 17:3c.

         c) Report of scripture fulfillment.
            17:4.

         d) Report of the reaction in heaven.
            17:5.

            (1) Report of the fear and amaze-
                ment. 17:5a.

            (2) Report of the reaction of the
                angels + corresponding scrip-
                tural prediction. 17:5b.

      4) Report of the closing of the heavens.
         17:6.

C. Report of the Descent from the Mountain with Prayer
   and Rejoicing over the Book of Life. 17:7.

BIBLIOGRAPHY

Abbadie, Antoine Thompson d'. Catalogue raisonné de
    manuscrits éthiopiens appartenant à Antoine d'Abbadie.
    Paris: Imprimerie Impériale, 1859.

Aland, Kurt. "The Problem of Anonymity and Pseudonymity
    in Christian Literature of the First Two Centuries."
    Journal of Theological Studies n.s. XII (1961):39-49.

Allenbach, J.; Benoit, A.; Bertrand, D.A.; Hanriot-Coustet,
    A.; Maraval, P.; Pautler, A.; Prigent, P. Biblia
    Patristica: Index des citations et allusions bibliques
    dans la littérature patristique, Vol. 1: Des origenes
    à Clément d'Alexandrie et Tertullien. Paris: Centre
    National de la Recherche Scientifique, 1975.

Altaner, Berthold. Patrology. New York: Herder and Herder,
    1960.

Amann, É. "Apocryphes du Nouveau Testament," in Supplément
    du Dictionnaire de la Bible, vol. 1,columns 460-533.
    Edited by Louis Pirot. Paris: Librairie Letouzey et
    Ané, 1928.

Anrich, Gustav. Das antike Mysterienwesen in seinem Einfluss
    auf das Christentum. Göttingen: Vandenhoeck und Ruprecht,
    1894.

Athanassakis, Apostolos N. The Orphic Hymns: Text, Trans-
    lation and Notes. Missoula: Scholars Press, 1977.

Aune, David Edward. The Cultic Setting of Realized Eschatology
    in Early Christianity. Leiden: E. J. Brill, 1972.

Bacon, Benjamin W. "The Transfiguration Story: A Study of
    the Problem of the Sources of our Synoptic Gospels."
    American Journal of Theology 6 (1902): 236-265.

Badham, F. P. "The New Apocryphal Literature." The Athenaeum,
    December 17, 1892, pp. 854-855.

_____. "The Origin of the Peter Gospel." The Academy
    (London) XLIV (July-December 1893): 91-93, 111-112.

446

Bakker, Adolphine. "Christ an Angel? A Study of Christian Docetism." Zeitschrift für die neutestamentliche Wissenschaft 32 (1933):255-265.

Baltensweiler, Heinrich. Die Verklärung Jesu: Historisches Ereignis und synoptische Berichte. Abhandlungen zur Theologie des Alten und Neuen Testaments no. 33. Zurich: Zwingli-Verlag, 1959.

Bardenhewer, Otto. Geschichte der Altkirchlichen Literatur. Vol. 4. Darmstadt: Wissenschaftliche Buchgeselschaft, 1924; reprint ed., 1962.

_____. Patrology. St. Louis: B. Herder, 1908.

_____. Die Petrusapokalypse. Geschichte der altkirchlichen Literatur. Vol. I. Darmstadt: Wissenschaftliche Buchgesellschaft, 2nd ed., 1913; reprint ed., 1962, 610-615.

Bardy, Gustav. "Faux et fraudes littérairies dans l'antiquite chrétienne." Revue d'histoire ecclesiastique 32 (1936): 5-23, 275-302.

_____. "Muratori (Canon de)," in Supplément du Dictionnaire de la Bible, vol. 5, columns 1399-1408. Edited by L. Pirot, A. Robert and H. Cazelles. Paris: Librairie Letouzey et Ané, 1957.

Barrett, C. K. "New Testament Eschatology." Scottish Journal of Theology 6 (1953):136-155.

Bartlet. Review of Theology and Philosophy, December 1911, pp. 334-6.

Batiffol, Pierre. "Apocalypses Apocryphes," in Dictionnaire de la Bible, vol. 1, columns 756-767. Edited by F. Vigouroux. Paris: Letouzey et Ané, 1912.

Bauckham, Richard. "The Worship of Jesus in Apocalyptic Christianity." New Testament Studies 27 (1981):322-341.

Bauer, Walter. A Greek-English Lexicon of the New Testament and Other Early Christian Literature. Edited and translated by William F. Arndt and F. Wilbur Gingrich. Chicago: University of Chicago Press, 1957; 2nd ed., revised and augmented by F. Wilbur Gingrich and Frederick W. Danker. Chicago: University of Chicago Press, 1979.

_____. Das Leben Jesu im Zeitalter der neutestamentlichen Apokryphen. Tübingen: J.C.B. Mohr (Paul Siebeck), 1907; reprint ed., Darmstadt: Wissenschaftliche Buchgesellschaft, 1967.

_____, "The Odes of Solomon." New Testament Apocrypha. Vol. 2. Edited by Edgar Hennecke. Rev. ed. by Wilhelm Schneemelcher. English translation by R. McL. Wilson. Philadelphia: The Westminster Press,1965, 808-810.

Baumgarten, A. I. "The Akiban Opposition." Hebrew Union College Annual 50 (1979):179-197.

Beare, F. W. The First Epistle of Peter. Oxford: Basil Blackwell, 1970. Additional Note "On the Literature Attributed to Peter in the Ancient Church," 228-229.

Beasley-Murray, G. R. A Commentary on Mark Thirteen. London: Macmillan and Co., 1957.

_____. Jesus and the Future. New York: St. Martin's Press, 1954.

Beck, Dwight M. "Transfiguration," in The Interpreter's Dictionary of the Bible, vol. 4, 686-687. Edited by George A. Buttrick. Nashville: Abingdon, 1962.

Becker, Ernest J. A Contribution to the Comparative Study of the Medieval Visions of Heaven and Hell, with Special Reference to the Middle-English Visions. Baltimore: John Murphy, 1899.

Beker, J. Christiaan. Paul the Apostle: The Triumph of God in Life and Thought. Philadelphia: Fortress Press, 1980.

_____. Paul's Apocalyptic Gospel: The Coming Triumph of God. Philadelphia: Fortress Press, 1982.

Ben-Yashar, Menachem. "Noch zum Migdaš 'Ādām in 4 Q Florilegium." Revue de Qumran 10 (1981):587-588.

Benz, Ernst. Die Vision: Erfahrungsformen und Bilderwelt. Stuttgart: Ernst Klett, 1969.

Berger, Klaus. Die Amen-Worte Jesu: Eine Untersuchung zum Problem der Legitimation in apokalyptischer Rede. Berlin: Walter de Gruyter, 1970.

_____. Die Gesetzesauslegung Jesu: Ihr historischer Hintergrund im Judentum und im Alten Testament. Teil I: Markus und Parallelen. n.p.: Neukirchener Verlag, 1971.

_____. Die Grieschische Daniel-Diegese: Eine
Altkirchliche Apokalypse. Leiden: E. J. Brill, 1976.

Bernardin, Joseph. "The Transfiguration." Journal of
Biblical Literature 52 (1933):181-189.

Bertholet, Alfred. Die Gefilde der Seligen: Ein akademischer
Vortrag. Tübingen: J.C.B. Mohr, 1903.

Bertram, Georg. Die Himmelfahrt Jesu vom Kreuz aus und der
Glaube an seine Auferstehung. Festgabe für Adolf Deiss-
mann zum 60. Geburtstag. Tübingen: J.C.B. Mohr (Paul
Siebeck), 1927, 187-217.

Best, Thomas F. "The Transfiguration: A Select Bibliography."
Journal of the Evangelical Theological Society 24 (1981):
157-161.

Bietenhard, Hans. Die himmlische Welt im Urchristentum
und Spätjudentum. Wissenschaftliche Untersuchungen
zum Neuen Testament no. 2. Tübingen: J.C.B. Mohr
(Paul Siebeck), 1951.

Bigg, Charles. A Critical and Exegetical Commentary on the
Epistles of St. Peter and St. Jude. International
Critical Commentary. 2nd ed. Edinburgh: T. & T. Clark,
1902.

Billerbeck, Paul and H.L. Strack. Kommentar zum Neuen
Testament aus Talmud und Midrasch. 6 vols. Munich:
Beck, 1922-1961.

Black, Matthew. Apocalypsis Henochi Graece. Leiden: Brill,
1970.

Le Blant, Edmond. "Mémoire sur les martyrs chrétiens et
les supplices destructeurs du corps." Academie des
inscriptions et belles-lettres 28 (1875):75-95.

Blinzler, Joseph. Die neutestamentliche Berichte über die
Verklärung Jesu. Münster: Aschendorff, 1937.

Bloch, Renée. "Midrash," in Supplément du Dictionnaire de
la Bible, vol. 5, columns 1263-1281. Edited by Louis
Pirot. Paris: Librairie Letouzey et Ané, 1957.

Bonsirven, Joseph. Palestinian Judaism in the Time of Jesus
Christ. Translated by William Wolf. New York: Holt,
Rinehart and Winston, 1964.

Bonwetsch, N. "Zur Apokalypse des Petrus." Theologisches
    Literaturblatt 33 (1912):121-123.

Boobyer, G. H. "St. Mark and the Transfiguration." Journal
    of Theological Studies 41 (1940):119-140.

_____. St. Mark and the Transfiguration Story. Edin-
    burgh: T. & T. Clark, 1942.

Bornkamm, Gunther. "The Acts of Thomas." New Testament
    Apocrypha. Vol.2. Edited by Edgar Hennecke. Rev. ed. by
    Wilhelm Schneemelcher. English translation by R. McL.
    Wilson. Philadelphia: The Westminster Press, 1965,
    425-531.

Bouriant, U. Fragments grecs du livre d'Enoch. Memoires
    publiés par les membres de la mission archeologique
    française au Caire, sous la direction de M.U. Bouriant.
    Vol. IX, fascicle 1. Paris: Ernest Leroux, 1893.

Bousset, Wilhelm. The Antichrist Legend: A Chapter in
    Christian and Jewish Folklore. Translated by A. H.
    Keane. London: Hutchinson and Co., 1896.

_____. Die Religion des Judentums im Späthellenisti-
    schen Zeitalter. 3rd ed. Edited by Hugo Gressmann.
    Tübingen: J.C.B. Mohr (Paul Siebeck), 1926; 4th ed.,
    1966.

Bowker, John. The Targums and Rabbinic Literature: An
    Introduction to Jewish Interpretations of Scripture.
    Cambridge: Cambridge University Press, 1969.

Bradner, L., Jr. "An Important Discovery of Mss." The
    Biblical World n.s. I (1893):33-35.

Brandon, S. G. F. The Judgement of the Dead: The Idea of
    Life after Death in the Major Religions. New York:
    Charles Scribner's Sons, 1967.

Brashler, James. "The Coptic Apocalypse of Peter: A Genre
    Analysis and Interpretation." Ph.D. dissertation under
    James M. Robinson. Claremont Graduate School, 1977.

Bratke, Eduard. "Handschriftliche Überlieferung und
    Bruchstücke der arabisch-aethiopischen Petrus-Apokalypse."
    Zeitschrift für wissenschaftliche Theologie 36 (1893):
    454-493.

_____. "Studien über die neu entdeckten Stücke der Jüdischen und altchristlichen Literatur." Theologisches Literaturblatt 14, no. 7 (February 17, 1893): columns 73-79 and no. 9 (March 3, 1893): columns 97-102.

Braun, Herbert. Spätjüdisch-häretischer und frühchristlicher Radikalismus: Jesus von Nazareth und die essenische Qumransekte. 2 vols. Beiträge zur historischen Theologie no. 24. Tübingen: J.C.B. Mohr (Paul Siebeck), 1957.

Brooke, George J. "The Ethiopic Apocalypse of Peter 15-17 and Mark 9:2-13." Research paper for William H. Brownlee, Claremont Graduate School, 1977.

Brown, Raymond E. The Community of the Beloved Disciple. New York: Paulist Press, 1979.

_____. The Epistles of John. Anchor Bible no. 30. Garden City, N.Y.: Doubleday, 1982.

Brown, Raymond E. and John P. Meier. Antioch and Rome: Cradles of Catholic Christianity. New York: Paulist Press, 1983.

Brownlee, William H. "Biblical Interpretation among the Sectaries of the Dead Sea Scrolls." Biblical Archaeologist 14 (1951):54-76.

_____. "The Habakkuk Midrash and the Targum of Jonathan." Journal of Jewish Studies 7 (1956):169-186.

_____. The Midrash Pesher of Habakkuk. Missoula: Scholars Press, 1979.

de Bruyne, Donatien. "Fragments retrouvés d'Apocryphes priscillianistes." Revue bénédictine 24 (1907):318-335.

_____. "Nouveaux Fragments des Actes de Pierre, de Paul, de Jean, d'André et de l'Apocalypse d'Élie." Revue bénédictine 25 (1908):149-160.

Buchanan, George Wesley. Revelation and Redemption: Jewish Documents of Deliverance from the Fall of Jerusalem to the Death of Naḥmanides. Dillsboro, N.C.: Western North Carolina Press, 1978.

Budge, E. A. Wallace. On the Illustrations of Ethiopic Manuscripts in the Lives of Maba Seyon and Gabra Krestos. London: published privately for Lady Meux, 1898, pp. XI-LXXXIII.

Bullard, Roger A., translator. "Apocalypse of Peter."
The Nag Hammadi Library In English. James M.
Robinson, general editor. San Francisco: Harper
& Row, 1977, 339-345.

Bultmann, Rudolf. The History of the Synoptic Tradition.
2nd ed. New York: Harper & Row, 1968. (English translation, with supplements from the 1962 edition of
Geschichte der synoptischen Tradition. Göttingen:
1931).

Burkert, Walter. Orphism and Bacchic Mysteries: New
Evidence and Old Problems of Interpretation. Berkeley:
Center for Hermeneutical Studies in Hellenistic and
Modern Culture, 1977.

Burkitt, F. C. Review of Woodbrooke Studies. nos. 1-4.
Journal of Theological Studies 33 (1932):311-315.

_____. "The Rivals of the Canonical Gospels."
The Gospel History and its Transmission. Edinburgh:
T. & T. Clark, 1906, 324-352.

Burnett, Fred W. The Testament of Jesus-Sophia: A Redaction-
Critical Study of the Eschatological Discourse in Matthew.
Lanham, Md: University Press of America. 1981.

Caird, George Bradford. Saint Luke. The Pelican Gospel
Commentaries. Baltimore: Penguin Books, 1963.

_____. "The Transfiguration." Expository Times 67
(1954):291-294.

Cameron, A. "The Exposure of Children and Greek Ethics."
Classical Review 46 (1932):105-114.

von Campenhausen, Hans Freiherr. Die Idee des Martyriums in
der alten Kirche. Göttingen: Vandenhoeck & Ruprecht,
1936.

Carlston, Charles Edwin. "Transfiguration and Resurrection."
Journal of Biblical Literature 80 (1961):233-240.

Carmignac, Jean. "Les Dangers de' l'eschatologie." New
Testament Studies 17 (1971):365-390.

_____. "Qu'est-ce que l'apocalyptique? Son emploi
a Qumrân." Revue de Qumran 10 (1979):3-33.

Chaine, Joseph. Les Épitres Catholiques. Paris: Librairie
    Lecoffre.

Chaîne, Marius. Catalogue des manuscrits éthiopiens de la
    collection Antoine d'Abbadie. Paris: Bibliotheque
    Nationale, 1912.

_____. Grammaire Éthiopienne. Beirut: Imprimerie
    Catholique, 1907; Nouvelle Édition, 1938.

Chapius, P. "L'Evangile et l'Apocalypse de Pierre." Revue
    de Theologie et de Philosophie (1893?):338-355.

Charles, R. H., ed. The Apocrypha and Pseudepigrapha of
    the Old Testament in English. 2 vols. Oxford: The
    Clarendon Press, 1913.

Charlesworth, James H., ed. The Odes of Solomon. Missoula:
    Scholars Press, 1977.

_____. The Pseudepigrapha and Modern Research.
    Missoula: Scholars Press, 1976.

Chase, F. H. "Peter, Second Epistle," in A Dictionary of
    the Bible, vol. 3, 796-818. Edited by James Hastings.
    New York: Charles Scribner's Sons, 1900.

Chavasse, Claude. "Jesus: Christ and Moses." Theology 54
    (1951):244-250, 289-296.

Chiappelli, Alessandro. "Il nuova frammento dell' Apocalisse
    di Pietro." Nuova antologia di scienze, lettre, et
    arti, ser. 3, 47 (1893):112-122.

Chilton, B. D. "The Transfiguration: Dominical Assurance
    and Apostolic Vision." New Testament Studies 27
    (1980):115-124.

Clark, Kenneth W. Checklist of Manuscripts in the Libraries
    of the Greek and Armenian Patriarchates in Jerusalem.
    Washington: Library of Congress, 1953.

Clark, William R., translator. "Methodius." The Ante-Nicene
    Fathers: Translations of the Writings of the Fathers
    down to A.D. 325. Vol. 6. Edited by A. Roberts and
    J. Donaldson. New York: Charles Scribner's Sons, 1925,
    305-402.

Clemen, Carl. Primitive Christianity and its Non-Jewish
    Sources. Translated by Robert G. Nisbet. Edinburgh:
    T. & T. Clark, 1912.

Cohn-Sherbok, Daniel. "The Jewish Doctrine of Hell."
Religion 8 (1978):196-209.

Collins, John J.   "The Apocalyptic Context of Christian
Origins." Michigan Quarterly Review 22 (1983):250-264.

_____. "Apocalyptic Eschatology as the Transcendence
of Death." Catholic Biblical Quarterly 36 (1974):21-43.

_____. "The Symbolism of Transcendence in Apocalyptic."
Biblical Research 19 (1974):5-22.

_____. "Introduction: Towards the Morphology of a
Genre," in Collins, John J., ed., Apocalypse: The
Morphology of a Genre. Semeia 14 (1979):1-20.

Conti Rossini, Carlo. "Notice sur les manuscrits éthiopiens
de la Collection d'Abbadie." Journal asiatique, ser.
X, 19 (1912):551-578 and ser.X, 20 (1912):5-72, 449-494
and ser.XI, 2 (1913):5-64 and ser.XI, 6 (1915):189-238,
445-493.

Cooper, James and Arthur John Maclean. The Testament of our
Lord. English. Edinburgh: T. & T. Clark, 1902.

Copleston, Frederick. A History of Philosophy. Vol. 1
Westminster, Md.: Newman Press, 1950, 463-464, 473-475.

Coppens, Joseph. "Le messianisme sacerdotal dans les écrits
du nouveau testament," Recherches bibliques no. 6.
Louvain: Desclée de Brouwer, 1962, 101-112.

Cranfield, C. E. B.   I & II Peter and Jude. Introduction
and Commentary. Torch Bible Commentaries. London:
SCM Press, 1960.

Cross, F. L. The Early Christian Fathers. London:
Duckworth, 1960.

Crossan, John Dominic. "A Form for Absence: The Markan
Creation of Gospel." Semeia 12 (1978):41-55.

_____. "The Hermeneutical Jesus." Michigan Quarterly
Review 22 (1983):237-249.

_____. "Perspectives and Methods in Contemporary
Biblical Criticism." Biblical Research 22 (1977):39-49.

Cumont, Franz. After Life in Roman Paganism. New Haven:
Yale University Press, 1922.

Curran, John T. "The Teaching of II Peter 1:20: On the Interpretation of Prophecy." Theological Studies 4 (1943):347-368.

Dabeck, P. "'Siehe, es erschienen Moses und Elias,' (Mt. 17,3)." Biblica 23 (1942):175-189.

Dalton, W. J. "2 Peter." A New Catholic Commentary on Holy Scripture. Reginald C. Fuller, general editor. Nashville: Thomas Nelson, 1975, 1252-1256.

Daniel, Felix Harry. "The Transfiguration (Mark 9:2-13 and Parallels): A Redaction Critical and Traditio-Historical Study." Ph.D. dissertation, Vanderbilt University, 1976.

Danielou, Jean. The Angels and their Mission According to the Fathers of the Church. Translated by David Heimann. Westminster, Md.: Newman Press, 1957.

Danker, Frederick W. Jesus and the New Age According to St. Luke. St. Louis: Clayton, 1972.

_____. "The Second Letter of Peter." Hebrews, James, 1 and 2 Peter, Jude, Revelation. Gerhard Krodel, general editor. Proclamation Commentaries. Philadelphia: Fortress Press, 1977, 81-91.

Davies, J. G. "The Prefigurement of the Ascension in the Third Gospel." Journal of Theological Studies n.s. 6 (1955):229-233.

Le Déaut, Roger. "Apropos a Definition of Midrash." Interpretation 25 (1971):259-282.

Delling, Gerhard. "ημερα," in Theological Dictionary of the New Testament, vol. 2, 947-953. Edited by Gerhard Kittel. Edited and translated by Geoffrey W. Bromiley. 9 vols. Grand Rapids: Eerdmans, 1964.

Denis, Albert-Marie. Introduction aux pseudepigraphes grecs d'ancien testament. Leiden: E. J. Brill, 1971.

Dib, S. D. "Les versions Arabes du ≪Testamentum domini nostri Jesu Christi≫." Revue de l'Orient chrétien 10 (1905):118-123.

_____. "Note sur deux ouvrages apocryphes arabes entitulés ≪Testament de notre-seigneur≫." Revue de l'Orient chrétien 11 (1906):427-430.

455

Dibelius, Martin. From Tradition to Gospel. New York: Charles Scribner's Sons, 1933.

Dickison, Sheila K. "Abortion in Antiquity." Review of Procurato aborto nel mondo greco romano by Enzo Nardi. Milan: Giuffre editore, 1971. Arethusa 6 (1973):159-166.

Dieterich, Albrecht. Nekyia: Beiträge zur Erklärung der neuentdeckten Petrusapokalypse. Leipzig: B. G. Teubner, 1893; 2nd edition with supplemental notes, 1913.

Dillmann, August. "Bericht über das Äthiopische Buch Clementinischer Schriften." Nachrichten von der Königliche Gesellschaft der Wissenschaften zu Göttingen: (1858):185-199, 201-215, 217-226.

_____. Chrestomathia Aethiopica edita et Glossario Explanata. 2nd ed. Lipsiae: 1866; reprint ed. with Addenda et Corrigenda by Enno Littmann, Darmstadt: Wissenschaftliche Buchgesellschaft, 1967.

_____. Ethiopic Grammar. 2nd ed. Enlarged and improved by' Carl Bezold. Translated by J. A. Chrichton. London: Williams and Norgate, 1907.

_____. Lexicon Linguae Aethiopicae cum Indice Latino. Leipzig: Weigel, 1865; reprint ed., New York: Ungar, 1955.

von Dobschütz. Review of Nekyia, by Albrecht Dieterich. Zeitschrift für Kulturgeschichte, ser.4, I (1894):340-348.

Dodd, C. H. "The Appearances of the Risen Christ: a Study in form-criticism of the Gospels." Studies in the Gospels: Essays in Memory of R. H. Lightfoot. London: Blackwell, 1957. Reprinted in More New Testament Studies. Grand Rapids: Eerdmans, 1968, 102-133.

Dölger, Franz Joseph. Sol Salutis. Gebet und Gesang im christlichen Altertum. Münster: Aschendorff, 1925.

Dubarle, A. M. "Le signe du temple." Revue Biblique 46 (1939):21-44.

Duensing, Hugo. "Apocalypse of Paul." New Testament Apocrypha. Vol.2. Edited by Edgar Hennecke. Rev. ed. by Wilhelm Schneemelcher. English translation by R. McL. Wilson. Philadelphia: The Westminster Press, 1965, 755-798.

_____. "Epistula Apostolorum." New Testament Apocrypha. Vol 1. Edited by Edgar Hennecke. Rev. ed. by Wilhelm Schneemelcher. English translation by R. McL. Wilson. Philadelphia: The Westminster Press, 1965, 189-227.

_____. Epistula Apostolorum nach dem Äthiopischen
und Koptischen Texte. Kleine Texte für Vorlesungen
und Übungen no. 152. Bonn: Marcus und Weber, 1925.

_____. "Ein Stücke der urchristlichen Petrusapokalypse
enthaltender Traktat der äthiopischen Pseudoklementischen
Literatur." Zeitschrift für die neutestamentliche
Wissenschaft und die Kunde der älteren Kirche 14 (1913):
65-78.

Edsman, Carl-Martin. Le baptisme de feu. Uppsala:
A.-B. Lundequistska Bokhandelm, 1940.

Ehrhard,Albert. Überlieferung und Bestand der hagiographischen
und homiletischen Literatur der Griechischen Kirche von
den Anfängen bis zum Ende des 16. Jahrhunderts. Leipzig:
J. C. Hinrichs, 1937.

Elliott, John H. and Raymond A. Martin. I-II Peter/Jude. James.
Augsburg Commentary on the New Testament. Minneapolis:
Augsburg, 1982.

Emmel, Stephen. "Post-Resurrection Dialogues Between Jesus
Christ and His Disciples or Apostles as a Literary
Genre." Research paper for Bentley Layton,
1980.

Enslin, Morton S. "Peter, Apocalypse of," in The Interpreter's Dictionary of the Bible, vol. 3, 758. Edited
by George A. Buttrick. Nashville: Abingdon, 1962.

Ernst, Josef. Die Eschatologischen Gegenspieler in den
Schriften des Neuen Testaments. Regensburg: Friedrich
Pustet, 1967.

Ewald, H. "Ueber die Aethiopischen Handschriften zu Tübingen."
Zeitschrift für die Kunde des Morgenlandes 5 (?):180-201.

Fallon, Francis T. "The Gnostic Apocalypses," in Collins,
John J., ed., Apocalypse: The Morphology of a Genre.
Semeia 14 (1979):123-158.

Fascher, Erich. "Petrusapokryphen," in Paulys Real-Encyclopädie
der classischen Altertumswissenschaft, vol. 19, part 2
(38th Halbband), columns 1373-1381. Edited by Wilhelm
Kroll. Stuttgart: J. B. Metzler, 1938.

de Félice, Philippe. L'autre Monde; mythes et légendes le
purgatoire de Saint Patrice. Paris: Honoré Champion, 1906.

Feuillet, A. "Les perspectives propres à chaque evangeliste dans les recits de la transfiguration." Biblica 39 (1958):218-301.

Findlay, Adam Fyfe. Byways in Early Christian Literature: Studies in the Uncanonical Gospels and Acts. Edinburgh: T. & T. Clark, 1923.

Finegan, Jack. Hidden Records of the Life of Jesus. Philadelphia: Pilgrim Press, 1969.

Fitzmyer, Joseph A. "Glory Reflected on the Face of Christ (2 Cor. 3:7-4:6) and a Palestinian Jewish Motif." Theological Studies 42 (1981):630-644.

_____. "The New Testament Title "Son of Man" Philologically Considered." A Wandering Aramean. Missoula: Scholars Press, 1979, 143-160.

Foakes-Jackson. The Rise of Gentile Christianity. New York: George H. Doran, 1927.

Fornberg, Tord. An Early Church in a Pluralistic Society. A Study of 2 Peter. Lund: Gleerup, 1977.

Frend, W. H. C. Martyrdom and Persecution in the Early Church. New York: New York University Press, 1967.

Funk. Fragmente des Evangeliums und der Apokalypse des Petrus. Theologische Quartalschrift 75 (1893):255-288.

Garnsey, Peter. Social Status and Legal Privilege in the Roman Empire. Oxford: The Clarendon Press, 1970.

Gärtner, Bertil. The Temple and the Community in Qumran and in the New Testament. Cambridge: Cambridge University Press, 1965.

Gaster, Moses. The Chronicles of Jerahmeel or, The Hebrew Bible Historiale. London: Royal Asiatic Society, 1899.

_____. "Hebrew Visions of Hell and Paradise." Journal of the Royal Asiatic Society of Great Britain and Ireland (1893):571-611.

von Gebhardt, Oscar. Das Evangelium und die Apokalypse des Petrus. Leipzig: J. C. Hinrichs'sche Buchhandlung, 1893.

Gertner, M. "Midrashim in the New Testament." Journal of Semitic Studies 7 (1962):267-292.

458

Gese, Hartmut. "Wisdom, Son of Man, and the Origins of
    Christology." *Horizons in Biblical Theology* 3 (1981):23-57.

Gibson, Margaret Dunlop. *Apocrypha Arabica*. Studia
    Sinaitica no 8. London: C. J. Clay, 1901.

Gifford, E. H., translator. "The Catechetical Lectures of
    S. Cyril Archbishop of Jerusalem." *A Select Library
    of Nicene and Post-Nicene Fathers of the Christian Church*.
    Vol. 6, 1-157. Edited by Philip Schaff and Henry Wace.
    1893; reprint ed., Grand Rapids: Eerdmans, 1952.

Glasson, T. Francis. *The Second Advent. The Origin of the
    New Testament Doctrine*. 3rd and revised ed. London:
    Epworth Press, 1963.

_____. "What Is Apocalyptic?" *New Testament Studies* 27
    (1980):98-105.

Goetz, Karl Gerold. *Petrus als Gründer und Oberhaupt der
    Kirche und Schauer von Gesichten nach den altchristlichen
    Berichten und Legenden*. Untersuchungen zum Neuen Testa-
    ment no. 13. Leipzig: J. C. Hinrichs, 1927.

Goguel, Maurice. *La foi à la résurrection de Jésus dans le
    christianisme primitif*. Paris: Ernest Leroux, 1933.

_____. "A propos du texte nouveau de l'Apocalypse de
    Pierre." *Revue de l'histoire des religions* 89 (1924):
    191-209.

_____. *Au Seuil de l'Évangile Jean-Baptiste*. Paris:
    Payot, 1928.

Goodspeed, Edgar J. *A History of Early Christian Literature*.
    Revised and enlarged by Robert M. Grant. Chicago:
    University of Chicago Press, 1966.

Gorman, Michael. *Abortion and the Early Church*. New York:
    Paulist Press, 1982.

Goss, James. "Eschatology, Autonomy, and Individuation: The
    Evocative Power of the Kingdom." *Journal of the American
    Academy of Religion* 49 (1981):363-381.

Grabe, Johann Ernst. *Spicilegium ss. patrum ut et haereticum*.
    Vol. 1. Oxoniae: theatro Skedoniano, 1689-90, 74-77.

Grébaut, Sylvain. "Littérature Éthiopienne pseudo-clémentine: III traduction du Qalêmentos." _Revue de l'Orient chrétien_ 16 (1911):72-84, 167-175, 225-233; 17 (1912): 16-31, 133-144, 244-252, 337-346; 18 (1913):69-78; 19 (1914):324-330; 20 (1915-1917):33-37, 424-430; 22 (1920-1921):22-28; 113-117; 395-400; 26 (1927-1928): 22-31 (with Alcide Roman).

_____. "Littérature Éthiopienne pseudo-clémentine." _Revue de l'Orient chrétien_ 12 (1907):139-151, 285-287, 380-392; 13 (1908):166-180, 314-320; 15 (1910):198-214, 307-323, 425-439.

_____. "Sargis d'Aberga." _Patrologia Orientalis_ vol. 3, fascicle 4 (1909):548-643.

_____. Supplément au Lexiçon Linguae Aethiopicae de August Dillmann (1865) et Édition du Lexique de Juste d'Urbin (1850-1855). Paris: Imprimerie Nationale, 1952.

Guerrier, L. "Le Testament en Galilee de Notre-Seigneur Jesus-Christ; edité et traduit en Français. _Patrologia Orientalis_ vol. 9, fascicle 3 (1912):141-236.

_____. "Un "Testament de notre-seigneur et sauveur Jésus-Christ" en Galilee." _Revue de l'Orient chrétien_ 12 (1907):1-8.

Guthrie, W. K. C. _The Greeks and Their Gods_. Boston: Beacon Press, 1955.

_____. _Orpheus and Greek Religion_. New York: W. W. Norton, 1952; reprint of revised ed., 1966.

van Haelst, Joseph. _Catologue des papyrus littéraires juifs et chrétiens_. Paris: La Sorbonne, 1976.

Hahn, F. _Christologische Hoheitstitel_. Göttingen: Vandenhoeck und Ruprecht, 1963.

Haile, Getatchew. "A Catalogue of Ethiopian Manuscripts Microfilmed for the Ethiopian Manuscript Microfilm Library, Addis Ababa, and for the Hill Monastic Manuscript Library, Collegeville. Vol. 4: Project Numbers 1101-1500." Collegeville, Minn.: Hill Monastic Manuscripts Library, 1979.

Hamerton-Kelly, R. G. "The Temple and the Origins of Jewish Apocalyptic." _Vetus Testamentum_ 20 (1970):1-15.

Hammerschmidt, Ernst. Äthiopische Handschriften vom Tānāsee, vol. I. Verzeichnis der orientalischen Handschriften in Deutschland no. 21, part 1. Weisbaden: Franz Steiner, 1973.

_____. Äthiopischen liturgische Texte der Bodleian Library in Oxford. Deutsche Akademie der Wissenschaften zu Berlin Institut für Orientforschung no. 38. Berlin: Akademie, 1960.

_____. Ethiopien Studies at German Universities. Weisbaden: Steiner, 1970.

_____. "Das Pseudo-Apostolische Schrifttum in Äthiopischer Überlieferung." Journal of Semitic Studies 9 (1964):114-121.

Hands, A. R. Charities and Social Aid in Greece and Rome. Ithaca, N.Y.: Cornell University Press, n.d.

Hanson, Paul D. "Apocalypse, Genre," in The Interpreter's Dictionary of the Bible, supplementary volume, 27-28. Edited by Keith Crim. Nashville: Abingdon, 1976.

_____. "Apocalypticism," in The Interpreter's Dictionary of the Bible, supplementary volume, 28-34. Edited by Keith Krim. Nashville: Abingdon, 1976.

Harden, J. M. An Introduction to Ethiopic Christian Literature. London: SPCK, 1926.

Hare, Douglas R. A. The Theme of Jewish Persecution of Christians in the Gospel According to St. Matthew. Cambridge: Cambridge University Press, 1967.

von Harnack, Adolf. "Bruchstücke des Evangeliums und der Apokalypse des Petrus." Sitzungsberichten der Königlich Preussischen Akademie der Wissenschaften zu Berlin 1892:895-903, 949-965. Reprinted in Kleine Schriften zur alten Kirche: Berliner Akademieschriften 1890-1907. Leipzig: Zentralantiquariat der D.D.R., 1980, 83-108.

_____. "Bruchstücke des Evangeliums und der Apokalypse des Petrus." Texte und Untersuchungen zur Geschichte der Altchristlichen Literatur no. 9, fascicle 2. Leipzig: J.C. Hinrichs, 1893. 2nd ed. Reprinted in Kleine Schriften zur alten Kirche: Berliner Akademieschriften 1890-1907. Leipzig: Zentralantiquariat der D.D.R., 1980.

461

_____. Geschichte der altchristlichen Literatur bis
Eusebius. 2 vols. Lepizig:J. C. Hinrichs, 1893 and 1897;
reprint ed., 1958.

_____. "Kritik des Neuen Testaments von einem griechischen
Philosophen des 3 Jahrhunderts." Texte und Untersuchungen
zur Geschichte der altchristlichen Literatur no. 37, fascicle
4. Leipzig: J.C. Hinrichs, 1911.

_____. "Die Petrusapokalypse in der alten abendländischen
Kirche." Texte und Untersuchungen zur Geschichte der
altchristlichen Literatur no. 13 (1895):71-73. Leipzig:
J. C. Hinrichs, 1895.

_____. "Die Verklärungsgischichte Jesu, der Bericht des
Paulus (I.Kor.15,3ff) und die beiden Christusvisionen
des Petrus." Sitzungberichten der Königlich Preussischen
Akademie der Wissenschaften zu Berlin 1899:878-891. Reprinted in Kleine Schriften zur alten Kirche: Berliner
Akademieschriften 1890-1907. Leipzig: Zentralantiquariat
der D.D.R., 1980.

_____. "Vorläufige Bemerkungen zu dem jüngst syrisch und
lateinisch publizierten «Testamentum domini nostri Jesu
Christi." Sitzungberichten der Königlich Preussischen
Akademie der Wissenschaften zu Berlin 1899:878-891. Reprinted in Kleine Schriften zur alten Kirche: Berliner
Akademieschriten 1890-1907. Leipzig: Zentralantiquariat
der D.D.R., 1980.

Harris, J. Rendel. "The Odes of Solomon and the Apocalypse of
Peter." The Expository Times 42 (1930):21-23.

Harris, J. Rendel and A. Mingana. The Odes and Psalms of
Solomon. 2 vols. New York: Longmans, Green & Co., 1916
and 1920.

Harrison, A.R.W. The Law of Athens. The Family and Property.
Oxford: The Clarendon Press, 1968.

Hartstock, Reinhold. Visionsberichte in den synoptischen
Evangelien. Ein Beitrag zur Frage der Glaubwürdigkeit
der synoptischen Ueberlieferung. Festgabe für D. Dr.
Julius Kaftan zu seinem 70. Geburtstage 30 September
1918 dargebracht von Schülern und Kollegen. Tübingen:
J.C.B. Mohr (Paul Siebeck), 1920, 130-145.

Haug, Martin and Edward William West. The Book of Arda Viraf.
1872; reprint ed., Amsterdam: Oriental Press, 1971.

Hayes, John H. "The Resurrection as Enthronement and the
Earliest Church Christology." Interpretation 22 (1968):
333-345.

Headlam, Arthur C. "The Akhmim Fragments." The Classical
    Review 7 (1893):458-463.

Hengel, Martin. The Son of God: The Origin of Christology and
    the History of Jewish-Hellenistic Religion. Philadelphia:
    Fortress Press, 1976.

Hilgenfeld, Adolphus. Novum Testamentum extra canonem receptem.
    fascicle 4. Lipsiae: T. O. Weigel, 1884.

Himes, Norman E. Medical History of Contraception. Baltimore:
    Williams and Wilkins, 1936; reprint ed., New York: Schocken,
    1970.

Hoffmann, J.G.H. Jésus messie juif. Aux sources de la tradition
    chrétienne. Mélanges offerts à M. Maurice Goguel à l'occasion
    de son soixante-dixième anniversaire. Neuchatel: Delachaux
    & Niestlé, 1950, 103-112.

Hoffman, Manfred. Der Dialog bei den christlichen Schrift-
    stellern der ersten vier Jahrhunderte. Berlin: Akademie-
    Verlag, 1966.

Hofmann, Josef. "Limitations of Ethiopic in Representing Greek."
    The Early Versions of the New Testament by Bruce M. Metzger.
    Oxford: Oxford University Press, 1977, 240-256.

Höller, Josef. Die Verklärung Jesu: Eine Auslegung der
    neutestamentlichen Berichte. Freiburg im Breisgau:
    Herder & Co., 1937.

Hopkins, Keith. "Contraception in the Roman Empire." Compar-
    ative Studies in Society and History 8 (1965):124-151.

van der Horst, P.W. "Pseudo-Phocylides and the New Testament."
    Zeitschrift für die neutestamentliche Wissenschaft und die
    Kunde der älteren Kirche 69 (1978):187-202.

Houghton, Herbert Pierrepont. "The Coptic Apocalypse."
    Aegyptus Rivista Italiana di Egittologia e di Papirologia
    39 (1959):40-91.

_____. "The Coptic Apocalypse. Part III. Akhmimice;'The
    Apocalypse of Elias.'" Aegyptus Rivista Italiana de
    Egittologia e di Papirologia 39 (1959):179-210.

Hupper, William G. "Additions to 'A 2 Peter Bibliography.'"
    Journal of the Evangelical Theological Seminary 23 (1980):
    65-66.

Ignatius Ephraim II Raḥmani. Testament of Our Lord. Latin and Syriac. Moguntiae: F. Kirchheim, 1899.

James, Montague Rhodes. Apocrypha Anecdota: A Collection of Thirteen Apocryphal Books and Fragments. Texts and Studies. Contributions to Biblical and Patristic Literature. Vol.2, no. 3. Cambridge: Cambridge University Press, 1893.

_____. The Apocryphal New Testament. Oxford: Oxford University Press, 1924; reprint ed., 1975.

_____. The Lost Apocrypha of the Old Testament. New York: The Macmillan Co., 1920.

_____. "A New Text of the Apocalypse of Peter." The Journal of Theological Studies 12 (1911):36-55, 157, 362-383, 573-583.

_____. "The Rainer Fragment of the Apocalypse of Peter." The Journal of Theological Studies 32 (1931):270-279.

_____. "The Recovery of the Apocalypse of Peter." The Church Quarterly Review 80 (1915):1-36.

_____. Review of Woodbrooke Studies vol.III, by A. Mingana. Journal of Theological Studies 33 (1932):76-77.

_____. The Second Epistle General of Peter and the General Epistle of Jude. Cambridge: Cambridge University Press, 1912.

_____. The Testament of Abraham. Texts and Studies. Contributions to Biblical and Patristic Literature. Vol. 2, no. 2. Cambridge: Cambridge University Press, 1892.

James, Montague Rhodes. See also Robinson, J. Armitage and M. R. James.

Jellinek, Ad. Bet ha-Midrasch. Sammlung kleiner Midraschim und vermischter Abhandlungen aus der ältern jüdischen Literatur. Vol 5. Vienna: Brüder Winter, vorm. Herzfeld & Bauer, 1873.

de Jonge, M. "Jewish Expectations about 'Messiah' according to the Fourth Gospel." New Testament Studies 19 (1972/3):246-270.

de. Jonge M. and A.S. van der Woude. "11 Q Melchizedek and the New Testament." New Testament Studies 12 (1965/66):301-326.

Julicher, Adolf. An Introduction to the New Testament. New York: G. P. Putnam's Sons, 1904.

Kähler, Ernst. Studien zum Te Deum und zur Geschichte des 24. Psalms in der Alten Kirche. Göttingen: Vandenhoeck & Ruprecht, 1958.

Käsemann, Ernst. "An Apologia for Primitive Christian Eschatology." Essays on New Testament Themes. Studies in Biblical Theology no. 41. London: SCM Press, 1964.

_____. Commentary on Romans. Translated and edited by Geoffrey W. Bromiley. Grand Rapids: Eerdmans, 1980. (Translation of An Die Romer. Tübingen: J.C.B. Mohr (Paul Siebeck), 1980).

_____. "The Faith of Abraham in Romans 4." Perspectives on Paul. Translated by Margaret Kohl. Philadelphia: Fortress Press, 1969, 79-101.

Kee, Howard Clark. "Mark's Gospel in Recent Research." Interpretation 32 (1978):353-368.

_____. "The Transfiguration in Mark: Epiphany or Apocalyptic Vision?" Understanding the Sacred Text. Edited by John Reuman. Valley Forge: Judson Press, 1972, 135-152.

Kelly, J. N. D. A Commentary on the Epistles of Peter and of Jude. Harper's New Testament Commentaries. New York: Harper and Row, 1969.

Kline, Leslie L. The Sayings of Jesus in the Pseudo-Clementine Homilies. SBL Dissertation Series, no. 14. Missoula: Scholars Press, 1975.

Klostermann, Erich, ed. Apocrypha I. Reste des Petrus-evangeliums, der Petrus-apokalypse und des Kerygma Petri. Kleine Texte für Vorlesungen und Übungen no. 3. Berlin: Walter de Gruyter, 2nd ed., 1908; 3rd reprint ed., 1933.

_____. "Zur Petrusapokalypse." Hundert Jahre A. Marcus und E. Webers Verlag 1818-1918. Bonn: Marcus und Weber, 1919, 77-78.

Kniff, Michael A. The Ethiopic Book of Enoch. 2 vols. Oxford: The Clarendon Press, 1978.

Knopf, R. Die Briefe Petri und Judä. 7th ed. Göttingen: Vandenhoeck und Ruprecht, 1912.

Koch, Klaus. The Rediscovery of Apocalyptic. Naperville, Ill.: Allenson, 1972.

Koester, Helmut. "Apocryphal and Canonical Gospels." Harvard Theological Review 73 (1980):105-130.

_____. "GNOMAI DIAPHOROI. The Origin and Nature of Diversification in the History of Early Christianity." Trajectories through Early Christianity by James. M. Robinson and Helmut Koester. Philadelphia: Fortress Press, 1971, 114-157. Originally in Harvard Theological Review 58 (1965):279-318.

_____. Introduction to the New Testament. Philadelphia: Fortress Press, 1982.

_____. "Literature, Early Christian," in The Interpreter's Dictionary of the Bible, supplementary volume, 551-556. Edited by Keith Crim. Nashville: Abingdon , 1976.

_____. "The Theological Aspects of Primitive Christian Heresy." The Future of our Religious Past. Edited by James M. Robinson. Translated by C. E. Carlston and R. P. Scharlemann. New York: Harper and Row, 1971, 65-83.

Krenkel, Werner A. "Erotica I. Der Abortus in der Antike." Wissenschaftliche Zeitschrift der Universitat Rostock 20 (1971):443-452.

Kretzenbacher, Leopold. "Richterengel und Feuerstrom." Zeitschrift für Volkskunde 59 (1963):205-220.

Kühl, Ernst. Die Briefe Petri und Judae. Göttingen: Vandenhoeck & Ruprecht, 1897.

Kümmel, W. G. Promise and Fulfillment. 2nd ed. Translated by Dorothea M. Barton. Studies in Biblical Theology, First Series, no. 23. London: SCM Press, 1961. (Translation of Verheissung und Erfüllung. 3rd ed. Zürich: Zwingli-Verlag, 1956).

Kurfess, Alfons. "Christian Sibyllines." New Testament Apocrypha. Vol. 2. Edited by Edgar Hennecke. Rev. ed. by Wilhelm Schneemelcher. English translation by R. McL. Wilson. Philadelphia: The Westminster Press, 1965, 703-745.

_____. "Oracula Sibyllina I/II." Zeitschrift für die neutestamentliche Wissenschaft und die Kunde der Alteren Kirche 40 (1941):151-168.

Lacau, Pierre. "Remarques sur le manuscrit akhmimique des apocalypses de Sophonie et d'Élie." Journal asiatique 254 (1966):169-195.

Lacey, W. K. The Family in Classical Greece. Ithaca, N.Y.: Cornell University Press, n.d.

Lambdin, Thomas O. Introduction to Classical Ethiopic (Ge'ez). Missoula: Scholars Press, 1978.

Lampe, G. W. H., ed., A Patristic Greek Lexicon. Oxford: The Clarendon Press, 1961.

Lake, Kirsopp, translator. Eusebius: The Ecclesiastical History. 2 vols. The Loeb Classical Library no. 153. Cambridge: Harvard University Press, 1926 and 1932.

Leahy, Thomas W. "The Second Epistle of Peter," in The Jerome Biblical Commentary, vol. 2, 494-498. Edited by Raymond E. Brown; Joseph A. Fitzmyer; and Roland E. Murphy. Englewood Cliffs, N.J.: Prentice-Hall, 1968.

Leivestad, Ragnar. "Exit the Apocalyptic Son of Man." New Testament Studies 18 (1971-2):243-267.

Lévi, Israel. "Apocalypses dans le Talmud." Revue des Études juives 1 (1880):108-114.

_____. "Le Repos sabbatique de Ames damnées." Revue des Études juives 25 (1892):1-13.

Lewis, Charlton T. An Elementary Latin Dictionary. Oxford; Oxford University Press, 1891; reprint ed., 1977.

Licht, Hans. Sexual Life in Ancient Greece. London: Abbey Library, 1932.

Lieberman, Saul. "On Sins and Their Punishment." Texts and Studies. New York: KTAV, 1974, 29-51. Originally in Louis Ginzberg Jubilee Volume. New York: KTAV, 1945.

_____. "Some Aspects of After Life in Early Rabbinic Literature." Texts and Studies. New York: KTAV, 1974, 235-272. Originally in Harry A. Wolfson Jubilee Volume. Jerusalem: 1965.

Lindars, Barnabas. "The Apocalyptic Myth and the Death of Christ." Bulletin of the John Rylands Library 57 (1974/5): 366-387.

_____. "The New Look on the Son of Man." Bulletin of the John Rylands Library 63(1981):437-462.

467

_____. "Re-enter the Apocalyptic Son of Man." New
Testament Studies 22 (1975/6):52-72.

Lindblom, Johannes. Gesichte und Offenbarungen: Vorstellungen
von Göttlichen Weisungen und übernatürlichen Erscheinungen
im Ältesten Christentum. Lund: Gleerup, 1968.

Littmann, Enno. "Die Äthiopischer Handschriften im griechischen
Kloster zu Jerusalem." Zeitschrift für Assyriologie und
Verwandte Gebiete 15 (1900):133-161.

Lods, Adolphe. L'Évangile et l'Apocalypse de Pierre. Le Texte
Grec du livre d'Énoch. Mémoires publiés par les membres
de la Mission Archéologique Française au Caire. Vol. IX,
fascicle 3. Edited by M. U. Bouriant. Paris: Ernest Leroux,
1893.

_____. L'évangile et l'apocalypse de Pierre publiés pour
la 1re fois d'apres le photographies du manuscrit de Gizéh.
Paris: Ernest Leroux, 1893.

_____. Evangelii secundum Petrum et Petri Apocalypseos
quae supersunt ad fidem codicis in Aegypto nuper inventi.
Paris: Ernest Leroux, 1892.

Lohfink, Gerhard. Die Himmelfahrt Jesu: Untersuchungen zu den
Himmelfahrts- und Erhöhungstexten bei Lukas. München: Kösel
Verlag, 1971.

Lohmeyer, Ernst. Das Evangelium des Matthäus. Göttingen:
Vandenhoeck & Ruprecht, 1956.

_____. "Die Idee des Martyriums im Judentum und Urchris-
tentum." Zeitschrift für systematische Theologie (1927/28):
232-249.

Lohse, Eduard. History of the Suffering and Death of Jesus
Christ. Translated by Martin O. Dietrich. Philadelphia:
Fortress Press, 1967.

Longenecker, Richard N. The Christology of Early Jewish
Christianity. Naperville, Ill.: Alec R. Allenson, 1970.

Loofs, Friedrich. "Descent to Hades (Christ's)," in Encyclo-
paedia of Religion and Ethics, vol. 4, 654-663. Edited
by James Hastings. New York: Charles Scribner's Sons, 1911.

Lüdemann, H. "Kirchengeshichte bis zum Nicänum." Thologischer
Jahresbericht. Vol. 13 (for 1893):171-183; Vol. 14 (for
1894):184-187. Edited by H. Holtzmann. Braunschweig: C.A.
Schwetschke.

Ludolf, Job. <u>Lexicon Aethiopico-Latinum</u>. London, 1661.

Luecke, George Lewis. "A Reconstruction of the Text of the Apocalypse of Peter." M.A. dissertation, University of Chicago, 1921.

Lührmann, Dieter. "POx 2949: EvPt 3-5 in einer Handschrift des 2./3. Jahrhunderts." <u>Zeitschrift für die neutestamentliche Wissenschaft und die Kunde der älternen Kirche</u> 72 (1981): 216-226.

MacCulloch, John Arnott. "Descent to Hades (Ethnic)," in <u>Encyclopedia of Religion and Ethics</u>, vol. 4, 648-654. Edited by James Hastings. New York: Charles Scribner's Sons, 1911.

_____. <u>Early Christian Visions of the Other-World</u>. Edinburgh: St. Giles, 1912.

_____. <u>The Harrowing of Hell: A Comparative Study of an Early Christian Doctrine</u>. Edinburgh: T. & T. Clark, 1930.

MacMahon, J. H., translator. "The Refutation of All Heresies." <u>The Ante-Nicene Fathers</u>. Vol. 5. Edited by A. Roberts and J. Donaldson. New York: Charles Scribner's Sons, 1926, 9-153.

M'Neile, Alan Hugh. <u>The Gospel According to St. Matthew</u>. London: Macmillan and Co., 1961.

Macomber, William F. "A Catalogue of Ethiopian Manuscripts Microfilmed for the Ethiopian Manuscript Microfilm Library, Addis Ababa, and for the Hill Monastic Manuscript Library, Collegeville. Vol. 3: Project Numbers 701-1100." Collegeville, Minn.: Hill Monastic Manuscripts Library, 1978.

Macurdy, G. H. "Platonic Orphism in the Testament of Abraham." <u>Journal of Biblical Literature</u> 61 (1942):213-226.

Maier, Johann. <u>Die Tempelrolle vom Toten Meer</u>. Munchen: Ernst Reinhardt, 1978.

Manson, T. W. Some Reflections on Apocalyptic. Aux sources de la tradition chrétienne. <u>Mélanges offerts à M. Maurice Goguel à l'occasion de son soixante-dixième anniversaire</u>. Neuchatel: Delachaux & Niestlé, 1950, 139-145.

Marmorstein, A. "Jüdische Parallelen zur Petrusapokalypse." <u>Zeitschrift für die neutestamentliche Wissenschaft und die Kunde der älteren Kirche</u> 10 (1909):297-300.

Marshall, I. Howard. The Gospel of Luke: A Commentary on the Greek Text. The New International Greek Testament Commentary. Grand Rapids: Eerdmans, 1978.

Marxsen, Willi. The Beginnings of Christology. Translated by Paul J. Achtemeier and Lorenz Nieting. Philadelphia: Fortress Press, 1979. (Translation of Anfangsprobleme der Christologie and Das Abendmahl als christologisches Problem. Gütersloher Verglagshaus, Gerard Mohn, 1960 and 1963 respectively).

Maurer, Ch. "Apocalypse of Peter." New Testament Apocrypha. Vol. 2. Edited by Edgar Hennecke. Rev. ed. by Wilhelm Schneemelcher. English translation by R. McL. Wilson. Philadelphia: The Westminster Press, 1965, 663-683.

Mayor, Joseph P. The Epistles of Jude and II Peter. New York: Macmillan & Co., 1907; reprint ed., Grand Rapids: Baker Book House, 1979, cxxx-cxxxiv.

McArthur, Harvey K. "Parousia," in The Interpreter's Dictionary of the Bible, vol. 3, 658-661. Edited by George A. Buttrick. Nashville: Abingdon, 1962.

McGinn, Bernard, translator. Apocalyptic Spirituality. New York: Paulist Press, 1979, 17-80.

McNamara, Martin. The Apocrypha in the Irish Church. Dublin: Dublin Institute for Advanced Studies, 1975.

Menoud, Philippe H. Remarques sur les textes de l'ascension dans Luc-Actes. Neutestamentliche Studien für Rudolf Bultmann. Berlin: Alfred Töpelmann, 1957, 148-156.

Mercer, Samuel A. B. Ethiopic Grammar with Chrestomathy and Glossary. Rev. ed. New York: Frederick Ungar, 1961.

Merklein, Helmut. "Die Auferweckung Jesu und die Anfänge der Christologie (Messias bzw. Sohn Gottes und Menschensohn)." Zeitschrift für die neutestamentliche Wissenschaft und die Kunde der älteren Kirche 72 (1981):1-26.

Metzger, Bruce M. The Early Versions of the New Testament. Oxford: Oxford University Press, 1977.

_____. "The Ending of the Gospel According to Mark in the Ethiopic Manuscripts." Understanding the Sacred Text. Edited by John Reumann. Valley Forge: Judson Press, 1972, 165-180.

_____. "Literary Forgeries and Pseudepigrapha." Journal of Biblical Literature 91 (1972):3-24.

Michaelis, Wilhelm. Die Apokryphen Schriften zum Neuen Testament. 2nd ed. Bremen: Carl Schünemann, 1958, 464-481.

Michel, Otto. "οιϰοσ," in Theological Dictionary of the New Testament, vol. 5, 119-159. Edited by Gerhard Kittel. Edited and translated by Geoffrey W. Bromiley. 9 vols. Grand Rapids: Eerdmans, 1964.

Michl, J. "Apokalypsen, apokryphe, II. A. des N.T.," in Lexicon für Theologie und Kirche, vol. 1, columns 698-704. 2nd ed. Edited by Josef Höfer and Karl Rahner. Freiburg: Herder, 1957.

Migne, J. P. Sozomeni, Historia Ecclesiastica. Patrologia Graeca. Vol. 64, columns 843-1630. Paris: Bibliothecae Cleri universae, 1864.

Milgrom, Jacob. "Further Studies in the Temple Scroll." The Jewish Quarterly Review 71 (1980):89-106.

_____. "The Temple Scroll." Biblical Archaeologist 41 (1978):105-120.

Milik, J. T. The Books of Enoch: Aramaic Fragments of Qumrân Cave 4. Oxford: The Clarendon Press, 1976.

Miller, Merrill P. "Midrash," in The Interpreter's Dictionary of the Bible, supplementary volume, 593-597. Edited by Keith Crim. Nashville: Abingdon, 1976.

_____. "Targum, Midrash and the Use of the Old Testament in the New Testament." Journal for the Study of Judaism in the Persian, Hellenistic and Roman Period 2 (1971):29-82.

Minear, Paul S. And Great Shall Be Your Reward: the Origins of Christian Views of Salvation. New Haven: Yale University Press, 1941.

_____. Christian Eschatology and Historical Methodology. Neutestamentliche Studien für Rudolf Bultmann zu seinem siebzigsten Geburtstag am 20. August 1954. Berlin: Alfred Töpelmann, 1957, 15-23.

Mingana, A. "The Apocalypse of Peter." Woodbrook Studies. Bulletin of the John Rylands Library 14 (1931):fascicle 6,182-297 and fascicle 7,423-562 and 15(1932):fascicle 8, 179-279.

Müller, Hans-Peter. "Die Verklärung Jesu: Eine motivgeschicht-
    liche Studie." Zeitschrift für die neutestamentliche
    Wissenschaft und die Kunde der älteren Kirche 50-51 (1960/61):
    56-64.

Munck, Johannes. Discours d'adieu dans le Nouveau Testament
    et dans la littérature biblique. Aux sources de la tradi-
    tion chrétienne. Mélanges offerts à M. Maurice Goguel à
    l'occasion de son soixante-dixième anniversaire. Neuchatel:
    Delachaux & Niestlé, 1950, 155-170.

Nardi, Enzo. Procurato Aborto nel monde Greco Romano. Milan:
    Giuffrè, 1971.

Nau, F. "Clementins (apocryphes),"in Dictionnaire de Théologie
    Catholique, vol. 3, columns 201-223. Edited by A. Vacant
    and E. Mangenot. Paris: Letouzey et Ané, 1908.

_____. "Note sur ⟨⟨Un nouveau texte de l'Apocalypse de
    Saint Pierre⟩⟩. Revue de l'Orient chrétien 15 (1910):
    441-442.

Neyrey, Jerome H. "The Apologetic Use of the Transfiguration
    in 2 Peter 1:16-21." Catholic Biblical Quarterly 42 (1980):
    504-519.

Nicholson, Edward W. B. "The Revelation of Peter." The
    Academy 43 (1893):14.

Nickelsburg, George W. "Enoch, Levi and Peter: Recipients of
    Revelation in Upper Galilee." Journal of Biblical Litera-
    ture 100 (1981):575-600.

_____. Resurrection, Immortality and Eternal Life in
    Intertestamental Judaism. Cambridge: Harvard University
    Press, 1972.

Noonan, John T., Jr. Contraception. A History of Its Treatment
    by the Catholic Theologians and Canonists. Cambridge:
    Harvard University Press, 1966.

Norden, Eduard. "Die Petrus-Apokalypse und ihre antiken
    Vorbilder." Beilage 98 zur Allgemeinen Zeitung 107
    (1893):1-6. Reprinted in Kleine Schriften zum klassischen
    Altertum. Berlin: Walter de Gruyter, 1966, 218-233.

Norris, John Massillon. "The Functional New Testament of
    Clement of Alexandria." Ph.D. dissertation, University
    of Chicago, 1942.

Nösgen, D. "Der Fund von Akhmim." Evangelische Kirchen-
    zeitung, no. 8, February 19, 1893, columns 125-128;
    no. 9, February 26, 1893, columns 141-144; no. 10, March 8,
    1893, columns 149-156.

Pagels, Elaine. The Gnostic Gospels. New York: Random House,
    1979.

Perkins, Pheme. The Gnostic Dialogue: The Early Church and
    the Crisis of Gnosticism. New York: Paulist Press, 1980.

_____. "Peter in Gnostic Revelation." SBL 1974 Seminar
    Papers. Edited by George MacRae. Cambridge: SBL, 1974.

Pesch, Rudolf. Simon Petrus. Geschichte und geschichtliche
    Bedentung des ersten Jüngers Jesu Christi. Stuttgart:
    Anton Hiersmann, 1980.

Peterson, Erik. "Das Martyrium des hl. Petrus nach der
    Petrus-Apokalypse." Miscellanea G. Belvederi. Rome:
    1953, 181ff. Reprinted in Frühkirche, Judentum and
    Gnosis. Freiburg: Herder, 1959, 88-91.

_____. "Die Taufe im acherusischen See." Vigiliae
    Christianiae 9 (1955):1-20. Reprinted with some revision
    and expanded notes in Frühkirche, Judentum und Gnosis.
    Freiburg: Herder, 1959, 310-332.

Piccolomini, E. "Sul testo dei frammenti dell'evangelio e
    dell'apocalissi del pseudo-pietro." Rendicoti della reale
    accademie dei Lencei 8 (1899): fascicles 7-8, 389-404.

Polotsky, H. J. "Aramaic, Syriac, and Ge'ez." Journal of
    Semitic Studies 9 (1964):1-10.

Pomeroy, Sarah B. Goddesses, Whores, Wives, and Slaves.
    New York: Schocken Books, 1975.

Praetorius, Franz. Aethiopische Grammatik mit Paradigmen,
    Litteratur, Chrestomathie, und Glossar. 1886; reprint
    ed., New York: Frederick Ungar, 1955.

Preuschen, Erwin. Antilegomena: Die Reste der auuserkanonischen
    Evangelien und urchristlichen Uberlieferungen. 2nd ed.
    Gieszen: Alfred Töpelmann, 1905.

Prümm, K. "De genuino apocalypsis Petri textu examen testium
    iam notorum et novi fragmenti Raineriani." Biblica 10
    (1929):62-80.

Quasten, Johannes. Patrology. 3 vols. Westminster, Md.:
The Newman Press, 1953-1962.

Quispel, G. and R. M. Grant. "Note on the Petrine Apocrypha."
Vigiliae Christianae 6 (1952):31-32.

Ramsey, Arthur Michael. The Glory of God and the Transfiguration
of Christ. New York: Longmans, Green & Co., 1949.

Reicke, Bo. The Epistlesof James, Peter, and Jude. 2nd ed.
Garden City, N. Y.: Doubleday, 1978.

_____. The New Testament Conception of Reward. Aux sources
de la tradition chrétienne. Mélanges offerts à M. Maurice
Goguel à l'occasion de son soixante-dixième anniversaire.
Neuchatel: Delachaux & Nièstle, 1950, 195-206.

Reitzenstein, R. "Religionsgeschichte und Eschatologie."
Zeitschrift für die neutestamentliche Wissenschaft und
die Kunde der älteren Kirche 13 (1912):1-28.

Rice, David G. and John E. Stambaugh. Sources for the Study
of Greek Religion. Missoula: Scholars Press, 1979.

Riesenfeld, Harald. La descente dans le mort. Aux sources de
la tradition chrétienne. Mélanges offerts à M. Maurice
Goguel à l'occasion de son soixante-dixième anniversaire.
Neuchatel: Delachaux & Nièstle, 1950, 207-217.

_____. Jésus Transfiguré. Lund: Hakan Ohlsson, 1947.

Rigaux, Béda. La Secende Venu de Jésus. La Venue du Messie.
Messianisme et Eschatologie. Recherches bibliques no. 6.
Louvain: Desclée de Brouwer, 1962, 173-216.

Rieβler, Paul. Altjüdisches Schrifttum auβerhalb der Bibel.
Augsburg: Dr. Benno Falser Verlag, 1928.

Rist, Martin. "Antichrist," in The Interpreter's Dictionary
of the Bible, vol. 1, 140-143. Edited by George A. Buttrick.
Nashville: Abingdon, 1962.

Robinson, J. Armitage and Montague Rhodes James. The Gospel
According to Peter and the Revelation of Peter. London:
C.J. Clay and Sons, 1892.

Robinson, James M. "Jesus: From Easter to Valentinus (or to
the Apostles' Creed)." Journal of Biblical Literature 101
(1982):5-37.

Robinson, James M. and Helmut Koester. Trajectories Through
Early Christianity. Philadelphia: Fortress Press, 1971.

Robinson, John A. T. "The Most Primitive Christology of all?" Journal of Theological Studies n.s.7 (1958):177-189.

Rohde, Erwin. Psyche: The Cult of Souls and Belief in Immortality among the Greeks. Translated from the 8th German edition by W. B. Hillis. 2 vols. 1893; rev. ed. 1897; 1925; reprint ed., New York: Harper and Row, 1966.

Rollins, Wallace Eugene and Marion Benedict Rollins. Jesus and His Ministry. Greenwich, Conn.: Seabury, 1954.

Rowland, Christopher. The Open Heaven. A Study of Apocalyptic in Judaism and Early Christianity. New York: Crossroad, 1982.

_____. "The Vision of the Risen Christ in Rev. i.13ff.: The Debt of an Early Christology to an Aspect of Jewish Angelology." Journal of Theological Studies n.s. 31 (1980): 1-11.

_____. "The Visions of God in Apocalyptic Literature." Journal for the Study of Judaism in the Persian, Hellenistic, and Roman Periods 10 (1979):137-154.

Rowley, H. H. The Relevance of Apocalyptic. New York: Association, 1964.

Rudolph, Kurt. Der gnostische 'Dialog' als literarische Genus. Probleme der koptischen Literatur. Edited by Peter Nagel. Halle: Wissenschaftliche Beiträge der Martin-Luther Universität Halle-Wittenberg 1968/1 (K 2), 1968, 85-107.

Rupp, George. "Incarnation and Apocalyptic: Christology in the Context of Religious Pluralism." Word and World 3 (1983): 41-50.

Ruppert, Lothar. Der leidende Gerechte: Eine motivgeschichtliche Untersuchung zum Alten Testament und zwischentestamentlichen Judentum. Forschung zur Bible no. 5. Würzburg: Echter Verlag, 1972.

Russell, D. S. The Method and Message of Jewish Apocalyptic. Philadelphia: The Westminster Press, 1964.

Rutherford, Andrew. "The Revelation of Peter." The Ante-Nicene Fathers. Vol. 10. Edited by Allan Menzies. Grand Rapids: Eerdmans, 1951, 141-147. Reprint of edition of 1897.

Sabbe, Maurice. La rédaction du récit de la transfiguration. Recherches bibliques no. 6. Louvain: Desclés de Brouwer, 1962.

Saldarini, Anthony J. "The Uses of Apocalyptic in the Mishna and Tosepta." Catholic Biblical Quarterly 39 (1977):396-409.

Salmon, George. A Historical Introduction to the Study of the Books of the New Testament. 7th ed. London: John Murray, 1894.

Salmond, S. D. F., translator. "Against Plato, On the Cause of the Universe." The Ante-Nicene Fathers. Vol. 5. Edited by Alexander Roberts and James Donaldson. New York: Charles Scribner's Sons, 1926, 221-223.

Sanday, W. Inspiration. Eight Lectures on the Early History and Origin of the Doctrine of Biblical Inspiration. New York: Longmans, Green & Co., 1894.

Sanders, E. P. The Tendencies of the Synoptic Tradition. Society for New Testament Studies Monograph Series no. 9. Cambridge: Cambridge University Press, 1969.

Sandy, D. Brent. "Transformed Into His Image." Grace Theological Journal 2 (1981):227-237.

de Santos Otero, Aurelio. "Apocalypse of Thomas." New Testament Apocrypha. Vol. 2. Edited by Edgar Hennecke. Rev. ed. by Wilhelm Schneemelcher. English translation by R. McL. Wilson. Philadelphia: The Westminster Press, 1965, 798-803.

_____. "The Pseudo-Titus Epistle." New Testament Apocrypha. Vol. 2. Edited by Edgar Hennecke. Rev. ed. by Wilhelm Schneemelcher. English translation by R. McL. Wilson. Philadelphia: The Westminster Press, 1965, 141-166.

Schäfer, Peter. Der Bar Kokhba Aufstand. Studien zum zweiten jüdischen Krieg gegen Rom. Tübingen: J.C.B. Mohr (Paul Siebeck), 1981.

Schmidt, Carl. Gespräche Jesu mit seinen Jüngern nach der Auferstehung. Leipzig: J. C. Hinrichs, 1919.

_____. Review of Nekyia, by Albrecht Dieterich. Theologische Literaturzeitung 19 (1894):columns 560-565.

Schmidt, David H. "The Peter Writings: Their Redactors and Their Relationships." Ph.D. dissertation, Northwestern University, 1972.

Schmithals, Walter. The Apocalyptic Movement. Nashville: Abingdon, 1975.

Schneemelcher, Wilhelm. "General Introduction." New Testament Apocrypha. Vol. 1. Edited by Edgar Hennecke. Rev. ed. by Wilhelm Schneemelcher. English translation by R. McL. Wilson. Philadelphia: The Westminster Press, 1963, 19-68.

_____. "Later Apocalypses, Introduction." New Testament Apocrypha. Vol. 2. Edited by Edgar Hennecke. Rev. ed. by Wilhelm Schneemelcher. English translation by R. McL. Wilson. Philadelphia: The Westminster Press, 1965, 751-754.

Schneider, Johannes. "προσερχομαι," in Theological Dictionary of the New Testament, vol. 2, 683-684. Edited by Gerhard Kittel. Edited and translated by Geoffrey W. Bromiley. 9 vols. Grand Rapids: Eerdmans, 1964.

Schrage, Wolfgang. Die Elia-Apokalypse. Jüdische Schriften aus hellenistisch-römischer Zeit no. 5. Gütersloh: Gerd Mohn, 1980.

von Schubert, Hans. "Neue Funde auf dem Gebiete der urchristlichen Litteratur. 1. Das Evangelium des Petrus. 2. Die Apokalypse des Petrus." Die christliche Welt, no. 1, December 29, 1892, columns 7-12; no. 3, January 12, 1893, columns 50-55.

Schurrer, Emil. Review of Fragments grecs du livre d'Énoch, by U. Bouriant. Theologische Literaturzeiting 17, no. 25 (December 10, 1892):columns 609-612.

_____. Review of "Bruchstücke des Evangeliums und der Apokalypse des Petrus," by Adolf Harnack. Theologische Literaturzeitung 17, no. 25 (December 10, 1892):columns 612-614.

_____. Review of The Gospel According to Peter, And the Revelation of Peter, by J. Armitage Robinson and Montague Rhodes James, "Evangelii secundum Petrum et Petri Apocalypseos quae supersunt ad fidem codicis in Aegypto nuper inventi," by Adolphe Lods, and "Bruchstücke des Evangeliums und der Apokalypse des Petrus, 2nd ed., by Adolf Harnack. Theologische Literaturzeitung 18, no. 2 (January 21, 1983): columns 33-37.

_____. Review of "L'évangile et l'apocalypse de Pierre publies pour la 1re fois d'apres le photographies du manuscrit de Gizeh," by Adolphe Lods. Theologische Literaturzeitung 18, no. 7 (April 1, 1893):columns 187-188.

_____. Review of "Das Evangelium und die Apokalypse des Petrus," by Oscar von Gebhardt. Theologische Literaturzeitung 18, no. 19 (September 16, 1893):columns 477-478.

Schwartz, Daniel R. "The Three Temples of 4Q Florilegium." Revue de Qumran 10 (1979):83-91.

Schweizer, Eduard. Church Order in the New Testament. Translated by Frank Clarke. London: SCM Press, 1961.

_____. "The Son of Man Again." New Testament Studies 9 (1962/63):256-261.

Scott, R. B. Y. "Behold, He Cometh With Clouds." New Testament Studies 5 (1958/59):127-132.

Senior, Donald. 1 and 2 Peter. Wilmington, Del.: Michael Glazier, 1980.

Sidebottom, E. M. James, Jude, 2 Peter. Grand Rapids: Eerdmans, 1967; reprint ed., 1982.

Simms, A. Ernest. "Second Peter and the Apocalypse of Peter." The Expositor (London), ser. 5, VIII (1898):460-471.

Simon, Marcel. Retour du Christ et reconstruction du Temple dans la pensée chrétienne primitive. Aux sources de la tradition chrétienne. Mélanges offerts à M. Maurice Goguel à l'occasion de son soixante-dixième anniversaire. Neuchatel: Delachaux & Niestle, 1950, 247-257.

Sint, Josef A. Pseudonymität im Altertum. Ihre Formen und Ihre Gründe. Innsbruck: Universitätsverlag Wagner, 1960.

Smith, Morton. Clement of Alexandria and a Secret Gospel of Mark. Cambridge: Harvard University Press, 1973.

_____. "The Origin and History of the Transfiguration Story." Union Seminary Quarterly Review 36 (1980):39-44.

Speyer, Wolfgang. Die Literarische Fälschung im heidnischen und christlichen Altertum. München: C. H. Beck'sche Verlagsbuchhandlung, 1971.

_____. "Religiöse Pseudepigraphie und literarische Fälschung im Altertum." Jahrbuch für Antike und Christentum 8/9 (1965/66):88-125.

Spitta, Friedrich. "Die evangelische Geschichte von der Verklärung Jesu." Zeitschrift für wissenscaftliche Theologie 54 (1911):97-167.

_____. "Die Petrusapokalypse und der zweite Petrusbrief." Zeitschrift für die neutestamentliche Wissenschaft und die Kunde der älteren Kirche 22 (1911):237-242.

de Ste. Croix, G. E. M. "Why Were the Early Christians Persecuted?" Past and Present 26 (1963):6-38.

Stein, Robert H. "Is the Transfiguration (Mark 9:28) a Misplaced Resurrection-Account?" Journal of Biblical Literature 95 (1976):79-96.

Stocks, H. "Quellen zur Rekonstruktion des Petrusevangeliums." Zeitschrift für Kirchengeschichte 34 (1913):1-57.

Stone, Michael E. "Apocalyptic - Vision or Hallucination?" Milla-wa-Milla. The Australian Bulletin of Comparative Religion 14 (1974):47-60.

_____. Signs of the Judgement, Onomostica Sacra, and the Generations from Adam. University of Pennsylvania Armenian Texts and Studies no. 3. Chico, Ca.: Scholars Press, 1981.

Strack, Hermann L. Introduction to the Talmud and Midrash. New York: Atheneum, 1969.

Sundberg, Albert C. "Muratorian Fragment," in The Interpreter's Dictionary of the Bible, supplementary volume, 609-610. Edited by Keith Crim. Nashville: Abingdon, 1976.

Surkau, Hans-Werner. Martyrien in jüdischer und frühchristlicher Zeit. Göttingen: Vandenhoeck & Ruprecht, 1938.

Taylor, Vincent. The Gospel According to St. Mark. New York: Macmillan & Co., 1966; reprint ed., Grand Rapids: Baker Book House, 1981.

Teeple, Howard M. The Mosaic Eschatological Prophet. Philadelphia: Society of Biblical Literature, 1957.

Telford, William R. The Barren Temple and the Withered Tree. Sheffield: Journal for the Study of the New Testament, supplement series I, 1980.

Theisohn, Johannes. Der auserwählte Richter. Untersuchungen zum traditionsgeschichtlichen Ort der Menschensohngestalt der Bilderreden des Äthiopischen Henoch. Göttingen: Vandenhoeck & Ruprecht, 1975.

Thelwall, S., translator. "A Strain of the Judgement of the Lord." The Ante-Nicene Fathers. Vol. 4. Edited by A. Roberts and J. Donaldson. New York: Charles Scribner's Sons, 1925, 135-141.

Thoma, Clemens. "Jüdische Apokalyptik am Ende des ersten nachchristlichen Jahrhunderts." Kairos: Zeitschrift für Religionswissenschaft und Theologie 11 (1969):134-144.

von. Tischendorf, Konstantin. Apocalypses Apocryphae. Leipzig: 1866; reprint ed., Hildesheim: George Olms, 1966.

Towner, Wayne Sibley. The Rabbinic "Enumeration of Scriptural Examples." Leiden: E. J. Brill, 1973.

Trites, Allison A. "The Transfiguration of Jesus: The Gospel in Microcosm." The Evangelical Quarterly 51 (1978):67-79.

Ullendorf, Edward. Ethiopia and the Bible. Oxford: Oxford University Press, 1968.

_____. The Ethiopians. An Introduction to Country and People. 2nd ed. London: Oxford University Press, 1965.

Vaganay, Léon. L'Évangile de Pierre. 2nd ed. Paris: Librairie Lecoffre (J. Gabalda et Fils), 1930.

Vailhé, S. "La Mosaique de la transfiguration au Sinai est-elle de Justinien?" Revue de l'Orient chrétien 12 (1907):96-99.

VanderKam, James C. "Some Major Issues in the Contemporary Study of I Enoch: Reflections on J. T. Milik's The Books of Enoch: Aramaic Fragments of Qumran Cave 4." MAARAV 3/1 (January, 1982):85-97.

Vermes, Geza and K. P. Bland, et al., "Interpretation, History of," in The Interpreter's Dictionary of the Bible, supplementary volume, 436-456. Edited by Keith Crim. Nashville: Abingdon, 1976.

Vielhauer, Philipp. "Apocalyptic in Early Christianity 1. Introduction." New Testament Apocrypha. Vol. 2. Edited by Edgar Hennecke. Rev. ed. by Wilhelm Schneemelcher. English translation by R. McL. Wilson. Philadelphia: The Westminster Press, 1965, 608-642.

_____. "Introduction." New Testament Apocrypha. Vol. 2. Edited by Edgar Hennecke. Rev. ed. by Wilhelm Schneemelcher. English translation by R. McL. Wilson. Philadelphia: The Westminster Press, 1965, 581-607.

_____. "Die Petrus-Apokalypse." Geschichte der urchristlichen Literatur: Einleitung in das Neue Testament, die Apokryphen und die Apostolischen Väter. Berlin: de Gruyter, 1975, 507-513.

Volz, Paul. Die Eschatologie der jüdischen Gemeinde.
Tübingen: J.C.B. Mohr (Paul Siebeck), 1934; reprint ed.,
Hildesheim: Georg Olms, 1966.

Vööbus, Arthur. Early Versions of the New Testament: Manuscript Studies. Stockholm: The Estonian Theological
Society in Exile, 1954, 243-269.

Waiz, Hans. "Apokryphen des Neuen Testaments," in Herzog-
Hauck, Realencyklopädie fur protestantische Theologie und
Kirche, vol. 23, 101-103. 3rd ed. Leipzig: J.C. Hinrichs, 1913.

Wallis, Ernest, translator. "On The Glory of Martyrdom."
The Ante-Nicene Fathers. Vol. 5. Edited by A. Roberts and
J. Donaldson. New York: Charles Scribner's Sons, 1926,
579-587.

Wallis, R. E., translator. "The Martyrdom of Perpetua and
Felicitas." The Ante-Nicene Fathers. Vol. 3. Edited by
A. Roberts and J. Donaldson. New York: Charles Scribner's
Sons, 1926, 691-706.

Walzer, R. Galen on Jews and Christians. London: Oxford
University Press, 1949.

Weil, Henri. Review of Nekyia, by Albrecht Dieterich. Journal
des Savants (1895):213-225, 303-319, 552-564.

Weinel, Heinrich. "Offenbarung des Petrus." Handbuch zu den
Neutestamentliche Apokryphen. Edited by Edgar Hennecke.
Tübingen: J.C.B. Mohr, 1904, 285-290.

_____. "Offenbarung des Petrus." Neutestamentliche
Apokryphen. Edited by Edgar Hennecke. Tübingen: J.C.B.
Mohr, 1904, 211-217.

_____. "Offenbarung des Petrus." Neutestamentliche
Apokryphen. 2nd ed. Edited by Edgar Hennecke. Tübingen:
J.C.B. Mohr, 1924.

_____. Die spätere christliche Apokalyptik. Ευχαριστηριον.
Studien zur Religionen und Literatur des Alten und Neuen
Testaments. Festschrift für Hermann Gunkel. Edited by
Hans Schmidt. Göttingen: Vandenhoeck und Ruprecht, 1923,
141-173.

Wessely, Charles. "Les plus anciens monuments du Christianisme:
Ecrits sur Papyrus II." Patrologia Orientalis 18 (1924):
345-511.

White, H. J. "On the Saying Attributed to Our Lord in John II.19." The Expositor (London), ser. 8, XVII (1919):415-423.

Widengren, Geo. The Ascension of the Apostle and the Heavenly Book. Uppsala: A.B. Lundequistske, 1950.

von Wilamowitz-Möllendorff, U. Index scholarum in Academie Georgus Augustus per Semester aestos anni 1893 Habdendarum, pp. 31-33.

Wilmart, André. "Un Anonyme Ancien De X Virginibus." Bulletin d'ancienne litterature et archéologie chrétiennes 1 (1911): 35-49, 88-102.

Winstanley, Edward William. "The Outlook of Early Christian Apocalypse." The Expositor (London), ser. 8, XIX (1920/21): 161-184.

Wright, Addison G. The Literary Genre Midrash. New York: Alba House, 1967.

Wright, William. Catalogue of the Ethiopic Manuscripts in the British Museum Acquired since the Year 1847. London: British Museum, 1877.

Wünsche, August. Aus Israels Lehrhallen. Vol. 3. 1907; reprint ed., Hildesheim: Georg Olms, 1967.

Yadin, Yigael. Bar Kokhba. Jerusalem: Weidenfeld and Nicholson, 1971.

_____. "Bar Kochba," in The Interpreter's Dictionary of the Bible, supplementary volume, 89-92. Edited by Keith Crim. Nashville: Abingdon, 1976.

Yarbro Collins, Adela. "The Early Christian Apocalypse," in Collins, John J., ed., Apocalypse: The Morphology of a Genre. Semeia 14 (1979):61-121.

Zahn, Theodor. Geschichte des neutestamentlichen Kanons. Vol. I, part 1, 307-310. Vol. 2, part 2, 810-820. Erlangen: Deichert, 1888 and 1892.

_____. Grundriss der Geschichte des neutestamentlichen Kanons. 2nd ed. Leipzig: A. Deichert'sche, 1904.

_____. Introduction to the New Testament. Vol. 2. Translated by Melanchton W. Jacobus, et. al. Edinburgh: T. & T. Clark, 1909.

_____. "Kanon des Neuen Testaments," in Herzog-Hauck, Realencyklopädie für protestantische Theologie und Kirche, vol. 9, 768-796. 3rd ed. Leipzig: J.C. Hinrichs, 1901.

_____. "Kanon Muratori," in Herzog-Hauck, Realencyklopädie für protestantische Theologie und Kirche, vol. 9, 796-806. 3rd ed. Leipzig: J.C. Hinrichs, 1901.

Zuntz, Günther. Persephone: Three Essays on Religion and Thought in Magna Graecia. Oxford: Oxford University Press, 1971.

The following works in Ge'ez have been used:

ወንጌል ፡ ቅዱስ The New Testament in Ge'ez first published in Leipzig in 1899, and now distributed in a reprinted edition by the American Bible Society.

መዝሙረ ፡ ዳዊት The Psalms in Ge'ez, a traditional prayer book available in Ethiopia from the Ethiopian Orthodox Church. Addis Ababa, no date.

Good texts in Ge'ez are hard to come by. Dr. Gustav Aren of Mekane Yesus Seminary in Addis Ababa has supplied me with two volumes which are recognized as more traditional by the Orthodox in Ethiopia. They are the product of an Ethiopian reform movement called Mahebere Hawaryat. This reform movement is led by the nibureid Dimetrios Gebre-Mariam, at one time the temporal and spiritual head of Axum, who was kind enough to supply Dr. Aren with these texts at my inquiry. Therefore I list the following two volumes with special gratitude to Dr. Aren and Nebureid Dimetrios.

ብሉይ ፡ ኪዳን The Old Testament in Ge'ez, Volume One, Genesis-Ruth and Jubilees. Addis Ababa, no date.

ወንጌል ፡ ቅዱስ The New Testament in Ge'ez. Addis Ababa, no date.